United States
Department of Agriculture

Forest Service

Rocky Mountain
Research Station

General Technical Report
RMRS-GTR-135-vol. 2.

September 2005

Assessment of Grassland Ecosystem Conditions in the Southwestern United States: Wildlife and Fish

I0411458

Volume 2

Editor
Deborah M. Finch

Abstract

Finch, Deborah M., Editor. 2005. **Assessment of grassland ecosystem conditions in the Southwestern United States: wildlife and fish—volume 2**. Gen. Tech. Rep. RMRS-GTR-135-vol. 2. Fort Collins, CO: U.S. Department of Agriculture, Forest Service, Rocky Mountain Research Station. 168 p.

This report is volume 2 of a two-volume ecological assessment of grassland ecosystems in the Southwestern United States. Broad-scale assessments are syntheses of current scientific knowledge, including a description of uncertainties and assumptions, to provide a characterization and comprehensive description of ecological, social, and economic components within an assessment area. Volume 1 of this assessment focused on the ecology, types, conditions, and management practices of Southwestern grasslands. Volume 2 (this volume) describes wildlife and fish species, their habitat requirements, and species-specific management concerns, in Southwestern grasslands. This assessment is regional in scale and pertains primarily to lands administered by the Southwestern Region of the USDA Forest Service (Arizona, New Mexico, western Texas, and western Oklahoma). A primary purpose of volume 1 is to provide information to employees of the National Forest System for managing grassland ecosystems and landscapes, both at the Forest Plan level for Plan amendments and revisions, and at the project level to place site-specific activities within the larger framework. This volume should also be useful to State, municipal, and other Federal agencies, and to private landowners that manage grasslands in the Southwestern United States.

Key words: grasslands, ecological assessment, Southwestern United States, ecosystem conditions, wildlife, fish, birds, mammals, Arizona, New Mexico

Acknowledgments

This project is a collaborative effort between the Rocky Mountain Research Station and the Southwestern Region of the U.S. Department of Agriculture, Forest Service. In early 2000, a Southwestern Grassland Ecosystem Sustainability Team was formed to determine the assessment approach and general content. By 2001, the team had evolved into a core group that finalized the assessment topics and authored the report. This current work is volume 2 of a two-volume report. Volume 1 was published in September 2004.

The core team members are:

Robert Calamusso, Southwestern Region, Tonto National Forest
Cathy Dahms, Southwestern Region, Ecosystem Analysis and Planning (retired)
Deborah Finch, Rocky Mountain Research Station
Reggie Fletcher, Southwestern Region, Ecosystem Analysis and Planning (retired)
Paulette Ford, Rocky Mountain Research Station
Gerald Gottfried, Rocky Mountain Research Station
Burt Pendleton, Rocky Mountain Research Station
Rosemary Pendleton, Rocky Mountain Research Station
Deborah Potter, Southwestern Region, Ecosystem Analysis and Planning
Carol Raish, Rocky Mountain Research Station
Bryce Rickel, Southwestern Region, Wildlife, Fish and Rare Plants
Wayne Robbie, Southwestern Region, Ecosystem Analysis and Planning
Michele Merola-Zwartjes, Rocky Mountain Research Station

We acknowledge Art Briggs (Southwestern Region), Jim Saveland (Rocky Mountain Research Station), Dave Stewart (Southwestern Region), and George Martinez (Southwestern Region) for their early role in the team's development, and Alison Hill (Rocky Mountain Research Station), Bob Davis (Southwestern Region), Amy Unthank (Southwestern Region), and Don DeLorenzo (Southwestern Region) for assisting in seeing both volumes through.

We thank Louise Kingsbury and her staff for assistance in editorial work and layout of chapters in preparation for publication. We thank Nora Altamirano for help in formatting the document. The team also recognizes the valuable input provided by other team members and by numerous manuscript reviewers. We thank Carl and Jane Bock, Rob Beltars, John Rinne, Janet Ruth, Fred Samson, John Sidle, and Amy Unthank for reviewing manuscripts for volume 2. We also acknowledge helpful input from Fritz Knopf, Christopher Rustay, Troy Corman, Bill Howe, and Sartor O. Williams on one or more chapters.

Support for this project was provided by USDA Forest Service's Southwestern Region, and by the Forest Service's Rocky Mountain Research Station (Ecology, Recovery, and Sustainability of Grassland and Riparian Ecosystems in the Southwest, Cultural Heritage Research, and Ecosystem Management Southwestern Borderlands).

Editor's Note

Assessment of Grassland Ecosystem Conditions in the Southwestern United States: Wildlife and Fish

Volume 2

Editor
Deborah M. Finch

USDA Forest Service
Rocky Mountain Research Station
333 Broadway SE, Suite 115
Albuquerque, New Mexico 87102

Cover photos clockwise from upper left: Black-tailed prairie dog (photo by Jeff Vanuga, USDA Natural Resources Conservation Service). Pronghorn (photo by Gary Kramer, USDA Natural Resources Conservation Service). Spikedace (photo by James E. Johnson, U.S. Fish and Wildlife Service). Lesser prairie chicken (photo by Gary Kramer).

The Authors

Bob Calamusso has a B.S. degree in fish and wildlife management from Montana State University, Bozeman, 1983 and an M.S. degree in fisheries science from New Mexico State University, Las Cruces, 1996. Bob has worked in the fisheries management field with the Montana Department of Fish, Wildlife, and Parks throughout Montana. He has worked in the fisheries management area in Alaska, New Mexico, and Arizona with the Forest Service and has also conducted research in affiliation with the Rocky Mountain Research Station in New Mexico and Arizona. The majority of Bob's work in Region 3 has been focused on the conservation of native fishes and their ecosystems on National Forest properties and adjoining lands.

Deborah M. Finch is a Research Wildlife Biologist and Project Leader with the USDA Forest Service's Rocky Mountain Research Station in Albuquerque, NM. She is also Research Associate Professor in the Department of Biology at University of New Mexico. She received her B.S. degree in wildlife management from Humboldt State University, California, her M.S. degree in zoology from Arizona State University, and her Ph.D. degree in zoology from the University of Wyoming. Deborah's research interests include neotropical migratory bird ecology and reproduction, bird migration, endangered species, riparian and grassland ecosystem ecology and conservation, and relationships between commodity use and natural resources. Deborah has published more than 125 articles and journal papers and is an active member of several professional societies. Since 1998, she has served as Leader of the Technical Subgroup of the Recovery Team for the Southwestern willow flycatcher.

Michele Merola-Zwartjes is a Fish and Wildlife Biologist and is working for the U.S. Fish and Wildlife Service, Division of Endangered Species Recovery, Region 1, Portland, OR. She was a postdoctoral Research Wildlife Biologist with the Rocky Mountain Research Station in Albuquerque, NM. She holds a B.A. degree in communications from the University of California, San Diego, and a Ph.D. degree in biology from the University of New Mexico. Amongst her varied work experiences, Michele has served as a conservation planner for The Nature Conservancy and taught in the Wildlife Department of Humboldt State University. Michele's interests include ornithology, conservation of threatened, endangered, and sensitive vertebrate species, animal behavior, wildlife management, and natural resource management issues.

Bryce W. Rickel received a B.S. degree in general biology and an M.S. degree in fishery biology from the University of Arizona. He has worked for the USDA Forest Service for 23 years as a Fishery and Wildlife Biologist in Arizona, Alaska, Utah, and New Mexico. Currently, he is the Regional Wildlife and Fish Habitat Coordinator for the Southwestern Region. His interests are in developing GIS applications and in using artificial intelligence for species habitat quality models and for habitat relationships programs.

Preface

This report is volume 2 of a two-volume ecological assessment of grassland ecosystems in the Southwestern United States, and it is part of a series of planned publications addressing major ecosystems of the Southwest. Volume 1, *An Assessment of Grassland Ecosystem Conditions in the Southwest* (Finch, editor, 2004), focused on the ecology, types, conditions, and management practices of Southwestern grasslands. The second volume (herein) describes wildlife and fish species, their habitat requirements, and species-specific management concerns, in Southwestern grasslands.

The first Southwestern ecological assessment, General Technical Report RM-GTR-295, emphasized forested ecosystems and was titled, *An Assessment of Forest Ecosystem Health in the Southwest* (by Dahms and Geils, editors, 1997). Given the complexities of grassland ecology and the increasing number of challenges facing grassland managers, the USDA Forest Service Southwestern Region, in partnership with the agency's Rocky Mountain Research Station, focused on grasslands in its second assessment. The assessment is regional in scale and pertains primarily to lands administered by the Southwestern Region (Arizona, New Mexico, Texas, and Oklahoma) of the U.S. Department of Agriculture, Forest Service.

Broad-scale assessments are syntheses of current scientific knowledge, including a description of uncertainties and assumptions, to provide a characterization and comprehensive description of ecological, social, and economic components within an assessment area (USDA Forest Service 1999b). A primary purpose of volume 2 of the grassland assessment is to provide information to employees of the National Forest System for managing habitats and lands for wildlife and fish populations, both at the Forest Plan level for Plan amendments and revisions, and at the project level to place site-specific activities within the larger framework. This volume should also be useful to State, municipal, other Federal agencies, and to private landowners that manage or regulate wildlife and fish populations and their habitats in the Southwestern United States. The assessment is not a decision document because it identifies issues and risks to grassland ecosystems that provide the foundation for future changes to Forest Plans or project activities, but it does not make any site-specific decisions or recommendations.

To conduct the entire assessment, we assembled a team of authors from the Southwestern Region and the Rocky Mountain Research Station whose expertise focused on or included grassland ecosystems. An outline of chapter titles and chapter contents was prepared using a group consensus process. Authors volunteered to write specific chapters that were then reviewed by the team. Following team review, each individual chapter was sent to a minimum of two peer reviewers for critique. This volume then went through an editorial process by myself, and by the Rocky Mountain Research Station's Publishing Services Office.

I thank the authors of volume 2 for writing and rewriting their chapters, and I repeat my thanks to authors of volume 1 for their contributions. Authors and I thank reviewers of volume 2 chapters for their helpful and constructive comments and advice. These reviewers were John Sidle and Mark Rumble (USDA Forest Service, Rocky Mountain Research Station) and Fred Samson (USDA Forest Service, Northern Region) for chapters 1, 2, and 3; Carl and Jane Bock (University of Colorado) and Janet Ruth (U.S. Geological Survey) for chapter 4; and Rob Bettaso (Arizona Game and Fish Department), John Rinne (USDA Forest Service, Rocky Mountain Research Station, Flagstaff, AZ), and Amy Unthank (USDA Forest Service, Southwest Region) for chapter 5. We also thank all members of the grassland assessment team for their contributions to the team planning effort. On behalf of the team, I express thanks to Don DeLorenzo, Art Briggs, Cathy Dahms, and Bob Davis of the Southwest Regional Office, and to Alison Hill of the Forest Service's Rocky Mountain Research Station for supporting this project. In addition, I am pleased to acknowledge Louise Kingsbury and her staff for publication editing and layout, and to Nora Altamirano for assistance in assembling and formatting the report.

Deborah Finch, Editor
USDA Forest Service
Rocky Mountain Research Station
Albuquerque, NM

Contents

Chapter 1: Wildlife 1
  Bryce Rickel

Chapter 2: Large Native Ungulates 13
  Bryce Rickel

Chapter 3: Small Mammals, Reptiles, and Amphibians 35
  Bryce Rickel

**Chapter 4: Birds of Southwestern Grasslands: Status,
Conservation, and Management** 71
  Michele Merola-Zwartjes

**Chapter 5: Fishes of Southwestern Grasslands: Ecology,
Conservation, and Management** 141
  Bob Calamusso

Bryce Rickel

Chapter 1: Wildlife

Introduction

This volume addresses the wildlife and fish of the grasslands in the Southwestern Region of the USDA Forest Service. Our intent is to provide information that will help resource specialists and decisionmakers manage wildlife populations within grassland ecosystems in the Southwestern United States. The information and analysis presented is at a Regional scale.

Many of the references and examples in this volume are from grassland types and/or States outside the Region but are applicable to our discussions. Some species are addressed at length, either because information is available, the species are threatened, endangered, being considered for listing, are sensitive, have special management requirements, or play or have played a special ecological role.

An underlying theme in managing wildlife residing in grassland ecosystems is that wildlife and their environments have evolved together over millennia. Each wildlife species has an important role and function to fill in its grassland environment. The challenge of managing grassland-adapted wildlife species is to sustain or restore, where possible, the processes, attributes, and habitat structures that have codeveloped with populations over time and that may be required by individual wildlife species.

Many human activities have significant effects on wildlife of grasslands, but two in particular are notable and frequently identified in the literature: habitat loss in relation to private farming, and habitat alteration from grazing by domestic livestock. Much of the literature addressing grassland wildlife can be classified under range management topics, especially as it relates to grazing effects and management of livestock.

Historic Conditions

As pioneers moved west in the United States century and a half ago, they found large expanses of prairie comprising grasses suitable for livestock forage, and level ground with soils amenable to growing domestic crops. The development of ranches, farms, towns, railroads, and roads began to fragment and change native grasslands, and this trend continues today. This advancement of civilization has placed an increasing demand on natural resources as fundamental as space, water, air, minerals, water, plants, and animals. Humans cleared native grasses and trees and planted new species. They combated and then controlled a natural process that was considered to be destructive—wildfire. Fire suppression changed various system processes that were important for the maintenance of grasslands. Because early pioneers found water to be a limiting factor in the Southwest, they drilled wells, built dams, and redirected water to meet their needs. As this development of the West progressed, the face of the landscape changed. The combination of fire suppression, water control, and

USDA Forest Service Gen. Tech. Rep. RMRS-GTR-135-vol. 2. 2005

1

habitat conversion and fragmentation significantly altered native grasslands and respective ecosystem processes that wildlife depended on.

The topic of grassland-associated wildlife in the Southwestern Region of the Forest Service is complex. The grasslands in the Region are subdivided into three distinct areas: the Great Plains, the Great Basin, and the desert grassland. While there are some similarities among wildlife species across the grassland types, each grassland has unique species with unique requirements and roles in its respective ecosystems.

The Great Plains grasslands include the shortgrass steppes of southeastern Colorado and northeastern New Mexico, northwestern Texas, western Oklahoma, and western Kansas. The desert grasslands are in southeastern Arizona, southwestern New Mexico, and Mexico. The Great Basin, a cold desert, is bounded by the Sierra Nevada on the west and Colorado Rockies on the east, and by the Idaho batholith of central Idaho on the north and a vegetation line defined by creosote bush (*Larrea divaricata*)—a warm desert species—and Great Basin sagebrush (*Artemisia tridentata*) in the south. The Great Basin, which is similar to other desert grasslands in the Southwest, was once dominated by perennial grasses but is currently dominated by desert shrubs (Hastings and Turner 1965, Hanley and Page 1982), including creosote (*Larrea tridentata*), tarbush (*Flourensia cernua*), mesquite (*Prosopsis juliflora*), Mormon tea (*Ephedra trifurca*), and acacia (*Acacia* spp.).

The Great Plains, Great Basin, and Desert Grassland remarkably differ in climate. The desert grasslands and the Great Basins are semiarid, whereas the Great Plains is wetter and colder. The grassland ecosystems of Western North America are climatically diverse with differences in productivity, seasonality, and disturbance regimes. These environmental dissimilarities have resulted in different fauna. If our goal is to sustain grasslands, we must understand the climatic and evolutionary constraints operating in each ecosystem and the resulting differences in resilience of these ecosystems and the wildlife species therein.

The grassland ecosystems discussed here are usually described as homogenous types of grass, tallgrass, shortgrass, mixed grass, interspersed with many smaller ecosystems, including wetlands, playas, riparian areas, shrublands, rocky outcrops, and in some locations, scattered trees and shrubs. Each system has a unique fauna, management problems, and needs. Consequently, only the major groups of wildlife and a few of the more important species can be discussed in any detail. By addressing species groups and some key species most of the management needs of other species will, we hope, be met. Most of the species groups and single species will be addressed in relation to functions within their respective grassland ecosystems and with respect to various anthropogenic activities that occur on the grasslands.

Many issues need to be considered when managing wildlife on grasslands, such as:

- Habitat fragmentation caused by urban development, agriculture (farming), changes in plant structure and composition, fencing, and roads.
- The use of chemicals such as pesticides and urban contaminates that have affected wildlife, directly or indirectly.
- Changes in the abundance and types of water sources. For example, playas have been drained to create farmlands, streams have been dammed, diverted, impacted by grazing or have dried up due to lowering water tables, and destruction and changes in riparian zones.
- Population declines of several wildlife species that have played important ecological functions (keystone species) such as bison (*Bison bison*), and prairie dogs (*Cynomys* spp.). Some grassland wildlife species are to the point of being listed or being considered for listing.
- Competition between domestic and wild species. Competition will be of sufficient interest throughout the following discussions that more explanation is merited. Some general definitions of competition as they apply in this report follow.

Factors Influencing Wildlife Populations

Competition

Competition can occur in one of two ways. The first way involves direct use of a common limited resource by the same or different species (Miller 1967, Nelson 1982). On the grasslands, the common resource is vegetation. Many factors influence competition for edible plants between wildlife and domestic herbivores (Vavra and others 1989). Nelson (1982) lists eight ways species could compete for vegetation:

- consumption equivalence
- dietary overlap
- forage quantity and quality
- forage use
- timing of use
- height of foraging reach
- density or stocking rate of animals
- spatial and temporal distribution of animals

These factors are not independent; they can interact in multiple ways to heighten or minimize the actual degree of competition.

The second way competition can occur involves active defense of a territory or other spatial resources by one animal against another Nelson (1982). This can

2

USDA Forest Service Gen. Tech. Rep. RMRS-GTR-135-vol. 2. 2005

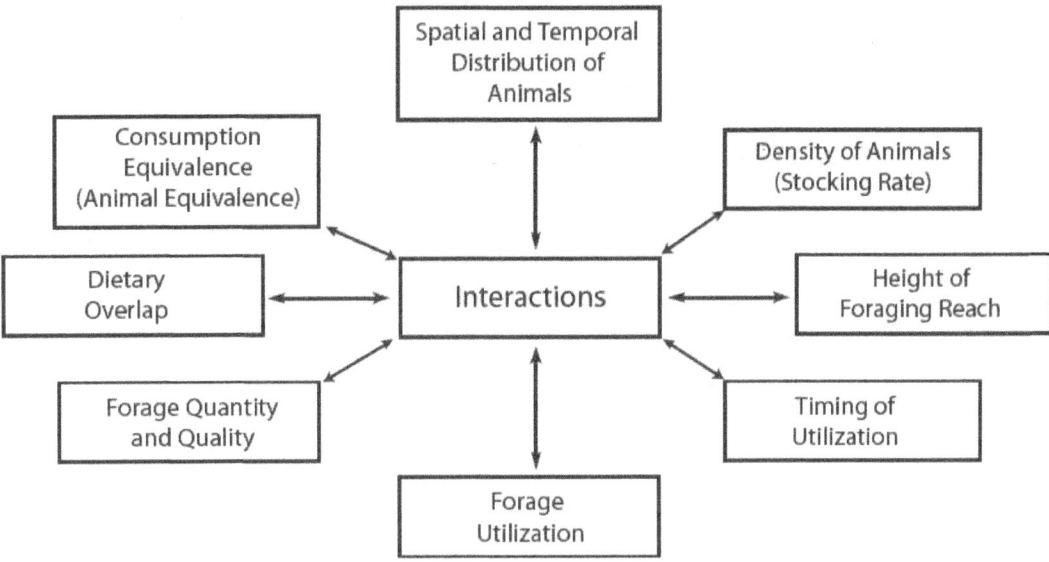

Figure 1-1. Potential interactions among variables that affect ungulate competition for food. Interactions can heighten or reduce the potential for competition in a myriad of ways that are not predicted (Wisdom and Thomas 1996).

also take a more passive form known as disturbance competition, when the mere presence of an animal intimidates or annoys another animal into leaving the area (Nelson 1982).

Figure 1-1 illustrates the competitive interactions among such native ungulates as elk, deer, and such exotic ungulates as cattle and sheep. Although, figure 1-1 depicts general competitive interactions between ungulates, both native and exotic, it is also a good representation of competition between many wildlife and domestic species.

Predators

In all of the grassland ecosystems, predators play an important function of controlling prey populations that may include other predators. Many of the large top carnivorous predators—bears, mountain lions, wolves—have been extirpated from the grasslands.

Important predators in contemporary desert grasslands include coyotes (*Canis latrans*), hawks, owls, bats, the insectivorous desert shrew (*Notiosorex crawfordi*), the grasshopper mouse, snakes, lizards, and toads. Local distributions and numbers of predators can often be linked to prey abundance. For example, studies of coyote and jackrabbit populations in the Great Basin desert showed that jackrabbit abundance rises and falls on a decadal cycle and that coyote populations track the jackrabbit cycle with a 1 to 2 year lag time (Stoddart 1987a,b). Predators are also known to regulate prey populations. Range caterpillar populations have been reduced by as much as 50 percent by rodent predators, as have been various darkling (*Tenebrionidae*) and ground beetles (*Carabidae*) (Parmenter and MacMahon

1988a,b). Insectivorous birds can have a similar impact on grasshoppers as rodent predators (Joern 1986).

Habitat Modification and Fragmentation

Grasslands have been subjected to various kinds of modifications, fire events, climate changes, wildlife uses, and other influences, for millions of years (Colbert and Morales 1992). In the grasslands of North America, native wildlife habitats have been modified, removed completely, or replaced with other kinds of vegetation by humans. As a result, native habitats in some areas have become more disjointed and the vegetation composition and structure have changed. Volume 1 of this assessment describes the causes and consequences of grassland alterations and landscape fragmentation in relation to plant communities, and the following chapters in this volume 2 document many of the effects of habitat modification and fragmentation on wildlife.

Studies of native mammals in disturbed grassland situations reveal that some animals have adapted remarkably well to these changes; for example, coyotes (*Canis latrans*) now use urban areas. However, many larger herbivores, such as bison, elk, antelope, and their respective predators, have not been able to adapt as well to grassland alterations as smaller herbivores. An explanation may be that large herbivores cannot readily adapt to habitat fragmentation because they depend on large geographic ranges and expanses of continuous open grasslands, whereas smaller animals may be able to adjust to fragmented habitats because they have smaller ranges and need smaller amounts of continuous habitat.

USDA Forest Service Gen. Tech. Rep. RMRS-GTR-135-vol. 2. 2005

3

Influence of Large Mammals

Effects of large herbivores (ungulates) on plant community composition and structure have been studied in many grasslands worldwide (Frank and McNaughton 1992). Ungulate activities affect many aspects of grassland structure and function, including the physical structure of the environment and the rates of certain ecosystem-level processes, for example, fire frequency and erosion probability (Frank and Evans 1997). The grazing habits of large herds of American bison, for example, resulted in a mosaic pattern of grazed and ungrazed areas. This pattern in turn influenced the occupancy patterns of other mammals in the areas.

Role of Riparian Areas in Grassland Environments

Riparian vegetation, trees, grasses, sedges, and rushes provide shade, cover, and food for many wildlife species. Streamside vegetation filters and traps sediments, which improves water quality and helps to maintain water temperatures and oxygen levels. Leaves, bark, and rotting wood provide homes and food for many insects and many vertebrate species. Insects are prey for birds, small mammals, reptiles, amphibians, and fish. Riparian habitats are important migratory corridors for birds and bats and travel corridors for large mammals such as elk and deer. Fragmented riparian habitats can also lead to isolated populations of animal species preventing both population expansion and gene flow (Ohmart and Zisner 1993).

The management of riparian ecosystems within the Southwestern Region is a special concern because of their importance to so many wildlife species (table 1-1). About three-fourths of the vertebrates in the Southwest, for example, depend on riparian areas for some portion of their life history (Johnson 1989). In the Southwestern Region, 57 percent of the terrestrial vertebrate species on National Forest lands occur in riparian systems (estimated from the Southwest

Table 1-1. The total number of birds, mammals, amphibians, and reptiles and their respective number in riparian habitats, and the percent of the totals on the 11 National Forests in the Southwestern Region. (Data compiled from the Southwest Wildlife Information System, Rickel 2002)

Species group	Total	Riparian	Percent
Birds	458	252	55
Mammals	203	153	75
Amphibians	34	15	44
Reptiles	114	41	36
Totals	**809**	**461**	**57**

Wildlife Information System 2001). The significance of this habitat type to wildlife becomes even more important when considering that riparian habitats comprise just less than 2 percent of the National Forests in the Southwestern Region (estimated from the Southwest Wildlife Information System 2001).

Because livestock spend much of their time in riparian zones, where ecological stakes are high, many of the adverse impacts of grazing are magnified in these habitats (Fleischner 1994). Destruction of vegetation adjacent to riparian streams has resulted in siltation of streambed gravels, warming of the water, and elimination of aboveground flows during summer and fall. The United States General Accounting Office (1988) reported that degradation of riparian and aquatic areas was the most serious threat to biodiversity in the West.

Role and Effects of Fire

One of the most important ecological processes of the grasslands has been fire. Fire has occurred either by lighting naturally, or by humans. Anthropologic fires were set by Native Americans and then by pioneers for various reasons; for example, to clear a piece of land for farming, to renew land for farming, to herd large mammals for hunting, and for warfare. Once the grasslands were settled, fires were viewed as more of a setback than a tool, and fire suppression commenced. Fire suppression altered the frequency of wildfire events, causing many grassland ecosystems to shift in plant species composition from areas composed primarily of grasses to areas having increasing numbers of shrubs and trees.

Birds—Some birds react to fire directly; raptors, for example, are attracted to fire and smoke. This response appears to be related to vulnerability and ease of capturing prey that are forced to escape a fire. Raptors are also attracted to burned areas where insects and small mammals are often plentiful and are easy prey. Other bird species are attracted to recently burned grasslands (Clark 1935, Handley 1969, Komarek 1969, Kramps and others 1983, Lyon and Marzluff 1984, Tombak 1986). The attraction is the increased forb composition. Seed production after fire is beneficial to avian herbivores and granivores (Bock and Bock 1990, Bock and others 1976, Lawrence 1966, Wirtz 1977).

Other effects of fire on birds include increased habitat heterogeneity. In shrub-grass complexes, bird diversity and abundance are enhanced if shrub cover and nesting sites are interspersed with open grassy areas maintained by fire (Baldwin 1968, Kramp and others 1983). Fire can have a cleansing effect on bird populations by lowering the numbers of parasites that affect health and vigor of individuals (Kramp and others 1983, Lyon and Marzluff 1984).

4

USDA Forest Service Gen. Tech. Rep. RMRS-GTR-135-vol. 2. 2005

Species that use shrubby habitat for nesting and perching are likely to be negatively impacted by fire if shrubs are destroyed. The shrub-associated common yellowthroat (*Geothlypis trichas*), for example, was found to reach highest abundance on unburned areas in mixed-grass prairie (Madden 1995).

Some bird species exhibit both negative and positive response to fires. This dual response is a consequence of requiring different habitats for different purposes. They may be attracted to recently burned grasslands for feeding if productivity of grasses and forbs has been improved. However, they may require shrub-dominated habitats for cover and nesting (Brown 1978, Komarek 1969, Kramp and others 1983, Renwald and others 1978, Wolfe 1973).

Fire or the lack of fire may affect the distribution of bird species. Populations of Baird's sparrow (*Ammodramus bairdii*), grasshopper sparrow (*Ammodramus bairdii*), LeConte's sparrow (*Ammospiza leconteii*), and Sprague's pipit (*Anthus spragueii*) were common to abundant in mixed-grass prairie, where fire has been used as a habitat management tool since the 1970s, but are virtually absent from unburned prairie (Madden 1995). Fire suppression in grasslands can lead to habitat type replacement, with plant community complexes comprising grass species replaced by shrub communities over time. This habitat conversion is likely to have beneficial effects on some bird (and other wildlife) species but detrimental effects on other species. Table 1-2 lists a few grassland bird species and their responses to fire.

Mammals—How mammals respond in the short term to fire is a function of mammal size and mobility. Large mobile mammals such as deer and elk can easily avoid injury during fire (Boeker and others 1972, McCulloch 1969, Dills 1970, Hallisey and Wood 1976). Young ungulates that are less mobile are frequently killed by large fires (Daubenmire 1968, Kramp and others 1983). Most small mammals escape fires by hiding in burrows or rock crevices (Howards and others 1959, Heinselman 1973). Bendell (1974) indicates that soil provides insulation from fire for burrowing animals (Kramp and others 1983).

The most common fire-related deaths for small mammals are from a combination of heat effects and asphyxiation, physiological stress caused by overexertion during escape, trampling by stampeding large mammals, and predation during and after escape from fire (Kaufman and others 1990).

Fires that temporarily remove food and cover may be detrimental to small rodents immediately after fire (Daubenmire 1968, Kaufman and others 1990). However, repopulation of burned areas by small rodents is reported to be nearly complete within 6 months (Cook 1959). Small mammal populations often increase after fire. This response is due to increased availability of forb seeds and insects (Lyon and others 1978). Burned areas often support more diverse animal populations than comparable unburned sites due to increased habitat diversity (Beck and Vogl 1972, Wirtz 1977). Omnivores and carnivores are attracted to burns owing to increased plant diversity and associated small prey populations (Gruell 1980).

Kaufman and others (1990) suggests that most of the effects of fire on small mammals in grasslands are not neutral but instead are either positive or negative. Fire-negative mammals (table 1-3) include species that forage on invertebrates in the litter layer, species that hide in dense vegetation and eat foliage, and species that use, at least partially, aboveground nests of plant debris. Fire-positive mammals (table 1-3) include species that feed on seeds and/or insects (Kaufman and others 1990). They exhibit an increase in populations and habitat use after fire because of an increased availability of forb seeds, insects, new green vegetation, the creation of open areas in otherwise dense habitat, and eventually an increase in forb cover. Increases can be immediate or can occur gradually as the areas begin to revegetate and habitat diversity increases. Carnivores of the southern Great Plains increase in population and habitat use in response to fire-enhanced rodent populations (prey) (Gruell 1980, Kramp and others 1983, Wirtz 1977). Most native ungulates, bison, white-tailed deer, elk, and pronghorn, increase in populations and habitat use after fire. These population responses are due to an increase in forage quality and quantity in newly burned areas.

Ecological Perspective

In this section, the ecosystem management issues of biodiversity, scale, fragmentation, population viability, and keystone species are discussed.

Resource managers must remember that biodiversity, scale, fragmentation, viability, and keystone species are not exclusively separate but are all closely interrelated and interconnected facets of ecosystems, and consequently it is difficult to understand and manage for one issue without understanding how they interact with others.

Biodiversity

Probably one of the most widely cited definitions of biodiversity comes from *Technologies to Maintain Biological Diversity* (Office of Technology Assessment 1987: 9): "Biological diversity refers to the variety and variability among living organisms and the ecological complexity in which they occur." Biodiversity has become one of the focal points of much discussion about ecosystem management. One of today's leading scientists, E.O. Wilson, predicted that, worse than

USDA Forest Service Gen. Tech. Rep. RMRS-GTR-135-vol. 2. 2005

5

Table 1-2. Some grassland birds their response to fire and description of their habitat (Kaufman and others 1990).

Species	Response to fire	Habitat description
Common yellowthroat *Geothlypis trichas*	Negative	Shrubs are required for nesting and perching, but nests are destroyed by fire. Yellowthroats were found to reach highest abundance on unburned areas in mixed-grass prairie, where prescribed fire has been used as a management.
Northern bobwhite *Colinus virginianus*	Both negative and positive.	Is attracted to recently-burned grasslands and is most productive in grass-forb habitat. However, it requires scattered woody plants for cover, and populations decrease in shrub-dominated habitats.
Eastern meadowlark *Sturnella magna*	Both negative and positive.	May be attracted to recent burns, but fires that destroy all shrub cover may be detrimental.
White-crowned sparrow *Zonotrichia leucophrys*	Both negative and positive.	Depends on shrub cover, and may decrease habitat use on some burns. But it also aggregates in large groups to feed in open burns.
Lark sparrow *Chondestes grammacus*	Both negative and positive.	Reportedly benefits from litter removal in grasslands and reduction but not complete removal of shrubs.
Baird's sparrow *Ammodramus bairdii* LeConte's sparrow *Ammospiza leconteii* Sprague's pipit *Anthus spragueii* Western meadowlark *Sturnella neglecta*	Positive	These birds were the most common, and abundant birds, overall, in mixed-grass prairie, where fire has been used as a habitat management tool since the 1970s, but were all completely absent from unburned prairie. Baird's sparrow was found to reach high densities in areas that had been frequently burned. The areas were characterized by low litter and high cover variability of forbs and bunchgrass.
Montezuma quail *Cyrtonyx montezumae*	Positive	The decline of Montezuma quail has been linked with widespread replacement of grassland with shrubland in the last 150 years. It may benefit from fires that decrease shrub cover.
Burrowing owl *Anthene cumicularia*	Positive	Populations of the burrowing owls have reportedly declined on grasslands with increases in litter cover. This suggests that the use of fire to reduce litter cover may be beneficial to this species
Lesser prairie-chicken *Tympanuchus pallidicinctus*	Positive	The lesser prairie-chicken is also a grassland species reported to be declining in the Southwest because of decreased grassland habitat due to suppression of grassland.
Sandhill crane *Grus Canadensis*	Positive	Regrowth of grasses, reduced litter, and decreased shrub cover in grasslands following fire is beneficial for the crane.

destruction caused by war, is the loss of genetic and species diversity in destruction of natural habitats because such loss will take millions of years to repair (Wilson 1984). An eloquent quote from Aldo Leopold (1949: 190) captures the same thought:

> The last word in ignorance is the man who says of an animal or plant: "What good is it?" If the land mechanism as a whole is good, then every part is good, whether we understand it or not. If the biota, in the course of eons, has built something we like but do not understand, then who but a fool would discard seemingly useless parts? To keep every cog and wheel is the first precaution of intelligent tinkering.

Biological diversity is of particular interest since our activities affect both vegetative and wildlife diversity. People alter the biodiversity of plant and animal communities both directly and indirectly.

Managing Wildlife Diversity—To maintain suitable grassland conditions for the variety of wildlife species adapted to southwestern grasslands, managers would benefit by developing a comprehensive approach for conserving and enhancing biological diversity, taking into account both species and ecosystem functions and processes (Probst and Crow 1991). In developing such an approach, three interrelated elements of ecosystem diversity must be analyzed and incorporated into management plans and desired future conditions (Crow and others 1993):

- *Compositional diversity*—The diversity of various components of an ecosystem, namely species, communities, and ecosystems within larger systems. The effective protection of these components usually depends on the next two components.

Table 1-3. Examples of mammals that have positive or negative response to fire (Kaufman and others 1990).

Hispid cotton rat (*Sigmodon hispidus berlandieri*)	Negative
Bailey's pocket mouse (*Chaetodipus baileyi baileyi*)	Negative
Pinyon mouse, (*Peromyscus truei truei*)	Negative
White-tailed antelope squirrel (*Ammospermophilus leucurus*)	Negative
Southern red-backed vole (*Clethrionomys gapperi*)	Negative
Western harvest mouse (*Reithrodontomys megalotis*)	Negative
Meadow vole (*Microtus pennsylvanicus modestus*)	Negative
Deer mouse (*Peromyscus maniculatus*)	Positive
White-footed mouse (*Peromyscus lleucopus*)	Positive
Merriam's kangaroo rat (*Dipodomys merriami*)	Positive
Southern grasshopper mouse (*Onychomys torridus*)	Positive
Nuttall's cottontail (*Sylvilagus nuttallii*)	Positive
Thirteen-lined ground squirrel (*Spermophilus tridecemliniatus*)	Positive
Hispid pocket mouse (*Chaetodipus hispidus*)	Positive
Bison (*Bison bison*)	Positive
Elk (*Cervus elaphus*)	Positive
White-tailed deer (*Odocoileus virginianus*)	Positive
Pronghorn (*Antilocapra americana*)	Positive

- *Structural diversity*—The diversity of habitats and how they are arranged relative to each other spatially and temporally. Structural diversity includes the size, shape, and distribution of species and habitat types, communities across landscapes, and patterns of successional change.
- *Functional diversity*—This refers to the diversity of ecological processes that maintain and are dependent on the other components of diversity. Functional diversity includes, for example, competition, predation, parasitism, and other biological interactions, as well as other processes, such as, nutrient retention and cycling. The ecological processes represented by functional diversity provide the "ecological services" necessary to support all organisms, including humans.

As resource managers develop approaches for applying the concepts of biodiversity and communities to designing desired future conditions, they should avoid oversimplifying the complexity of a landscape and wildlife habitat relationships. Communities with similar resources may still vary in the number of species because of different degrees of niche overlap. Niche overlap is the degree two species exploit the same resource; for example, cattle and deer. Communities differ in species requirements for a variety of reasons: differences in climatic stability and predictability, completion, predation, and disturbances (Solbrig 1991). Consequently, as management plans are developed, good field inventories will be needed.

Scale

One of the most significant changes and challenges in moving from traditional management to ecosystem management is to analyze and manage systems at multiple spatial and temporal scales, simultaneously (Fischer and others 2004). In order to maintain and/or restore grassland ecosystem conditions for wildlife, such management approaches need to be developed and implemented with scale in mind (Crist and others 2003, Su and others 2004).

A hierarchical (multiple-scaled) perspective emphasizes three strategic concerns in an analysis of landscape patterns:

- To detect patterns and define their spatial and temporal scales; in other words, define functional patches at a specific scale for a species (Crist and others 2003, Fischer and others 2004, Kotliar and Wiens 1990).
- To infer which factors generate these patterns.
- To relate these patterns to adjacent levels" (Urban and others 1987, Fischer and others 2004).

Spatial Scale—The scale at which nature is viewed determines the patterns and processes detected. Fischer and others (2004) explain that organisms are affected by ecological processes operating at multiple scales, different habitat variables vary over different spatial scales, and some species reflect habitat at one, but not all, spatial scales. For any management needs or problem, spatial and temporal scales must

USDA Forest Service Gen. Tech. Rep. RMRS-GTR-135-vol. 2. 2005

7

both be carefully defined. There is no "best" scale at which to manage for. The appropriate scale depends on management needs (Noss 1992) and the requirements of the species. When developing plans for managing landscapes, it is essential for managers to address scaling in relation to specific questions and needs.

Temporal Scale—Problems in time correspond to our limited temporal scale of concern in conservation strategies. In many cases these problems involve disturbance. In general, most human impacts on biodiversity represent a change in the environment and/or an increased rate of change. Changes in disturbance regimes threaten biodiversity when they introduce stresses or events either qualitatively or quantitatively different from the disturbance or stresses to which organisms have adapted over evolutionary time (Noss 1992).

Over long time spans, centuries or millennia, grasslands of any size never remain the same. Changes in species distributions most typically result from variation in disturbance regimes and changes in climate. Because species migrate at different rates, grassland communities are ephemeral and unlikely to attain equilibrium (Davis 1981).

Managing Wildlife at Different Scales—Only by examining wildlife populations along habitat gradients encompassing environmental variations within species' ranges can wildlife be effectively managed. Species exhibiting ecological differences in habitat use among areas will likely require different types of management, depending on location. Species that exhibit specific habitat requirements having little variation across their range may require only one set of management strategies (Block and Morrison 1991).

Biodiversity should be considered at a regional scale where attention is paid to species composition as well as diversity. Even if management concerns are strictly focused on a local area, regional ecological processes as well as local processes must be taken into account. Failure to consider regional processes that control local biodiversity may result in the disruption of these processes, as when habitat fragmentation eliminates opportunities for species to migrate in response to changing climate or human activities. Conservation strategies, even for single species, will be most effective when they address ecological phenomena at multiple spatial scales and levels of organization (Noss 1992).

Management practices can often be effective when they mimic natural disturbances, and these practices can account for frequency, intensity, and seasonality of disturbances over multiple spatial scales. Managers are more likely to maintain native biodiversity by using practices that create a variety of habitats required by a range of wildlife species than when they create conditions unlike those occurring in "natural" landscapes (Noss 1992). For example, using prescribed fire to simulate naturally occurring wildfires may help to stimulate growth of suppressed plants, restore lost species, reduce numbers of invasive shrubs, and reduce amounts of senescent vegetation.

Fragmentation

The problem of fragmentation cannot be understated or underestimated. Rosenberg and Rapheal (1986) state that perhaps the most critical problem facing wildlife, worldwide, is the systematic shrinking and fragmentation of their habitat. Fragmentation is the process where patches of habitats are reduced in size and/or isolated from one another by natural disturbances such as fire, earthquakes, or flooding, or by human development (McLellan and others 1986). Although most of the research and literature has focused on forested lands, the concerns and many of the fundamental principles and theories apply to grasslands. Often fragmentation of grasslands and its effects on wildlife and ecosystem processes and functions are subtle. The size and shape of a habitat patch, and species composition and structure of the patch vegetation, determine the wildlife species that occupy any given site. The number and kinds of edge and interior species are typically correlated with patch size and shape.

Population Viability

A fundamental problem for wildlife management is assuring long-term viability of populations of different species. Population viability refers to the probability of continued existence of geographically well-distributed population over a specified period (Marcot and Murphy 1996). Managing viable populations is more complex than simply maintaining minimum population sizes needed for populations to survive over time with random fluctuations. To assess population dynamics accurately, resource managers must consider demographics, ability to disperse, and habitat quantity and quality (Probst and Crow 1991).

Central to all planning efforts that involve population viability analysis is provision of well-distributed and interconnected habitats (Noss and Harris 1986). Although some species' distributions are naturally patchy, in general, the maintenance of distributions and connectivity is the key to sustaining genetically diverse and demographically healthy populations. A population or habitat is well-distributed if it is maintained over the long term across at least its existing range of geographic, environmental, and ecological conditions (Marcot and Murphy 1996).

Keystone Species

An ecological concept that needs explanation before moving on to the rest of this volume is that of keystone

8

USDA Forest Service Gen. Tech. Rep. RMRS-GTR-135-vol. 2. 2005

species and their role within ecosystems. This understanding of keystone species will be important as various wildlife species and their management are discussed.

Where did the term "keystone species" come from? While Robert Paine, an ecologist, was studying the pattern of life among the intertidal rock species along the coast of Washington State in the 1960s, he found that one species of starfish preyed so skillfully on mussels that it effectively kept the mussels from monopolizing space on the rock. When he removed the starfish from sections of the shoreline, the mussels began to multiply, crowding out limpets, barnacles, and other marine organisms from the rock surfaces. In the absence of the starfish, the total number of species living on the rock (other than the mussels) decreased by half (Baskin 1997). Paine (1969) coined the term "keystone species" to describe species such as the starfish. He presented the characteristics required for a species to be given keystone status: (1) It provides top-down effects (for example, predation) on lower tropic levels, and thus (2) it prevents the monopolization of a critical resource in lower tropic levels. And (3) the synergy of this dualistic top-down (for example, predation) and bottom-up (for example, competition) interaction must stabilize community diversity. This narrowly defined keystone process is relatively rare and functionally nonredundant in ecosystems, making keystone species of great ecological significance (Davic 2002). A keystone species is one whose impacts on its community or ecosystem are large and greater than would be expected from its relative abundance or total biomass (Keystone Species Hypothesis 1969).

Research has shown that not all species are ecologically equal in their importance to a system. Species that are abundant, that dominate space and resources or contribute to controlling processes are not necessarily the most influential in a system. Sometimes, keystone species are less conspicuous and can even be rare (Baskin 1997). Their contribution to the system is disproportionate to other species in the community, and their removal creates ripple effects that might both change the community and also alter ecological processes (Baskin 1997). These community changes can have drastic consequences. If a keystone species becomes extinct, the other species that are dependent on the keystone species may also become extinct. Keystone species help to support the ecosystem of which they are a part (Jain and Krishna 2002, Keystone Species Hypothesis 1969).

Keystone species may be top carnivores that keep prey in check, large herbivores that shape the habitat in which other species live, important plants that support particular insect species that are prey for birds, bats that disperse the seeds of plants, and many other types of organisms (Keystone species 2004). Keystone species may occur at any level of the ecosystem, from plants and herbivores, to carnivores and detritivores.

In many systems, "keystone groups" of species rather than individual species assume the role of keystone species (De Leo and Levin 1997).

Functions of Keystone Species—Keystone species can occur in four ways. The first way is when organisms control potential dominants. In terrestrial systems, large and small herbivores play major roles in maintaining vegetation structure and species composition. The effect of herbivores is often to suppress potentially dominant plant species, reducing competitive exclusion of less competitive species, and promoting greater vegetation diversity (Ernest and Brown 2001, Payton and others 2002). A second way a species can be a keystone is to provide a vital resource or resources to a range of organisms (Payton and others 2002). A third way species may be keystone is when mutualism exists. Mutualism is where two species are jointly dependent, and the elimination of one will result in the demise of the other. In this situation they act as keystones for each other. What might be more in keeping with the multispecies concept of keystone species is "group mutualisms." True group keystones arise where there is dependency of several species on a single mutualist, for example, pollinators and groups of plants (Payton and others 2002). The fourth way an organism can be a keystone species is by being an ecosystem engineer. These species modify the physical characteristic of the environment, for example, burrowing, excavating nests, and so forth, providing resources for other species. These groups are not mutually exclusive, and individual species may exhibit characteristics of more than one type (Payton and others 2002).

Management Significations of Keystone Species—Natural resource managers are faced with complex issues and problems and an array of species, communities, and ecosystems. Faced with this complexity and ever-increasing demands for limited resources, the question is: How do I as a land manager adequately maintain these resources? (Payton and others 2002)

Protecting keystone species has become a priority for conservationists. Unfortunately, the keystone functions of a species may not be known until it is too late, that is, when it is listed or is extirpated. Where a keystone species has been identified, efforts to protect it also will help protect the other species in delicately balanced ecosystems (Keystone species 2004).

To determine the ecological importance of a species, a manager's attention must be directed to individual species or groups of species whose decline or removal may result in dramatic changes in the structure and functioning of its biological community (De Leo and Levin 1997).

In assessing the keystone role of an organism it is not always possible to distinguish clearly between the effects it may have as a keystone. For example, a good

USDA Forest Service Gen. Tech. Rep. RMRS-GTR-135-vol. 2. 2005

9

case could be made for considering large grazers as both keystone ecosystem engineers and as herbivores. By suppressing invasion of woody species and maintaining open grassland vegetation, large grazers profoundly alter the physical structure of the community. Even the classic keystone predator, the starfish, exerts its influence not just as a predator but as the incidental creator of bare patches, which provide recruitment sites for other species. Most organisms probably alter their environment in some way that can be exploited by other species. Whether the engineer can be considered a keystone species is a matter of degree: how profound the physical effect is, how disproportionate it is, how many other species benefit, and how great their dependence on the alteration is (Payton and others 2002).

Monitoring is a major issue and a need the manager has. There have been two basic monitoring approaches employed: single-species (for example, indicators (MIS), umbrellas, or flagships) or whole ecosystems (for example, focals). Each tactic has its advocates and detractors. Single-species monitoring focuses on one species. In contrast, ecosystem or landscape-scale approaches emphasize ecological processes and habitats rather than individual species (Payton and others 2002).

It has been suggested that the keystone species concept may allow managers to combine the best features of single-species and ecosystem-based management approaches. Monitoring keystone species retains a single-species focus while avoiding the need to examine every species, and it emphasizes the mechanisms that directly rather than indirectly control biodiversity. Where it is possible to identify a keystone species that is critical for the continued survival (or demise) of many other species in its community, management of that keystone may be an efficient means of managing a much wider range of biodiversity (Payton and others 2002).

By themselves, keystone species are unlikely to provide a panacea for managers. Not all ecosystems may contain keystone species, and even where keystones are identified they may not be easily managed as part of a conservation strategy (Payton and others 2002).

Summary

During the 19th and early 20th centuries, people moving westward saw the grasslands as a land that could fulfill their dreams of new homes, new opportunities, and new freedoms. The settlement of the grasslands brought many changes that affected wildlife. These changes include conversion of wild habitats to agriculture and urban areas, and the dissecting of the landscape with roads, fences, and rails. This land conversion and dissection have resulted in habitat loss and fragmentation.

Another drastic change to the grassland has been the alteration or loss of riparian habitats and wetlands, affecting many wildlife species that use riparian areas or are riparian obligates. Introduction of farm and ranch livestock has imposed another change by subjecting native species to competition pressures that they had not evolved with. Natural predator-prey relationships have been disrupted as many predators were greatly reduced in number or extirpated because they prey on livestock. Conversely, populations of some prey species have been reduced, at times intentionally, because they were and are deemed as a pest and a nuisance.

Another change that has altered grassland ecosystems has been fire suppression. Suppression of fire has result in changes in the structure and species composition of the vegetation and, consequently, has influenced the wildlife species of the grasslands.

In light of the many, often dramatic, changes people have made to the grassland ecosystems mentioned above and which will be discussed in more detail in the following chapters, it is worth repeating the words of Aldo Leopold (1949: 190):

> The last word in ignorance is the man who says of an animal or plant: "What good is it?" If the land mechanism as a whole is good, then every part is good, whether we understand it or not. If the biota, in the course of eons, has built something we like but do not understand, then who but a fool would discard seemingly useless parts? To keep every cog and wheel is the first precaution of intelligent tinkering.

Over time, many of the wheels and cogs (biological diversity, predator-prey relationships, competition, wild habitats, and so forth) in the grassland ecosystem have been changed, broken, or replaced, resulting in a system that does not work as well as it had originally evolved to work. Consequently, it is wise for land managers to work with the components of the system that are present and strive to have them working as well as possible.

The information in this volume is intended to help manage the wildlife and fisheries components of the grassland ecosystems.

Acknowledgments

I thank Mark A. Rumble, Fred B. Samson, and John Sidle for reviewing this chapter and providing insightful comments. I express my appreciation to Deborah M. Finch for editing the chapter and to Nora C. Altamirano for helping prepare this chapter for publication.

References

Baldwin, J.J. 1968. Chaparral conversion on the Tonto National Forest. Tall Timbers. Fire Ecology Conference. 8: 203-208

10

USDA Forest Service Gen. Tech. Rep. RMRS-GTR-135-vol. 2. 2005

Baskin, Y. 1997. The work of nature: how the diversity of life sustains us. Natural History. 106(1):48-52. URL: [online] http://www.anapsid.org/nature.html

Beck, A.M.; Vogl, R.J. 1972. The effects of spring burning on rodent populations in a brush prairie savannah. Journal of Mammalogy. 5 3(2): 336-345.

Bell, R.H.V. 1971. A grazing ecosystem in the Serengeti. Scientific American. 225: 86-93.

Bendell, J.F. 1974. Effects of fire on birds and mammals. In: Fire and Ecosystems. T.T. Kozlowski and C.E. Ahlgren, eds. New York: Academic Press. 545 p.

Berg, W.A. 1986. Effect of 20 years of low N rate pasture fertilization on soil acidity. Journal of Range Management. 39: 122-124.

Bock, C.E.; Bock, J.H. 1978. Response of birds, small mammals and vegetation to burning sacaton grasslands in southeastern Arizona. Journal of Range Management. 31: 296-300.

Bock, C.E.; Bock, J.H. 1990. Effects of fire on wildlife in southwestern lowland habitats. In: Effects of fire management of southwestern natural resources. Gen. Tech. Rep. RM-191. Fort Collins, CO: U.S. Department of Agriculture Forest Service Rocky Mountain Forest and Range Experiment Station: 50-59.

Bock, J.H.; Bock, C.E.; McKnight, J.R. 1976. The study of the effects of grassland fires at the Research Ranch in southeastern Arizona. Arizona Academy Science. 11: 49-57.

Boeker, E.L.; Scott, V.E.; Reynolds, H.G.; Donaldson, B.A. 1972. Seasonal food habitats of mule deer in southwestern New Mexico. Journal of Wildlife Management. 36(1): 56-63.

Bradley, W.G.; Mauer, R.A. 1973. Rodents of a creosote brush community in southern Nevada. Southwestern Naturalist. 17(4): 333-344.

Brown, D.E. 1978. Grazing, grassland cover and gamebirds. Transactions of the North American Wildlife Conference. 34: 477-485.

Brown, D.E.; Lowe, C.H. 1980. Biotic communities of the Southwest. Gen.Tech.Rep. RM-78. Fort Collins, CO: U.S. Department of Agriculture Forest Service Rocky Mountain Forest and Range Experiment Station.

Cable, D.W. 1967. Fire effects on semi-desert grasses and shrubs. Journal of Range Management. 20(3): 170-176.

Clark, H.W. 1935. Fire and bird populations. Condor. 37:16-18.

Colbert, E. H.; Morales, M. 1992. Evolution of the vertebrates: A history of the backboned animals through time. New York: John Wiley & Sons. 470 p.

Cook, S.F. 1959. The effects of fire on a population of small rodents. Ecology. 40(1): 102-108.

Crist, T.; Veech, J.A.; Gering, J.C.; Summerville, K.S. 2003. Partitioning species diversity across landscapes and regions: a hierarchical analysis of , , and diversity. American Naturalist. 162(6): 734-743.

Daubenmire, R. 1968. Ecology of fire in grasslands. In: Advances in Ecological Research. Vol. 5. New York: Academic Press: 209-273.

Davic, R.D. 2002. Herbivores as keystone predators. Conservation Ecology 6(2): r8. [online] URL: http://www.consecol.org/vol6/iss2/resp8

Davies, N.B. 1979. Ecological questions about territorial behaviour. In: J. R. Krebs and N. B. Davies, eds. Behavioural ecology, an evolutionary approach. London, UK: Blackwell Scientific: 317-350.

De Leo, G.A.; Levin, S. 1997. The multifaceted aspect of ecosystem integrity. Conservation Ecology 1(1):3. [online] URL: http://www.conecol.org/vol1/iss1/art3

Dills, G.G. 1970. Effects of prescribed burning on deer browse. Journal of Wildlife Management. 34(3): 540-545.

Ernest S.K.M.; Brown, J.H. 2001. Delayed compensation for missing keystone species by colonization. Science. 291(5514):101-104

Fischer, J.; Lindenmayer, D.B.; Cowling, A. 2004. The challenge of managing multiple species at multiple scales: reptiles in an Australian grazing landscape. Journal of Applied Ecology. 41:32-44.

Fleischner, T.L. 1994. Ecological costs of livestock grazing in western North America. Conservation Biology. 8: 629-644.

Ford, P.L.; McPherson, G.R. 1996. Ecology of fire in shortgrass prairie of the southern Great Plains. In: D.M. Finch, ed. Ecosystem disturbance and wildlife conservation in western grasslands – A symposium proceedings, September 22-26, 1994; Albuquerque, NM. Gen. Tech. Rep. RM-GTR-285. Fort Collins, CO: U.S. Department of Agriculture Forest Service Rocky Mountain Forest and Range Experiment Station. 82 p.

Frank, D.A.; McNaughton, S.J. 1992. The ecology of plants, large mammalian herbivores, and drought in Yellowstone National Park. Ecology. 73: 2043-2058.

Geier, A. R.;Best, L.B. 1980. Habitat selection by small mammals of riparian communities: Evaluating effects of habitat alterations. Journal of Wildlife Management. 44(1): 16-24.

Gruell, G.E. 1980. Fire's influence on wildlife habitat on the Bridger-Teton National Forest, Vol. II. Gen. Tech. Rep. INT-252. Ogden, UT: U.S. Department of Agriculture Forest Service Intermountain Forest and Range Experiment Station. 35 p.

Hallisey, D.M.; Wood, G.W. 1976. Prescribed fire in scrub oak habitat in central Pennsylvania. Journal of Wildlife Management. 40(3): 507-516.

Handley Jr., C.O. 1969. Fire and mammals. Tall Timbers Fire Ecology Conference. 9: 151-159.

Hanley, T.A.; Page, J.L. 1982. Differential effects of livestock use on habitat structure and rodent populations in Great Basin communities. California Fish and Game. 68: 160-174.

Hanson, E.E. 1978. The impact of a prescribed burn in a temperate subalpine forest upon the breeding bird and small mammal populations. M.S. thesis. Ellensburg, WA: Central Washington University.

Hastings, J.R.; Turner, R.M. 1965. The changing mile. Tucson: University of Arizona Press.

Heinselman, M.L. 1973. Fire in the virgin forests of the Boundary Waters Canoe Area, Minnesota. Quaternary Research. 3: 329-382.

Howards, W.E.; Fenner, R.L.; Childs Jr., H.E. 1959. Wildlife survival in brush burns. Journal of Range Management. 12: 230-234.

Jain, S.; Krishna, S. 2002. Large extinctions in an evolutionary model: The role of innovation and keystone species. PNAS. 99(4): 2055-2060.

Joern, A. 1986. Experimental study of avian predation on coexisting grasshopper populations (Orthoptera: Acrididae) in a sandhill grassland. Oikos. 46: 243 249.

Johnson, A.S. 1989. The thin green line: riparian corridors and endangered species in Arizona and New Mexico. In: G. Mackintosh, ed. In defense of wildlife: preserving communities and corridors. Washington, DC: Defenders of Wildlife: 35-46.

Kaufman, D.W.; Finck, E.J.; Kaufman, G.A. 1990. Small mammals and grasslands fires. In: S.L.Collins and L.L. Wallace, eds. Fire in North American Tallgrass Prairies, Norman and London: University of Oklahoma Press: 46-80.

Keay, J.A.; Peck, J.M. 1980. Relationship between fires and winter habitat of deer in Idaho. Journal of Wildlife Management. 44(2): 372-380.

Keystone Species. 2004. [online] URL: http://www.bagheera.com/inthewild/spot_spkey.htm

Keystone Species Hypothesis. 1969. [online] URL: http://www.washington.edu/researchlpathbreakers/l969g.htm1

Komarek Sr., E.V. 1969. Fire and animal behavior. Tall Timbers Fire Ecology Conference. 9: 161-207.

Kotliar, N.B.; Wiens, J.A. 1990. Multiple scales of patchiness structure: a hierarchical framework for the study of heterogeneity. Oikos. 29: 253-260.

Kramp, B.F.; Patton, D.R.; Brady, W.W. 1983. The effects of fire on wildlife habitat and species. Run Wild Wildlife Habitat Relationships. Wildlife Unit Tech. Rep. Washington, DC: U.S.Department of Agriculture Forest Service. 29 p.

Lawrence, G.E. 1966. Ecology of vertebrate animals in relation to chaparral fire in the Sierra Nevada foothills. Ecology. 47(2): 278-290.

Leopold, A. 1949. A Sand County almanac, and sketches from here and there. New York: Oxford University Press. 226 p.

Lowe, P.O.; Ffolliott, P.F; Dieterich, J.H.; Patton, D.R. 1978. Determining potential wildlife benefits from wildfire in Arizona ponderosa pine forests. Gen. Tech. Rep. RM-52. Fort Collins, CO: U.S. Department of Agriculture Forest Service Rocky Mountain Forest and Range Experiment Station. 12 p.

Lyon, L.J.; Crawford, H.S.; Czuhai, E.; Fredriksen, R.L.; Harlen, R.F.; Metz, L.J.; Pearson, H.A. 1978. Effects of fire on fauna: A state-of-knowledge review. Gen. Tech. Rep. WO-6. Washington, DC: U.S. Department of Agriculture Forest Service. 22 p.

USDA Forest Service Gen. Tech. Rep. RMRS-GTR-135-vol. 2. 2005

11

Lyon, L.J.; Marzluff, J.M. 1984. Fire's effects on a small bird population. In: J.E. Lotan and J.K. Brown, comp. Fire's effects on wildlife habitat-symposium proceedings. Washington, DC: U.S. Department of Agriculture Forest Service: 16-22.

Madden, L. 1995. Ecological effects of prescribed fire on prairie songbird communities. Abstract: International Conference and Training Workshop on Conservation and Ecology of Grassland Birds & 1995 Annual Meeting of the Association of Field Ornithologists. 26-28 October 1995. Tulsa, OK.

Marcot, B.G.; Murphy, D.D. 1996. On population viability analysis and management. In: R.C. Szaro and D.W. Johnston, eds. Biodiversity in managed landscapes theory and practice. New York and Oxford: Oxford University Press: 58-76.

Mazurek, E.J. 1981. Effect of fire on small mammals and vegetation on the Upper Sonoran Desert. M.S. thesis. Tempe: Arizona State University.

McCulloch, C.Y. 1969. Some effects of wildfire on deer habitat in pinyon-juniper woodland. Journal of Wildlife Management. 33(4): 778-784.

McLellan, C.A.; Dobson, A.P.; Wilcove, D.S.; Lynch, J.F. 1986. Effects of forest fragmentation on new- and old-world bird communities: empirical observations and theoretical implications. In: Wildlife 2000: Modeling habitat relationships for terrestrial vertebrates. J. Verner, M.L. Morrison, and C.J. Ralph, eds. Madison: University of Wisconsin Press: 305-314.

McNaughton, S.J. 1985. Ecology of a grazing system: the Serengeti. Ecological Monographs. 55: 259-294.

Miller, R.S. 1967. Patterns and process in competition. Advance Ecological Research. 4: 1-74.

Nelson, J.R. 1982. Relationships of elk and other large herbivores. In: J.W. Thomas and D.F. Toweill, eds. Elk of North America, ecology and management. Harrisburg, PA: Stackpole Books: 415-44.

Noss, R.F. 1992. Issues of scale in conservation biology. In: P.L. Fiedler and S. K. Jam, eds. Conservation Biology - The theory and practice of natural conservation preservation and management. New York: Chapman and Hall.

Noss, R.F.; Harris, L.D. 1986. Node, networks, and MUMs: preserving diversity at all scales. Environmental Management. Vol. 10(3): 299-309.

Odum, F. P. 1971. Fundamentals of ecology. Philadelphia, PA: W.B. Saunders Co. 574 p.

Ohmart, R.D.; Zisner, C.D. 1993. Functions and values of riparian habitat wildlife in Arizona a literature review. Arizona Game and Fish Department. 213 p.

Paine, R.T. 1969. A note on trophic complexity and species diversity. American Naturalist 100: 91—93.

Parmenter, R.R.; MacMahon, J.A. 1988a. Factors influencing species composition and population sizes in a ground beetle community (Carabidae): predation by rodents. Oikos. 52: 350-356.

Parmenter, R.R.; MacMahon, J.A. 1988b. Factors limiting populations of arid-land darkling beetles (Tenebrionidae): predation by rodents. Environmental Entomology. 17: 280-286.

Payton, I.J.; Fenner, M.; Williams, G.L. 2002. Keystone species: the concept and its relevance for conservation management in New Zealand. Science for Conservation 203. 29 p.

Probst, J.R.; Crow, T.R. 1991. Integrating biological diversity and resource management. Journal of Forestry. February.

Renwald, J.D.; Wright, H.A.; Flinders, J.T. 1978. Effects of prescribed fire on bobwhite quail habitat in the rolling plains of Texas. Journal of Range Management. 31(1): 65-69.

Roppe, J.A.; Hem, D. 1978. Effects of fire on wildlife in a lodgepole pine forest. Southwestern Naturalist. 23(2): 279-288.

Rosenberg, K.V.; Rapheal, M.G. 1986. Effect of forest fragmentation on vertebrates in Douglas-fir forests. In: Wildlife 2000: Modeling habitat relationships for terrestrial vertebrates.

Rowe, J.S.; Scotter, G.W. 1973. Fire in the Boreal Forest. Quaternary Research. 3: 444-464.

Stoddart, L.C. 1987a. Relative abundance of coyotes, jackrabbits and rodents in Curlew Valley, Utah. Final Report, U.S. Department of Agriculture Project DF-931.07. Denver, CO: Denver Wildlife Research Center.

Stoddart, L.C. 1987b. Relative abundance of coyotes, lagomorphs, and rodents on the Idaho National Engineering Laboratory. Final Report, U.S. Department of Agriculture Project DF-931.07. Denver, CO: Denver Wildlife Research Center.

Su, J.C.; Debinski, D.M.; Jakubaushas, M.E.; Kindscher, K. 2004. Beyond species richness: community similarity as a measure of cross-taxon congruence for coarse-filter conversation. Conservation Biology. 18(1):167-173.

Thomas, D.B.; Werner, F.G. 1981. Grass feeding insects of the western ranges: an annotated checklist. Tech. Bull. Tempe: University of Arizona Agricultural Experiment Station. 243 p.

Thomas, J.W. 1979. Wildlife habitat in managed forests of the Blue Mountains of Oregon and Washington. Forest Service Agricultural Handbook 53. Portland, OR: U.S. Department of Agriculture Forest Service Pacific Northwest Forest and Range Experiment Station. 512 p.

Thomas, W.; Toweill, D.F. eds. 1982. Elk of North America, ecology and management. Harrisburg, PA: Stackpole Books.

Tomhack, D.F. 1986. Post-fire regeneration of krummholz whitebark pine: a consequence of nutcracker seed caching. Madrono. 33: 100-110.

Urban, D.L.; O'Neill, R.O.; Shugart, H.H. 1987. Landscape ecology. BioScience. Vol. 37, No. 2: 119-127.

Vavra, M.; Mclnnis, M.; Sheehy, O. 1989. Implications of dietary overlap to management of free-ranging large herbivores. Proceedings Western Section American Society Animal Science. 40: 489-495.

Williams, 0. 1955. Distribution of mice and shrews in a Colorado montane forest. Journal of Mammalogy. 36(2): 221-231.

Wilson, E.O. 1984. Biophilia, the human bond with other species. Cambridge, MA: Harvard University Press l7 p.

Winter, M. 1995. The impact of fire on Baird's sparrow habitat. Abstract: International Conference and Training Workshop on Conservation and Ecology of Grassland Birds & 1995 Annual Meeting of the Association of Field Ornithologists. 26-28 October 1995. Tulsa, OK.

Wirtz, W.O. 1977. Vertebrate post-fire succession. In: Proceedings of the symposium on the environmental consequences of fire and fuel management in Mediterranean ecosystems. Gen. Tech. Rep. WO-3. Washington, DC: U.S. Department of Agriculture Forest Service: 46-57 p.

Wisdom, M.J.; Thomas, J.W. 1996. Elk. In: Range Wildlife, Kausmann, P.R., ed. Denver, CO: The Society of Range Management. 440 p.

Wolfe, C.W. 1973. Effects of fire on a sand hills grassland environment. Tall Timbers Fire Ecology Conference. 12: 241-255.

Bryce Rickel

Chapter 2:
Large Native Ungulates

Introduction

This chapter addresses the large native ungulates (American bison (*Bos bison*), elk (*Cervus elaphus*), white-tailed deer (*Odocoileus virginianus*), mule deer (*Odocoileus hemionus*), and pronghorn (*Antilocapra americana*) of the grasslands. The information presented includes historical background, description of the species' biology and ecology, and management in relation to domestic animals.

American Bison

Historically bison were widespread in North America from Alaska and Western Canada across the United States into Northern Mexico (fig. 2-1). They are currently found in isolated units throughout and external to historical range. Three separate subspecies are recognized: the Armican bison (*Bos bison*), the wood bison (*Bos bison athabascae*), and the bison (*Bos bison bison*).

The wood bison and bison are primarily distributed in Canada (NatureServe 2004). Population size of bison in North America may have been between 30 million to 60 million about the time of Euro-American settlement and reduced to about 1,650 by 1903. The population in 1983 was estimated at 75,000 (Meagher 1986). In Yellowstone National Park, the herd was estimated at 3,000 to 3,500 in 1996 (Keiter 1997); however, more than 1,000 were killed during the winter

Bison on prairie dog site. (Photo by Paulette Ford.)

of 1996 to 1997 by agency personnel (NatureServe 2004). Populations of American bison have fluctuated dramatically during the 11,000 years of the present interglacial (the Holocene) and probably were at their peak in the Great Plains when Europeans first arrived in the 16th century (Parmenter and Van Devender 1995). A prolonged drought in the mid-19th century in concert with greater hunting pressures from Native American residents and American settlers and increasing competition with domestic livestock (notably horses and cattle) for riparian winter grazing lands, brought the bison to the brink of extinction. Today,

USDA Forest Service Gen. Tech. Rep. RMRS-GTR-135-vol. 2. 2005

13

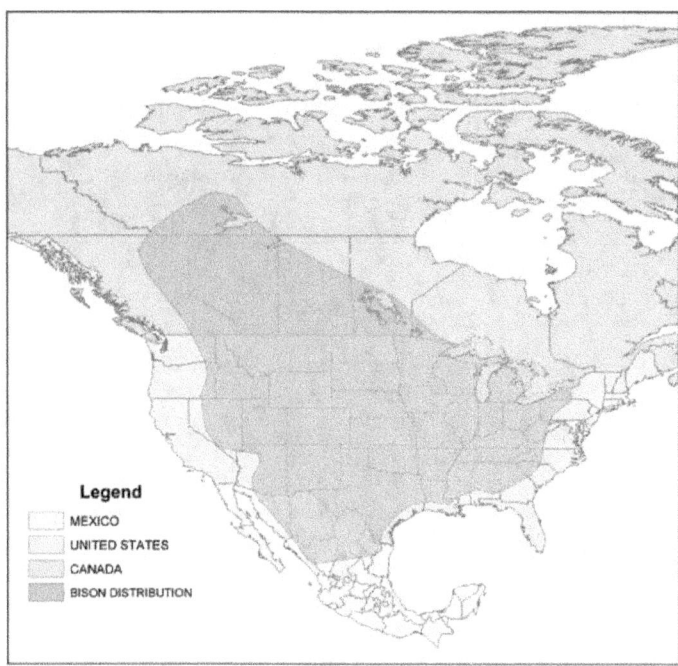

Figure 2-1. Map of the historic range of bison (NatureServe 2004).

there are approximately 30,000 bison in North America (Parmenter and Van Devender 1995). Bison currently play only a small role in the ecology of the grasslands of the Southwestern Region. They are discussed here because historically they had influence on some of the Great Plains grasslands and possibly on the desert grasslands (fig. 2-2) in the Region and because of their relationships with other wildlife species. They are also discussed because of their role as herbivores and the comparison with cattle.

Bison were common on the eastern plains of New Mexico in early historic times, although they did not inhabit the Rio Grande Valley or country to the west. Formerly abundant, and an important source of meat for Pueblo peoples, bison were essentially gone from New Mexico by 1860. Strips of buffalo skin kept among the Taos Indians were highly prized and were still being used primarily for decoration and ornamentation. Supposedly at this time, a fine buffalo robe would be saved by one of the Indian men for his burial. As with many Pueblo Tribes, the Taos Indians had among them a buffalo clan. The buffalo dance was one of the principal dances of the tribe, and it was set to music of drum and voice to represent the low hum of the grazing herd, and the thunder of a stampede (BISOM-M 2005). Unconfined herds of bison in the early 19th century moved over extensive areas of the Great Plains. Historical evidence shows that bison were present year round on short-grass, tallgrass, and mixed-grass regions. Herd movements were localized

and flexible, indicating that movements were in response to changing forage quantity and quality, making regular, long-range migrations unnecessary (Shaw 1996).

Currently in the Southwestern Region, there are no large herds of bison. Where they do exist, the herds are comparatively small and are reintroductions or transplants managed for hunting or recreation or to maintain the species.

How Bison Modify Habitat

Bison have been identified as keystone species in the Great Plains (Knapp and others 1999). As a keystone species, bison had a principal role in the formation and maintenance of grassland ecosystems.

Grazing—Bison are primarily graminoid feeders (Shaw 1996, Wisdom and Thomas 1996) and avoid forbs and woody species. Thus, within a bison grazing area, forbs are often conspicuously left ungrazed and are surrounded by grazed grasses (Knapp and others 1999).

Bison and large herbivores influenced landscapes at multiple scales. Therefore, in their planning, managers should consider the role these large herbivores had historically on grasslands. At broad scales, watershed and landscape, the long-term consequences of bison activities included cover reduction, and changes in dominance of plant species and productivity of grasses. Bison grazing may result in a competitive release of many subdominant plant species resulting in an increase in the abundance of forbs, an overall increase in plant species richness and diversity, and increased spatial heterogeneity (Hartnett and others 1996).

Although alterations in plant community composition can be attributed to the direct effects of grazing by bison, increased plant species richness is also likely to be a product of increased microsite diversity generated by nongrazing activities, such as dung and urine deposition, trampling, and wallowing. These and other bison activities contribute significantly to the increase in the spatial heterogeneity that is characteristic of grazed tallgrass prairie (Knapp and others 1999).

Bison use of grasslands alters nutrient cycling processes and patterns of nutrient availability. Their effects on nitrogen cycling are critical because nitrogen availability often limits plant productivity in these grasslands and influences plant species composition (Knapp and others 1999). Bison and other ungulates in grasslands consume plant biomass that is difficult to digest and return labile forms of nitrogen (that is, urine) to soils (Knapp and others 1999). Nitrogen in bison urine is largely urea, which can be hydrolyzed to ammonium in a matter of days, facilitating nitrogen cycling in the grasslands (Knapp and others 1999). The

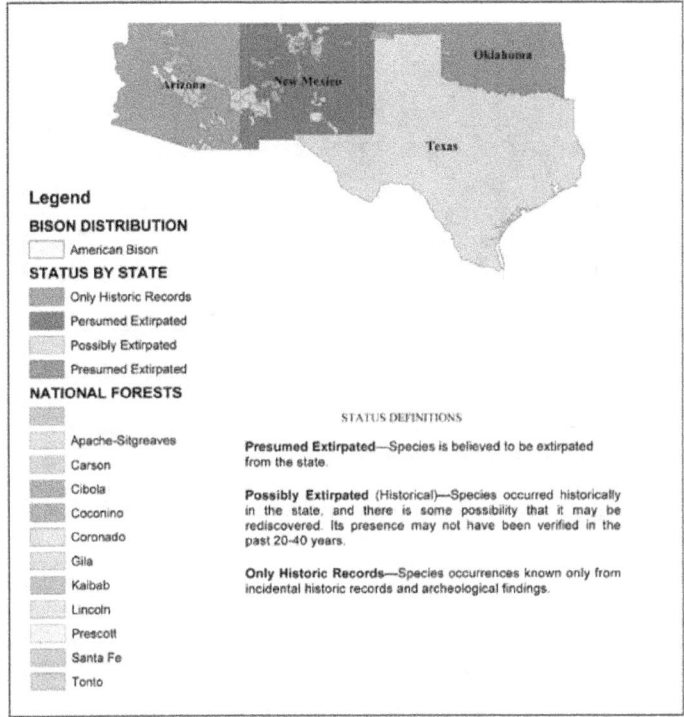

Legend

BISON DISTRIBUTION

☐ American Bison

STATUS BY STATE

◼ Only Historic Records

◼ Persumed Extirpated

☐ Possibly Extirpated

◼ Presumed Extirpated

NATIONAL FORESTS

☐

◼ Apache-Sitgreaves

◼ Carson

◼ Cibola

◼ Coconino

◼ Coronado

☐ Gila

◼ Kaibab

◻ Lincoln

☐ Prescott

◼ Santa Fe

◻ Tonto

STATUS DEFINITIONS

Presumed Extirpated—Species is believed to be extirpated from the state.

Possibly Extirpated (Historical)—Species occurred historically in the state, and there is some possibility that it may be rediscovered. Its presence may not have been verified in the past 20-40 years.

Only Historic Records—Species occurrences known only from incidental historic records and archeological findings.

Figure 2-2. Map showing the historic range of bison overlaid by the States within the USDA Forest Service Southwestern Region, and the status of bison within each State (NatureServe 2004) and the National Forests within the Region.

net effect of bison grazing on nutrient cycling appears to be increased rates of nitrogen cycling, coupled with an increase in spatial heterogeneity in nitrogen availability (Knapp and others 1999).

Are Bison and Cattle Functional Equivalents in Tallgrass Prairie?—Studies that have focused exclusively on cattle generally concur that their grazing activities can increase spatial heterogeneity and enhance plant species diversity, as long as stocking density is not too high (Hartnett and others 1996). Because bison grazing in tallgrass prairie has a similar effect, one could conclude that either herbivore can alter resource availability and heterogeneity and reduce the cover of the dominant grasses sufficiently to enhance the success of the subdominant species. Perhaps of greater importance than differences in foraging patterns between bison and cattle, however, are the numbers of nongrazing activities, such as wallowing and horning (rubbing on trees) that are associated exclusively with bison (Hartnett and others 1996). These activities, when combined with the spatial redistribution of nutrients and selective consumption of the dominant grasses, may further increase plant species richness and resource heterogeneity, particularly at the landscape scale.

Nevertheless, it is likely that because bison and cattle are functionally similar as large grass-feeding herbivores, management strategies (stocking intensity and duration) will have a greater influence on the degree of ecological equivalency achieved than inherent differences in these ungulates (Hartnett and others 1996). The degree of overlap in diet and foraging patterns is greater between bison and cattle than between cattle and other historically important native herbivores (Hartnett and others 1996) such as antelope, deer, and elk.

The important elements of bison grazing activities can and should be incorporated into conservation and restoration strategies for remnant prairies (Knapp and others 1999). One approach to accomplish this goal is the substitution of cattle for bison. In Knapp and others (1999), an argument was presented that the choice of whether to use cattle or bison as a management tool in grasslands is scale- and context-dependent. Clearly, reintroducing bison may not be appropriate for small prairie remnants with public access and low economic resources. But cattle, managed for their ecological rather than their economic value, may be suitable in such cases.

Relationship of Bison with Other Herbivores

Elk have such wide feeding niches that they use some of the same forages as bison (Shaw 1996). Diets of domestic sheep overlap partially with those of bison (Shaw 1996). Diets of mule deer and white-tailed deer do not converge with those of bison under normal conditions. Deer favor browse, forbs, and mast, whereas bison concentrate on graminoids. Deer favor woodier habitats while bison more frequently use open meadows and grasslands. Pronghorn share common ranges and habitats with bison but have divergent diets. Pronghorns eat almost exclusively forbs and browse. Horses forage on a wide range of plant foods, and their diets can overlap with those of bison (Shaw 1996).

Bison in the Desert Grasslands

The role bison played in desert grasslands is not clear. We do know that they occurred in the Southwest, but to what extent is still a question. An extinct bison (*Bison antiquus*) with massive widespread horns was prevalent in Arizona and Sonora, Mexico, during the last Ice Age, the Wisconsin Glacial Period (Parmenter and Van Devender 1995). There have been several archaeological findings that indicate bison where in the Southwest (Parmenter and Van Devender 1995).

USDA Forest Service Gen. Tech. Rep. RMRS-GTR-135-vol. 2. 2005

15

- The last confirmed hunting record of native bison in eastern New Mexico was in 1884 (Findley and others 1975).
- Bison horn cores, teeth, and bones were recovered in the excavation of Snaketown, a Hohokam settlement in the Gila River valley in Pinal County south of Phoenix that was occupied from before the birth of Christ until A.D. 1200 (Parmenter and Van Devender 1995).
- Bison bones associated with the years A.D. 1200 and 1380 were identified from two rooms in a 1968 excavation of the Hohokam Las Colinas site in Maricopa County near Phoenix (Parmenter and Van Devender 1995).
- Bison bones, some of them painted, found in a Babocomari Village excavation, were dated to A.D. 1200 through 1450 (Parmenter and Van Devender 1995). The Babocomari River, a tributary of the San Pedro River, flows through desert grassland on the north end of the Huachuca Mountains east of Elgin in Cochise County, Arizona. In the 1970s, a bison skull was found eroding out of sediments in the same area (Parmenter and Van Devender 1995).
- At Murray Springs, in the desert grasslands in the San Pedro River valley near Sierra Vista on the eastern base of the Huachucas in Cochise County, bones of extinct bison were found. This desert grassland site was likely dominated by grasses prior to 1890 but is presently covered with velvet mesquite (*Prosopis velutina*). At the same excavation, the skeleton of a female bison with a near-term fetus inside was discovered (Parmenter and Van Devender 1995) and radiocarbon-dated to A.D. 1700.

Not only were bison an archeological part of the desert grassland fauna, they were present according to historical accounts at least into the 17th and even into the 19th century. Parmenter and Van Devender (1995) present a postulate that the bison expanded its range into Arizona from the desert grassland valleys of northwestern Chihuahua during cooler, moister climatic fluctuations. It is a mystery why bison disappeared from desert grasslands before Euro-Americans began recording their observations in the 1820s (Parmenter and Van Devender 1995).

Bison have been introduced into Arizona and New Mexico since the early 1900s (Chung-MacCoubrey 1996, Findley and others 1975). Several small bison herds now exist in the desert grasslands of the Southwest.

Elk

Elk are an important herbivore in North American rangelands. Their large body size, herding behavior, pioneering habits, and high mobility make them a

Elk photo by Lane Eskew.

conspicuous wildlife species on open grasslands. The potential for elk to compete with livestock makes them an obvious source of controversy between ranchers, farmers, and wildlife advocates (Wisdom and Thomas 1996).

Elk use a broad spectrum of habitats including alpine, conifer, hardwood and mixed forests, grasslands, savanna, and shrubland/chaparral. They often frequent open areas such as alpine pastures, marshy meadows, river flats, and aspen parkland, as well as open meadows in coniferous forests, brushy clear cuts or forest edges, and semidesert areas. On more level terrain, they seek wooded hillsides in summer and open grasslands in winter. No special calving ground is typically used; calves are born in valleys or in areas as high as alpine tundra. Newborn initially may be hidden in rough terrain or dense cover.

Historical Distribution of Elk

The elk that live in North America today are direct descendants of red deer that migrated from Asia approximately 120,000 years ago. Currently, most biologists consider all the elk in North America to be the same species as the red deer in Asia and Europe (Rocky Mountain Elk Foundation 2004). Before European settlement, elk were among the most common and widely distributed of the wild ungulates in North America (Shaw 1996, Wisdom and Thomas 1996, Yoakum and others 1996). Historically, six subspecies of elk inhabited areas from the Atlantic to the Pacific Coasts. The Eastern elk (*Cercus elaphus Canadensis* extinct) once lived in Ontario, southern Quebec, and over much of the Eastern United States. Roosevelt elk (*Cervus elaphus roosevelti*) are found in the Pacific Northwest coastal forests of northern California,

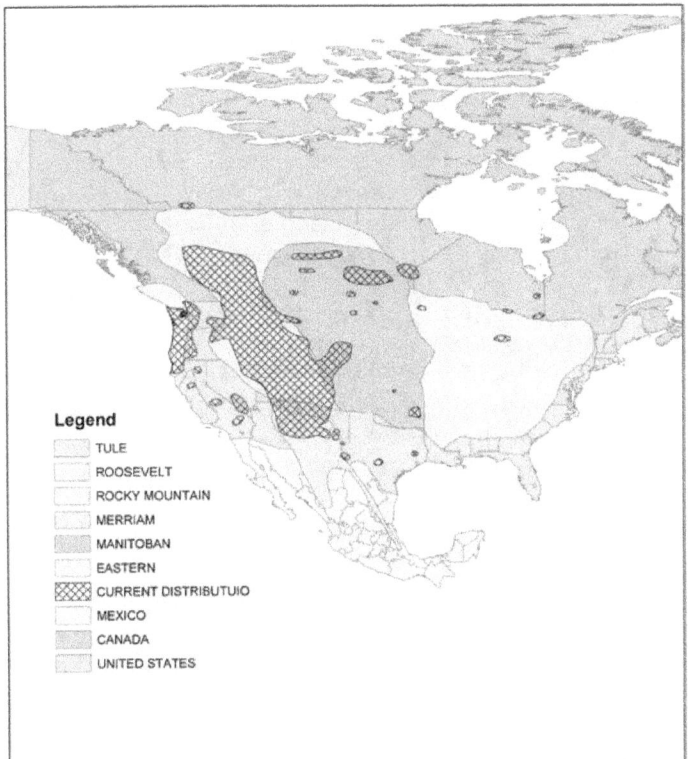

Figure 2-3. Historic distribution of elk in North America (Bryant and Maser 1982, in Wisdom and Thomas 1996) and the current distribution (NatureServe 2004).

Oregon, Washington, and Vancouver Island. The smallest of the subspecies is the Tule or California elk (*Cervus elaphus nanodes*), which once lived in large numbers in California's San Joaquin and Sacramento Valleys and has adapted to semidesert conditions. The Rocky Mountain elk (*Cervus laphus nelsoni*) ranges from New Mexico to Northcentral British Columbia and through the Intermountain region. It has been introduced into many places in North America and elsewhere in the world. Merriam elk (*Cevus elaphus marriami* extinct) once lived in the mountains and chaparrals of western Texas, New Mexico and mountains of Arizona. Manitoban elk (*Cervus elaphus manitobensis*) ranges from the southern Prairie Provinces of Canada to North Dakota. (fig. 2-3) (North American Elk Subspecies 2004, Rocky Mountain Elk Foundation 2004, Wisdom and Thomas 1996).

Controversy exists on whether elk once occupied rangelands of the Great Basin and Desert Southwest. This controversy centers on recent transplants of elk and/or recent colonization by elk into these areas (Yoakum and others 1996) and the potential for competition with livestock.

According to Yoakum and others (1996) and Wisdom and Thomas (1996), elk originally occupied most of the grasslands throughout Western North America, including major areas of the Great Basin and Desert

Southwest. However, lack of permanent water likely restricted elk distribution in the driest portions of these regions, and these dry areas presumably are outside the historical range of the species (fig. 2-3). This agrees with evidence that large, wild ungulates historically were absent from or sparsely distributed across large areas of the Intermountain West (Wisdom and Thomas 1996).

Population Declines and Extirpations

Shaw (1996) estimated numbers of North American elk at 10 million before the arrival of Euro-American settlers. By contrast, with the exception of the Rocky Mountain and Roosevelt subspecies in the West, elk are now distributed in small, disjunct populations across much of their former range (Wisdom and Thomas 1996) (fig. 2-3).

Elk numbers declined as Euro-American settlers moved west in the 17th, 18th, and 19th centuries. By the early 1800s, the eastern subspecies was likely extinct (Wisdom and Thomas 1996). Populations of Tule elk, once abundant in valleys and bottomlands of California, were reduced to approximately 100 animals by 1875 (Wisdom and Thomas 1996). The Merriam subspecies was extirpated from the Southwest by 1906 (Wisdom and Thomas 1996). By the early 1900s, Manitoban elk of the northern prairies were close to extinction (Wisdom and Thomas 1996). During the same period, populations of Rocky Mountain and Roosevelt elk were reduced to scattered, isolated pockets within their former range (Wisdom and Thomas 1996). Unregulated hunting, overgrazing by livestock, and conversion of habitat to agriculture and city land led to these broad-scale declines and extirpations (Parmenter and Van Devender 1995, Wisdom and Thomas 1996).

Current Abundance and Distribution

In 1910, an estimated 60,000 elk remained in North America, with fragmented populations present in seven Western States. By this time, most States had enacted legislation that prohibited the hunting of elk. Then, efforts to recover elk populations were initiated through programs of translocation. From 1892 to 1939, more than 5,000 elk were live-trapped and transported from the Yellowstone area for release in 36 States and parts of Western Canada (Wisdom and Thomas 1996).

By the 1930s, elk numbers and distribution increased substantially, with the population estimated at 165,764 by 1937 and 236,787 by 1941. In the 1960s, elk populations had grown to approximately 440,000 and increased to 500,000 by the late l970s and 600,000 by 1987 (Wisdom and Thomas 1996).

Today an estimated 700,000 elk exist in North America. Populations are generally increasing and

USDA Forest Service Gen. Tech. Rep. RMRS-GTR-135-vol. 2. 2005

17

translocations continue. Elk are present in at least 22 States (fig. 2-3). Native predators, particularly wolves (*Canis* spp.), have been extirpated throughout the Southwestern range of elk except in limited reintroduction areas, and therefore, elk numbers are no longer naturally regulated. Hunting has replaced predation as a means for maintaining elk populations.

Elk on Public Versus Private Lands

Before Euro-American settlement, elk often made expansive seasonal movements in response to annual changes in weather and forage availability (Wisdom and Thomas 1996). Such movements are not possible today. Many seasonal habitats used historically by elk are now privately owned and managed exclusively for agriculture, livestock, and timber production (Wisdom and Thomas 1996). Elk use of these areas is not tolerated or tolerated only minimally. In other cases, historic habitats have been converted to cities, industrial developments, and recreation areas (Wisdom and Thomas 1996). Elk now reside in "ecologically incomplete" or "ecologically compressed" habitats across much of their historic range (Wisdom and Thomas 1996).

Patterns of land ownership in the Western United States exemplify the problem. In the West, more than 90 percent of elk use public lands during summer while they use privately owned lands for the majority of their winter range. Large numbers of elk are produced on publicly owned summer range, where they are valued for hunting and viewing. Elk then migrate to privately owned ranges at lower elevations during the winter. On such lands, elk often encounter severe shortages of habitat features and active programs of population control to minimize competition with livestock and damage to crops (Wisdom and Thomas 1996).

Efforts to control elk damage and consumption of crops and cattle forage on privately owned lands are intense and varied. Activities include providing landowners elk hunting permits to sell to hunters, government financial compensation for loss of revenue due to damages caused by elk, permission to landowners to kill "nuisance" elk, special hunts, fencing to exclude animals from private ranges, and leasing or acquisition of additional winter range to maintain winter carrying capacity.

The shortage of year-round, ecologically complete habitats for elk and other wild ungulates poses significant management problems on North American rangelands. Many of today's management problems can be attributed to fragmented ownerships and the associated differences in land use goals between public and private lands (Wisdom and Thomas 1996).

Other Economic and Social Values

Elk hunting and viewing are highly valued experiences, both aesthetically and economically. New sources of revenue from consumptive and nonconsumptive users of elk and other wildlife, combined with growing political influences of such users, are causing shifts in economic and social values that affect management of public lands (Wisdom and Thomas 1996).

Elk-Livestock Interactions

Grazing by elk and livestock is perhaps the most significant land use issue affecting management of both species on public and private lands. Issues of forage allocation and competition are subjects of unending debates (Wisdom and Thomas 1996).

In relation to dietary overlap between elk and cattle, the following 12 generalizations can be made (Wisdom and Thomas 1996):

- The potential for competition between elk and cattle is highest on winter and spring-fall ranges where either forage quantity or quality is limited and where both species can commonly share "ecologically compressed habitats" on low-elevation bottomlands or foothills.
- Competition between elk and cattle is usually low on high-elevation summer ranges where forage of moderate to high quality is readily available during late spring and summer and where animals have a more expansive land base from which to make optimal grazing choices with carryover effects into winter and spring.
- The potential for competition between elk and cattle increases during late summer and fall on high elevation summer ranges following the onset of prolonged seasonal drought and the subsequent decline in forage quality.
- Elk and cattle often distribute themselves spatially in a manner that minimizes competition.
- Elk and cattle can distribute themselves temporally (seasonally) in a manner that minimizes or heightens competition between the two.
- On ranges where spatial or temporal distributions overlap, differences in the diets of elk and cattle can sometimes minimize competition.
- The potential for competition between elk and cattle is high on unproductive rangelands, especially in arid ecosystems. Potential for competition also is high on rangelands grazed to full or maximum use by elk or cattle, and on rangelands experiencing a declining trend in condition.

Table 2-1. How elk respond to various grazing regimes (Wisdom and Thomas 1996).

Grazing system	Result
Season-long, deferred-rotation (in northeastern Oregon)	Elk preferred ungrazed areas and showed no difference in their use of season-long versus deferred-rotation pastures.
Season-long, deferred-rotation grazing (in northeastern Oregon)	Higher elk use under season-long than deferred-rotation grazing with cattle light stocking. The opposite preference was found when stocking was high.
Rest-rotation grazing, season-long grazing (in Montana)	Elk preferred pastures in rest and avoided pastures actively grazed by cattle. However, overall use by elk was not significantly different under rotation grazing than that observed under season-long grazing.
Season-long, rest-rotation grazing (in east-central Idaho)	No changes were found in population trends of elk following a change from season-long to rest-rotation grazing. It was concluded that elk preferred pastures in rest and avoided those actively grazed by cattle.

- High densities of elk may induce negative effects on forage conditions similar to that caused by high stocking rates of cattle, resulting in lower animal performance. Intraspecific competition among elk, and resultant negative effects on forage, likely are density-dependent and manifested at high population densities.

- Elk show an aversion to the presence of cattle that may or may not restrict their grazing choices.

- On productive rangelands that were grazed historically by native herbivores, systems of cattle grazing can be designed to enhance forage or foraging conditions for elk. Likewise, grazing by elk can enhance conditions for cattle.

- Competition can be high at a given time and place during a year and low or nonexistent in the same place and time in subsequent years.

- Perception is rarely reality when judging competitive interactions between elk and cattle.

Elk and other Native Large Herbivores

Distributional overlap can occur with mule and white-tailed deer, bison, pronghorn, and bighorn sheep, which apparently partition forage and habitat resources to minimize competition in areas of overlapping distribution such as Yellowstone National Park (Shaw 1996). Often, patterns of foraging and habitat use are complementary. Grazing by elk can enhance forage conditions for pronghorn and mule deer (Shaw 1996).

Regardless, competition does occur in some situations (Wisdom and Thomas 1996). In contrast to mule deer and bighorn sheep, elk generally are more opportunistic and varied in their diet selection. Elk more easily digest forage of low quality, are more mobile and wide-ranging, and form larger herds, all of which may result in a competitive edge when resources are limited, presuming that elk out-compete mule deer on winter ranges that are limited in size and forage availability. Wisdom and Thomas (1996) also believed that mule deer would leave

or avoid areas of heavy use by elk, even if forage was available and dietary overlap with elk is low.

Grazing Management Trade-Offs Between Elk and Livestock

Type of Grazing System—Little data exist about elk response to various systems of livestock grazing because there are few tests of elk response under experimental replication. Most research focuses on the effect of livestock grazing. The information that is available is inconclusive regarding elk preference for or aversion to any particular grazing system. Table 2-1 summarizes how elk respond to various grazing schemes.

Effect of Stocking Rate—Stocking rate of livestock, more than any other grazing variable, influences the composition, quantity, and nutritive value of forage ungulate (Wisdom and Thomas 1996). This premise, combined with the potential for forage competition between elk and cattle, provides a framework for describing the effect of stocking rate on forage conditions for elk:

- Regardless of the grazing system used, the composition, quantity, and quality of forage available to elk is determined largely by the stocking rate of cattle, interacting with the density of elk, the inherent characteristics of the site, and weather.

- Light stocking rates of cattle can be neutral or positive in their influence on the composition and nutritive value of forage for elk.

- Moderate stocking rates of cattle, with allowable use of key species between 25 and 60 percent, can be positive, neutral, or negative in their effect on elk forage. Much depends on the timing of grazing, the physiological response of key forage plants to grazing, and the inherent productivity of the range and its condition.

- On relatively unproductive rangelands of the Great Basin and Desert Southwest, it is likely that cattle use more than 25 percent will negatively affect forage conditions for elk.

- High stocking rates of cattle invariably heighten the potential for competition with elk for limited forage. Similarly, high densities of elk may induce intraspecific competition for forage (Shaw 1996, Wisdom and Thomas 1996), magnifying potential competition with cattle.

- Regardless, cattle use of key species at levels 60 percent or higher may significantly reduce or eliminate key forage plants for elk and cattle on nearly all range types (Wisdom and Thomas 1996). The remaining forage will likely be abundant but of low nutritive value, or scarce but of high nutritive value.

- On desert rangelands, both low quantity and quality of vegetation may result from overgrazing, negatively affecting both elk and cattle. These effects on elk forages may explain the inverse relationship between stocking rates of cattle and habitat use by elk (Wisdom and Thomas 1996). This relationship generally holds true for all types of grazing systems that have been studied.

Water Developments—Water is considered limiting to elk on many arid and semiarid rangelands. Elk may concentrate near water sources in extremely dry areas. Increasing the distribution and availability of water on many of the driest grasslands will likely enhance elk use of such areas, especially during dry seasons or years (Wisdom and Thomas 1996).

However, water development can be a "double-edged sword" if livestock have access to the water. Livestock use is usually highest within 1.6 km of water; this is the zone of most direct competition between elk and livestock. Improving the distribution of water—that is, making water more evenly and readily available throughout a pasture—will also result in a more even distribution of livestock (Wisdom and Thomas 1996) when all things are equal. This may increase the potential for competition with elk, or reduce elk use in favor of cattle use for two reasons: First, most water developments have road access; elk avoid areas near roads. Road densities and traffic will likely to increase with an increase in number and distribution of water developments. Elk are especially vulnerable to human harassment during hunting seasons when roads facilitate hunting (Wisdom and Thomas 1996). The second reason is that elk avoid livestock but return to grazed areas after livestock have left. A more even distribution of livestock, resulting from a more even distribution of water, may hinder grazing choices by elk unless livestock-free areas also are available within a herd's seasonal home range.

Roads—Wherever elk occur, they consistently and dramatically avoid areas near roads that are open to motorized traffic (Perry and Overly 1977, Wisdom and Thomas 1996). Implications of this relationship cannot be underestimated. All of the positive elk management that could be accomplished could be partially or wholly offset by the negative effects of open roads. This is especially true in areas of open grasslands and gentle terrain; here, vegetation and topography provide limited hiding and security from human activities. Aggressive programs of road management, obliteration and closure, is necessary to facilitate elk use of grasslands.

Conflict Resolution of Elk-Livestock Problems

Ecosystem Management of Elk—Elk are mobile, adaptive, and opportunistic; they use a variety of habitats that span many jurisdictions and land ownerships. Their annual movements can encompass hundreds of square kilometers, bringing them into contact with a multitude of landowners and land uses.

At the same time, human development continues unabated on elk ranges. Traditional users of rangelands, such as farmers and livestock growers, are generally intolerant of high elk numbers. Hunters, wildlife viewers, and urbanites value these same rangelands, desiring more elk for hunting and watching. Given these conditions, elkland use conflicts will continue to grow in frequency and intensity.

If polarized interest parties can adopt an ecosystem or a landscape approach to elk management, all of them will benefit. The geographic scale must change from that of an individual pasture, watershed, landowner, or allotment to that of an entire herd range, such as 10,000 ha or more. Within each herd range, partnerships such as those under way in Colorado (Wisdom and Thomas 1996) must be forged. Such partnerships are politically effective and provide an ecological basis upon which all interested parties can plan and implement the proper combination of land treatments and hunting regimes necessary to achieve the desired demography and distribution of elk across all land ownerships in time and space.

Deer

White-Tailed Deer

Of all the big game animals in North America, the white-tailed deer is the most widespread and numerous member of the deer family, *Cervidae*. It is also the most important big game species recreationally and economically. It occurs in all States except California, Nevada, and Utah (fig. 2-4) (Southeastern Cooperative Wildlife Disease Study 1982). There are 38 races or subspecies ranging from southeastern Alaska through parts of

20

USDA Forest Service Gen. Tech. Rep. RMRS-GTR-135-vol. 2. 2005

Figure 2-4. White-tailed deer distribution in North America (NatureServe 2004).

Legend
- WHITE-TAIL DEER
- CANADA
- UNITED STATES
- MEXICO

The requirements of white-tailed deer are met in practically every ecological type, including grasslands, prairies and plains, mountains, hardwood, coniferous and tropical forests, deserts, and even farmland where it associates with woodlots and riverine habitats (Teer 1996).

Woody vegetation used by deer for cover and often for browse and mast is not an absolute requirement of deer habitats, although white-tailed deer are most often associated with brushlands and forested habitats. The species does occur in low densities in open pasturelands and grasslands. White-tailed deer in open grassland habitats occur in areas having screening or protective cover nearby for escape. Cover in such habitats may be herbaceous. Woody cover may be available in riparian zones associated with grasslands and plains.

White-tailed deer are also reported to use hardwood draws that often surge down into grasslands and mesic shrublands (Teer 1996). They often use these habitats during summer.

Management of Livestock for White-Tailed Deer—White-tailed deer and livestock are compatible and even synergistic, if livestock are managed for deer. Livestock can change the quantity and quality of forage by affecting erosion processes and nutrient losses, and consequently, even change the quality of the soil on which the feed is produced (Teer 1996). No other factors in deer ecology and management, outside of poaching and the plow, have influenced the habitat and productivity of deer on rangelands more than livestock (Teer 1996).

Traditionally, the economic worth of livestock made them the animals of choice, the priority, in grasslands. Livestock were often stocked in combinations on common-use ranges where browse, forbs, and grasses provide preferred foods. Until recently, white-tailed deer and other wildlife species were not considered in livestock management. Changes that have occurred in management of rangeland for wildlife have been the result of commercialization of hunting, recreation, and, more recently, the growing interest in wildlife viewing. The changes from traditional uses of grasslands, particularly of public lands, are due to environmental groups challenging many of the traditional uses in favor of management of wildlife.

Competition for Resources—Competition between deer and domestic livestock is important when populations are dense. Sheep and goat competition with deer can be especially severe because the seasonal and dietary overlaps of these species are almost 100 percent. Cattle are less competitive with deer because their diets are primarily grasses and grasslike plants, whereas, deer use grasses sparingly (Teer 1996).

southern Canada into practically all of the contiguous United States and through Central America and as far south as northern South America (Teer 1996).

The ecology and management of the different races of white-tailed deer are similar across the various ecosystems they inhabit. Therefore, management is habitat- and herd-specific and must be adapted to the vegetation type and other elements of their habitat.

Unlike those in forested habitats, white-tailed deer numbers in the grasslands in the western United States have increased as a result of encroachment of woody vegetation and agricultural fields. In the Great Plains, deer were associated primarily with riparian systems but began to extend their ranges into upland habitats in the 1940s. In prairie-agricultural habitat in east-central Montana, white-tailed deer selected riparian habitat and its interspersion with cropland and rangeland habitats (Teer 1996). White-tailed deer on the lower Yellowstone River are associated with grassland (Teer 1996) and use adjacent farmland. Their numbers are positively related to density of riparian cover.

Habitat—White-tailed deer are extremely adaptable. They thrive in close association with humans and their agricultural and industrial developments.

USDA Forest Service Gen. Tech. Rep. RMRS-GTR-135-vol. 2. 2005

21

Good deer habitat consists of diverse vegetation. Availability of seasonal food sources is imperative in satisfying the whitetail's nutritional requirements. White-tailed deer reach their greatest numbers in rangeland communities where seral stages are below climax. Thus, disturbed land is often the best deer range because the habitat contains an array of annual and perennial herbaceous plants that serve as food, and woody plants provide food and protection from enemies and weather (Teer 1996).

Behavioral Relationships with Livestock—It is not clear if whitetails avoid cattle in pastures that are grazed. Deer on the Welder Wildlife Foundation in southern Texas avoided pastures stocked with cattle. Deer did not alter their home ranges but chose pastures in unstocked portions of their range. Avoidance was mostly in heavily stocked, short-duration grazing pastures. Similar avoidance occurred with greater distances between deer and cattle than between deer and other cervids (Teer 1996).

Whitetails ignored cattle and commonly grazed with them. They also ignored riderless horses but avoided horses with riders. Deer avoided pastures where forage supply was decimated by heavy grazing (Teer 1996). Whitetails do not appear to avoid livestock when stocking is low or moderate. Deferred rotation pastures contained deer in higher numbers than pastures grazed more intensively.

In the past, criteria used by range and wildlife managers to judge carrying capacity or quality of the range for livestock had little relationship to quality of white-tailed deer habitat or other wildlife species' habitats. Great differences occur in food and cover requirements of various kinds of domestic animals and deer, and these differences were largely ignored in classification systems.

Several researchers have attempted to determine forage relationships between livestock and whitetails. Animal unit equivalents proposed on the Edwards Plateau of Texas were five sheep, or six goats, or six white-tailed deer to one 489 kg cow with calf at side (Teer 1996). Teer (1996) reported that 13 deer were equivalent to one cow on the King Ranch in southern Texas. These ratios are viewed as rough standards for interpreting stocking rates and for developing diet relationships among various herbivores.

The impact of stocking rates of livestock on white-tailed deer is a two-pronged relationship. Overgrazing is obviously harmful to deer habitat, and undergrazing can also reduce its quality. Light to moderate grazing promotes plant vigor and diversity and increases production (Teer 1996). When grasses dry, cattle will switch to woody plants, which affect the quality of browse for white-tailed deer.

In addition to the effects grazing may have on the quality of white-tailed deer habitat, ranching activi-ties also have an influence. Hood and Inglis (1974) found roundups disturbed white-tailed deer. Bucks reacted to roundups with long flights to adjacent pastures and, at times, extending their home range or left their home range for a time. Does, on the other hand, took a circuitous course that began and ended in their home range. Before the roundups the mean home range for does was 173 ha (427 acres), and after the disturbance the mean size of the home range had not change significantly, 190 ha (469 acres). The mean home range for bucks enlarged significantly from before the roundups, 285 to 402 ha (704 to 993 acres) (Hood and Inglis 1974). These before-disturbance home ranges are in close agreement to those determined by Rogers and others (1978) of a mean of 2.9 squire miles (751 acres) in semidesert grass-shrub community in Arizona.

Mule Deer

Population Trends and Changes with Habitat—Mule deer are found throughout Western North America (fig. 2-5). There is disagreement on how common they were prior to Euro-American settlement. Diaries and journals from the period 1820 to 1834 of early Euro-American explorers and mountain men indicate that mule deer were seen only incidentally. Also, researchers estimate that no more than five million, and possibly fewer, mule and black-tailed deer occupied the western United States during pre-Columbian times (Teer 1996).

Human settlement, unrestricted hunting, drought, severe blizzards, and the conversion of habitat to agriculture caused declines in mule deer populations. By the early 1900s, mule deer were generally scarce throughout much of the West. Widespread and intensive livestock grazing, logging, and burning proved beneficial to mule deer. Plants that were more palatable to mule deer than those that originally dominated native vegetation either invaded or increased in abundance (Teer 1996). This improvement in habitat along with strict hunting regulations, control of predators, and perhaps favorable weather conditions allowed populations to increase to all-time highs during the 1920s through the 1950s (Peek and Krausman 1996).

Since those high population levels, a variety of factors including overpopulation, the aging of shrub habitats to less productive seral stages, liberalized hunting regulations, and severe winters and drought led to declines in mule deer populations. By the mid-1960s and early 1970s, mule deer populations in many areas of the West had declined sharply (Peek and Krausman 1996).

The vegetation communities that supported mule deer have been subjected to livestock grazing, fire

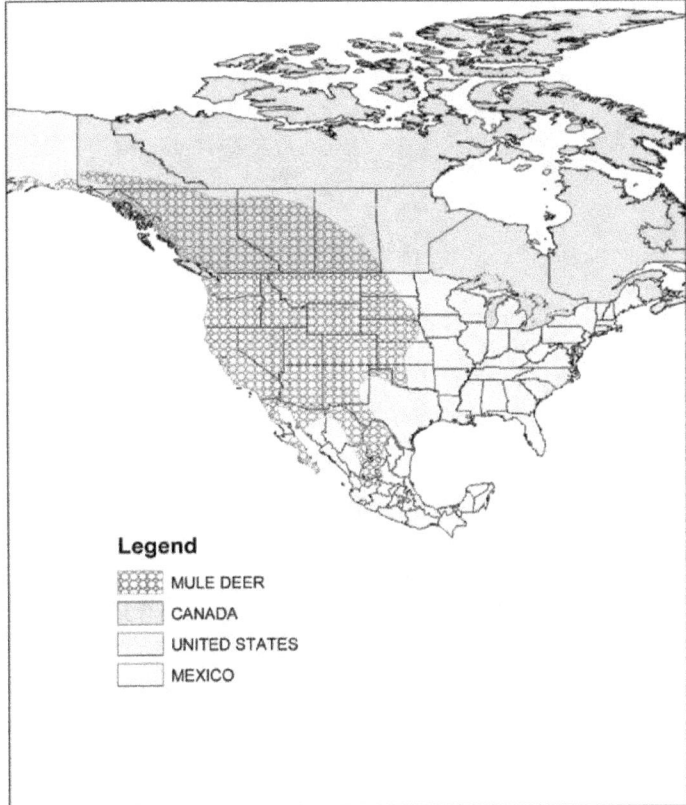

Figure 2-5. Mule deer distribution in North America (Nature-Serve 2004).

Legend

- MULE DEER
- CANADA
- UNITED STATES
- MEXICO

not woody browse for mule deer. Fire, mechanical manipulation, and herbicides are all employed to control and eradicate woody species. Because only a part of mule deer diet is composed of woody plants it is difficult to establish how these treatments have impacted mule deer numbers (Peek and Krausman 1996).

Predation—Predators include coyotes (*Canis latrans*), bobcats (*Felis rufus*), golden eagles (*Aquila chrysaetos*), wolf (*Canis* spp.), mountain lion, grizzly bear (*Ursus arctos*), and black bear (*Ursus americanus*) (Peek and Krausman 1996, Shawn and Dood 1984). The effect of predators, alone or in combination, on the dynamics of ungulate populations will vary with relative size of the predator and ungulate populations, ungulate dispersion patterns, sex and age, and general health of the populations. The effects of predation are difficult to isolate from all the factors concurrently acting on populations.

Deer population size will often influence the role predation plays. Predators, particularly those whose numbers are only slightly influenced by prey density, generally will have a relatively greater effect on deer populations whose numbers have been reduced by other factors (Wisdom and Thomas 1996).

Grazing and Mule Deer—Livestock grazing may interact with mule deer by altering plant succession to favor or reduce deer forage and cover. Changes in plant productivity caused by livestock grazing may also affect mule deer. Kie (1996) found that when cattle stocking rates increased during the fall and early winter when herbaceous forage was limited, then mule deer maximized energy by spending less time feeding. And when herbaceous plants began to grow rapidly there appeared to be no competition between deer and cattle, and increased cattle stocking rates had no effect on the time deer spent foraging.

Mule deer can also be directly disturbed by livestock and associated human activity. Mule deer responses may include changes in distribution patterns and habitat use, modification of activity, or alteration in population density (Peek and Krausman 1996).

Forage Choice by Mule Deer and Cattle—Peek and Krausman (1996) describe winter mule deer diet as consisting of an average of more than 74 percent shrubs and trees, 15 percent forbs, and 11 percent grasses and sedges and rushes (table 2-2). Spring diets include shrubs and trees (49 percent), grasses, sedges, and rushes (26 percent), and forbs (25 percent) (table 2-2). Summer diets include shrubs (49 percent) and forbs (46 percent) and minor proportions of grasses, sedges, and rushes. The fall diet showed an increase in dietary use of shrubs and trees to an average of 60 percent, while forbs declined to an average of 30 percent, and grasses, sedges, and rushes were 9 percent (table 2-2).

suppression, uncharacteristically hot wildfires, and logging. These factors combined with natural successional processes have changed the natural habitats of mule deer. In some areas excessive grazing reduced grasses and brought about a reduction of fine fuels necessary to carry wildfires (Peek and Krausman 1996). This created a favorable environment for trees and shrubs, allowing many browse species to become larger and more vigorous and establish in higher densities. For example, important species such as bitterbrush (*Purshia tridentata*), sagebrush, curlleaf mountain-mahogany (*Cercocarpus ledfolius*), and rabbitbrush increased. Eventually, however, lack of fire or some other stand renewal process led to decadent/senescent older aged shrub stands that are less productive for mule deer. Dense, older aged shrub stands can restrict animal movements and browse availability (Peek and Krausman 1996).

Invasion by exotic annual grasses such as cheatgrass (*Bromus tectorum*) has caused range deterioration in some areas. Cheatgrass can out-compete native species and tends to burn frequently, thus eliminating the opportunity for woody browse species to become established. Ranchers and range managers encourage the production of grasses as forage for livestock and

USDA Forest Service Gen. Tech. Rep. RMRS-GTR-135-vol. 2. 2005

23

Table 2-2. Comparison of forage use by season between mule deer and cattle.

Season	Mule deer	Cattle
Winter		
Shrubs and trees	Averaged > 74% of (range = 27-100%)	Shrubs and trees typically receive light use.
Forbs	Averaged 15% (range = 0-43%)	
Grasses and grasslikes (sedges and rushes)	Average 11% (range = 0-53%)	
Spring		
Shrubs and trees	Average 49% (range = 6-92%)	Shrubs and trees typically receive light use.
Forbs	Average 25% (range = 0-43%)	Forbs appear to be used more in spring and when grazing is light.
Grasses and grasslikes (sedges and rushes)	Average 26% (range = 4-64%)	
Summer		
Shrubs	Average 49% (range = 12-95%)	Shrubs and trees typically receive light use.
Forbs	Average 46% (range = 3-77%)	
Grasses and grasslikes (sedges and rushes)	Very low	Grasses generally predominate in the summer diet of range cattle, but forbs may constitute a significant proportion in some areas.
Fall		
Shrubs and trees	Average 60% (range = 3-97%)	Shrubs and trees typically receive light use.
Forbs	Average 30% (range =2-78%)	
Grasses and grasslikes (sedges and rushes)	Average 9% (range = 0-24%)	

The general diet for mule deer shows high variability across the range depending on what is available. Habitat manipulations can stimulate changes in plant use. For example, burning or grazing that removes standing litter and stimulates early growth of bluebunch wheatgrass (*Agropyron spicaturn*) can increase wheatgrass palatability, encouraging use by mule deer (Peek and Krausman 1996).

Forage used by livestock changes with intensity of use of a range, between areas, seasons, and years, as with mule deer. Grasses generally predominate in the summer diet of cattle, but forbs may constitute a significant proportion of cattle diet in some areas (Peek and Krausman 1996). Forbs are used more in spring diet of cattle and when grazing is light. Highest forb use occurred in late spring on eastern Oregon grasslands (Wisdom and Thomas 1996). Foraging use of shrubs and trees by cattle is light during all seasons, but woody plants may be a significant part of the diet during some years and in some areas.

The contrast between cattle and mule deer forage preferences is best exemplified by their usages of grasses. Cattle concentrate on the most abundant grasses that are often dominants in the ecosystem while mule deer tend to use subdominant species such as the bluegrasses, fine-leafed species such as fescues, or tips of leaves of species such as crested wheatgrass.

Potential Overlaps in Forage Choice—Drought and intensity of grazing are significant factors that influence the potential for competition for forage between mule deer and livestock (Julander 1955). When the highly palatable forb yellow sweetclover (*Melilotus officinalis*) was reduced in abundance because of low precipitation, greater use of shrubs and grasses by deer and cattle resulted (Bowyer 1986). If grazing is heavy, then cattle and mule deer may be forced to compete for scarce forage. Diet choice may be expected to vary between years for both species, depending upon what is available and what is palatable. Managing for several plant species may provide the level of nutrients needed. In maintaining mule deer habitat, it is important to provide a variety of forage choices and species diversity in plant communities. Heavy grazing or drought that reduces plant diversity or plant productivity can increase the potential for forage competition among the different grassland wildlife species (Peek and Krausman 1996). Forage availability in early summer is much higher than later in the season when forages become senescent. While range managers cannot anticipate the weather, the implications are to keep grasslands productive with a diversity of forage so animals have opportunities to exercise free choice and minimize potential competition.

In winter, forage use and species abundance are influenced by snow depth (Peek and Krausman 1996).

Mule deer photo by Lane Eskew.

Although mule deer may forage on a combination of forbs, grasses, and browse plants during snow-free periods, snow conditions may limit the use of forbs and grasses covered with snow that might otherwise be selected. Releasing livestock on winter ranges prior to snowfall should help to minimize reductions in available forage for mule deer.

Plant Succession—Sagebrushes may compose a moderate to heavy part of the winter and spring diet of mule deer (Peek and Krausman 1996) when forbs are unavailable and grasses are cured. Mule deer using less nutritious woody browse forage will switch to green grasses and forbs when they appear in spring without shifting to new habitats.

Mule deer graze many exotics plants, including cheatgrass, tansy mustard, filaree (*Erodium cicutariurn*), and tumble mustard. Wyethia, dandelion, salsify (*Tragopogon dubius*), and the eriogonums (*Eriogonurn* spp.), which would be expected to increase with cattle grazing, are also foraged by mule deer. However, balsom-root (*Balsamorhiza* spp.), tall asters (*Aster* spp.), bluebells (*Mertensia* spp.), and geraniums (*Geranium* spp.), which would be expected to decrease with livestock grazing, may be locally important mule deer foods (Peek and Krausman 1996).

The semidesert grasslands of the Southwest have also been subject to extensive modifications due to grazing and reduction of fire (Peek and Krausman 1996). There has been a general trend from grass-dominated communities in semidesert grasslands to shrub-dominated communities, but this trend has occurred in both grazed and ungrazed areas. An increase in shrubs is attributed to a hotter and drier climatic trend (Bock and Bock 1996). These grasslands are extremely important mule deer habitats and probably have become more so as shrubs have proliferated.

Rangeland conditions have generally improved since the drought of the 1930s (Peek and Krausman 1996). However, "improvement" is often interpreted in relation to livestock forage and might not reflect improvement for mule deer. Increases in livestock forage may mean that ground cover has improved, even if numbers of palatable mule deer forage species have declined. Mule deer habitat may benefit in some circumstances where plant species diversity is enhanced (Peek and Krausman 1996).

Grazing Systems and Their Influence on Mule Deer—This section includes some recommendations that will benefit mule deer (Peek and Krausman 1996):

- Construct fences that will permit passage of deer. These fences can be constructed to minimize interference with movement between pastures.
- Water developments may be used by deer, and guidelines exist to accommodate wildlife (Boroski and Mossman 1966, Peek and Krausman 1996, Rickel and others 1996). However, water development may allow cattle or other native ungulate species to graze areas previously not grazed and may displace deer.
- Forage use by livestock must be kept at levels that will ensure enough food for mule deer or will enhance growth of forages palatable to deer following grazing. This assumes that the objective of the grazing system is merely to integrate grazing with retention of mule deer habitat. However, if objectives include improvement of habitat by increasing shrub production, then special grazing management is indicated.

Peek and Krausman (1996) suggests that dual use of range by cattle and mule deer, when effectively managed, can be efficient land use even when both herbivores are utilizing the same forage species.

Use of Livestock to Enhance Mule Deer Habitat—Complete removal of livestock may not maintain nor increase needed shrub production on mule deer winter ranges, and efforts to enhance shrub retention and growth require active manipulation of plant cover (Peek and Krausman 1996). Fire and grazing management are logical tools for manipulating cover. They are relatively economical to apply, and managers have experience in their use.

Livestock grazing can be used to improve vegetation conditions for mule deer. Early observations that browsing stimulated production of additional twigs showed the potential for retention or improvement by grazing, recognizing that cattle might be used to alter shrub form and productivity to promote use by mule deer. The following objectives may be achieved by gazing livestock on mule deer habitat (Peek and Krausman 1996):

USDA Forest Service Gen. Tech. Rep. RMRS-GTR-135-vol. 2. 2005

25

- Removing old growth to stimulate new growth palatable to deer.
- Reducing shrub heights to levels that are available to deer.
- Removing old growth that blocks access to palatable forage for deer.
- Using forage less palatable to deer, and consequently reducing competition with forage used by deer.

Timing of grazing is important where mule deer and livestock may have similar diet preferences. Timing of livestock grazing can be adjusted to influence forage production to benefit deer. Spring grazing may be appropriate to support shrubs that compose the major part of mule deer's winter diet. On ranges where the grass-forb components are important for deer, fall grazing is more appropriate. It has been found that sheep grazing from early summer to late summer improves forage quality in fall and increases forage quantity in spring for deer in Oregon's Coast Range. Springtime sheep grazing of a Utah winter range increased bitterbrush current annual growth and reduced the standing dead grass cover, which allowed mule deer to select a more nutritious diet that included more herbaceous material (Fulgham and others 1982). Longhurst and others (1983) explains that grazing maintained oak-woodland vegetation in a productive seral stage for deer by promoting growth and production of important deer forages. Cattle grazing could be used to drive plant composition in ways similar to sheep management (Peek and Krausman 1996). These results demonstrate how livestock can manipulate forage composition and productivity to achieve mule deer habitat objectives, suggesting that complete exclusion of livestock may not be necessary.

Long-term changes in vegetation composition may occur when special grazing treatments are used, and these changes should be monitored to ensure that trends in rangeland conditions are detected and modifications of grazing, if necessary, are timely (Peek and Krausman 1996). Manipulation of timing and species of livestock to enhance mule deer range has been effectively demonstrated and should be more broadly applied in future habitat management programs for mule deer and other wildlife. While such range management programs may require more flexibility and coordination, benefits derived may more than offset the added efforts. We can now purposefully manage grasslands to benefit livestock, mule deer, and rangeland vegetation by establishing suitable objectives and developing grazing programs that are flexible and tailored to the specific situation (Peek and Krausman 1996).

Deer Management

Herd and Population Management—Maintenance, growth, and reproductive states require different nutritional intakes. Three seasons of the year are particularly critical for mule deer: fall, winter, and spring. Fall is important for putting on fat and for fetus development during the winter. A good winter diet is important for survival during the cold months. Then in spring, the plants that are early spring growers are critical for fetus development and lactation. Plus, aside from forage requirements, fawns need tall vegetation for hiding from predators. The importance of diets for fall, winter, and spring is similar for all Cervidea. Healthy growth of fawns after weaning is dependent on protein in their diets. Males have higher protein requirements than females. During latter stages of pregnancy, protein requirements are intermediate between that of growth and maintenance (Teer 1996).

Although deer can subsist for long periods on water obtained from vegetation, free water is an important component of deer habitat. Rickel and others (1996), in modeling mule deer habitat, concluded that the maximum traveling distance to water for fawns was 1 mile, for does 2 miles, and for bucks 3 miles. Water is usually supplied by natural water areas or can be provided through stock ponds and troughs used to water livestock.

Starvation results from the exhaustion of food resources and is a consequence of poor deer herd management or of no management. If the habitat will not support the herd and if the annual crop of deer is not removed by other means, starvation will remove it. This is an axiom in deer management. Natural regulation of herbivore populations is difficult when natural systems have been disrupted by man.

Predator Control—Predators are often cited as the chief cause of deer declines by the general public. Coyotes, mountain lions, bobcats, and other carnivores do kill deer, and their impacts on deer numbers can be important. However, quality of habitat and hunting may be much more important than predation.

Whether predators can control numbers of deer has been the subject of long debate. Now, however, considerable evidence has accumulated to show that coyotes, mountain lions, and other predators can substantially impact, if not control, herd numbers in certain situations (Teer 1996).

Coyotes are omnivorous and opportunistic in relation to diet. They take vegetable materials (that is, fruits, mast) when available and animal prey when abundant and easily caught (Teer 1996). Deer fawns are a large proportion of coyote diets especially when cover is sparse and other foods are scarce.

Control of predators through some kind of bounty system or other subsidized control program is often

26

USDA Forest Service Gen. Tech. Rep. RMRS-GTR-135-vol. 2. 2005

the remedy called for by misinformed citizenry. Bounty systems by government agencies have often been abused by those engaged in predator management. Cost and benefit evaluations of the bounty system indicate it is ineffective in preventing predation or encouraging deer numbers (Teer 1996).

Predation along with sport hunting can be used to control deer populations. Conversely, when deer numbers are to be increased or protected, predator control may be an important activity (Teer 1996). A blanket recommendation cannot be made about predator control; each situation must be addressed separately.

Pronghorn

The pronghorn is one of the key herbivores on both the plains and desert grasslands (fig. 2-6). The pronghorn's scientific name, *Antilocapra americana*, means "American antelope goat." However, the deer-like pronghorn is neither an antelope nor a goat. They evolved in North America and are the sole surviving members of an ancient family dating back 20 million years (The Pronghorn 2004, Yoakum and others 1996). Pronghorn existed with bison in legendary numbers when Lewis and Clark made their historic journey across the continent (fig. 2-6).

Today, an estimated 98 percent of pronghorn share their habitat with domestic livestock (Yoakum and others 1996). An estimated 60 percent of all pronghorn live on private lands and the remainder on Federal or State government-administrated lands.

Pronghorn Distribution

When Euro-Americans began to explore North America, they found pronghorn from the plains of south-central Canada (Alta., Saskatchewan, Manititoba), south through most of the Western United States and into Mexico (fig. 2-6). Herds ranged from the Mississippi River to the Pacific Ocean in central California. Herds extended from the Gulf of Mexico in Texas to the Pacific Ocean in lower California.

Pronghorn populations reached greatest densities with bison on grasslands of the Great Plains. Smaller populations occupied Intermountain and desert regions. They did not occur east of the Mississippi River (Yoakum and others 1996). Pronghorn now occupy many of their historic grasslands but in greatly reduced numbers. Contemporary herds are confined to smaller isolated habitats (fig. 2-6), unable to make historical seasonal movements because of freeways, railroads, fencing, and other anthropogenic constraints. The pronghorn is the most representative big game species dependent upon Western grasslands (Yoakum and others 1996).

Pronghorn Abundance

Yoakum and others (1996) estimated there were 30 to 60 million pronghorn at the beginning of the 19th century. Some reports indicate they were as numerous or possibly more abundant than bison (Shaw 1996, Yoakum and others 1996). During the late 1800s, sport and commercial hunters hunted pronghorn herds and killed animals regardless of sex or age. Much of the best habitat was lost to the plow, and pronghorn movements became increasingly restricted by fences and other human-made impediments. Pronghorn also were subjected to livestock diseases and parasites to which they had little resistance. Numbers dropped from an estimated 35 million in 1800, to perhaps 13,000 in 1910 (Yoakum and others 1996). Public concern arose, protective laws were enacted, and supporting conservation and management practices were implemented. Within a decade, populations more than doubled and have continued to recover. Currently, pronghorn antelope number approximately 1 million (Pronghorn 2004). They are now second only to deer in large herbivore abundance and harvest in the United States.

Two subspecies—Sonoran pronghorn (*A. a. sonoriensis*) and Chihuahuan (Mexican) pronghorn (*A. a. mexicana*)—are found in the southern part of Arizona and New Mexico. The Sonoran pronghorn is Federally endangered. Of the total pronghorn population in North America, less than 1 percent is classified as

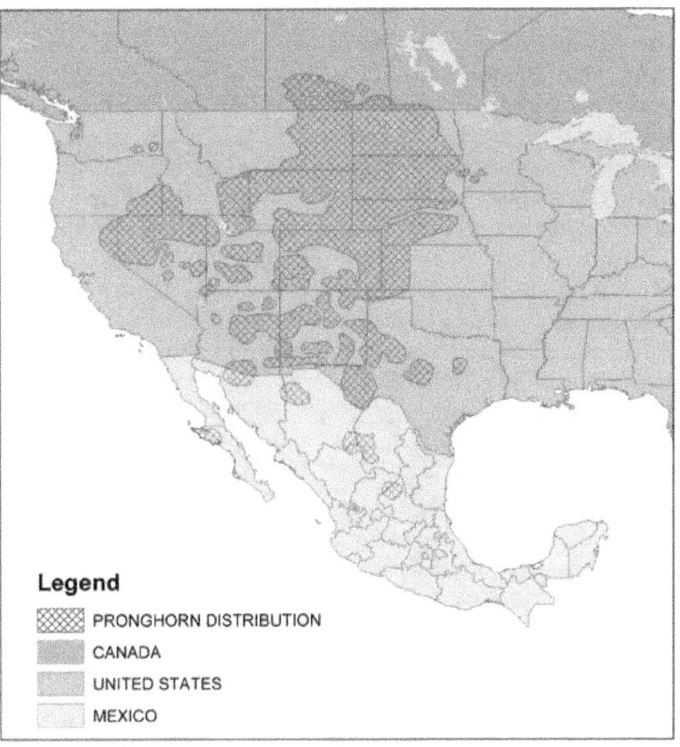

Figure 2-6. Pronghorn antelope distribution in North America (NatureServe 2004).

USDA Forest Service Gen. Tech. Rep. RMRS-GTR-135-vol. 2. 2005

27

endangered (Yoakum and others 1996). The endangered populations are on the grasslands along the Mexico-United States border (BISON-M 2005, Ockenfels and others 1996, Yoakum and others 1996).

Chihuahuan (Mexican) Pronghorn—Historically this subspecies ranged throughout southeastern and south-central Arizona and inhabited grass-shrub valleys and grasslands. In Arizona by 1900, Chihuahuan pronghorn populations had been reduced, and they were not reported in Arizona after the 1920s (BISOM-M 2005). Chihuahuan pronghorn populations in Arizona were probably extirpated by uncontrolled subsistence hunting and changing land-use patterns (BISON-M 2005). Populations were reintroduced from Texas stock in several areas within historic range from 1981 through 1985 and 1987, including Empire Ranch near Sonoyta, San Bernardino Valley, Fort Huachuca, and Buenos Aires National Wildlife Refuge (most western extent of its range) (Arizona's Natural Heritage Program: Heritage Data Management System 2005).

The Chihuahuan pronghorn in Arizona are classified as big game, permitting it to be hunted. Only bucks are harvested annually (Arizona's Natural Heritage Program: Heritage Data Management System 2005).

Sonoran Pronghorn—Sonoran pronghorn has been described as the smallest of the five subspecies. Some females lack horns (Arizona's Natural Heritage Program: Heritage Data Management System 2005).

The historic range is difficult to determine because the subspecies was not described until 1945, many years after the population had declined and marginal populations were extirpated (BISON-M 2005). Herds that were observed along the lower Gila River, Arizona, by early travelers are presumed to have been Sonoran pronghorn. They are thought to have ranged from Hermosillo to Kino Bay, Mexico, to the south; Highway 15, Mexico to the east; Altar Valley and the Tohono O'odham Indian Reservation to the North; and Imperial Valley, California to the west (BISON-M 2005).

Presently, in Arizona, they are found on the Cabeza Prieta National Wildlife Refuge, the Organ Pipe Cactus National Monument, the Luke Air Force Barry M. Goldwater Gunnery Range, and possibly the Tohono O'odham Indian Reservation. In Mexico, they are believed to be confined to the northwest part of Sonora (Arizona's Natural Heritage Program: Heritage Data Management System 2005).

Based on a study conducted in 1984 using collared Sonoran pronghorn, four males had home ranges ranging from 64.5 km^2 to 1,213.6 km^2 (24.9 miles^2 to 468.6 miles^2) an average of 799.7 km^2 (179.8 miles^2), while six females had home ranges ranging from 40.7 km^2 to 1,143.7 km^2 (150.7 miles^2 to 441.6 miles^2) and an average of 465.7 km^2 (176.3 miles^2). The large variation

A doe and buck pronghorn. (Courtesy of NatureServe© Larry Master)

in home range size for this study appears to be tied to forage and possibly water availability (BISON-M 2005). These animals must use large tracts of land to obtain adequate forage.

Sonoran pronghorn exhibit the same social doe/fawn, territorial, and flight behaviors as noted for other pronghorn. A heightened response to human traffic has been noted. Once aware of an observer, Sonoran pronghorn are quick to leave the area (BISON-M 2005).

Fawning for Sonoran pronghorn takes place from February to May, and as early as January for populations in Mexico. Although the stress of summer rutting on pronghorn is higher, spring drop is desirable to coincide with temperate weather and spring forage. Sonoran pronghorn fawns are nursed for 60 days, unlike northern populations, which nurse up to 90 days (Arizona's Natural Heritage Program: Heritage Data Management System 2005).

Sonoran pronghorn were observed browsing on forbs, shrubs, and cacti. Forbs and cholla (*Cactaceae* ssp) were browsed on during the summer and fall seasons, while shrubs, cholla, and ocotillo were browsed on the remainder of the year (Arizona's Natural Heritage Program: Heritage Data Management System 2005). Cholla appears to be a key succulent forage item in their diet during the summer, constituting nearly 50 percent of their diet, apparently to meet their water requirements (Arizona's Natural Heritage Program: Heritage Data Management System 2005).

Free-standing water is limited within range of the Sonoran pronghorn in Arizona. In 1984, collared Sonoran pronghorn were observed at water troughs in November, January, and August. Tracks were observed leading up to, then away from, seasonal potholes during the monsoon season. The collared pronghorn exhibit movements apparently tied to water, as well as forage, availability. During a study conducted in 1995 using collared animals, Sonoran pronghorn were observed using an ephemeral supply of water on a daily basis in a crater on the Barry M. Goldwater Gunnery Range

28

USDA Forest Service Gen. Tech. Rep. RMRS-GTR-135-vol. 2. 2005

(Arizona's Natural Heritage Program: Heritage Data Management System 2005).

In Arizona, the reason for population decline is attributed mainly to loss of habitat and drought. The drying of major rivers and overgrazing significantly altered Sonoran pronghorn habitat in southwestern Arizona by the 1930s. The population has not recovered since the establishment of three large public land withdrawals and the removal of cattle from these areas in the early 1980s (Arizona's Natural Heritage Program: Heritage Data Management System 2005). The only significant loss of habitat in recent years in Arizona occurred on the Tohono O'odham Indian Reservation where severe overgrazing by cattle, coupled with drought, resulted in the loss of large areas of pronghorn habitat (Arizona's Natural Heritage Program: Heritage Data Management System 2005). In Mexico, it is believed that economic exploitation of habitat (grazing and agriculture) and poaching are still causing population and habitat losses (Arizona's Natural Heritage Program: Heritage Data Management System 2005).

Measures have been taken to protect and enhance this endangered pronghorn. The establishment of three large public land withdrawals in Arizona, Cabeza Prieta National Wildlife Refuge, Organ Pipe Cactus National Monument, and Luke Air Force Gunnery Range (Barry M. Goldwater Gunnery Range). The removal of hunting from these sites, and the restriction of vehicle traffic further protects the Sonoran pronghorn. The removal of fencing between the Cabeza Prieta NWR and Organ Pipe Cactus NM, and within the Cabeza Prieta NWR in the 1990s has allowed for easier natural movement of Sonoran pronghorn (Arizona's Natural Heritage Program: Heritage Data Management System 2005).

Predators

Predators of all pronghorn include coyotes, bobcats, mountain lions, golden eagles, and wild dogs. Coyotes are the primary predator of fawns in Arizona and New Mexico. Losses of pronghorn due to predation vary with pronghorn and predator numbers, habitat type, and availability of alternative food sources for predators. A pronghorn's speed and exceptional eyesight are its main defense from predators; pronghorn can detect movement up to 4 miles away. A fawn's best defense from predators is to choose good cover to lay down and to lie motionless (Arizona's Natural Heritage Program: Heritage Data Management System 2005, BISON-M, Yoakum and others 1996).

Pronghorn Habitat Requirements

Currently, 68 percent of the herds inhabit grasslands, 31 percent shrub-steppes, and 1 percent deserts (Arizona's Natural Heritage Program: Heritage Data Management System 2005, BISON-M, Yoakum and others 1996)). Most populations historically occurred in grasslands and shrub-steppes with large expanses of flat or low rolling terrain without major physical barriers to seasonal movements.

Pronghorn forage studies show that pronghorn prefer forbs, then shrubs, and that grasses were the least preferred forage. Thus, pronghorn management should promote an abundance of preferred forb species. However, an abundance of less preferred forbs and reduced grass cover resulting from excessive livestock grazing is detrimental to pronghorn.

Pronghorn select palatable, nutritious, succulent forage, and being selective, take small bites of preferred leaves, flowers, and terminal parts. Rarely do they feed extensively in one place but move frequently as they forage. Pronghorn consume less then 1 percent of forage produced on Western grasslands in the United States (Yoakum and others 1996).

The quality and quantity of vegetation appear to be major factors affecting pronghorn densities and production. Habitat quality is directly related to proper percentages, quantities, and distribution of physiographic and vegetative characteristics; too little or too much of any component may limit pronghorn production and survival. Pronghorn population dynamics between the shrub-steppes of the Great Basin and the grasslands of the Great Plains were compared, showing that fecundity was 190 fawns per 100 producing does for both ecosystems (Yoakum and others 1996). But fawn survival was twice as high, and grass and forb production was higher on the Great Plains than in the Great Basin. Nutritive values (particularly protein) of grasses and forbs were greater than shrubs during late spring and early summer when fawning occurred. Fawn survival was higher on the Great Plains because of abundant, nutritious grasses and forbs during late gestation and early lactation (Yoakum and others 1996). The lesser amount of grasses and forbs in the Great Basin, partly because of livestock grazing, apparently resulted in grasslands of lower carrying capacity for pronghorn.

Pronghorn Relationships with Other Grassland Wildlife

Prairie Dogs—Because forb production is high in the centers of prairie dog colonies, it is speculated that prairie dogs (*Cynomys* spp.) may enhance grasslands for pronghorn by consuming grasses and disturbing soils, thereby increasing the abundance and variety of forbs (Yoakum and others 1996).

Predators—Predatory birds and mammals kill some pronghorn, but predation usually is significant only on marginal grasslands or sites where predator numbers are high in relation to pronghorn numbers. Most predator losses occur among fawns 1 to 3 weeks

USDA Forest Service Gen. Tech. Rep. RMRS-GTR-135-vol. 2. 2005

29

Table 2-3. Dietary overlap for forage classes between pronghorn and bison, white-tailed deer, mule deer, and elk (Yoakum and others 1996).

Species	Location	Biome	% dietary overlap			
			Grasses	Forbs	Shrubs	Annual
Bison	Wichita Mountain National Wildlife Refuge, OK	Grassland	1	1		2
	Pawnee Grasslands, CO	Grassland	41	3	0	44
	National Bison Range, MT	Grassland	2.8	1.4	0.1	4.3
Elk	Wichita Mountain National Wildlife Refuge ,OK	Grassland	0.1	24	0	24.1
	National Bison Range, MT	Grassland	2.9	4.6	3.8	11.3
	Trickel Mountain, CO	Shrub-steppe	3.5	11.5	45.5	60.5
Whitetailed deer	Wichita Mountains National Wildlife Refuge, OK	Grassland	0	99	0	99
	National Bison Range, MT	Grassland	2.9	24.8	18.5	46.2
Mule deer	Yellowstone National Park, WY	Shrub-steppe	16.6	9.2	52	77.8
	National Bison Range, MT	Grassland	2.3	27.1	33.3	62.7
	Northeast California, northwest Nevada	Shrub-steppe	2.3	4.2	82.3	88.8
	Trickle Mountain, CO	Shrub-steppe	3.5	10.2	79.5	93.2
	Sheldon National Wildlife Refuge, NV	Shrub-steppe	5	31	39	75

of age, while separated from their dams (Yoakum and others 1996).

Bison—Bison and pronghorn shared the same range, foraging and watering on the vast grassland prairies (Yoakum and others 1996). Apparently bison did not coexist with pronghorn historically in the Great Basin or on deserts. In comparing diets of bison and pronghorn in Colorado, diet differences were attributed to the species rather than to the grasslands (Yoakum and others 1996). Diets of bison and pronghorn studied in Montana overlapped minimally: bison consumed mostly grasses while pronghorn ate forbs and shrubs (table 2-3) (Shaw 1996). Bison disturbed dominant grass communities by trampling, wallowing, and grazing that resulted in greater production of forbs and shrubs favored by pronghorn.

Elk—There were larger range and habitat overlaps between elk and pronghorn historically than now. Elk and pronghorn have been observed foraging together with no acts of aggression and little dietary overlap (table 2-3) (Yoakum and others 1996). There is little overlap in habitat use between elk and pronghorn in Montana and little competition for space, water, or forage (Yoakum and others 1996). Elk forage primarily on grasses, whereas pronghorn prefer forbs and shrubs; consequently, dietary overlap was low.

Deer—Pronghorn occur on grasslands with whitetail and mule deer; however, their distributions usually do not overlap (Yoakum and others 1996.). All have similar diets (primarily forbs and shrubs) but overlaps are minimal (table 2-3) because of differences in habitat occupancy patterns. Behavioral interactions are also minimal because pronghorn are generally diurnal while deer are crepuscular and nocturnal.

Pronghorn Relationships with Livestock

Pronghorn and Livestock Forage Competition—An estimated 98 percent of pronghorn populations share grasslands with domestic or feral livestock during some of the year (Yoakum and others 1996). Livestock on Western grasslands are either domestic animals such as cattle, sheep, and horses, or feral stock, primarily horses. Table 2-4 is a summary of the dietary overlaps between pronghorn and cattle, horses, and domestic sheep on grasslands and shrub-steppes.

Livestock grazing may alter pronghorn habitats more than any other human-controlled activity by changing vegetation structure and composition (Shaw 1996). When pronghorn and livestock grazed grasslands in southeastern New Mexico, they used many of the same forage species. Pronghorn did not switch to less preferred forage classes and were adversely affected when forbs and shrubs were depleted through drought or heavy livestock grazing (Shaw 1996).

Pronghorn use of plants noxious to livestock has been well documented (Shaw 1996), and for this reason pronghorn may be considered beneficial to livestock on grasslands. Spines of bull thistle (*Cirsium* spp.), Russian thistle (*Salsola* spp.), and cacti are less palatable to livestock, but pronghorn frequently eat them. Other noxious plants that livestock do not eat but are consumed by pronghorn include: in Oregon— woolly locoweed (*Astragalus mollissimus*), larkspur (*Dephinium* spp.), lupine (*Lupinus* spp.), death camas (*Zigadimus* spp.) (Shaw 1996); in Texas—locoweed (*Astragalus* spp.), woody senecio (*Senecio* spp.), Riddell groundsel (*Senecio* spp.), (Yoakum and others 1996); in Colorado—cocklebur (*Xanthium* spp.), snakeweed (*Gutierrezia* spp.), bull thistle, Russian thistle, cacti,

Table 2-4. Forage class dietary overlap among pronghorn and cattle, horses, and domestic sheep (Yoakum and others 2006).

Class of livestock	Location	Biome	Percent dietary overlap			
			Grasses	Forbs	Shrubs	Annual
Cattle	Trans-Pecos, TX	Grassland	4	7	9	20
	Southwest, MT	Grassland	3	20.3	1.6	24.9
	Winnett, MT	Shrub-steppe	3	13	0	16
	Rawlins, WY	Shrub-steppe	7.1	0.2	39.4	46.7
	Pawnee, CO	Grassland	46.3	2	6	54.3
	Northeast California, northwest Nevada	Shrub-steppe	4.1	3.4	3.7	11.2
	Southwest, UT	Shrub-steppe	0	0	27	27
	Roswell, NM	Grassland	4	15.2	1.3	20.5
	Panhandle, TX	Grassland	2.5	19	8.5	30
	Trickle Mountain, CO	Shrub-steppe	3.5	5	14	22.5
	Little Lost-Birch Creek, ID	Shrub-steppe	3	2	11	16
	Burns Junction, OR	Shrub-steppe	9.4	4.6	0.2	14.2
	Sheldon National Wildlife Refuge, NV	Shrub-steppe	5	9	1	15
Horse	Sheldon National Wildlife Refuge, NV	Shrub-steppe	3	23	2	28
	Northeast California, northwest Nevada	Shrub-steppe	2.5	5.2	5	12.7
	Trickle Mountain, CO	Shrub-steppe	3.5	2	31	36.5
	Burns Junction, OR	Shrub-steppe	13.5	2.1	0.3	15.9
	Sheldon National Wildlife Refuge, NV	Shrub-steppe	5	6	0	11
Sheep	Trans-Pecos, TX	Grassland	4	19	10	33
	Red Desert, WY	Shrub-steppe	3.2	2.6	28.4	34.2
	Southeast, MT	Grassland	3	27.3	25.3	55.6
	Rawlins, WY	Shrub-steppe	7.1	1.2	39.9	48.2
	Pawnee, CO	Grassland	46.3	18	3.3	67.6
	Southwest, UT	Shrub-steppe	0	0	46	46
	Little Lost-Birch Creek, ID	Shrub-steppe	3	14	39	56
	Roswell, NM	Grassland	4	50.2	6	60.2

chokecherry (*Prunus* spp.) (Hoover and others 1959); in Texas—tarbush (*Flourensia cernua*) (Hailey 1979); and in Utah—halogeton (*Halogeton* spp.) (Shaw 1996).

A potential exists for forage competition between pronghorn and domestic sheep. Yoakum and others (1996) reported intense competition for preferred forbs. A study of pronghorn and domestic sheep forage competition conducted during the early 1980s in New Mexico determined that livestock used as much as 40 percent of available forbs (Shaw 1996). As forbs declined in number or decreased in moisture content, livestock increased their use of grasses, increasing the potential competition for forbs. Overlap is highest when forbs are most available and lowest when they are least available. Yoakum and others (1996) reported that moderate use of shrubs on the cold desert of southwestern Utah by domestic sheep during winter created unfavorable conditions for pronghorn until the spring regrowth occurred.

Horses predominantly feed on grasses while pronghorn prefer forbs and shrubs. Five studies listed dietary overlap as low to moderate (11 to 36 percent) (table 2-4), suggesting that competition for food was limited.

Pronghorn and Livestock Behavioral Relationships—The behavioral relationship between pronghorn and livestock is nonaggressive while both species are feeding, drinking, or resting. Pronghorn does avoided cattle during fawning, resulting in selection of less favorable fawn-production sites (Shaw 1996).

Domestic and feral horses occupy grasslands with pronghorn (Yoakum and others 1996). Both animals have been observed to water together, with pronghorn giving ground only when directly approached by horses (Shaw 1996). Pronghorn and feral horse relationships in the Great Basin have shown various instances where pronghorns were displaced by horses.

Pronghorn and Livestock Diseases—Exposure to diseases is a concern when pronghorn and cattle share grasslands because their spatial distributions usually overlap. There is concern that either species may serve as a reservoir for diseases that affect the health of the other (Yoakum and others 1996). Blue tongue is probably the most serious disease of pronghorn, and cattle are a primary agent for spreading this disease to pronghorn. Blue tongue is fatal to domestic sheep. Neither pronghorn nor sheep are important reservoirs

USDA Forest Service Gen. Tech. Rep. RMRS-GTR-135-vol. 2. 2005

31

for this disease because few animals survive to become carriers (Yoakum and others 1996). Leptospirosis causes some mortality in pronghorn, but evidence is insufficient to implicate either pronghorn or cattle as a primary reservoir of infection (Yoakum and others 1996).

Pronghorn had higher rates of parasitism on grasslands grazed by domestic sheep than grasslands grazed by cattle. In Wyoming, illness and deaths of pronghorn fawns have been attributed to parasitic infections that were prevalent on grasslands grazed heavily by sheep (Yoakum and others 1996).

Pronghorn Management

Grassland management practices and improvements can be beneficial or detrimental to pronghorn populations, depending upon how they are planned and implemented. If the biological requirements of pronghorn are not met, then any management action could be detrimental.

Effective management systems should consider the control of livestock and range improvements for livestock, determine how many livestock will use certain grasslands, and take into account seasons of livestock use, results of monitoring studies, physiology of plants, and the effects and needs of wildlife on the grasslands.

For grasslands used by pronghorn and livestock, the following guidelines are recommended for designing livestock grazing systems (Yoakum and others 1996):

1. When allotting forage, the habitat requirements of pronghorn should be considered.

- Adequate amounts of preferred plant species should be reserved as forage for pronghorn. These include grasses, forbs, and shrubs determined from diet studies in the same or similar ecosystems. Consideration should be given to proper use of key forbs and shrubs. Make sure that these are not grazed beyond their physiological tolerance levels.

- Natural vegetation should be managed to provide an abundance and variety of forage classes. Most livestock graze grasses; pronghorns primarily consume forbs and shrubs. Grasslands producing mixtures of grasses, forbs, and shrubs will best serve livestock and wildlife. The challenge is to maintain existing grasslands in good ecological condition comprised of native vegetation. When deteriorated sites require rehabilitation, practices that restore vegetation to natural diversity are more desirable than practices that bring about monocultures and other unnatural conditions.

- Practices that increase availability of long-term drinking water sites are highly beneficial to both animal groups. Water should be available every 1.5 to 6.5 km. Water improvements can be designed in a number of ways; however, those that simulate natural waters are favored and cause fewer problems.

- Both pronghorn and livestock experience problems with predation, diseases, and parasites. Managers need to recognize how these factors affect the animals and coordinate control techniques beneficial to both groups.

2. Drinking water should be available during all seasons that pronghorn are in the area.

3. Fence construction should meet specifications to allow movements year-round for all pronghorn age classes.

4. When livestock grazing systems are designed using the "key plant species" concept, forbs and/or shrubs preferred by pronghorn should be included as key species.

5. Livestock use should be limited on pronghorn natal areas during the fawning season.

6. Livestock grazing systems that restrict, alter, limit, or deleteriously affect the habitat requirements of pronghorn should include mitigating measures and alternate procedures for enhancing pronghorn habitat.

Acknowledgments

I thank Mark A. Rumble, Fred B. Samson, and John Sidle for reviewing this chapter and providing insightful comments. I express my appreciation to Deborah M. Finch for editing the chapter and to Nora C. Altamirano for helping prepare this chapter for publication. A thank you also goes to Kerry Mich for help on the range maps.

References

Arizona's Natural Heritage Program: Heritage Data Management System (HDMS). 2005. [Online] http://www.azgfd.gov/w_c/edits/species_concern.shtml.

BISOM-M, New Mexico Game and Fish. Biota Information System of New Mexico. 2005.

[Online] http://nmnhp.unm.edu/bisonm/bisonquery.php

Bock, C.E.; Bock, J.H. 1996. Factors controlling the structure and function of desert grasslands: a case study from southeastern Arizona. In: The future of arid grasslands: identifying issues, seeking solutions. B. Tellman, D.M. Finch, C. Edminster, and R. Hamre, eds. Proc. RMRS-P-3. Fort Collins, CO: U.S. Department of Agriculture, Forest Service, Rocky Mountain Research Station.

Boroski, B.B.; Mossman, A.S. 1966. Distribution of mule deer in relation to water sources in northern California. Journal of Wildlife Management. 60(4)770-776.

Bowyer, R.T. 1986. Habitat selection by southern mule deer. California Fish and Game Bulletin: 72(3): 153-169.

Chung-MacCoubrey, A.L. 1996. Grassland bats and management in the Southwest. In: D.M. Finch, ed. 1996 Ecosystem disturbance and wildlife conservation in western grasslands – A symposium proceedings, September 22-26, 1994; Albuquerque, NM. Gen. Tech. Rep. RM-GTR-285. Fort Collins, CO: U.S. Department of Agriculture, Forest Service, Rocky Mountain Forest and Range Experiment Station. 82 p.

Findley, J.S.; Harris, A.H.; Wilson, D.E.; Jones, C. 1975. Mammals of New Mexico. A.buquerque: University of New Mexico Press.

Fulgham, K.0.; Smith, M.A.; Malachek, J.C. 1982. A compatible grazing relationship can exist between domestic sheep and mule deer. In: I.M. Peek and P.D. Dalke, eds. Wildlife-livestock relationships symposium: proceedings 10. Moscow: University of Idaho, Forestry, Wildlife and Range Experiment Station: 458-478.

Hailey, T.L. 1979. A handbook for pronghorn antelope management in Texas. Houston: Texas Parks and Wildlife Department. 59 p.

Hood, R.E.; Inglis, J.M. 1974. Behavior responses of white-tailed deer to intensive ranching operations. Journal of Wildlife Management. 38(3): 488-478.

Julander, 0. 1955. Deer and cattle range relations in Utah. Forest Science. 1: 130-139.

Keiter, R.B. 1997. Greater Yellowstone's Bison: unraveling of an early American Wildlife Conservation achievement. Journal of Wildlife Management. 61: 1-11.

Kie, J.G. 1996. The effects of cattle grazing on optimal foraging in mule deer (*Odocoileus hemionus*). Forest Ecology and Management. 88(1996): 131-138.

Knapp, A.K.; Blair, J.M.; Briggs, J.M.; Collins, S.L.; Hartnett, D.C.; Johnson, L.C.; Towne, E.G. 1999. The keystone roll of bison in North American tallgrass prairie. BioScience vol. 49 no 1: 39-50.

Meagher, M. 1986. Bison. Mammalian Species. 266: 1-8.

NatureServe. 2004. [online] http://www.natureserve.org/explorer

North American Elk Subspecies. 2004. Pennsylvania Elk Herd [online] http://www.pennsylvaniaelkherd.com/elk00076.htm

Ockenfels, R.A.; Ticer, C.L.; Alexander, A.; Wennerlund, J.A.; Hurley, P.A.; Bright, J.L. 1996. Statewide evaluation of pronghorn habitat in Arizona. W-78-R Final Rep. Phoenix: Arizona Game and Fish Department Fed Aid Wildife. Rastoration Project. 296 p.

Parmenter, R.R.; Van Devender, T.R. 1995. Diversity, spatial variability, and functional roles of vertebrates in desert grasslands. In: The Desert Grasslands. M.P. McClaran and T.R. Van Devender, eds. Tucson, AZ: The University of Arizona Press: 196-230.

Peek, M; Krausman, J.M. 1996. Grazing a mule deer. In P.R. Krausman, ed. Rangeland Wildlife. Denver, CO: The Society of Range Management: 183-192.

Perry, C.; Overly, R. 1977. Impact of roads on big game distributions in portions of the Blue Mountains in Washington. 1972-1973. Appl. Res. Bull. Olympia: Washington Department of Game. 39 p.

Pronghorn. 2004. Great Plains Nature Center. [online] http://www.gpnc.org/pronghor.htm

Rickel, B.W.; Anderson, B.; Pope, R. 1996. Using Fuzzy systems object-oriented programming, and GIS to evaluate wildlife habitat. AI Applications. 12(1-3):31-40.

Rocky Mountain Elk Foundation. 2004. [online] http://www.rmef.org

Shaw, J.H. 1996. Bison. In: P.R. Krausman, ed. 1996. Rangeland Wildlife. Denver, CO: The Society of Range Management: 227-235.

Shawn, J.R.; Dood, A.R. 1984. Summer movements, home range, habitat use, and behavior of mule deer fawns. Journal of Wildlife Management. 48(4): 1302-1310.

Southeastern Cooperative Wildlife Disease Study. 1982. White-tailed deer populations 1980. A map prepared in cooperation with the Emergency Programs, Veterinary Services, Animal and Plant Health Inspection Service, U.S. Department of Agriculture, through cooperative agreement 12-16-5-2230. Athens: University of Georgia. 1 p.

Teer, J.G. 1996. The white-tailed deer: natural history and management. In: P.R. Krausmann, ed. 1996. Rangeland Wildlife. Denver, CO: The Society of Range Management: 193-209.

The Pronghorn. 2004. Desert USA. [online] http://www.desertusa.com/mag99/may/papr/pronghorn.html

Wisdom, M.J.; Thomas, J.W. 1996. Elk. In: P.R. Krausmann, ed. 1996. Rangeland Wildlife. Denver, CO: The Society of Range Management: 157-181.

Yoakum, J.D.; O'Gara, W.; Howard, V.W. 1996. Pronghorn on the western rangelands. In: P.R. Krausmann, ed. 1996. Rangeland Wildlife. Denver, CO: The Society of Range Management: 211-226.

USDA Forest Service Gen. Tech. Rep. RMRS-GTR-135-vol. 2. 2005

33

Bryce Rickel

Chapter 3:
Small Mammals, Reptiles, and Amphibians

Introduction

This chapter focuses on small mammals, reptiles, and amphibians that inhabit the grasslands within the Southwestern Region of the USDA Forest Service. The chapter is not intended to be an all inclusive list of species, but rather to address the species that play important roles in grassland ecosystems and that often are associated with the management of grasslands. Among the larger rodents discussed here are prairie dogs and pocket gophers. The small rodents include deer mice, voles, kangaroo rats, and pocket mice. Nonrodent species described in this chapter include the endangered black-footed ferret, as well as cottontail rabbits, jackrabbits, and bats. The herpetofauna include turtles and tortoises, lizards, snakes, frogs, toads, and salamanders.

The species discussed in this chapter serve important ecological roles and are considered important to the health and function of grassland ecosystems. Some species—for example, prairie dogs and kangaroo rats—are frequently identified as keystone species by scientists and ecologists because they influence ecosystems processes and populations of other species.

Distribution maps included in this chapter provide assistance to managers as to what species may be of concern when managing grasslands. All of the species distribution maps can be downloaded from a NatureServe's Web site: http://www.natureserve.org/getData/animalData.jsp.

Rodents are the largest and most diverse component of the mammalian faunas on grasslands. They range from the small harvest mouse (*Reithrodontomys* spp.) and pocket mouse (*Perognathus* spp.) to the large porcupine (*Erethizon dorsatum*) and beaver (*Castor canadensis*). The diets of small mammals reflect a diverse selection of food types that vary by mammal species, behavior, activity schedule, habitat, and location. Small mammal species range from being strictly herbivorous to omnivorous to mostly carnivorous. Rodents are nocturnal, diurnal, and crepuscular, depending on species. Most grassland rodents are strictly terrestrial and mostly fossorial (burrowing), while others are semiaquatic. Jones and Manning (1996) demonstrated that general habitat type (for example, riparian, tallgrass, shortgrass) influenced species distribution of rodents more than either the presence or absence of particular species of plants. Many of the heteromyid rodents (pocket mice and kangaroo rats) inhabit overgrazed areas and sparsely vegetated areas on sandy soils. The pocket mouse (*Chaetodipus hispidus*) occurs frequently in areas of early seral stage. In the arid Southwest, the species composition of rodent communities can be habitat-specific (Findley 1989, Parmenter and Van Devender 1995).

Rodents have important roles in influencing habitat structure and composition of grasslands. These roles include dispersal of seeds, consumption and shredding of vegetation contributing to the deposition of humus, and mixing and aeration of soils by burrowing

USDA Forest Service Gen. Tech. Rep. RMRS-GTR-135-vol. 2. 2005

35

activities. In addition, numerous rodents are major sources of food for predators.

General Effects of Grazing on Rodents and Other Small Mammals

Effects of livestock grazing on small mammals can be variable, depending on the level of grazing, the type of grassland, and the particular small mammal species involved. Moderate grazing may have little or even a positive effect on many species, but overgrazing depresses populations of most small mammals. For example, heavy grazing and repeated fires in sagebrush range caused the establishment of nearly pure stands of annual grasses (Fagerstone and Ramey 1996, Jones and Manning 1996) that support only a few species of deer mice (*Peromyscus maniculatus*) and Great Basin pocket mice (*Perognathus parvus*). In southern Idaho, rodent burrow numbers were significantly higher on ungrazed than on heavily grazed pastures. In a seldom-grazed pasture in Arizona, the total rodent population was roughly twice as high as on a heavily grazed pasture (Fagerstone and Ramey 1996). On grasslands that are grazed heavily and are used continuously for decades, as they have been in areas of the Southwest, the resulting soil erosion reduces the quality of habitat for even grazing-tolerant species such as kangaroo rats (*Dipodomys* spp.) and prairie dogs (*Cynomys* spp.).

Results from studies suggest that the general composition of small mammal communities is determined primarily by structural attributes of the habitat. Livestock grazing affects many aspects of grassland ecosystems, including plant cover or biomass, plant species composition and diversity, primary productivity, soil compaction, and soil moisture. Plant cover probably has the most influence on small mammal populations because it provides food, nests, and protection from predators. Plant cover also influences behavioral interactions such as fighting and dispersal, and moderates ground level humidity, temperature, and soil moisture. There has been reported a significant positive relationship between small mammal abundance and canopy cover in sagebrush-grass grassland in Montana, where all areas were managed on a rest-rotation grazing system. Research has also shown that the percentage of forb cover was most consistently correlated with small-mammal species abundances, grass coverage was of lesser importance, and tree cover was not related to species abundance. These findings were consistent with that of other researchers, who reported that rodent abundance and diversity increased with vegetation cover and density and that overgrazing by cattle decreased vegetation complexity (Fagerstone and Ramey 1996).

Small mammal population responses to grazing depend on site characteristics and original composition of mammal species, and therefore, responses differ greatly among grassland types. Where there is sufficient vegetation in ungrazed grasslands to support herbivorous, litter-dwelling species, for example voles (*Microtus* spp. and *Clethrionomys* spp.), the small mammal communities are changed significantly by a reduction in cover caused by grazing. These changes in rodent communities are true for tallgrass and montane grasslands, which have significantly greater standing vegetation, greater annual net primary production, and greater abundance of mammals than shortgrass and bunchgrass grasslands (Fagerstone and Ramey 1996).

Often when there are habitat modifications, small mammal communities shift in species composition and abundance. Decreases in vegetation cover in tallgrass and montane grasslands result in a decrease in total number of small mammals, an increase in small mammal species diversity, and a shift from litter-dwelling species with relatively high reproductive rates to surface-dwelling species with relatively low reproductive rates (Fagerstone and Ramey 1996). Microtines—voles and lemmings—dominated ungrazed tallgrass habitats (Payne and Caire 1999), with cricetines—harvest mice, deer mice, grasshopper mice, and woodrats—roughly half as abundant as microtines. In contrast, grazed tallgrass habitats were dominated by sciurids (chipmunks, marmots and squirrels) and heteromyids (pocket mice and kangaroo rats). In montane grasslands, grazing-induced reduction in cover resulted in similar decreases in total small mammal biomass and changes in species composition from litter-dwelling species to surface dwelling species, but the reduction in cover also resulted in a decrease rather than an increase in mammal species diversity. At montane sites, microtines dominated the ungrazed area, but cricetines dominated the grazed area. In shortgrass and bunchgrass grasslands, numbers of small mammal species and abundance were not changed drastically by reduction in vegetation cover by grazing (Fagerstone and Ramey 1996).

Small mammal communities of shortgrass and bunchgrass often are composed primarily of surface-dwelling, granivorous, and omnivorous species adapted to open habitats. On bunchgrass sites, sciurids and heteromyids were dominant, and on shortgrass sites, biomass was greatest for cricetines and sciurids, followed by heteromyids. A reduction in cover resulting from grazing may improve conditions for granivorous mammal species by promoting the abundance and seed production of annual grasses and forbs rather than perennial grasses (Fagerstone and Ramey 1996).

By affecting plant species diversity and vegetation structure, livestock grazing can influence rodent

Table 3-1. Rodent populations in three grazed and ungrazed riparian habitats (Fagerstone and Ramey 1996).

Community type	Mammals/ha	
	Grazed	Ungrazed
Hawthorne (Crataegus spp.)	800 to 83	690 to 136
Meadow	450 to 60	235 to 463
Cottonwood-mixed conifer	129 to 42	118 to 254

species diversity. The effects of grazing on rodents can vary by habitat. Despite long-term protection from grazing, vegetation patterns on desert grasslands do not return to their original grass cover. This is because recovery takes a long time in desert (xeric) environments and because, once established, woody plants may competitively restrict the reestablishment of herbaceous cover and perennial grasses. For example, granivorous foragers such as the least chipmunk (*Tamias minimus*), Great Basin pocket mouse (*Perognathus parvus*), and deer mouse (*Peromyscus maniculatus*) have increased most in mesic habitats. In contrast, reduction of herbaceous vegetation by livestock grazing has resulted in a reduction in plant diversity and rodent diversity in xeric communities (Fagerstone and Ramey 1996).

Research has demonstrated that small mammals that used riparian areas may be significantly impacted by grazing. In a comparison of small mammal populations before and after late season (late August to mid-September) grazing, population estimates were lower in all grazed riparian habitats than in ungrazed habitats (table 3-1). The significant difference between small mammal populations in grazed versus ungrazed riparian areas was apparently related to loss of cover due to forage removal. Reduced cover resulted in increased predation on small mammals and their emigration from grazed habitats into neighboring ungrazed habitats (Fagerstone and Ramey 1996).

Sylvatic Plague

Sylvatic (bubonic) plague (*Yersinia pestis*) has been in the United States for approximately 100 years and in black-tailed prairie dog populations for approximately 50 years. This exotic disease was first observed in wild rodents in North America near San Francisco, CA, in 1908. The first reported incidence of plague in black-tailed prairie dogs (*Cynomys ludovicianus*) occurred in Texas in 1946 (Gober 2002). Some rodents may act as hosts or carriers of the disease and show little or no symptoms, but prairie dogs do not develop effective antibodies or immunity to the disease (Gober 2002). The plague is transmitted by fleas and decimates prairie dogs (Knowles 2002). It has spread through

the West and Southwest where a variety of rodent species serve as reservoirs for passing the disease to humans and wildlife (Brand 2002). Of the three major factors (habitat loss, poisoning, and disease) that currently limit the abundance of black-tailed, white-tailed (*C. leucurus*), Gunnison's (*C. gunnisoni*), and Utah (*C. parvidens*) prairie dogs, sylvatic plague is the one that is currently beyond human control (Cully and Williams 2002). When colonies are infected, the mortality of prairie dogs is often as high as 90 to 100 percent (Brand 2002).

The plague has the potential to reduce prairie dogs to levels lower than encountered during organized poisoning campaigns. And directed prairie dog poisoning, in concert with the plague, has the potential of extirpating prairie dogs from large areas, resulting in fragmented and isolated prairie dog populations persisting over the long term. Repeated catastrophic events (plague epizootics and poisoning) will progressively drive prairie dog populations toward extinction (Knowles 2002).

The plague is the major reason for the declines in Gunnison's prairie dog populations today. The only area where plague appears not to have had an impact is possible Aubrey Valley, Arizona, which has no documented plague outbreaks and retains large prairie dog colonies. Plague entered the range of the Gunnison's prairie dog during the late 1930s to the late 1940s. Published accounts for Gunnison's prairie dogs show that mortality from plague frequently exceeds 99 percent. Bureau of Land Management biologists who have Gunnison's prairie dogs within their area of jurisdiction have reported that, due to plague, there are no large colonies, 200 acres (81 ha) being the upper size limit of a colony (Knowles 2002).

Some populations have had no significant recovery, such as Gunnison's prairie dogs in South Park, CO. In northern New Mexico, Gunnison's prairie dogs partially recovered following an initial plague epizootic but failed to recover following a second epizootic. Other reports suggest a sequence where colonies are regularly lost due to plague, then new colonies develop and grow in other areas; this pattern may yield populations that are stable over a larger geographic area. Similar reports have come from northern Arizona, where there have been substantial declines due to plague. However, at the same time, Arizona's largest complex has been increasing 8 percent annually since 1992. There are concerns that plague cycles result in successive population peaks that are progressively lower than the previous peak. There are also concerns that with each new epizootic, the loss of colonies from plague will exceed the rate of establishment of new colonies (Knowles 2002).

Observations of these patterns to date are largely anecdotal and not based on careful mapping. However,

USDA Forest Service Gen. Tech. Rep. RMRS-GTR-135-vol. 2. 2005

37

in New Mexico and Colorado, plague impacts for the Gunnison's prairie dog are well documented. South Park, CO, was described as containing 913,000 acres (369,480 ha) of Gunnison's prairie dog colonies in 1941 prior to the advent of plague. Plague entered this area in 1947, and by only 2 years later plague had reduced the prairie dog acreage by more than 95 percent. Epizootics of plague continued in this area through the 1950s and 1960s and prairie dogs were nearly eliminated from South Park. Currently this area contains only a few hundred acres of prairie dog colonies. Former colonies are now occupied by Wyoming ground squirrels (*Spermophilis elegans*) and thirteen-lined ground squirrels (*Spermophilis trzdecemlineatus*) (Knowles 2002).

The black-tailed prairie dog is less susceptible to plague than the Gunnison's species (Knowles 2002). Plague affects black-tailed prairie dog populations by reducing colony size, increasing population variance within colonies, and increasing intercolony distances within colony complexes. In the presence of plague, black-tailed prairie dogs will probably survive in complexes of small colonies greater than 3 km (1.9 mi) from their nearest neighbor colonies or colonies that undergo severe population fluctuations (Cully and Williams 2002).

Currently plague is widespread throughout 66 percent of the historic range of the black-tailed prairie dog including all of Arizona, Colorado, Montana, New Mexico, Texas, and Wyoming, and portions of Kansas, Nebraska, North Dakota, and Oklahoma. South Dakota is the only State within the range of the species where plague in black-tailed prairie dogs has not been documented, although plague antibody titers (Knowles 2002) have been detected in badger (*Taxidea taxus*), coyote (*Canis latrans*), and red fox (*Vulpesfulva*) collected in the southwestern portion of the State (Gober 2002).

The endangered black-footed ferrets (*Mustela nigripes*) are extremely susceptible to sylvatic plague (CBSG 2004, Hatfield-Etchberger and others 2002). The threat to the black-footed ferret comes from both direct mortality from plague and indirectly from decimation of prairie dogs, their sole food source (Brand 2002).

Plague can infect humans also. Some 10 to 15 cases of plague in humans have been reported each year in the United States since 1975. Wild rodents, particularly rock squirrels (*Spermophilus variegatus*), are frequently shown or implicated to be the reservoir for infecting fleas that then transmit the plague bacterium to humans via domestic cats. Increased risk for plague in humans is associated with expansion of residential areas into areas populated by rodent reservoirs, and with pastoral human life styles, particularly among Native Americans on reservations in the southwestern United States.

Plague control in wildlife in the United States has been attempted on numerous occasions in direct response to human cases of plague or proactively to reduce risk of transmission to humans within a relatively localized geographic area. These programs often involve rodent and vector population suppression in addition to public education and medical surveillance. While these efforts to reduce the incidence of plague have met with varying degrees of success, in general they do not contain the disease for long periods or over broad geographical areas.

Large Rodents

Prairie Dogs

Prairie dogs (*Cynomys*) are unique to North America. Five species within the genus inhabit grasslands of central North America from southern Canada to northeastern Mexico (Hof and others 2002, Wagner and Drickamer 2004). The Mexican prairie dog is the only one that does not occur in the United States. The four species that do reside in the United States are the black-tailed prairie dogs and three species of white-tailed prairie dogs—white-tailed prairie dog, Gunnison's prairie dog, and Utah prairie dog. Black-tailed and Gunnison's prairie dogs occur in the Southwestern Region of the Forest Service. Populations of the black-tailed prairie dog are distributed in New Mexico, Texas, Oklahoma, Kansas, and Colorado grasslands; Gunnison's prairie dogs are found in Arizona and New Mexico (fig. 3-1) (Fagerstone and Ramey 1996). In New Mexico, black-tailed prairie dogs occurred historically in the southwestern, southeastern, and northeastern parts of the State, while Gunnison's and Utah prairie dogs occurred in the Great Basin.

Prairie dogs typically live in towns of 1,000 acres (400 ha) or larger. The rodent occupied up to 700 million acres of western grasslands in the early 1900s. The largest prairie dog colony on record, in Texas, measured nearly 25,000 square miles (65,000 km^2) and contained an estimated 400 million prairie dogs (Knowles 2002). Larger towns are divided into wards by barriers such as ridges, lines of trees, and roads. In a ward, each family or "coterie" of prairie dogs occupies a territory of about 1 acre (0.4 ha). A coterie usually consists of an adult male, one to four adult females, and any of their offspring that are less than 2 years old. Members of a coterie maintain unity through a variety of social activities, for example calls, postures, displays, grooming, and other forms of physical contact (Hygnstrom and Virchow 1994).

Prairie dogs are largely herbivorous, feeding preferably on grasses, 62 percent to 95 percent of their diet, and on forbs when they are the dominant vegetation. During certain periods of the year, they

38

USDA Forest Service Gen. Tech. Rep. RMRS-GTR-135-vol. 2. 2005

Figure 3-1. Distribution of black-tailed (*Cynomy ludovicianus*) and Gunnison's (*C. gunnisoni*) prairie dogs in North America (adapted from Fagerstone and Ramey 1996).

Legend
- Black-tailed Prairie Dog
- Gunnison's Prairie Dog

Vernon Bailey, working for the U.S. Biological Survey, traveled from Deming to Hachita and through the Animas and Playas Valleys in what is now southern Hidalgo County. He reported that the area was one continuous prairie dog town, and estimated that the county contained 6.4 million animals. In numerous trips through exactly the same region from 1955 through 1972, workers from the Museum of Southwestern Biology never saw a single prairie dog. Similar devastation has occurred in many parts of the mammal's former range. In this respect, black-tail prairie dogs have suffered more than Gunnison's. The latter species may be seen more or less regularly in various parts of northwestern New Mexico. Both species are subject to the plague and are periodically decimated by the disease (Sevilleta LTER: Data 1998c). Population increases have been observed in the 1970s and 1980s, possibly due to the increased restrictions on and reduced use of toxicants (Hygnstrom and Virchow 1994).

Early accounts of the black-tailed prairie dog suggest that this was an abundant species on the Great Plains. Although we lack similar accounts of the white-tailed and Gunnison's prairie dogs, it is assumed that these were also highly successful within their distributional range (Knowles 2002). The 1900s saw drastic declines for all prairie dog species. Although the prairie dog distributional range has not contracted greatly, it is estimated that overall black-tailed prairie dog populations have declined by 98 to 99 percent (Hof and others 2002, Knowles 2002, Wagner and Drickamer 2004).

In addition to the plague and poisoning, recreational shooting has affected prairie dog densities and populations (Knowles 2002). Pauli (2005), in his study on the effects of recreational shooting on black-tailed prairie dogs, found shooting caused a reduction in a colony of 30 percent in 1 year. He also found:

- Survivors exhibited an eight-fold increase in alert behavior.
- Aboveground activity was reduced by 66 percent, which reduced the time spent foraging.
- These behavioral changes resulted in 35 percent decrease in the body condition of the survivor.
- Flea load increased 30 percent.
- Fecal corticosterone—a steroid hormone produced in the adrenal glands that functions in the metabolism of carbohydrates and proteins—increased 80 percent.
- After shooting, the pregancy rates declined 50 percent, and the reproductive output decreased by 76 percent.

The results from Pauli's study indicate that the stress caused by the shooting is long lasting and affects the colony and not just individuals.

may feed heavily on seeds (Hygnstrom and Virchow 1994, Knowles 2002). All prairie dogs are capable of living without free water, obtaining their water from what they eat. Gunnison's prairie dogs are hibernators and may even estivate during late summer (Knowles 2002).

Prairie dogs are most active during the day. In the summer during the hottest part of the day, they go below ground where it is cooler. Black-tailed prairie dogs are active all year, but may stay under ground for several days during severe winter weather. The Gunnison's prairie dogs hibernate from October through February (Hygnstrom and Virchow 1994, Sevilleta LTER: Data 1998c).

Since 1900, prairie dog populations have been reduced by as much as 98 percent in some areas and totally eliminated in others. This demise is largely the result of cultivation of prairie grasslands and control programs implemented in the early and mid-1900s (Hof and others 2002, Hygnstrom and Virchow 1994) and the plague (Brand 2002). Because prairie dogs feed upon gasses and upon a variety of annuals, they compete with domestic livestock for food. As a result, humans have made great efforts to eliminating the "pest" from rangeland, chiefly by poisoning. For example, in 1908,

USDA Forest Service Gen. Tech. Rep. RMRS-GTR-135-vol. 2. 2005

39

Importance of Prairie Dogs—Knowles (2002) appropriately states that the importance of prairie dogs to the grassland ecosystems of North America is matched only by the degree to which that importance is misunderstood, misrepresented, and minimized. They probably had a more profound influence on the physiognomy and composition of native grassland communities than most other mammal species (Fagerstone and Ramey 1996, Hof and others 2002). Probably the only other species that played such a significant role in grassland structure on the Great Plains was the bison. Prairie dog colonies often encompassed huge grassland expanses and their maintenance of these areas for colonial use influenced both abiotic and biotic conditions (Fagerstone and Ramey 1996).

Prairie dogs are identified as keystone species in the ecosystems they inhabit (Cook and others 2003, Kotliar 2000). A keystone species is one whose impact on its community or ecosystem is large, and disproportionately large relative to its abundance (Payton and others 2002) (see discussion in chapter 1). Prairie dogs play a keystone role in maintaining grassland ecosystems. For example, dozens of species of mammals, birds, reptiles, and amphibians are dependent to one degree or another on prairie dogs for food, shelter, or both. Without the prairie dog, the vast American grassland ecosystems cannot survive (Knowles 2002). Much of the research on these associated species has been conducted within the range of the black-tailed prairie dogs. Reports of up to 117 wildlife species associated with prairie dogs may overestimate the total number, but many species are benefited by prairie dogs. These close associates appear to use white-tailed and Gunnison's prairie dog colonies, as well as black-tailed prairie dog colonies (Knowles 2002).

Effects of Prairie Dogs on Grassland—Prairie dogs colonize sites where the vegetation is low due to heavy grazing or to other disturbance that reduce vegetation height and density, thus allowing a good view of predators. In well-established prairie dog colonies, large areas of bare soil are common. Where there is low vegetation, they often clip shrubs and other tall vegetation to maintain a condition where plant species composition, biomass, and productivity of vegetation differ from uncolonized areas (Fagerstone and Ramey 1996).

High densities of prairie dogs may negatively influence native perennial grasses by causing shifts in plant species composition toward shorter grasses and, ultimately, toward annual and short-lived perennial forb species (Fagerstone and Ramey 1996, Severe 1977). Often buffalograss (*Buchloe dactyloides*) is the dominant plant on prairie dog colonies, and the taller western wheatgrass (*Agropyron smithii*) and blue grama (*Bouteloua gracilis*) are most common on uncolonized mixed-grass prairie sites. In areas with

Black-tailed prairie dog. (Photo by Jeff Venuga)

the greatest prairie dog activity, annual forbs, shrubs, and cacti often replace most of the original grass cover. The formation of forb-dominated communities in prairie dog colonies is related to the length of time since colonization and the level of prairie dog activity; forb domination is usually greatest in the center of the colony (Fagerstone and Ramey 1996). They will forage on the following forbs: scarlet globe- mallow (*Sphaeralcea coccinea*), prickly pear (*Opuntia* spp.), kochia (*Kochia scoparia*), peppergrass (*Lepidium* spp.), and wooly plantain (*Plantago patagonica*) (Hygnstrom and Virchow 1994).

Positive effects of prairie dogs on grassland productivity include greater soil aeration, changes in community structure, increased plant species diversity, and greater forb production. It has been postulated that burrowing decreases soil compaction, increases water absorption, aerates soil, and promotes soil formation. Soils in prairie dog colonies are richer in nitrogen, phosphorus, and organic matter than soils in adjacent grasslands (Fagerstone and Ramey 1996, Severe 1977).

Prairie dog foraging removes aging leaves and may stimulate growth of new plant tissue, which usually has a higher nutritional value (increased nitrogen concentration) than older tissue. Prairie dog colonies, therefore, have been found to contain better quality forage and growing conditions than uncolonized areas (Fagerstone and Ramey 1996).

On February 4, 2000, the USDI Fish and Wildlife Service announced its 12-month finding for a petition to list the black-tailed prairie dog as Threatened throughout its range under the Endangered Species Act

40

USDA Forest Service Gen. Tech. Rep. RMRS-GTR-135-vol. 2. 2005

of 1973. They determined that listing was warranted but precluded by other higher priority actions. The black-tailed prairie dog was added to the candidate species list.

Competition Between Prairie Dogs and Cattle—The degree of dietary competition and overlap between prairie dogs and cattle can be high. Both eat mainly grasses, followed by forbs and shrubs. However, eliminating prairie dogs has had little effect on increasing the amount of food available for cattle (Fagerstone and Ramey 1996). At a prairie dog repopulation rate of 30 percent, controls have not been economically feasible, and annual maintenance costs are greater than the amount of forage gained. Controlling black-tailed prairie dogs on depleted grasslands in western South Dakota did not increase the amount of forage produced after 4 years, whether or not cattle were allowed to graze (Fagerstone and Ramey 1996). To improve range conditions, long periods, up to 10 years, of total exclusion from prairie dogs and livestock may be required when the range is in a low condition class. In a study discussed by Fagerstone and Ramey (1996), prairie dog-cattle competition was found to have no differences in forb production on steers-only pastures compared to pastures with steers and prairie dogs. They did find significant reductions in availability of blue grama, sand dropseed (*Sporobolus cryptandrus*), and other grasses on pastures with prairie dogs. Uresk and Paulson (1988) estimated the carrying capacity and forage utilization for cattle in western South Dakota when prairie dogs were present, but pastures were maintained in good condition at a near climax stage of mixed perennial cool-season grasses. They found that carrying capacity for cows and for cow-calf units decreased as the number of hectares occupied by prairie dog colonies increased; the decrease was approximately three AUMs or two cow-calf units for every additional 20 ha of prairie dogs. The researchers showed that on such sites, needle leaf sedge (*Carex eleocharis*) and needlegrasses (*Stipa* spp.) could become major limiting factors in determining cow carrying capacity.

Interactions Between Prairie Dogs and Other Wildlife Species—As a keystone species, prairie dogs have great influence on other wildlife species. Through modifications of aboveground vegetation, prairie dogs influence the densities, foraging patterns, and nutritional dynamics of other animals. Because these habitat modifications can be extensive, researchers refer to "prairie dog ecosystems"—that is, they are systems comprised of prairie dogs and other associated plants and animals. Studies have reported 64 to 163 vertebrate species associated with prairie dog colonies (Fagerstone and Ramey 1996, Hygnstrom and Virchow 1994). Five classes of invertebrates were identified on prairie dog colonies in South Dakota, which may explain why more insectivorous rodent species are found on prairie dog colonies than on surrounding grassland (Fagerstone and Ramey 1996, Hygnstrom and Virchow 1994).

One of the most important features of a prairie dog colony is the burrow system. Prairie dog burrows serve as homes for various small mammals, reptiles, birds, amphibians, and invertebrates whose numbers are usually higher on prairie dog colonies (Fagerstone and Ramey 1996, Hygnstrom and Virchow 1994, Knowles 2002). On mixed-grass sites in South Dakota and Oklahoma, small rodent abundance was found to be greater on than off colonies, but small rodent species richness was significantly lower. Lower species richness can probably be attributed to changes in vegetation structure and composition in colonies (Fagerstone and Ramey 1996).

Prairie dogs are also important prey for some mammalian predators. The black-footed ferret has been historically an important predator of prairie dogs. The population decline of black-footed ferrets to the point where they are now listed as Federally Endangered is related to the decrease in prairie dog populations. In the absence of ferrets, the badger (*Taxidea taxus*) is the main prairie dog predator (Fagerstone and Ramey 1996). Others mammalian predators include coyotes (*Canis latrans*), bobcats (*Lynx rufus*), foxes (*Vulpes* spp.), occasionally mink (*Mustela vison*), and long-tailed weasels (*Mustela frenata*) (Fagerstone and Ramey 1996). Many avian predators feed on prairie dogs, including golden eagles (*Aquila chrysaetos*), bald eagles (*Haliaeetus leucocephalus*), Ferruginous hawks (*Buteo regalis*), red-tailed hawks (*B. jamaicensis*), rough-legged hawks (*B. lagopus*), marsh hawks (*Circus cyaneus*), and other species (Fagerstone and Ramey 1996). Young prairie dogs may be taken by prairie rattlesnakes (*Crotalus viridis*) and bullsnakes (*Pituophis catenifer*), but rarely are adult prairie dogs prayed upon by snakes (Hygnstrom and Virchow 1994).

Bird species diversity and abundance are significantly higher on prairie dog colonies than on mixed-grass sites (Fagerstone and Ramey 1996). They attributed the higher numbers to "patchiness" or structural diversity on prairie dog colonies, to increased forb seed production, and to lower amounts of mulch and lower vegetation height, which may result in greater visibility of macroarthropods and seeds. Bird species that are significantly more abundant on prairie dog colonies include horned larks (*Eremophila alpestris*), mourning doves (*Zenaidura macroura*), killdeer (*Charadrius vociferus*), barn swallows (*Hirundo rustica*), and burrowing owls (*Athene cunicularia*) (Fagerstone and Ramey 1996).

Prairie Dog Management Programs—Land managers are learning to account for the positive and negative effects of prairie dogs on grasslands and on other wildlife species in land management planning.

USDA Forest Service Gen. Tech. Rep. RMRS-GTR-135-vol. 2. 2005

41

Recognizing the important ecological roles prairie dogs play within grasslands is critical for the overall management of these ecosystems. Management of prairie dog colonies and grasslands should take into consideration a number of factors including range conditions and trends, season of livestock use, prairie dog and livestock densities, how much area is available for colony expansion, maintaining habitats with a large component of appropriate vegetation, and potential interactions with other species.

Prairie dogs most frequently colonize sites that have been overgrazed or otherwise disturbed. Intense livestock grazing promotes high prairie dog densities, and colonies tend to expand under heavy grazing. Depending on climatic factors, prairie dog colony expansion rates can be decreased by increasing vegetation cover around colonies through reducing grazing and human disturbance.

Pocket Gophers

Pocket gophers are fossorial (burrowing) rodents that have gnawing teeth for chewing (Pocket Gopher 2005c, Wiscomb and Messmer 1988). The name pocket gopher comes from the pouches on their cheeks. They belong to the family Geomyidae (Geomyidae 2005, Pocket Gophers 2005a). There are 33 species of pocket gophers represented by five genera in the western hemisphere. The two primary genera of pocket gophers discussed here are *Geomys* spp. and *Thomomys* spp. *Geomys* are present from the Rocky Mountains east to the Mississippi River, and from southern Canada to southern Texas. The three main *Geomys* species in North America are the plains pocket gopher (*Geomys bursarius*), the desert pocket gopher (*G. arenarius*), and the Texas pocket gopher (*G. personatus*). The plains pocket gopher is the most widespread (fig. 3-2). *Thomomys* species occur generally in the Western States. The northern pocket gopher (*T. talpoides*) (fig. 3-2) is widely distributed from Canada south to northern California and New Mexico, and from the West Coast east to the Dakotas (fig. 3-2) (Fagerstone and Ramey 1996).

Pocket gophers occur on pastures, grasslands, prairies, roadsides, and railroad rights-of-way (Pocket Gopher 2005c) or any disturbed land. They live in a broad range of habitats from deserts to mountain meadows, in soils ranging from sand to clay, with loam preferred. In valleys and mountain meadows, they prefer loamy soil, but some occur in sandy or rocky situations. The soil in which a gopher will dig its burrow seems to be dependent on the size of the animal and related to depth and friability of the soils. Larger

Figure 3-2. Distribution of the northern (*Thomomys talpoides*), plains (*Geomys burarius*), and desert (*G arenarius*) pocket gophers (NatureServe 2005).

gophers lived in deep, soft soils and small animals in shallow, rocky ones (Sevilleta LTER: Data 1998b).

In Arizona and New Mexico, botta's pocket gophers live in nearly every habitat within the States so long as sufficient tuberous roots and plant material are available and soil is suitable for digging tunnels. They are found near sea level up to 11,000 feet. They live in extremely xeric deserts through all of the vegetative types to near timberline in the mountains (Sevilleta LTER: Data 1998b, Sullivan 2005).

These rodents, weighing less than a pound, are living mining machines. Where the digging is easy, they are able to tunnel as much as 200 to 300 feet (61 to 91 m) in a single night. A burrow may be occupied by the same animal for several years, and burrows may occur in densities of up to16 to 20 per acre (6.4 to 8 per ac). Burrow systems consist of a main tunnel from 4 to 18 inches (10 to 46 cm) below the surface with a number of lateral tunnels branching off from the main tunnel (Forest Preserve District of Cook County 1973, Pocket Gophers 2005c, Sullivan 2005). Lateral tunnels end at the surface where the soil mound is created.

Pocket gophers usually construct one nest that contains a number of toilets and a number of food cache chambers in deeper tunnels that branch off from the main tunnel. A nest chamber also is lined with vegetation. Nest chambers and food caches have been found as deep as 5 to 6 feet (1.5 to 1.8 m) below the surface. During the breeding season a male's burrow may be more linear because its sole purpose is to intercept a female's burrow. A single pocket gopher may construct as many as 300 soil mounds in a year while moving more than 4 tons (3629 kg) of soil. Burrows are continually changing, with old tunnels being sealed off and new ones excavated. A single tunnel system may consist of as much as 200 yards (183 m) of tunnels. In habitat with poorer vegetation, longer tunnels must be excavated to meet food needs (Forest Preserve District of Cook County 1973). Gophers seal the openings to the burrow system with earthen plugs (Pocket Gophers 2005b,c, Sullivan 2005).

Pocket gophers feed on a wide variety of herbaceous material (Pocket Gopher 2005c, Sevilleta LTER: Data 1998b, Wiscomb and Messmer 1988). Above ground, from the vicinity of burrow openings, they take leafy vegetation, generally preferring herbaceous plants, shrubs, and trees to grass; most commonly they feed on roots and fleshy portions of plants while digging underground devouring succulent roots and tubers. They often prefer forbs and grasses, but diet shifts seasonally according to the availability and needs for nutrition and water. For example, water-laden cactus plants may become a major dietary component during the hot and dry summer months in arid habitats. Gophers will pull entire plants into their burrow from below. In snow-covered areas they may feed on bark several feet up a tree. Pocket Gophers are active all year, day and night, and guard their burrows and territories fiercely (Pocket Gopher 2005a,b,c, Forest Preserve District of Cook County 1973, Wiscomb and Messmer 1988). Gophers do not hibernate (Pocket Gopher 2005b, c). Although pocket gophers are usually solitary (Pocket Gopher 2005c, Sevilleta LTER: Data 1998b), occasionally a male and female will be found in the same burrow on the same day. This probably occurs most frequently during their breeding season. A male probably mates with several females, especially those with burrow systems adjacent to his. This polygamous behavior results in a large number of females in the population. Some males practice serial monogamy; researchers found four cases where a male and female were sharing a nest (Sevilleta LTER: Data 1998b).

Gophers are prayed upon by hawks, owls, snakes, badgers, foxes, and coyotes (Sullivan 2005). Badgers and coyotes hunt pocket gophers by digging out their burrows, while weasels and snakes may pursue them underground. Other predators include skunks, owls, bobcats, and hawks (Desert USA 2005).

Pocket gophers are found throughout most of the grasslands in the United States (Fagerstone and Ramey 1996, Pocket Gopher 2005c). That pocket gophers play a vital role in the functioning of grassland ecosystems becomes evident as we consider their roles as an ecosystem engineer and prey species, their influence in loosening, stirring, and enriching the soil (Forest Preserve District of Cook County 1973, Pocket Gophers 2005a, Reichman 2004), their effects on microtopography and in creating habitat heterogeneity, their effects on plant species diversity and primary production, and their role as providers of habitat for other wildlife species, such as, rabbits, ground squirrels, mice, skunks, snakes, lizards, and toads (Pocket Gophers 2005a, Sullivan 2005).

Gopher's Effects on Grasslands—Pocket gophers are an important element controlling ecosystem structure and development. It has been argued that Geomyidae is a dynamic force to direct the biogeochemical attributes of the North American grasslands. The activities of gophers may provide an explanation for the genesis of North American Prairie soils. Native plant life on hill and mountainside in canyon and mountain meadow would soon begin to depreciate if gopher populations were to be completely destroyed (Huntly and Inouye 1988).

Gopher effects on the productivity, heterogeneity, and trophic structure of ecosystems, of various temporal and spatial scales have been described. Gophers influence the physical environment, altering patterns and rates of soil development and nutrient availability, microtopography, and the consequent abiotic environment. They affect the demography and abundance of plant species, changing vegetational patterns and diversity. They affect the behavior and abundance of other herbivores, from grasshoppers and ground squirrels to large grazers (Huntly and Inouye 1988).

Pocket gophers may be a keystone species in grasslands. The plains pocket gopher (Geomys bursarius) turns over as much as 5 percent of the tallgrass prairies per year. This disturbance creates openings in the grassland canopy that may allow seedlings to establish. It has been demonstrated that gopher mound building negatively affects the activity of meadow voles (Microtus pennsylvanicus), a major aboveground herbivore. This, in turn, allows a greater proportion of seedlings to escape predation by voles. Thus, through these direct and indirect effects, gophers may be instrumental in structuring the prairie plant and animal communities as well as maintaining prairie diversity (Geomyidae 2005).

Pocket gophers affect grassland in three important ways: (1) by burying plants; (2) by transporting nutrients to the soil surface during burrowing and mound formation activities; and (3) by feeding, which decreases biomass of forage plants and alters plant species composition. Pocket gophers compete directly with livestock by consuming range plants, above and below ground. Consumption of forage by gophers is much higher than

USDA Forest Service Gen. Tech. Rep. RMRS-GTR-135-vol. 2. 2005

43

for other small mammals (Fagerstone and Ramey 1996, Forest Preserve District of Cook County 1973).

Pocket gophers may be the primary non-ungulate consumer of forage in grasslands, frequently harvesting and storing more vegetation than they actually eat. What they do not eat, they store in underground food caches (Forest Preserve District of Cook County 1973, Pocket Gophers 2005a,b). The plains pocket gopher differs from other pocket gophers in that forbs comprise a smaller portion of their diet (Fagerstone and Ramey 1996). In contrast to *Thomomys* species, *Geomys* species frequently thrive in grassland areas with few forbs. Various studies have shown that grasses were either the majority or near majority portion of *Geomys* diet (Fagerstone and Ramey 1996).

Several studies demonstrate that pocket gophers can decrease grassland forage production by consumption, clipping, burying litter and vegetation, and reducing plant vigor. The decrease in production varies between shortgrass and tallgrass and between range condition classes within sites. Plains pocket gophers have been shown to significantly impact forage production on western Nebraska grasslands, decreasing overall production between 18 percent and 49 percent. In Texas, biomass increased 22 percent when plains pocket gophers were excluded from grasslands (Fagerstone and Ramey 1996).

Besides changing forage availability, pocket gophers can alter the vegetation species composition of grasslands by feeding, burying herbage, and by altering the microenvironment. Plant species favored by gophers tend to decrease on grasslands while unpalatable species increase. Pocket gopher feeding and burrowing activity promotes the presence of annual grasses, annual forbs, and perennial forbs, while decreasing the frequency of perennial grasses. These changes in plant composition are related to precipitation. The greatest changes occur in areas with low precipitation. Pocket gophers have been known to cause major changes in vegetation composition on high mountain grasslands, suppressing productivity of some livestock forage species such as common dandelion (*Taraxacum officinale*), lupine (*Lupinus* spp.), agoseris (*Agoseris glauca*), and aspen peavine (*Lathyrus leucanthus*), and increasing production of orange sneezeweed (*Helenium hoopesi*), which is poisonous to sheep and unpalatable to cattle. Two grass species palatable to livestock, slender wheatgrass (*Agropyron pauctflorum*) and mountain brome (*Bromus carinatus*), benefited from gopher activity. Range condition may decline following pocket gopher occupation as desirable perennial grasses decline, accompanied by an increase in annual grasses and forbs. This decline may cause gophers to move into previously unoccupied areas and abandon the weedy areas (Fagerstone and Ramey 1996).

As pocket gophers dig, they deposit soil that may bury vegetation and prevent growth of the underlying vegetation. Subsequent plant succession on denuded areas may be slow and may continually provide colonization sites for early successional species. Vegetation density on pocket gopher mounds increases rapidly over time as perennial species replace less desirable annuals and forbs. The first plants to appear are usually annuals, followed by perennial dicots. It has been observed that herbaceous perennial dicots benefit from pocket gopher disturbance by germinating and surviving in greater numbers on mounds than off mounds (Fagerstone and Ramey 1996).

Digging by gophers may cause higher erosion rates than those attributed to other processes in an area. Most digging occurs in late summer and fall when young gophers establish their own burrow systems and when adults extend their burrows in search of underground food. Estimates on the amount of soil brought to the surface by pocket gophers range from 4,483 kg to 85,200 kg (4.9 to 94 tons). This huge variance in displacement of soil by gophers may result in formation of mima mounds (Fagerstone and Ramey 1996, Geiger 2002). Such mounds are usually 0.3 to 0.9 m (1 to 3 ft) high and 4.5 to 30 m (14.7 to 98.4 ft) in diameter and are formed over decades of gopher burrowing activities that tend to move soil toward the nest. The soil on mima mounds may differ considerably from adjacent soils, having a lower bulk density, higher water permeability, higher organic matter content, and a lack of definite structure in the topsoil. Stones of the sizes pocket gophers can move are concentrated in mounds, and vegetation on mounds is usually denser and more effective in retarding soil erosion than that off mounds. In a Colorado range seeding project, grasses produced two to five times more herbage on mounds than between mounds (Fagerstone and Ramey 1996).

Results from different studies conflict as to how nutrient cycling may be affected by deposition of soil by pocket gophers. Increases in organic matter, nitrogen, and phosphorus in areas occupied by pocket gophers have been reported. In contrast, other researchers reported reduced nutrients in occupied areas. Still other studies looked at the nutrient content of soil samples from old mounds, new mounds, and away from mounds (controls), and found that old mounds were often significantly lower in nutrient concentrations than new mounds, which were lower than control sites. Gophers reduced the average nitrogen concentration near the soil surface and increased the variability in soil nitrogen. Soil deposited by pocket gophers was lower in nutrients (that is, phosphorus, nitrate, and potassium) than randomly collected samples, possibly because nutrients were leached out or drawn from soil by plant roots. Deficiency of nutrients in mounds may also occur because mounds lack the litter layer that

44

is important in holding moisture and nutrients near the surface (Fagerstone and Ramey 1996).

Pocket gophers may benefit grasslands by loosening compacted soil, allowing better aeration, improving water infiltration, and increasing soil fertility by adding excrement and burying vegetation. The decrease in plant biomass caused by mound-building was partly compensated for by increased production in areas immediately adjacent to mounds, where production was higher than vegetative production near the edge of mounds. Researchers hypothesized that increased density of vegetation near mounds was a response to increased nutrient availability caused by leaching of nutrients from mounds into surface soil (Fagerstone and Ramey 1996).

Grazing Effects on Pocket Gophers—Pocket gophers are attracted to grasslands in good to excellent range condition where they use vigorous plants with large root systems. Their densities appear to be dependent on plant biomass. Lower plant biomass may require gophers to burrow more extensively to locate food. The impacts of grazing on pocket gophers are variable. In two studies of northern pocket gopher populations, no significant differences were found between grazed or ungrazed areas on mountain rangeland. Other studies have shown higher pocket gopher numbers on ungrazed areas. However, other comparisons involving grazing intensity have shown heavily grazed range to have higher gopher densities than lightly grazed range.

Although these results seem contradictory they may have a biological basis. During the summer grazing season, both sheep and cattle consume large quantities of forbs, which are also the preferred summer foods of northern pocket gophers. Forb availability may be highest for gophers on ungrazed range versus lightly or moderately grazed range and may allow for higher pocket gopher densities on the ungrazed areas. On the other hand, higher pocket gopher densities on heavily grazed range may be an effect of long-term heavy grazing, which can promote greater abundance of forb species than moderate or light grazing (Fagerstone and Ramey 1996).

Pocket Gopher Management—Range management can favor plains pocket gophers, which are attracted to areas of improving and good range condition, where gophers use vigorous plants. Once present, pocket gophers interact with grasslands and livestock in ways that can decrease grassland productivity by 25 to 50 percent. Managers should be aware that the presence of pocket gophers may require reduction in levels of livestock grazing to maintain good range condition (Fagerstone and Ramey 1996).

Even though grassland production is lowered by gophers, many researchers believe that gophers are not a significant problem on well-managed grasslands.

In some areas, such as high mountain grassland, the total ecological effects of pocket gopher populations may be beneficial rather than detrimental. In areas where livestock were excluded, grass biomass increased most at sites having pocket gophers; so it is possible that pocket gophers may actually improve depleted range (Fagerstone and Ramey 1996).

Pocket gopher control is rarely practiced on Western grasslands. Gopher control is more frequently recommended for improving deteriorated grasslands than for maintaining grasslands that are well managed and productive. Where range conditions are poor, it may be advantageous to reduce pocket gopher populations. The most widely used approach to control pocket gophers is poisoning. Control of forbs, which frequently have large underground storage structures, can be an effective method for minimizing damage to grassland by northern pocket gophers. Application of herbicides can indirectly reduce pocket gopher populations by 80 to 90 percent. Herbicide success is attributed to decreased forb production and resulting starvation of pocket gophers. Where vegetative composition after herbicide treatment remained relatively stable, with a grass dominance for 5 years, repopulation of pocket gophers in treated areas was slow (Fagerstone and Ramey 1996).

Small Rodents

Deer Mice

The deer mouse (*Peromyscus maniculatus*) belongs to the family Muridae and subfamily Sigmodontinae. The deer mouse is found almost everywhere in North America (fig. 3-3). Because it occurs over a large geographic area and range of habitats and is highly variable in appearance, more than 100 subspecies have been described (Mammals 2005). The deer mouse inhabits woodlands but it also turns up in desert areas (CDC 2004).

Like other small rodents, deer mice are heavily preyed upon and are quite secretive (Deer Mouse 2005). Because of their abundance, deer mice are a major food source for almost every bird and mammal predator. When predators are reduced or absent, the mice can become pests (Cato 2005).

They are primarily nocturnal emerging from their nest to feed (Deer Mouse 2005). They are energy efficient, reducing their body temperature when in their burrows. Lowering their metabolism means they need less food. Deer mice do not hibernate during the winter (Cato 2005). Deer mice usually make their nest in a cavity found inside a tree, stump, under logs, and sometimes even in abandoned squirrel nests. Their nests are often found under rocks, boards, and haystacks. The nest, about the size of two cupped hands, is made of

USDA Forest Service Gen. Tech. Rep. RMRS-GTR-135-vol. 2. 2005

45

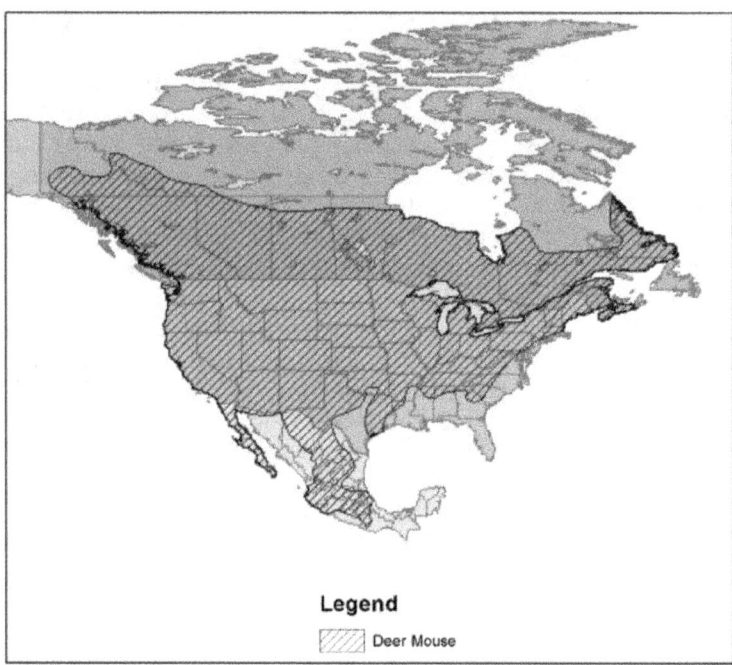

Legend

///// Deer Mouse

Figure 3-3. Distribution of the deer mouse (*Peromyscus maniculatus*) (NatureServe 2005).

coarse outer materials with a soft inner lining of plant fibers, fur, feathers, moss, shredded tree bark, leaves, and other material (Deer Mouse 2005, Forest Preserve District of Cook County 1974).

Deer mice are widespread and adaptable, with broad diets (Fagerstone and Ramey 1996). The food of the deer mouse is mostly seeds of grasses, weeds, and berries. Their diet may also include buds, insects, spiders, centipedes, land snails, and many other foods (Forest Preserve District of Cook County 1974, Mammals 2005). They will carry food in their cheek pouches and often store by the quart (0.9 l). These small rodents need more food in proportion to their weight than do larger warm-blooded animals. A 1 oz (28 grams) mouse will eat 0.5 oz (14 grams) of food per day (Forest Preserve District of Cook County 1974). Food selection is dependent on both habitat and season. Deer mice feed heavily on larvae from lepidopterans (moths and butterflies) and other insects in the spring. They can eat large volumes and are capable of ridding an area of many insects that may be detrimental to trees. In the fall, seeds become a major food source and are stored in caches for use during the winter (Cato 2005).

Their habitat selection ranges from native prairie to farm fields (Fagerstone and Ramey 1996). Throughout their range, they occur in nearly all ecological communities and life zones from the desert floor to the high mountains (Cato 2005). These small rodents are pioneer species that occur in most vegetation types during most stages of plant succession, but usually not in large numbers (Fagerstone and Ramey 1996). At times, they can be highly abundant, numbering as many as 10 per acre (4 per ha) (Cato 2005). They are sometimes referred to as a "weed" species because disturbances that result in early seral stages favor population increases. Deer mice usually are the most abundant small mammals in severely disturbed areas. Therefore, grazing is generally beneficial to deer mice, which select areas with low cover and are common in habitats with bare soil surface and open vegetation such as grazed prairie. Researchers have found that heavy grazing in big sagebrush habitat promotes an increase in deer mice numbers (Fagerstone and Ramey 1996). The total small mammal population declined in grazed communities, but the density estimates of deer mice increased; they were dominant after the grazing season whereas they were found in only minor proportions before. Deer mice have used microhabitats with high shrub density, which is sometimes a consequence of grazing (Fagerstone and Ramey 1996).

Range depletion does not always favor an increase in deer mouse populations in all habitats. Fagerstone and Ramey (1996) found increased deer mice populations with increasing forb cover. In some studies, more deer mice were found in ungrazed than in grazed riparian habitat, but fewer deer mice were found in ungrazed than in grazed short-grass prairie uplands (Fagerstone and Ramey 1996). From the different studies conducted on deer mice and grazing, it can be concluded that deer mice have differential responses to grazing, decreasing in the most xeric habitats and increasing in mesic habitats (Fagerstone and Ramey 1996).

Deer mice do not normally have noticable effects on grassland vegetation. However, seed predation by mice may be an important factor in grasslands. During reseeding efforts, deer mice may consume or cache considerable quantities of seeds, resulting in poor plant establishment. In contrast, Fagerstone and Ramey (1996) concluded that seed caches may result in clumps of seedlings, and that 50 percent of bitterbrush resulted from rodent seed caches.

Deer mice may be carriers of Hantavirus. When present, this virus is spread through the rodent's urine and feces. Although the mice do not become ill from the virus, humans can become infected when they are exposed to contaminated dust from the nests or droppings. Humans are advised to not camp nor sleep where mouse droppings are abundant and to clean indoor areas where mice live (Cato 2005).

People should eliminate or minimize contact with rodents in homes, workplaces, or campsites. If structures used by humans are inhospitable for mice, then humans will have less contact with mice. Recommendations include (1) Seal up holes and gaps in homes or garages. (2) Place traps in and around

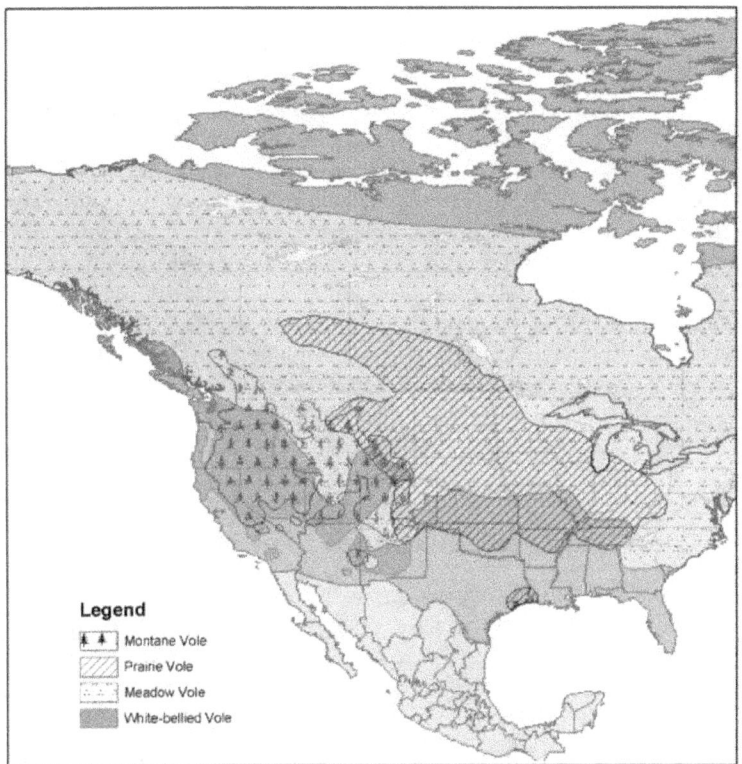

Figure 3-4. Distribution of long-tailed (*Microtus longicaudus*), montane (*M. montanus*), prairie (*M. ochrogaster*), and meadow (*M. pennsylvanicus*) voles (NatureServe 2005).

grasses, grasslike plants, or litter, and they are active day and night, year-round (Andelt and Ahmed 2004, Saimon and Gorenzel 2002). The meadow vole will inhabit stream and lake shores and is a good swimmer (Meadow Vole 2005).

Vole numbers fluctuate from year to year. Populations are influenced by dispersal, food quality, climate, predation, physiological stress, and genetics. Under favorable conditions their populations can increase rapidly (Andelt and Ahmed 2004, Saimon and Gorenzel 2002). In some areas their numbers are cyclical, reaching peak numbers every 3 to 6 years before dropping back to low levels. When populations go through a high, numbers can soar to several thousand per acre (Saimon and Gorenzel 2002). During cyclic population peaks, voles (*M. longicaudus*, *M. montanus*, and *M. pennsylvanicus*) can reach densities as high as 7,400 voles per ha (2960 per ac) (Fagerstone and Ramey 1996).

Voles make nests in clumps of grass, using materials such as dry grass, sedges, and weeds. From their nests, they build "runways", akin to tunnels beneath the grass and plants (Meadow Vole 2005). They construct many surface runways and underground tunnels with numerous burrow entrances. The surface or subsurface burrows and tunnels are 1 to 2 inches (2.5 to 5 cm) wide, in a relatively small area, and contain numerous adults and young. Home-range size is usually less than 0.25 acre (0.1 ha) and varies with habitat quality, food supply, population levels, and season (Andelt and Ahmed 2004, Bryan 2005, Saimon and Gorenzel 2002).

Voles are primarily herbivores and forage on grasses, flowers, vegetables, fruits, bulbs, and roots; on occasion they will eat insects and snails (Saimon and Gorenzel 2002). They eat virtually constantly, concentrating on green vegetation during the summer and switching to mostly grains and seeds in the fall (Meadow Vole 2005). During winter months, voles do not hibernate, but instead make tunnels beneath the snow and gnaw on shrubs and tree bark for nutrition (Andelt and Ahmed 2004, Meadow Vole 2005, Saimon and Gorenzel 2002).

Voles are an important part of the ecosystem. They are preyed upon by hawks, owls, foxes, cats, snakes, crows, herons, shrews, skunks, bullfrogs, snapping turtles, largemouth bass, and raccoons (Meadow Vole 2005).

Most vole species select sites with relatively high cover, so increased canopy cover is likely to increase *Microtus* populations. They do well in ungrazed or only lightly grazed grasslands but disappear from areas with moderate to heavy grazing (Fagerstone and Ramey 1996). In a study reported by Fagerstone and Ramey 1996, prairie voles were captured only on mixed

homes to decrease rodent infestation. (3) Clean up any easy-to-get food (CDC 2004).

Recent research results show that many people who became ill with HPS developed the disease after having been in frequent contact with rodents and/or their droppings around a home or a workplace. On the other hand, many people who became ill reported that they had not seen rodents or rodent droppings at all. Therefore, if you live in an area where the carrier rodents are known to live, try to keep your home, vacation place, workplace, or campsite clean (CDC 2004). Never vacuum or sweep mouse droppings; thoroughly wet the area with a disinfectant, then carefully wipe up the droppings with a wet cloth (Mammals 2005).

Voles

Voles (Microtus spp.), which are commonly known as meadow or field mice, belong to the rodent family Muridae. The range for each species is limited by specific habitat conditions. Four species of voles inhabit grasslands in Arizona and New Mexico: long-tailed vole (*Microtus longicaudus*), montane vole (*Microtus montanus*), prairie vole (*Microtus ochrogaster*), and meadow vole (*Microtus pennsylvanicus*) (fig. 3-4). The most widely distributed species is the meadow vole. Voles normally occupy areas with dense ground cover,

USDA Forest Service Gen. Tech. Rep. RMRS-GTR-135-vol. 2. 2005

47

grass prairie sites and did not occur on shortgrass sites such as prairie dog colonies. Mountain vole (*Microtus montanus*) was drastically reduced in numbers or disappeared from grazed habitats (Fagerstone and Ramey 1996). One hypothesis is that there may be a cover threshold required by voles before populations show significant fluctuations, and that a lower cover threshold may be needed before voles can establish resident breeding populations (Fagerstone and Ramey 1996). Researchers have postulated that cover provides favorable conditions for population buildups by providing food, reducing antagonistic contacts between voles, and moderating microhabitat humidity and temperature (Fagerstone and Ramey 1996).

During normal years, voles have little influence on grasslands, although they may have a direct impact on soil. Voles at a density of 200 to 400 per ha (600 to 900 per ac) probably dislodge 1,000 m^2 of earth per hectare (1196 $yard^2$ ac) per year. Because this activity is restricted to the top 40 cm (15 in) of soil, such activities have minimal influence on microtopography and surface water runoff (Fagerstone and Ramey 1996). They normally have little effect on vegetation cover because the amount of standing crop vegetation they remove is usually quite small (Fagerstone and Ramey 1996). However, after a literature review and after studying the California vole (*Microtus californicus*) in a field, Fagerstone and Ramey (1996) concluded that during the late increase and peak phases of a population cycle, grazing by voles can have a marked effect on vegetation cover. Grazing by microtine rodents removed current-season stem primordia of perennial grasses. In a series of exclosure experiments, grazing by voles kept the habitat open and increased plant species diversity; when voles were excluded, grasses, their preferred food, increased and became dominant. In some instances, voles can have severe effects on vegetation. Studies have found that a population of California voles that exceeded 1,500 voles per ha (3700 per ac) removed 85 percent of the volume of vegetation for wild oats (*Avenafatua*), Italian ryegrass (*Lalium mulhflorum*), and ripgut grass (*Bromus rigidus*). Heavy cropping by small rodents of plants during reproduction suppressed flowering and caused a 70 percent seed loss (Fagerstone and Ramey 1996). Seed predation by mice, including voles, may be an important regulating factor for some plant species (Janzen 1971).

During high population levels, voles can kill and damage sagebrush and other shrub species (Andelt and Ahmed 2004, Bryan 2005, Fagerstone and Ramey 1996, Mueggler 1967, Saimon and Gorenzel 2002) by stripping bark from plants and girdling stems and branches. Damage is greatest when a dense, ungrazed herbaceous understory exists that favors increases in vole populations, and when the snowpack persists throughout the winter (Fagerstone and Ramey 1996, Mueggler 1967). Usually voles kill only portions of the crowns of individual plants, but occasionally they kill entire plants. During 1962 to 1964, Mueggler (1967) observed an irruption of voles on southwestern Montana grassland that caused damage to a number of shrubs, including big and silver sagebrush (*Artemisia* spp.), sumac (*Rhus trilobata*), bitterbrush (*Purshia tridentata*), mountain mahogany, and serviceberry (*Amelanchier* spp.). Mueggler (1967) recorded crown kills of 35 to 97 percent of sagebrush on extensive areas. A similar population explosion of long-tailed voles (*M. longicaudus*) in Utah in 1969 killed 59 percent of sagebrush plants and damaged another 28 percent (Fagerstone and Ramey 1996). But as natives of the sagebrush-grass ecosystem, vole populations at normal levels have little impact on grassland function.

Kangaroo Rats and Pocket Mice

The Heteromyidae is a family of rodents consisting of kangaroo rats and pocket mice. Despite their names, they are neither rats nor mice; and in spite of their mouselike appearance, they are not closely related to any other species of North American rodent (Pocket Mice 2005). Most Heteromyidae live in complex burrows within the deserts and grasslands of western North America, though species within the *Heteromys* and *Liomys* genera are also found in forests and extend south as far as northern South America. They feed mostly on seeds and other plant parts, which they carry in their cheek pouches to their burrows. Although they are different in physical appearance, the closest relatives of the Heteromyidae are pocket gophers in the family Geomyidae (Heteromyidae 2005).

Kangaroo rats and pocket mice are all nocturnal, burrowing animals with external fur-lined cheek pouches for storing and transporting the seeds that are their primary food. They are all well adapted to living in arid environments and most of them never need to drink water. They also have efficient kidneys that can conserve fluids by concentrating the urine (Heteromyidae 2000).

Because there are many of these little rodents and they are closely related to each other, each species has evolved to have different foraging times and places, which minimizes competition. Bailey's pocket mouse (*Chaetodipus baileyi*), for example, climbs up into desert wash vegetation to find seeds and berries still on the plants, while the desert pocket mouse (*Chaetodipus penicillatus*) hunts along the ground in washes and open areas for seeds. Merriam's kangaroo rat (*Dipodomys merriami*), a creature of open, creosote flats, tends to dash from one clump of bushes to the next, overlooking seeds out in the open spaces, leaving those for other mice to find. In this way many species of heteromyid mice and rats can share the same environment (Heteromyidae 2000, Burgess 1996).

Pocket Mice—Pocket mice are well adapted to arid desert life (fig. 3-5). They seldom drink, and can conserve water in a number of ways. They spend the days underground in the burrow where in summer the humidity is higher and the temperature lower than aboveground. The entrance hole is usually plugged to keep the moisture from escaping to the dry air above. Their kidneys concentrate the urine to a viscous consistency, reducing water loss. When temperatures become extreme, some pocket mice go into a torpor state. They appear to be active through most of the year in the southern part of their range, but they probably "hibernate," or are at least holed up, in winter in northern Texas (Pocket Mice 2005). These animals are solitary and defend small territories, often fighting when they encounter each other (Heteromyidae, 2000).

They burrow in friable soil. Their holes have been described as resembling auger holes bored straight into the ground. Usually all the dirt excavated from the burrow system is piled near one opening. A burrow excavated in Brazos County, Texas, had two openings, neither of which was plugged, connected by a single tunnel that descended to a depth of about 40 cm (16 in). A side branch contained food and nest chambers. Another burrow was found opening under a log that served as a roof for the nest chamber. These mice have been known to inhabit deserted burrows, and in Texas they were using burrows of Mexican ground squirrels (*Spermophilus mexicanus*) (Pocket Mice 2005).

The nest of the Hispid pocket mouse (*Chaetodipus hispidus*) is composed of shredded dry grasses and weeds. In captivity, the mice pile the nesting material into a loose heap and then mat it down by sleeping on top of the structure. They seem to behave likewise in the wild (Pocket Mice 2005).

Although they feed almost entirely on vegetation, and principally seeds, gaillardia, cactus, evening primrose, and winecup are found in their caches, an additional 23 other species of plants have been utilized (Pocket Mice 2005). Animal matter makes up only a small part of their diet, including grasshoppers, caterpillars, and beetles (Pocket Mice 2005).

In farming areas, pocket mice can do considerable damage by digging up and carrying away planted seeds. In range and pasture lands they perform a service by eating seeds of weeds (Pocket Mice 2005). Some pocket mice species (*Chaetodipus* spp. and *Perognathus* spp.) prefer a heavy protective cover of grass and some shrubs (table 3-2) (Fagerstone and Ramey 1996). In desert grasslands, some favor cover forage under and around large shrubs and clumped

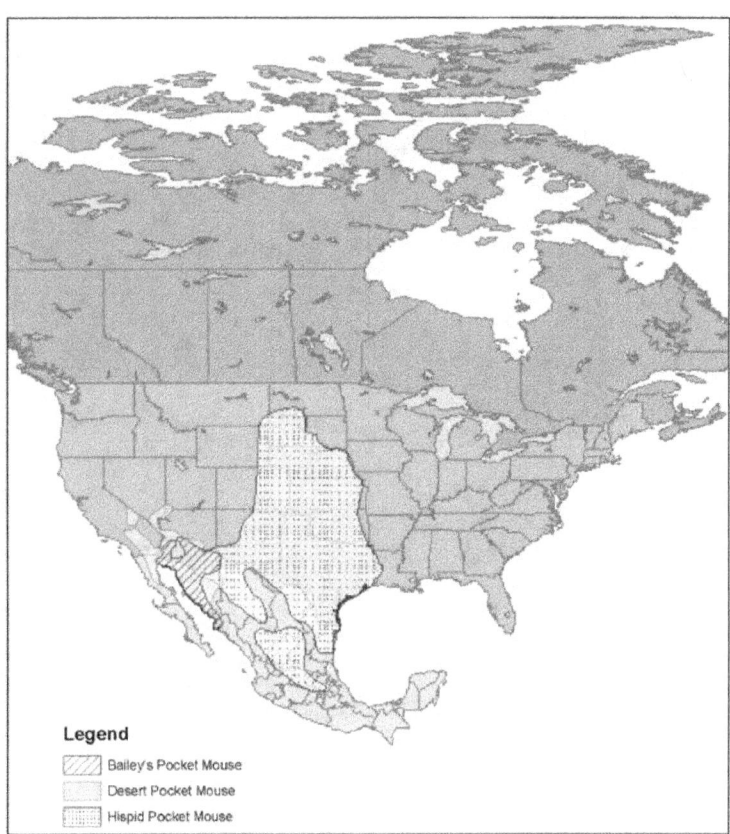

Figure 3-5. Distribution of Bailey's (*Chaetodipus baileyi*), desert (*C. penicillatus*), and Hispid (*C. hispidus*) pocket mice (NatureServe 2005).

vegetation (Fagerstone and Ramey 1996). Within these habitats, pocket mice densities are highest when soils are sandy, which allows for easier digging (Pocket Mice 2005, Fagerstone and Ramey 1996). Pocket mice are most common in nongrazed dense grass communities or areas that are lightly grazed with heavy cover and high seed production. Pocket mice populations are reduced in habitats with sustained heavy grazing (Fagerstone and Ramey 1996). Grazing itself, by reducing the height of bunchgrasses, produces a less favorable habitat, and lowers pocket mouse numbers.

Kangaroo Rats—There are 23 species of kangaroo rats (genus *Dipodomys*) in North America (fig. 3-6); 14 occur in the lower 48 States (Howard 1994). Kangaroo rats inhabit semiarid and arid regions throughout most of the Western and Plains States. The Ord's kangaroo rat is the most common and widespread of the kangaroo rats (Howard 1994). Throughout the Southwest, kangaroo rats occur in great numbers in desert shrub-grasslands. Several species of kangaroo rat inhabit Arizona and New Mexico, including the banner-tailed kangaroo rat (*Dipodomys spectabilis*), Merriam kangaroo rat, and the Ord's kangaroo rat (*D. ordii*), which has the widest range (Kangaroo Rat 2005a,

USDA Forest Service Gen. Tech. Rep. RMRS-GTR-135-vol. 2. 2005

49

Table 3-2. Selected pocket mice species, their response to grazing, and brief description of their habitats (Fagerstone and Ramey 1996).

Species	Response to grazing	Habitat description
Great Basin pocket mice *Perognathus parvus*	Positive	Reside only in relatively dense cover in sagebrush or greasewood communities.
Price pocket mice *Perognathus penicillatus* and Bailey pocket mice *P. baileyi*	Negative	Are most abundant in dense stands of perennial grasses. Their numbers are reduced on grazed ranges.
Arizona pocket mouse *P. amplus*	Positive	Associated with open habitat and with increased grazing.
Silky pocket mice *P. flavus*	Both negative and positive	They were found in greatest densities where there was the sparsest grass cover. Adversely affected by protection of the playa grassland from grazing.
Hispid pocket mice *Chaetodipus hispidus hispidus*	Positive	Are commonly found in areas with open vegetation or where the prairies are intensely grazed and erosion has removed much of the topsoil. Hispid pocket mice inhabit a wide variety of habitats, from native prairie to cropfields, and would be expected to be affected by disturbance. Severe disturbance limits their populations except in heavily grazed prairie dog colonies.

Sevilleta LTER: Data 1998d). Merriam's kangaroo rat inhabits warm deserts and grasslands in southern New Mexico where it is associated with mesquite or other leguminous shrubs (Sevilleta LTER: Data 1998d). In those areas of southern New Mexico where creosote bush dominates large areas of degraded grassland, Merriam's rat is one of the few mammals that occur with any regularity. The Ord's kangaroo rat has a wide distribution that includes revegetated habitats with low production and is most abundant where disturbed earth provides easy tunneling (Fagerstone and Ramey 1996).

Most kangaroo rats prefer areas with less dense herbaceous vegetation and soils that are sandy or sandy loam, which are easy for burrowing. Where Ord's kangaroo and Merriam's rats inhabit the same area, the latter are usually excluded from the more friable soils and are most common on desert pavements or other hardened, stonier soils. A common relationship is for Merriam's to occupy the gravelly bajadas and for Ord's to be found in the loose soils along arroyos or around wind-ablated playas (Sevilleta LTER: Data 1998d). Merriam's kangaroo rat will burrow on sandy soils, clays, gravels, and even among rocks, mostly in low deserts with scattered vegetation (Fagerstone and Ramey 1996, Kangaroo Rat 2005a,c, Sevilleta LTER: Data 1998d).

Banner-tailed kangaroo rat (*Dipodomys spectabilis*) inhabits well-developed grasslands, preferring heavier soils, and avoids basins where basal cover of grass is low. Light soils may be unable to support the fairly

complex and deep burrow systems usually constructed by these rats (Sevilleta LTER: Data 1998d).

Kangaroo rat burrows can be simple in design, shallow, and with openings near the base of shrubs, or quite extensive with separate living, nesting, and food storage areas. Nests are constructed of plant fibers. Rats live in these during the daytime and rear their families. Usually, only one adult occupies each burrow system. If burrows are occupied, entrance holes are plugged (Kangaroo Rat 2005c, Howard 1994). Tracy and Walsberg (2002) determined: (1) burrows are much hotter during the summer than previously thought, 30 to 35 °C (86 to 95 °F), (2) kangaroo rats remain in shallow burrows that are less than a meter (3 feet) below the surface at relatively high ambient temperatures (above 35 °C, 95 °F) throughout the daytime in summer instead of residing deep within the soil as once assumed, (3) they do not restrict their activity to the coolest periods of the night but are active immediately following sundown, during the hottest time of the night, (4) burrows are not persistently humid but can be quite dry, and (5) insects and succulent vegetation constitute a significant portion of a kangaroo rat's diet and may be key to their survival in the hot desert environment.

These nocturnal rodents are solitary rather than communal, with a home range of less than 0.5 acre (0.2 ha); the female's home territory is usually smaller than the male's (Kangaroo Rat 2005a,b). Kangaroo rats do not have large home ranges, 0.04 to 0.07 acres (0.02 to 0.03 ha) and rarely exceeding 0.14 acres (0.06 ha).

Figure 3-6. Distribution of banner-tailed (*Dipodomys specta-bilis*), Merriam's (*D. merriami*), and Ord's (*D. ordii*) kangaroo rats (NatureServe 2005).

found in their cheek pouches, as well as green vegetation, succulents, and insects (Howard 1994, Kangaroo Rat 2005a,b,c, Sevilleta LTER: Data 1998d, Tracy and Walsberg 2002). A study of Merriam's kangaroo rats in the Guadalupe Mountains showed that seeds made up 64 percent of the diet, with seeds of shrubs constituting 23 percent, those of forbs 24 percent, those of grasses 4.5 percent, and those of succulent plants 12 percent.

Kangaroo rats are opportunistic feeders. Green vegetation is most important in mid-summer, while insects are eaten in greatest abundance in winter (Kangaroo Rat 2005c). In the spring when annuals are producing seeds their pouches are filled with these seeds. In late summer, seeds of the perennial grasses are more abundant in their pouches. At some places and at some times, insects may make up as much as 15 to 20 percent of the diet. Green vegetation is sometimes consumed, especially during the breeding season (Sevilleta LTER: Data 1998d).

During winter, Merriam's kangaroo rats open surface caches where seeds are stored. Seeds may be cached as far as 200 feet from where they were found. Apparently Merriam's kangaroo rats do not normally store food within a burrow system but rather in separate caches on the surface (Sevilleta LTER: Data 1998d, Preston and Jacobs 2001). Kangaroo rats may harvest more than 75 percent of an entire seed crop (Parmenter and Van Devender 1995). In some years, Merriam kangaroo rats are sufficiently abundant to eat nearly all large perennial grass seed produced (Fagerstone and Ramey 1996).

Because grass seeds contain little water, adaptations have developed to conserve what little water rats take in. Their skin has no sweat glands and their urine is about three times more concentrated than humans (Kangaroo Rat 2005c). Even with their ability to conserve water, they still need to obtain water by eating insects and green plants (Tracy and Walsberg 2002).

Kangaroo rats are prey for owls, coyotes, foxes, badgers and snakes. Badgers and coyotes dig them out of the ground, and snakes may get some by entering their burrows (Kangaroo Rat 2005b,c).

Kangaroo rats are a keystone guild: through seed predation and soil disturbance they have major effects on biological diversity and biogeochemical processes, facilitating the establishment of annuals and shrubs by selectively foraging on large seeds, and by seed caching and burrowing activities(Sevilleta LTER: Research 2001). Fields and others (1999) showed that banner-tailed kangaroo rats have important effects on both species dominance and composition of different vegetation patch types and may provide a mechanism for small-scale dominance patterns at an ecotone. This

They may move nearly 1 mile (1.6 km) to establish a new home range (Howard 1994).

Kangaroo rats are generally solitary animals, although they often occur in aggregations that appear to have little if any social organization among them. Burrows are spaced to allow for adequate food sources within normal travel distances. Spacing of mounds will vary according to abundance of food, but well-defined travel lanes have been observed between neighboring mounds. Both the number of burrows and individuals per acre can vary greatly depending on locality and time of year. There are usually many more burrow openings than there are rats. Each active burrow system, however, will contain at least one adult rat. There could be as many as 35 rats per acre (14 per ha) in farmlands. In rangelands, 10 to 12 rats per acre (4 to 5 per ha) is more common (Howard 1994). These territorial rats will engage in fierce battles if a prowler is caught trying to pilfer from his neighbor's stores (Kangaroo Rat 2005a).

Their food, which is held within two cheek pouches, is almost entirely seeds. Seeds of mesquite, fescue grass, shadscale (*Atriplex confertifolia*), creosote bush (*Larrea tridentate, Cryptantha angustifolia*), purslane, ocotillo (*Fouquieria splendens*), desert scrubs, Russian thistle (*Salsola* spp.), and grama grass have been

USDA Forest Service Gen. Tech. Rep. RMRS-GTR-135-vol. 2. 2005

51

provids further support for their role as keystone species in desert grasslands.

Other Small Mammals_____

Black-Footed Ferret

The black-footed ferret (*Mustela nigripes*) is the most endangered mammal in North America and one of only three species of ferrets in the world (Black-Footed Ferret 1995). Even before their numbers declined, black-footed ferrets were rarely seen: they were not officially recognized as a species by scientists until 1851, following publication of a book by naturalist John James Audubon and Rev. John Baclunan. Even then, their existence was questioned because no other black-footed ferrets were reported for more than 20 years (Black-Footed Ferret 2005c, CBSG 2004).

Black-footed ferret is a member of the mustelid (musk-producing animals) family that includes mink, skunks, badgers, martens, fishers, stoats, polecats, and wolverines (Ferret Facts 2005). They are loners, except during breeding season, and are nocturnal predators, living in or near prairie dog colonies. They use prairie dog burrows for shelter and travel (Black-Footed Ferret 1997, 2005c,b, Fagerstone and Ramey 1996) and will move into vacant burrows or prey on the current resident and then move in (Black-Footed Ferret 1997). Prairie dogs make up the main staple of the ferret's diet although they occasionally eat mice and other small animals (Black-Footed Ferret 2005a,b, Fagerstone and Ramey 1996). They have also been seen chasing birds and catching moths (Black-Footed Ferret 2005a). A single family of four black-footed ferrets eats about 700 prairie dogs each year and cannot survive without access to large colonies of them (Black-Footed Ferret 2005c).

In the wild, black-footed ferrets spend 99 percent of their time underground (Black-Footed Ferret 2005b). During the night they hunt for prairie dogs that are sleeping in their burrows. Sometimes the ferret is the casualty when a group of prairie dogs attack and drag a ferret underground (Black-Footed Ferret 2005b). They will travel, from burrow to burrow, hunting for prairie dogs, sometimes traveling more than a mile in a night. They leave scent to mark their territory, which averages 150 acres (61 ha) for a female with a litter (Black-Footed Ferret 1997). The ferret is well adapted to slither around its prairie environment. Its color and markings blend so well in grassland soils and plants that it is hard to detect until it moves (Ferret Facts 2005).

Black-footed ferrets can be detected by looking for snow tracks or trenching. Because of their short legs, as ferrets dig, they cannot throw dirt between their legs like dogs do when they dig. They hold the dirt against their chests when they are digging, then back out of the hole, leaving a furrow of dirt. These trenches are usually made during winter, perhaps when ferrets dig after hibernating (Black-Footed Ferret 1997).

Ferrets are born in May or June, usually in a litter of three or four kits. Kits look like mice when they are born and their eyes are shut. When they are 6 to 8 weeks old, the mother starts taking the kits out of their burrow. Before winter, the kits are on their own, and they leave their home territory and their mother (Black-Footed Ferret 1997, 2004).

The original distributional range of the black-footed ferret corresponded closely to that of prairie dogs, and historically they were found throughout the Eastern and Southern Rockies and the Great Plains, from Southern Saskatchewan to Texas (Fagerstone and Ramey 1996, Black-Footed Ferret 1994, 2004, 2005b, Naylor 1994). This range included portions of 12 States (Naylor 1994).

The black-footed ferret is an important member of grassland ecosystems. As a predator, they kept prairie dog populations in check. As with all native species, it evolved having a unique niche within grassland ecosystems. The demise of the ferret and other prairie species is a reminder that the grassland ecosystem itself may be threatened (Naylor 1994).

The decline in black-footed ferret numbers is linked primarily to (1) reductions in prairie dog populations and to (2) secondary poisoning by eating poisoned animals—both programs to eradicate prairie dogs (Black-Footed Ferret 2004, CBSG 2004, Fagerstone and Ramey 1996). They are susceptible to the Sylvatic plague and canine distemper (Black-Footed Ferret 1995, 2004, CBSG 2004). They also are a casualty to plowing and fragmenting of the grasslands for agriculture (Black-Footed Ferret 2004, CBSG 2004). They are reported to be prey for owls and coyotes, and as with other wildlife, they become victims to vehicles (Black-Footed Ferret 2004).

Captive Breeding and Recovery Program—The black-footed ferret became extinct in the wild in Canada in 1937 (Black-Footed Ferret 2005c). In the United States, it was listed in 1967 as an endangered species. By the 1970s, only a few ferrets were known to exist, and by 1980 the species was feared to be extinct (Naylor 1994).

Then in 1981, a small population was discovered in Meeteetse, WY (Black-Footed Ferret 2005b,c, CBSG 2004, Naylor 1994). A black-footed ferret captive breeding program was initiated in October 1985 by the Wyoming Fish Department, in cooperation with the USDI Fish and Wildlife Service, and a year later a recovery plan for captive breeding and reintroduction of black-footed ferrets was formed. Six black-footed ferrets were captured near Meeteetse to start the program. The ferrets were taken to the Department's Sybille

52

USDA Forest Service Gen. Tech. Rep. RMRS-GTR-135-vol. 2. 2005

Wildlife Research Center near Wheatland, WY, and eventually all died of canine distemper (Black-Footed Ferret 1995, 1997, CBSG 2004). The disease was then confirmed among Meeteetse's wild ferrets (CBSG 2004, Saving a Species 2005).

Biologists launched an emergency effort to capture all remaining animals. Five were captured in late 1985, 12 more in 1986, and by February 1987, the last known wild black-footed ferret was captured. All the animals were vaccinated and quarantined, and all 18 survived (CBSG 2004, Saving a Species 2005).

No kits were born during the ferret breeding season in captivity in 1986. However, eight were born in 1987 at Sybille. Seven survived and were followed by 34 surviving kits in 1989 and 66 in 1990 (CBSG 2004, Saving a Species 2005).

In 1988, the USDI Fish and Wildlife Service developed the "Black-Footed Ferret Recovery Team" that emphasized species preservation through natural breeding, development reproductive technology, and establishment of multiple reintroduction sites. The objective of the captive breeding program was to maintain 240 ferrets (90 males, 150 females) of 1 through 3 years old and subdivide the captive population into different groups to avoid catastrophic loss at a single facility. The strategy for the reproductive program was to support captive breeding efforts by developing artificial insemination. One high priority for protecting genetic diversity was to have a frozen repository of sperm from genetically valuable males (CBSG 2004, Saving a Species 2005).

After evaluating eight Gunnison's prairie dog complexes across northern Arizona, the Aubrey Valley was selected as the best site for black-footed ferret reintroduction. In 1997, the prairie dog acreage estimate was 29,653 acres. With the release of 35 ferrets (nine kits, 26 adults) in 1996, Aubrey Valley in Arizona became the fourth reintroduction site and the first to develop and evaluate onsite acclimation pens to precondition release candidates. No ferrets were released in 1997, 26 in 1998, 52 in 1999, 19 in 2000, 12 in 2001, and six in 2002. Survivorship has been generally low. In 2001, the first wild-born black-footed ferret kits were found in Arizona following a spring release of animals bred prior to release (CBSG 2004).

Current Status—Captive-bred ferrets have been reintroduced to the Shirley Basin in Wyoming, UL Bend National Wildlife Refuge and the Fort Belknap Reservation in Montana, the Badlands National Park and Buffalo Gap National Grasslands in South Dakota, and Aubrey Valley in Arizona (Black-Footed Ferret 2005b,c, CBSG 2004). Approximately 1,000 black-footed ferrets live in captivity at breeding facilities, while another 80 exist in the wild following release by the Federal government (Black-Footed Ferret 2005b, Naylor 1994).

Despite these population gains in some areas of the country, both habitat loss and the continued decline of their prey base, the prairie dog, continue to threaten the black-footed ferret (Black-Footed Ferret 2005b). Conversion of grasslands to agricultural uses, widespread prairie dog eradication programs, and plague (Black-Footed Ferret 1995) have reduced ferret habitat to less than 2 percent of what once existed. Remaining habitat is now fragmented, with prairie dog towns separated by great expanses of cropland and human development (Ferret Facts 2005). Preservation of large prairie dog colonies will be essential for recovery of the black-footed ferret.

Rabbits and Hares

Approximately 50 species of rabbits and hares form the family Leporidae of the order Lagomorpha (Lagomorphs 2005b). This group of mammals is largely diurnal or crepuscular (Order Lagomorpha 2005). The order Lagomorpha, with a fossil history dating back to the Oligocene (33.8 to 23.7 million years ago), comprises two modern families: Ochotonidae (pikas) and Leporidae (hares and rabbits). Members of all genera except *Lepus* are usually referred to as rabbits, while members of *Lepus* are usually called hares (Fagerstone and Ramey 1996). Rabbits—as distinguished from the related hares—are altricial, having young that are born blind and hairless; many also live underground in burrows (Lagomorphs 2005b). No lagomorphs hibernate (Order Lagomorpha 2005). The distinction between these two common names does not correspond completely with current taxonomy, because the jackrabbits are members of *Lepus*, whereas members of the genera *Pronolagus* and *Caprolagus* are sometimes called hares (Lagomorphs 2005b).

Rabbits and hares feed almost entirely on vegetable matter—grasses, forbs, bark of trees and shrubs, and so forth. Because of their usually large size and food preference, lagomorphs frequently come into conflict with grazing, agriculture, and forestry interests (Order Lagomorpha 2005). Leporids are conspicuous mammals in various habitats on grasslands. These herbivores generally occur in areas where short grasses and herbs are abundant and clumps of tall grasses or brush are available for cover. Several taxa of lagomorphs are major components of the wildlife of grasslands. The mountain cottontail (*Sylvilagus nuttallii*) occurs on montane "islands"; the desert cottontail (*S. audubonii*) is an inhabitant of upland, grazed areas; the eastern cottontail (*S. floridanus*) seems restricted mostly to ungrazed, riparian-edge habitats. The white-sided jackrabbit (*Lepus callotis*) occurs in Southwestern desert grasslands; however, its current range in the United States apparently is restricted to about 120 km^2 (46 ac) in southwestern New Mexico (Jones and

USDA Forest Service Gen. Tech. Rep. RMRS-GTR-135-vol. 2. 2005

53

Manning 1996). The grassland habitats for some of these species have expanded as a result of alterations of the environment by humans.

Rabbits are prolific breeders and some, especially black-tailed jackrabbit (*L. californicus*), may become abundant enough that at times they contribute to overgrazing of grasslands and even become a nuisance to agricultural crops (Jones and Manning 1996). Rabbits are major dispersers of seeds of some important plants, especially dropseed (*Sporobolus* spp.), and they are important components of the food chain in that they serve as major prey species for some carnivores. Lagomorphs are even of some value to humans as food (Fagerstone and Ramey 1996).

Rabbits—Seven genera in the family are classified as rabbits, including the European rabbit (*Oryctolagus cuniculus*) and cottontail rabbits (*Sylvilagus* spp.) (Lagomorphs 2005b). They are well-known for digging networks of burrows, called warrens, where they spend most of their time when not feeding. Rabbits can be gregarious, while hares are often solitary. In areas with high densities of rabbits, females form dominance hierarchies, with the dominant females suppressing the reproduction of subdominants by denying them access to nest sites and by physical intimidation (Lagomorphs 2005a). Cottontail females (doe) and young share territory only until the young are independent (Eastern Cottontail 2005).

Rabbits are also well-known for their breeding rate, another factor that differentiates them from hares; in theory, a doe can produce from three to seven live young per month, during the first half of the year, although a more common rate is half that (Lagomorphs 2005b). In the warmer parts of their range, eastern cottontails can breed from the months of February through September, with three or four litters per year. The female rabbit is entirely responsible for her young. The doe makes a shallow nest that she lines with grasses, twigs, and fur she pulls from her own coat. She visits her nest only at dusk and dawn (Desert Cottontail 2005, Eastern Cottontail 2005).

Cottontails—Two primary species of cottontail rabbits are of interest to Southwestern grasslands: the eastern cottontail (*S. floridanus*) and the desert cottontail (*S. auduboni*). Cottontails are among the most widely distributed of North American mammals, with eastern cottontail the most widely distributed of the cottontail rabbits. Eastern cottontails are the most common rabbits in North America. The eastern cottontail is found from the Eastern Seaboard west to the Rocky Mountains and from southern Canada south to Costa Rica (fig. 3-7) (Eastern Cottontail 2005, Fagerstone and Ramey 1996). It occurs throughout the Plains region primarily in riparian ecosystems (Fagerstone and Ramey 1996) and ubiquitously in the Eastern deciduous forests.

Desert cottontails are distributed widely throughout the arid areas of Western North America, from Montana south to central Mexico, and from the High Plains of Oklahoma, Kansas, and Nebraska to the Pacific Coast (fig. 3-7) (Fagerstone and Ramey 1996). They occur in a wide variety of habitats, including dry desert grasslands and shrublands, riparian areas, and pinyon-juniper forests. They may occur in the same areas as black-tailed jackrabbits (*Lepus californicus*) (Desert Cottontail 2005).

Cottontails are preyed upon by a number of predators, including golden and bald eagles, great horned owls, ferruginous hawks, badgers, coyotes, foxes, bobcats, and humans. Badgers, weasels, and rattlesnakes may prey on the young (Desert Cottontail 2005).

Cottontails can be found almost anywhere, fields, woods, and farmlands but they especially inhabit areas where there are thickets and brush for shelter and for hiding (Eastern Cottontail 2005). Typical habitat in the Great Plains includes weedy margins of fields and pastures, brushy areas, and dry ravines.

Cottontail densities are positively correlated with increased biomass of herbaceous vegetation and with areas ungrazed by livestock (Fagerstone and Ramey 1996). Periodic cycles may have occurred in historic populations. For example, eastern cottontail population densities have been reported to be as high as 17 to 25 per hectare (42 to 62 per ac) with 8 to 10 years in cyclic tendencies (Fagerstone and Ramey 1996, Lagomorphs 2005a). However, recent land use changes have more profound impacts on population densities than any natural processes. For one thing, nesting density is habitat specific. A Pennsylvania study illustrated how human changes in the landscape can alter population densities: nests occurred every 1.5 acres (0.6 ha) in unkempt orchards, were 7 acres (2.8 ha) apart in hayfields, 13.5 acres (5.5 ha) apart in woodlands, and 14 acres (5.7 ha) in pasture lands (Lagomorphs 2005a).

Home range for eastern cottontails of 2.5 to 5 acres (1 to 2 ha) is normal, with a range from 1 to 10 acres (0.4 to 4 ha). The home range will depend on populations, habitat quality, season, and sex, with the male having a slightly larger range. Ranges for males are the largest in the main breeding period of late spring to early summer, while females have the smallest range at this same time. Dominant males have the largest ranges. Ranges are generally smaller in spring (before breeding) and in winter, reflecting lush vegetation and severe limiting weather. These mammals are not territorial, and their ranges often overlap (up to 50 percent for males and 25 percent for females in spring), especially in winter, when they tend to concentrate in areas offering the best combination of food and cover. Females have little or no overlap of home ranges during breeding season (Lagomorphs 2005a).

54

USDA Forest Service Gen. Tech. Rep. RMRS-GTR-135-vol. 2. 2005

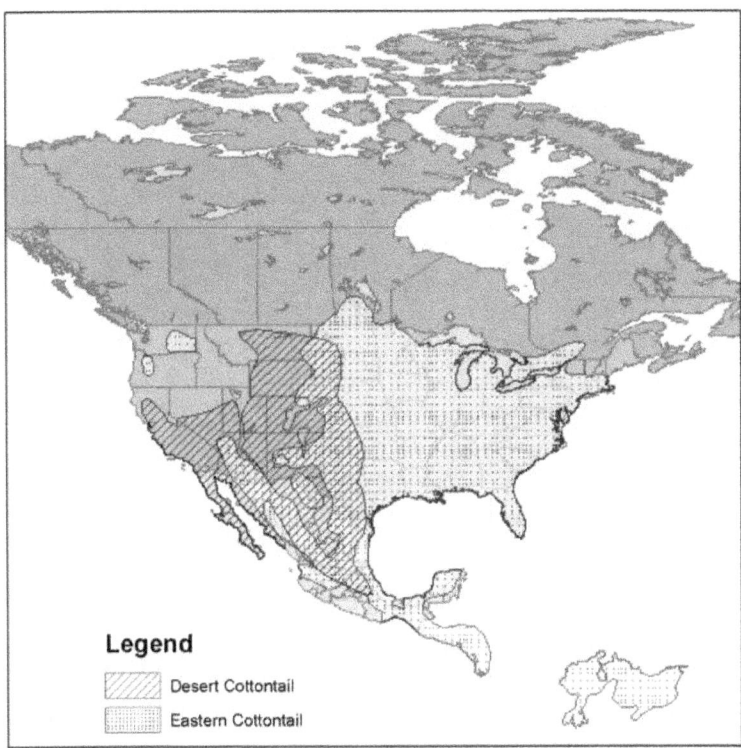

Figure 3-7. Distribution of the eastern cottontail (*Sylvilagus floridanus*) and the desert cottontail (*S. auduboni*) (Nature-Serve 2005).

Eastern cottontails, like most other rabbits, are solitary, generally not territorial, except for females in the immediate vicinity of a nest. Males have a dominance hierarchy in which the most dominant have more aggressive encounters with other males and do most of the mating. Dominance hierarchy of males allows the strongest males to fertilize more females than subordinates and also minimizes fighting. Most aggressive behavior is exhibited between the dominant male and the individual immediately below it in social status. Females have a less rigid hierarchy. Females exhibit dominance over males except during estrus (Lagomorphs 2005a).

Rabbits are herbivores, eating a wide range of vegetation. The diet of the eastern cottontail varies with habitat and seasonal availability of forage. Eastern cottontails prefer herbaceous plants when available during the growing season, including bluegrass, orchard grass (*Dactylis glomerata*), timothy (*Phleum pratense*), clover (*Trifolium* spp.), and alfalfa (Eastern Cottontail 2005, Fagerstone and Ramey 1996). Succulent new growth supplies much of the cottontail's water requirements. Woody species are preferentially eaten during the dormant season (Fagerstone and Ramey 1996).

The desert cottontail is a crepuscular to nocturnal forager. Desert cottontails can survive droughts by obtaining water from cacti and forbs (Desert Cottontail 2005, Fagerstone and Ramey 1996). They also can survive drought conditions because they are coprophagic, meaning they eat their own feces. Because grass is difficult to digest, the rabbits eat the first-formed set of pellets after a meal. These pellets, rich in protein and B vitamins, are reingested directly from the anus. Additional nutrition is extracted during the second digestive process. Pellets from the second set are hard, fibrous, and lack nutritive value (Desert Cottontail 2005, Lagomorphs 2005a). This practice allows the animals to spend relatively little time exposed to predators because while they are in the field feeding, they consume green vegetation rapidly and then make optimum use of it in the safety of their cover. This process is also called "pseudo-rumination" because it is functionally the same as cows chewing their cud. Coprophagy is also practiced by beaver and voles and, apparently, by some shrews.

Desert cottontail rely seasonally on grasses, sedges, rushes, shrubs (for example, black-berry [*Rubis allegheniensis*), and trees (for example, willow [*Salix* spp.] and oak [*Quercus* spp.]). Their annual diet is similar to that of prairie dogs and cattle in the kinds of plants eaten, but differs in the relative proportions preferred (Fagerstone and Ramey 1996).

Cottontail Economic Status—Eastern cottontails are the most widely hunted game mammals in the United States (Jones and others 1985), and their high reproductive rates allow them to withstand high hunting pressure. Eastern cottontails are responsible for 55 percent of tularemia cases reported in Americans, due to direct contact while skinning and dressing animals. A few cases of plague (*Pasteurella pestis*) have also been reported in cottontail rabbits. Cottontails are not an important contributor to grassland overgrazing. Overall, the ecological, economic and recreational benefits from hunting by humans outweigh the minor damage cottontails do to crops, nurseries, and orchards (Fagerstone and Ramey 1996).

As with other rabbits, cottontails disperse seeds widely owing to their high abundance, intensive use of small annual and perennial herbs, and production of fecal pellets. Seed dispersal by rabbits may influence the distribution and long-term dynamics of some plant species (Fagerstone and Ramey 1996).

Cottontail Association with Livestock—Cottontails were reported to be significantly greater on the un-grazed bottomlands paralleling the South Platte River in eastern Colorado and were almost nonexistent on grazed areas. The desert cottontail is negatively impacted when pinyon-juniper habitat is cleared during

USDA Forest Service Gen. Tech. Rep. RMRS-GTR-135-vol. 2. 2005

55

operations for increased livestock production (Fagerstone and Ramey 1996).

Cottontail Management—Habitat management to increase populations should emphasize moderate grazing, clumps of shrubs and small trees, and possibly rock and brush piles (Fagerstone and Ramey 1996). Because cottontails utilize successional vegetation primarily, habitat management techniques such as prescribed burning and sharecropping may be useful for controlling succession and increasing cottontail numbers.

When cottontails are found in high concentrations, they may damage crops, nurseries, and orchards. Controls include hunting and exclusionary methods such as tree trunk guards, fencing, repellents, habitat modifications, and trapping (Fagerstone and Ramey 1996).

Jackrabbits—Jackrabbits are a prominent grassland herbivore throughout the West. Two principal species occur on grassland: the black-tailed jackrabbit and the white-tailed jackrabbit (*L. townsoni*) (fig. 3-8). Jackrabbit densities are dependent on vegetation, climate, season, and other factors (Fagerstone and Ramey 1996). Reported densities have ranged from 0.01 per ha (0.025 per ac) in southeastern Colorado to 35 per ha (88 per ac) in agricultural areas in Kansas. Jackrabbit densities are significantly higher near cultivated crops than on isolated grassland (Fagerstone and Ramey 1996).

Fluctuations in jackrabbit density have been reported in the literature with cycles of approximately 5 to 10 years. Populations in local areas can become extremely large during population irruptions. Some researchers believe that the populations are not actually cyclic, but that drought and food availability or drought and overgrazing concentrate the jackrabbits. Evidence now suggests that the key parameters associated with population fluctuations are much more complex than previously thought. There appear to be geographic trends in jackrabbit frequency of fluctuations, and these include the interactions between many features of the jackrabbit habitat, for example, food availability, and natural phenomena such as weather (Fagerstone and Ramey 1996).

The black-tailed jackrabbit is the most common jackrabbit in the Western and Central United States (fig. 3-8), ranging from the Pacific Coast to western Missouri and Arkansas, and from the prairie and grassland regions of Idaho to South Dakota to the Mexican border (Dunn and others 1982, Fagerstone and Ramey 1996). Black-tailed jackrabbits occur in many diverse habitats but are primarily associated with shortgrass prairie and open country. Black-tailed jackrabbits avoid areas of heavy brush or woods,

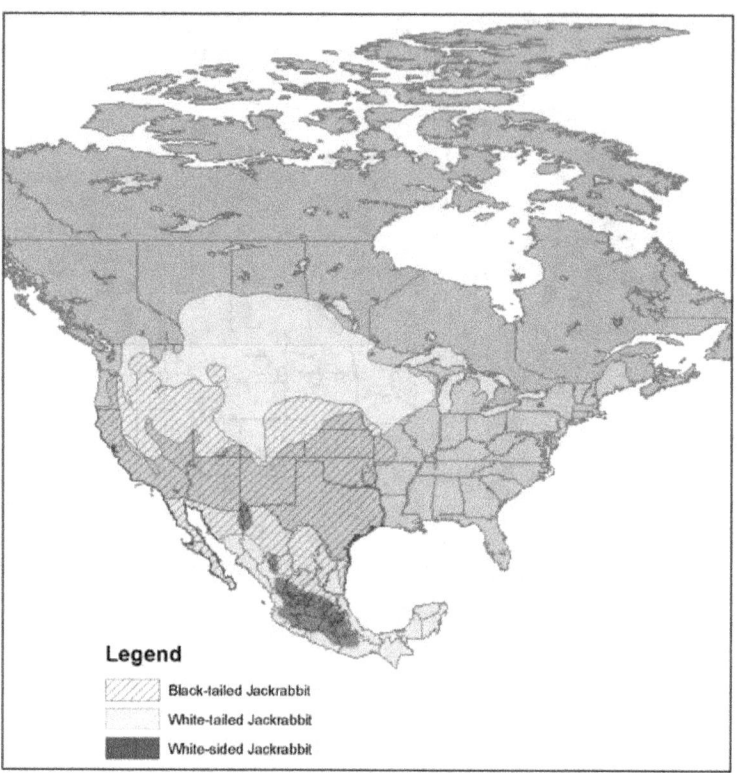

Figure 3-8. Distribution of the black-tailed jackrabbit (*Lepus californicus*), white-tailed jackrabbit (*L. townsoni*), and white-sided jackrabbit (*L. callotis*) (NatureServe 2005).

which limit their principal means of defense— keen eyesight and escape speed (Fagerstone and Ramey 1996, Mueggler 1967).

The white-tailed jackrabbit occurs in close association with the flora of the northern Great Plains and open areas of the Great Basin (Dunn and others 1982, Fagerstone and Ramey 1996). They range from Southern Canada to Colorado and from Michigan to the high mountain slopes of the Rockies, Cascades, and Sierras (fig. 3-8). White-tailed jackrabbits once ranged south across the Plains States to southern Kansas, but they now occur generally north of the Platte River (Fagerstone and Ramey 1996) and are considered imperiled in New Mexico.

White-tailed jackrabbits prefer large expanses of croplands and pastures interspersed with brush and heavy vegetation in open flats. In recent years, the white-tailed jackrabbit's range has declined, and it is now extirpated from Kansas and is rare in Missouri. These jackrabbits are not adapting to the general climatic warming of the Great Plains and are less able to use cultivated areas than are the black-tailed jackrabbits. Some researchers have theorized that the expansion of black-tailed jackrabbits into areas formerly occupied by white-tailed jackrabbits was due to the changing habitat associated with prairie cultivation by humans. When both species came into contact on the shortgrass prairie, white-tailed jackrabbits selected more sparsely vegetated upland habitats and occupied higher elevations than black-tailed jackrabbits. It has been suggested that the black-tailed jackrabbit is more efficient than the white-tailed jackrabbit in foraging. Thus, the black-tailed jackrabbit, with its greater adaptability and feeding efficiency, may be able to displace the white-tailed jackrabbit (Fagerstone and Ramey 1996).

Jackrabbits feed in open areas that have a supply of succulent young plants, interspersed with patches of dense weeds; the open areas allow them to detect danger, and the dense weeds serve as cover. Foraging begins during twilight, increases during early night, and begins to decrease as dawn approaches. This general pattern of foraging is influenced by season, ambient temperature, and phase of the moon (Fagerstone and Ramey 1996).

Although the plant species eaten vary throughout the jackrabbit's range, their diets have some seasonal features in common: they show greater use of shrubs in winter than in other seasons and greater use of grasses and forbs in the spring and summer. Various cereal crops and other cultivated crops (such as winter wheat [*Triticum aestivum*], alfalfa, crested wheatgrass [*Agropyron cristatum*]) are used when available. Plant phenology was a major factor in determining food preferences of grassland jackrabbits; 85 percent of their diet was composed of grasses in the spring, grasses and forbs were nearly equal in diets in early summer, and forbs and shrubs increased to 71 percent of the diets in late summer. Grasses and sedges composed 49 percent of their overall diet (Fagerstone and Ramey 1996).

In contrast, in arid areas of the Southwest, mesquite made up 54 percent of the annual diet. Needle-and-thread grass (*Stipa comata*) was preferred in sagebrush habitat, while yarrow (*Achillea lanulosa*) was preferred in bitterbrush habitat. Grasses are the largest component of jackrabbit diets in semidesert grassland, particularly during the summer growing season. Herbaceous weeds were not preferred dietary items. Most investigators agree that jackrabbits select plants for their succulence, particularly during times of water stress (Fagerstone and Ramey 1996).

Positive and Negative Effects of Jackrabbits—Black-tailed jackrabbits have both positive and negative relationships with humans. The following are the positive effects (Fagerstone and Ramey 1996):

- They are used for sport hunting, food, and fur.
- They are also an important part of the prairie ecosystem and a major food for mammalian predators, particularly coyotes.

- They are important to secondary succession on old fields and denuded ranges by dispersing seeds in fecal pellets.
- Jackrabbits are also important in increasing the viability of some seeds in their pellets by their digestive processes.

The following are the negative effects (Fagerstone and Ramey 1996):

- In some areas they cause extensive damage to agriculture. Cultivated crops adjacent to grassland are particularly vulnerable to damage by jackrabbits given the grassland provides daytime resting areas for them.
- Jackrabbits have been reported to cause damage to seedling trees, grains, and cotton, range rehabilitation efforts, and vegetables.

White-tailed jackrabbits are generally viewed as having positive effects. Some of the positive benefits of these jackrabbits have been associated with sport hunting, food, and fur. Their fur has had some commercial value. They are also important for maintenance of ecological balance, biodiversity, and aesthetics of grassland ecosystems.

Jackrabbit Association with Livestock—The relationship between livestock grazing and jackrabbit population numbers is not well understood, and there are mixed opinions as to the costs and benefits of cohabitation of jackrabbits and livestock. The varied conclusions noted in table 3-3 may be the result of differences in study areas, grazing systems, or other factors. Studies have shown the interactive relationship of herbivores and their pastures, and that herbivores affect the biomass, growth, and species composition of the pasture (Fagerstone and Ramey 1996). As the density of herbivores increases, a point is reached when plant species of low quality and palatability also increase and make the pasture less suitable for herbivores, including jackrabbits. The influences that range conditions have on the diets of jackrabbits and cattle (Lagomorphs 2005b) are: jackrabbit densities were highest on ranges that were in good condition (Eastern Cottontail 2005); range condition influenced the amount of forbs and shrubs in a jackrabbit's diet, but not the grass component; and jackrabbits consumed less grasses and more shrubs than cattle, producing a moderate dietary overlap (Order Lagomorpha 2005). In early studies of competition, scientists estimated the foraging capacity of black-tailed jackrabbits to be one cow equivalent to 148 black-tailed jackrabbits or 62 white-tailed jackrabbits, and one sheep equivalent to 6 black-tailed or 15 white-tailed jackrabbits. The greatest direct competition for forage between cattle and black-tailed jackrabbits was in early spring when both species preferred green forage such as western wheatgrass, needle-and-thread, and sunsedge (*Carex*

USDA Forest Service Gen. Tech. Rep. RMRS-GTR-135-vol. 2. 2005

57

Table 3-3. Some results of studies on the relationship between jackrabbits and livestock (Fagerstone and Ramey 1996).

Relationship	Explanation
Negative	The combination of livestock and jackrabbits can cause severe destruction to grassland.
Positive with heavy grazing	Some researchers believe heavy grazing of grassland increases suitable habitat for jackrabbits and encourages their presence.
Positive with moderate grazing	It has been reported that jackrabbits prefer moderately grazed pastures.
Positive with no grazing	It has been stated that jackrabbits prefer non-grazed grassland.

heliophila), and least in late fall and winter (Fagerstone and Ramey 1996).

The vegetation on various grasslands has changed during the past century, partly because of poor grazing practices (Fagerstone and Ramey 1996). Reports have documented shifts from grassland to shrub-dominated vegetation in New Mexico. In Great Basin shrub communities protected for 15 years from domestic sheep, with or without protection from jackrabbits, plant community changes were slow to nonexistent, and protection from jackrabbits had no effect (Burgess 1996, Fagerstone and Ramey 1996).

Bats

The more than 900 species of bats worldwide belong to the Order Chiroptera. Bats are found almost everywhere on Earth, except in extremely hot desert environments and the cold Polar Regions. The United States is known to have 15 genera, totaling 44 species of bats. Those that inhabit the Southwestern deserts comprise 11 genera and more than 18 species. The diverse habitats of New Mexico and Arizona support up to 28 species of bats (Parmenter and Van Devender 1995, Chung-McCoubrey 1996), many of which are found regularly or occasionally in grasslands.

Bats are unique in the animal kingdom because they are the only mammals to have evolved true flight. Bats are often thought of as flying mice, but they are more closely related to primates than to mice. As with most other mammals, their bodies are covered by hair, with the exception of their wings. Although bats have the same basic arm and hand bones found in humans and most other mammals, their hand and finger bones are long and slender, and there are only four digits. The skin between the arms, fingers, body, legs, and feet looks delicate, but it is extremely resistant to tearing by sharp objects.

The bats in temperate North America are nocturnal and are mostly insectivorous, but a few are nectarivorous and play an important role in the pollination of certain plants (Chung-MacCoubrey 1996). As insectivores, bats are important because they feed on nocturnal flying and terrestrial insects, and they likely play a role in regulating insect populations (Chung-McCoubrey 1996) and insect-related ecological processes. Bats help maintain balances of relationships within the insect community, and between insects and plants, animals, and other entities. Bat droppings (guano) support entire ecosystems of unique organisms, including bacteria useful in detoxifying wastes, improving detergents and producing gasohol and antibiotics. Bats are integral to the function and integrity of many ecosystems (Chung-McCoubrey 1996).

Mating may occur two or even three times a year, in late fall, just before hibernation, in midwinter if the roost is warm enough, and again in spring. Birth takes place in the spring or summer after a gestation period of 50 to 60 days in May, June, and July. Within a week after its birth, the female will carry her pup on nightly hunts; the pup grasps her fur and feeds at one of her two nipples. The young bats are weaned in 2 to 3 weeks, and then they may be fed on regurgitated food brought home by the mother. In 3 to 4 weeks, the young bat is hunting on its own and is only 5 weeks away from full growth. Females typically mate at the end of their first summer, males at the end of their second. Multiple births up to four occur in some species.

Many people see bats as a threat because they fear bats carry rabies. Like any other animal, a bat that contracts rabies will die. What is unique about bats with rabies is that they rarely become aggressive. Dogs and cats pose a far more dangerous threat as transmitters of rabies to humans. Humans are rarely endangered by bats except in cases where sick bats are handled.

Bat Habitat—Grassland habitats for bats are limited by the availability of roosting sites, such as, crevices, caves, trees, buildings, mines, bridges, other artificial structures, and by availability of water. The type of roosts selected varies by bat species. Their mobility allows them to select habitats at a large landscape level and to utilize habitats that are separated by significant distances (Chung-McCoubrey 1996). Their small size allows them to exploit a large variety of sheltered sites.

Roosts: The annual energy budget of bats makes it difficult for them to balance body size, energetic demands of flight, fat storage given limited ability, and response to seasonal abundance of prey. One of the keys to managing their energy expenditures is selection of roost sites (Chung-McCoubrey 1996). Roost sites typically have the following characteristics:

- Suitable microclimates that facilitate gestation and rapid growth of the young (Chung-McCoubrey 1996).
- Exposed to minimal disturbance.
- Relatively close to food and water.

Reproductive success and over-winter survival of individuals and populations may largely depend on suitable roosts (Chung-McCoubrey 1996). Winter hibernation sites minimize the potential for disturbance and arousal and maximize use of energy reserves. Other factors, such as threat by predators, distance to or availability of local hibernacula, and sensitivity to human disturbance may influence local distributions and sites

Bat roosts within grasslands include crevices in and under stones and rocks, excavated or natural holes in the ground, and the foliage of scattered shrubs and trees. Such habitats are interspersed within grasslands, patches of other habitat types such as rock escarpments, talus slopes, cliff faces, lava flows and tubes, caves, open mines, barns, and bridges, providing a host of different roost environments for grassland bats. In addition, bats may roost within the foliage, bark, and cavities of riparian vegetation along arroyos, tributaries, and rivers that pass through grasslands. Table 3-4 provides a summary of grassland bat species (including scientific names of bats) by Federal status and types of summer roosts (Chung-MacCoubrey 1996).

Water: Surface water for drinking is critical for bats. Due to their high protein diet, insectivorous bats require water to excrete toxic nitrogenous waste products. Bats residing in dry environments have high rates of evaporative water loss through wing membranes and respiratory exchange. Xeric species such as California myotis (*Myotis californicus*), western pipistrelle (*Pipistrellus hesperus*), pallid bat (*Antrozous pallidus*), and Mexican free-tailed bat (*Tadarida brasiliensis*) have high urine-concentrating abilities and are efficient at conserving water. Species that live in more mesic grasslands and deserts (for example, long-legged myotis (*Myotis volans*), fringed myotis (*Myotis thysanodes*), little brown myotis (*Myotis lucifugus*), Yuma myotis (*Myotis yumanensis*), and Townsend's big-eared bat (*Corynorhinus townsendii*)) have low urine-concentrating abilities and probably select habitats where water is readily available (Chung-McCoubrey 1996).

Historically, bats relied on naturally occurring water sources, sparsely distributed springs, seeps, and permanent water sources. Water availability may have limited the geographic distribution of species not adapted for water conservation or for long-distance flight. Construction of waterholes and stock tanks in Southwestern grasslands has increased the quantity and distribution of available water. Areas originally devoid of water may have become viable roosting and foraging habitat for bat species that were historically absent (Chung-McCoubrey 1996). Because few records document bat distributions prior to Euro-American development of the Southwest, it is impossible to confirm whether geographic ranges of such species—for example, fringed myotis and long-legged myotis—expanded into grasslands and deserts due to the increased number of water holes and stock tanks, or whether they were always present.

Food: Food along with water availability determine bat species distribution and habitat use. Insects may generally be so abundant as to preclude competition among bats (Fagerstone and Ramey 1996). Dietary partitioning may occur among insectivorous bats as evident from their wide range of sizes, flight styles, echolocating abilities, and the vertical and horizontal partitioning of space during foraging (Chung-McCoubrey 1996). Although bats forage on diverse insects, some select particular orders of insects. In New Mexico, California myotis, western pipistrelles, and long-legged myotis are classified as Lepidoptera (moths) strategists. Pallid bats, long-eared myotis, and fringed myotis are classified as Coleoptera (beetles) strategists (Chung-McCoubrey 1996). These species consume arthropods in addition to moths and beetles, including Orthoptera (grasshoppers), Hymenoptera (bees/wasps), Diptera (flies), Homoptera (leafhoppers), Hemiptera (true bugs), and Isoptera (termites) (Chung-McCoubrey 1996, Fagerstone and Ramey 1996). Diet composition reflects seasonal peaks of different arthropod species (Chung-McCoubrey 1996) and probably varies with habitat type.

Conservation—Bats have many natural enemies, and consequently large numbers of bats die while still young. Predators include great horned owls, some species of hawks, peregrine falcons, raccoons, house cats, and snakes. Bats can also be caught on barbed-wire fences, fall from roosts, or die if their roost site (for example, cave) is flooded. Some 40 percent of the bat species in the United States and Canada are endangered or candidates for such status. Even small disturbances in their habitats can seriously threaten bat survival. Agricultural insecticides are responsible for killing bats in great numbers. When bats consume chemical-laden insects, the bats become poisoned and die (Chung-MacCoubrey 1996).

Desert Grasslands

Desert grassland ecosystems impose many restrictions on its residents. Precipitation is scarce and unpredictable, and temperatures and wind velocities fluctuate greatly. Cover from weather and predators is scarce. Wildlife species in the harsh desert

USDA Forest Service Gen. Tech. Rep. RMRS-GTR-135-vol. 2. 2005

59

Table 3-4. Federal status and types of summer roosts by bats in Southwestern grasslands and short-grass prairies (Chung-Mc-Coubery 1996).

Species	USFWS Status	Type of summer roosts
Species more commonly associated with grasslands		
Small-footed myotis (*Myotis ciliolabrum*)	Species of concern	Cracks and crevices of cliffs and rocks, abandoned buildings and barns; under rock slabs and loose bark; possibly in caves and mine tunnels.
California myotis (*M. californicus*)		Cliffs, hillsides, rock outcrops, mine shafts, barns, houses, under tree bark and sign boards, amongst desert shrubs, and on the ground.
Cave myotis (*M. velifer*)	Species of concern	Primarily caves and tunnels; occasionally buildings, bridges, and under rocks.
Pallid bat (*Antrozous pallidus*)		Rocky outcrops, crevices, mine tunnels, buildings, and under rocks.
Western pipistrelle (*Pipistrellus hesperus*)		Canyon walls, cliffs, and other rock crevices; under rocks, in burrows and buildings.
Mexican free-tailed bat (*Tadarida brasiliensis*)		Caves, mines, bridges; occasionally in buildings.
Species found in grasslands given appropriate habitat		
Little brown bat (*M. lucifugus*)		Buildings, hollow trees, natural crevices, mines.
Yuma myotis (*M. yumanensis*)	Species of concern	Crevices, mines, caves, buildings.
Fringed myotis (*M. thysanodes*)	Species of concern	Caves, mine tunnels, rock crevices, old buildings.
Long-legged myotis (*M. volans*)	Species of concern	Abandoned buildings, cracks in ground, cliff face, and other crevices, under loose bark.
Long-eared myotis (*M. evotis*)	Species of concern	Tree hollows, loose bark, folds of wood/bark, rock crevices, abandoned buildings, mines.
Hoary bat (*Lasiurus cinereus*)		Foliage of trees and shrubs.
Silver-haired bat (*Lasionycteris noctivagans*)		Hollow trees, woodpecker holes, under loose bark, and in buildings.
Eastern red bat (*Lasiurus borealis*)		Foliage of trees and shrubs, clump of Spanish moss.
Big brown bat (*Eptesicus fuscus*)		Hollow trees, rock crevices, mine tunnels, caves, buildings: occasionally in cliff swallow nests.
Townsend's big-eared bat (*Plecotus townsendii*)	Species of concern	Caves, mine tunnels, and abandoned buildings.
Spotted bat (*Fuderma maculatum*)	Species of concern	Cracks and crevices in rocky cliffs or under loose rocks.
Big free-tailed bat (*Nyctinomops macrotis*)	Species of concern	Crevices in rocky cliffs, buildings.

environment have adapted morphologically, physiologically, and behaviorally to survive drought, heat, and cold.

A well-known and studied area in Socorro County in south-central New Mexico is the Sevilleta Long-Term Ecological Research Site (LTER) managed by the University of New Mexico. The LTER has a wide variety of vegetation types including desert grassland, Chihuahuan and Great Basin desert scrub, pinyon-juniper woodland, wetlands, riparian woodland, montane forest, and meadows. Scientists at the Sevilleta LTER have described the number of mammal species by

habitat type (table 3-5). A total of 56 mammal species have been observed in desert grasslands at the Sevilleta LTER and 51 species in desert-scrub. Fewer mammal species occupy other habitats at the LTER, suggesting that desert grasslands and scrub contribute greatly to the mammalian species diversity of the Southwest.

Effects of Grazing on Rodents, and Vice Versa

Desert shrub-grasslands in the Southwest are primarily used by humans for grazing cattle and

Table 3-5. The number of mammal species found in various habitats in Socorro County, central New Mexico (Parmenter and Van Devender 1995).

Family	Desert scrub	Desert grassland	Pinyon-juniper	Montane forest	Montane meadow	Riparian zone
Shrews (Soricidae)	2	1	2	1	2	1
Bats (Molossidae, Vespertilionidae)	9	10	7	12	12	8
Rabbits (Leporidae)	2	2	1	1	1	1
Squirrels (Sciuridae)	4	6	5	5		
Gophers (Geomyidae)	4	4	1	1	1	1
Kangaroo rats, pocket mice (Heteromyidae)	5	5	3			
Beaver (Castoridae)				1		
Mice, rats (Arvicolidae, Muridae, Cricetidae, Zapodidae)	9	13	10	8	8	6
Porcupine (Erethizontidae)	1	1	1	1	1	
Coyote, foxes (Canidae)	3	3	3	2	2	3
Bear (Ursidae)	1	1	1	1	1	1
Raccoon, ringtail (Procyonidae)	1	1	1	1	1	1
Weasels, badger, skunks (Mustelidae)	5	4	5	4	3	4
Cats (Felidae)	2	2	2	2	2	2
Deer, elk (Cervidae)	2	2	2	3	3	2
Sheep (Bovidae)				1	1	1
Pronghorn (Antilocapridae)	1	1	1			
Total	**51**	**56**	**46**	**43**	**38**	**31**

Note: SEV = Sevilleta National Wildlife Refuge (mixed-grassland-shrubland-woodland)
BDA = Bosque del Apache National Wildlife Refuge (riparian and wetlands)
MAG = Magdalena Mountains (montane forest and meadows)

secondarily for farming. These desert grasslands are characterized by seasonal bursts of vegetation productivity following sporadic rains (Fagerstone and Ramey 1996). Vegetation is composed of desert shrubs, drought resistant summer-growing perennial grasses, and annual plants. Seeds persist after green vegetation is gone.

As an example of the effect of grazing on wildlife, a look at kangaroo rats is helpful because kangaroo rats are a keystone guild. Through seed predation and soil disturbance they have major effects on biological diversity and biogeochemical processes, facilitating the establishment of annuals and shrubs by selectively foraging on large seeds, and by seed caching and burrowing activities (Sevilleta LTER: Research 2001). Fields and others (1999) showed that kangaroo rats have important effects on both species dominance and composition for different vegetation patch types and may provide a mechanism for small-scale dominance patterns at an ecotone.

Merriam kangaroo rats, as a further example, are favored by grazing. The range of this species matches with the distribution of creosote bush, low humidity and rainfall, high summer temperatures, and evaporation rates. They avoid sites with dense cover and prefer open areas with scattered woody plants and annual grasses. Consequently, they tend to inhabit lands that are managed on a sustainable basis for cattle grazing

(Fagerstone and Ramey 1996). On rangelands, the rats may do some damage by consuming seeds of desirable grazing grasses, but in general, losses attributable to them are negligible (Kangaroo Rat 2005c). Sound management of grazing on high elevation grasslands allows the maintenance of perennial grass with interspersed shrubs, sustains forage for livestock and reduces erosion. At lower, drier elevations, however, a shrubby cover may be all that can be sustained. When grasslands are improperly grazed, there is a gradual downward trend in perennial grass density and a corresponding increase in Merriam kangaroo rats. A corresponding invasion of mesquite is also observed at some localities where grass densities are reduced, and this vegetation shift is notably accompanied by an increase in Merriam kangaroo rat populations (Fagerstone and Ramey 1996).

The abundance of plant species whose seeds are favored foods of small mammals can be strongly affected by seed predation. Foraging by rodent granivores substantially reduces the standing crop of large-seeded winter annual plants (Fagerstone and Ramey 1996) that other small mammals or grazing animals may favor. After removal of rodents, densities of these plants increased as much as several thousand times.

Rodents are important to plant population recruitment in desert grasslands. Although rodents consume large amounts of seed, their seed caches are a major source of plant recruitment (Fagerstone and Ramey 1996, Pocket Mice 2005). Kangaroo rats cache seeds in a centrally located burrow, but they also often store seed in scattered caches just below the soil surface. Seed caches that are not recovered provide for recruitment of new plants. The establishment of small-seeded plants and of annuals and perennial grasses is influenced by pocket mice (Fagerstone and Ramey 1996), whereas, the establishment of large-seeded plants is affected by kangaroo rats.

Kangaroo rats have variable effects on range condition of desert or arid grasslands. When a range is in good to excellent condition, Merriam kangaroo rats have little effect on seed dispersal (Fagerstone and Ramey 1996). Good quality grassland is less favorable habitat for kangaroo rats because its increased cover produces obstacles for kangaroo rats when escaping from predators, and because large-seeded vegetation, their preferred food, is replaced by small-seeded plants. On grasslands in good to excellent condition, the seed-burying habits of heteromyid rodents are probably beneficial to grassland condition, given that large-seeded perennial grasses and tall shrubby plants have been shown to increase on areas where kangaroo rats were most abundant (Fagerstone and Ramey 1996). During a favorable seed year, and when range condition is such that the supply of large-seeded perennial grass seed is in excess of the needs of kangaroo rats, much more seed is cached by rats than is ever recovered (Fagerstone and Ramey 1996). Large seeded species have difficulty in germinating and establishing from seed on the soil surface. Such species may require burial in seed caches for seedling establishment to occur (LaTourette and others 1971). Because seed buried in the ground is in a more favorable environment for germination and seedling survival than seed lying on the ground surface, the rate of plant restocking may be enhanced by the presence of kangaroo rats (Fagerstone and Ramey 1996). Rodent caches of antelope bitterbrush (*Purshia tridentata*), snowbrush (*Ceanothus velutinus*), squawcarpet (*C. prostratus*), green rabbitbrush (*Chrysothamnus viscidiflorus*), eheatgrass, and Indian rice grass (*Oryzopsis hymenoides*) have been reported (Fagerstone and Ramey 1996). On recently burned or denuded pinyon-juniper and sagebrush sites, kangaroo rat caches created opportunities for germination of species such as bitterbrush and snowberry (*Symphoricarpos* spp.). Rodents also transport mycorrhizae associated with range plants and therefore may facilitate establishment of plant species and their mycorrhizae on denuded range sites (Fagerstone and Ramey 1996).

As grassland conditions decrease from fair to poor, the vegetation composition changes, woody perennial shrubs increase, and perennial grasses decline (Fagerstone and Ramey 1996). Increasing openness allows kangaroo rats to see and avoid predators (Fagerstone and Ramey 1996). Under these conditions, kangaroo rats can be an important factor in accelerating range deterioration. In poor grassland, kangaroo rat activities may prevent range recovery.

Reduction of kangaroo rat populations to increase forage is justified biologically only where the density of perennial grass is low and can be increased by grazing management or range improvement practices. Kangaroo rat control may also be warranted where artificial reseeding of large-seeded plants is hampered by kangaroo rats (Fagerstone and Ramey 1996).

Kangaroo rats may prevent grassland succession by maintaining sub-climax vegetation. Long-term removal of a guild of kangaroo rat species from a Chihuahuan Desert ecosystem led to the conversion of the habitat from shrubland to grassland (Fagerstone and Ramey 1996). And 12 years after removal, density of tall perennial and annual grasses increased approximately three times and rodent species typical of arid grassland colonized, including harvest mice.

Reptiles and Amphibians_____

To this point, this discussion of grassland animals has focused on mammals. As a group they are homoeothermic, "warm-blooded." Their body temperature is maintained within a narrow range, regardless of ambient temperature. The source of body heat is metabolic, powered by their food they eat. The skin is of great importance in conserving or disposing of excess heat from the body. Insulating layers of hair and/or fat prevent heat loss in cold weather. The sweat glands, when present, dissipate heat by evaporative cooling. (Mammals 1997).

The discussion now turns to reptiles and amphibians. By contrast to mammals, reptiles and amphibians are ectotherms, "cold-blooded" animals such as reptiles, fish, and amphibians, whose body temperature is regulated by their behavior or surroundings. They must bask in the sun or find a warm spot to get warm and become active, and they must find shade or a cool spot to cool off. In cold conditions they become sluggish and do not move around much, and some enter a state of inactivity or hibernation if it becomes cold for a long time (Reptiles 2005, Amphibians 2005).

Savage (1960) described a modern North American desert and plains herpetofauna whose boundaries are determined by zones of relatively rapid species transitions into different surrounding herpetofaunas. With the increasingly xeric climate of the late Miocene, the modern, unbroken grasslands began to form by coalescence of previously scattered and isolated fragments (Scott 1996). In marked contrast to mammalian faunas that experienced massive Pleistocene (1.8 million to about 10,000 years ago) extinctions, North

62

USDA Forest Service Gen. Tech. Rep. RMRS-GTR-135-vol. 2. 2005

American herpetofaunas have changed remarkably little since the Pliocene (5.3 million to 1.8 million years ago). Pleistocene herpetofaunas from Western North America were composed of most of the same species that are found now (Rogers 1982, Parmley 1990). A major difference between early herpetofaunas and modern ones is the loss of several tortoises of the genus Geochelone (Moodie and Van Devender 1979). Based on fossil evidence, the Great Plains herpetofauna have evolved *in situ* since at least the Miocene (23.8 million to 5.3 million years ago), with only minor east-west and north-south shifts that coincide with Pleistocene glaciations. This stability has produced a recognizable grassland herpetofauna that is relatively uniform across the North American plains.

The patterns of herpetofaunal diversity were accomplished mainly by the addition or deletion of species from a widespread suite of grassland forms. Most species are wide-ranging, supporting the notion that the grassland fauna is fairly homogeneous. For example, half (6 of 12) of the reptile and amphibian species found in the grasslands of Alberta and almost three-fourths (32 of 43) of the Kansas tallgrass species are also found in the grasslands of the Chihuahuan Desert, several hundred kilometers to the south (Scott 1996).

Reptiles

There are four main groups of reptiles: turtles and tortoises; lizards and snakes; crocodiles and alligators; and the tuatara. Many spend their time on land, but some reptiles spend most of the time in water, such as crocodiles, alligators, turtles, some species of snakes, and some species of lizards. Reptile species can be found in all types of habitats except polar ice and tundra (Reptiles 2005).

Most reptiles make nests or dig holes to lay their eggs in. Some stay to guard the nest and even facilitate the hatchlings start in life. But most female reptiles leave the nest once eggs are laid; the hatchlings are independent from the start and must find their own food and shelter (Reptiles 2005).

Reptiles, like other vertebrates, partition habitats according to their food and shelter, although competition between various species may also influence their relative abundance. For example, in Hidalgo County, southwestern New Mexico, desert spiny lizard (*Sceloporus magister*), side-blotched lizard (*Uta stansburiana*), tree lizard (*Urosaurus ornatus*), and western whiptail lizard (*Aspidoscelis tigris*) prefer habitat with greater densities of shrubs. Other species, including the greater earless (*Cophosaurus texanus*), Longnose Leopard lizard (*Gambelia wislizenii*), round-tailed horned (*Phrynosoma modestum*), and zebra-tailed lizards (*Callisaurus draconoides*), prefer more open areas with few shrubs (Parmenter and Van Devender 1995).

Habitat, food, and behavioral factors were examined to determine how four similar species of whiptail lizards could coexist in southeastern Arizona (Parmenter and Van Devender 1995). Each species used a slightly different part of the habitat. Little striped whiptail lizards (*Aspidoscelis inornata*) preferred areas dominated by mesquite. Desert grassland whiptails (*Aspidoscelis uniparens*) inhabited the ecotone between mesquite habitats and Arizona Upland Sonoran desertscrub. Two all-female (parthenogenetic) whiptail species were found in transition zones.

Parthenogenetic whiptail species typically occupy transitional ecotones between the habitats where their parent species occur. The desert grassland is an evolutionary center for all-female whiptails. Seven species are mostly or completely restricted to this habitat. Checkered (*A. tesselata*), Chihuahuan spotted (*A. exsanguis*), and New Mexican whiptails are common in desert grassland in Texas and New Mexico, while desert grassland and Sonoran whiptails are more common in southeastern Arizona. The Gila spotted whiptail (*A. flagellicauda*) is common in desert grassland-interior chaparral mosaics below the Mogollon Rim in central Arizona. The plateau whiptail (*A. velox*) lives in Great Basin grasslands on the Colorado Plateau above the Mogollon Rim (Parmenter and Van Devender 1995).

Turtles and Tortoises

The order Testudines, popularly known as the turtles, includes the tortoises and the terrapins. Testudines is an ancient clade dating back to the Triassic period, 248 million to 206 million years ago, and today are represented by more than 200 species. Populations of many turtle species have declined, and such endangered species as the Green Sea Turtle (*Chelonia mydas*) have become international symbols to environmentalists and conservationists (Turtles 2005).

All turtles retain the basic strategy of laying eggs in nests, always on land, either buried in sand or hidden in vegetation. This tactic of depositing eggs has been a major factor in the endangerment of many turtles. The eggs are abandoned to the mercy of predators. Juvenile turtles often play different ecological roles than their larger parents, especially as prey to predators. However, turtles in general have relatively long life spans and mate repeatedly and have a generalized life history strategy of producing many young (Turtles 2005).

Turtles have a wide range of diets and habitats, and thus fill a variety of ecological roles. The armored shells of turtles may seem impregnable, but still the turtles have their predators, including predatory birds, and some mammals, such as coyotes. Their tough shells are not a suit of invulnerability, though tortoises have been known to survive wildfires in grasslands by withdrawing into their shells. That same behavior doubtless frustrates many predators (Turtles 2005).

Box Turtles—All North American box turtles belong in the *Emydidae* family of turtles. This large family also includes the sliders, map turtles, and pond turtles from North America and Asia. Box turtles are separated from all the other turtles in this family into the genus *Terrapene* (Cook 1997). The western box turtle (*Terrapene ornata*) inhabits the grasslands of the Southwest. This turtle is found as far north and east as South Dakota, Michigan, and Indiana, south through southeastern Arizona, New Mexico, and Texas into northern Mexico (Western Box Turtle 2005a). In Arizona, the subspecies known as desert grassland box turtle (*Terrapene ornata luteola*) is common in certain areas (Parmenter and Van Devender 1995).

The western box turtle of grasslands are found in treeless plains to gentle hills with grass or low bushes and sandy soils. Their ranges may have developed along side the great herds of grazing animals on the North American Prairies (Cook 1997). They occasionally inhabit desert habitats (Western Box Turtle 2005a). This turtle tends to create shallow burrows in loose soils; it will also use mammal burrows and bannertail kangaroo rat mounds. These burrows are used to avoid temperature extremes and reduce desiccation (Western Box Turtle 2005a). Their powerful front legs and strong claws are perfectly made for tearing apart manure piles in search of dung beetles and grubs. Studies have shown that the Ornate box turtle's numbers are reduced when cattle are removed from that turtle's home range (Cook 1997).

The western box turtle is omnivorous, feeding on insects, especially beetles, berries, leaves, fruits, and sometimes carrion. It reproduces from March to November, laying two to eight eggs per clutch. Breeding strongly correlates with rainfall (Western Box Turtle 2005a).

Western box turtles are locally threatened by dangers associated with agriculture and increasing urbanization. Roads are major threats: hundreds of turtles may be killed by vehicles in a single year on certain Interstate Highways, and dozens may be run over on secondary roads. Machinery used to till farmland and grow crops and applications to improve farmlands and ranges can inadvertently injure or kill box turtles. For example, in Missouri, this species incurred a high rate of mortality as a result of prescribed burning of tallgrass prairie in late October (Western Box Turtle 2005b).

Box turtles are popular in the pet trade of Europe and Southeast Asia. Excessive exploitation for this trade may be a significant threat to box turtles, and their visibility on roads also increases their vulnerability to collectors (Western Box Turtle 2005b). They are listed by The Convention of International Trade in Endangered Species of Fauna and Flora (C.I.T.E.S.) as a threatened species. Permits for their export and import are required. Many States protect native box turtles and do not allow collection. These turtles are a long-lived species with low egg/clutch numbers, high hatchling mortality rates, and ever shrinking habitat. Their survival may depend on active conservation and research into their needs and demography (Cook 1997).

Lizards

Lizards typical of desert grassland include lesser earless (*Holbrookia maculata*), side-blotched (*Uta stansburiana*), southern prairie (*Sceloporus undulatus consobrinus*), and one or more species of whiptail (*Aspidoscelis* spp.) lizards. In dry, gravelly arroyos, greater earless and zebra-tailed lizards are usually found. In southeastern Arizona and southwestern New Mexico, the Gila monster (*Heloderma suspectum*) is occasionally found in rock outcrops in desert grassland (Parmenter and Van Devender 1995).

The Gila monster is one of only two venomous lizards known. The other venomous lizard is the Mexican beaded lizard (*Heloderma horridum*) in Mexico and Central America. Gila monsters are not aggressive or dangerous unless they are picked up and handled. They typically inhabit the lower slopes of mountains and nearby outwash plains, especially in canyons and arroyos where water is at least periodically present. In some areas, they frequent irrigated farmlands that adjoin those habitat types. Other cover in such areas often includes boulders, rock crevices, downed vegetation, and litter. Gila monsters dig burrows for shelter, or use those made by other animals or formed by nature. These shelters are occupied both as winter hibernacula and as warm-season retreats from the heat. Gila monsters are common to rocky slopes, and uncommon to mesquite-dominated bajada in the Sulphur Springs Valley of Arizona (Gila Monster 2005b,c, Mexican Beaded Lizard. 2005).

The diet of Gila monsters includes small mammals, snakes, lizards, the eggs of birds and reptiles, and invertebrates. They are a diurnal and occasionally nocturnal predator. They use their tongue to sample the air and substrate for molecules of substances that provide them information about the environment. This mechanism is apparently the principal method used to locate their prey. Coyotes, owls, hawks, and eagles may prey upon them, and other reptiles probably eat young Gila monsters as well (Gila Monster 2005b,c).

Gila monster populations have been exploited by commercial and private collectors, and have suffered from habitat destruction due to urbanization and agricultural development. They are often killed by people who believe they are dangerous and a hazard to the public. They are also one of the most commercially valuable reptile species in North America. Stringent

64

USDA Forest Service Gen. Tech. Rep. RMRS-GTR-135-vol. 2. 2005

prohibitions against commercial exploitation and unnecessary killing are needed. As a result of these threats, there is no question that the Gila monster is less widespread and less abundant than it was formerly. Habitat preservation is important, especially the protection of den sites. Gila monsters are protected under California and Arizona law, and the species is listed as endangered in New Mexico (Gila Monster 2005a,b,c).

The horned lizards or "horny toads" (*Phrynosoma* spp.) are an interesting looking group of ant-eating reptiles. They are not like typical long slender lizards but are flat and chunky. Round-tailed horned lizard, regal horned lizard (*P. solare*), and Texas (*P. cornutum*) horned lizards are common in desert grasslands from western Texas to southeastern Arizona (Parmenter and Van Devender 1995).

Snakes

Common nonvenomous snakes of the desert grasslands include the gopher snake or bullsnake (*Pituophis catenifer*, and *P. c. sayi*), coachwhips (*Masticophis flagellum cingulum*, *M. f. lineatulus*, *M. f. piceus*, and *M. f. testaceus*), desert grassland kingsnake (*Lampropeltis getulus splendida*), Great Plains Rat snake (*Elaphe guttata emoryi*), western hognose snake (*Heterodon nasicus*), Trans-Pecos ratsnake (*E. subocularis*), and western hooknosed snake (*Gyalopion canum*). The Mexican vine snake (*Oxybelis aeneus*), green rat snake (*E. triaspis*), and desert hooknosed snake (*Gyalopion quadrangulare*) are tropical species occasionally found in desert grassland in the Atascosa and Santa Rita Mountains of Pima and Santa Cruz Counties, south-central Arizona (Parmenter and Van Devender 1995).

Four venomous snakes widespread in desert grassland are the Mohave (*Crotalus scutulatus*), the prairie (*C. viridis viridis*), western diamondback (*C. atrox*) rattlesnakes, and the desert grassland massasauga (*Sistrusrus catenatus edwardsi*). The diminutive Arizona coral (*Micruroides euryxanthus*), a member of the cobra family (Elapidae), reaches desert grassland in southeastern Arizona and southwestern New Mexico (Parmenter and Van Devender 1995).

Amphibians

There are about 5,500 known species of amphibians, divided into three main groups: slamanders, newts, and mudpuppies; caecilians; and frogs and toads. They are animals that live part of their lives in water and part on land. Amphibians are ectothermic and cannot regulate their own body heat as mammals do. They depend on heat from sunlight to become warm and active. They also cannot cool down on their own, so if they get too hot, they have to find shade. In cold weather, they tend to be sluggish and do not move around much (Amphibians 2005).

Young amphibians do not look like their parents. They are generally called larvae, and as they develop, they change in body shape, diet, and lifestyle, a process called metamorphosis. Frogs are familiar examples. After hatching from eggs, they start out as tadpoles with gills to breathe underwater and a tail to swim with. As they grow, they develop lungs, legs, and a different mouth. Their eyes also change position and they lose their tails. At this point they are adult frogs, which spend most of their time hopping on land (Amphibians 2005).

Most amphibians have soft, moist skin that is protected by a slippery secretion of mucus. They also tend to live in moist places or near water to keep their bodies from drying out. Many adult amphibians also have poison-producing glands in their skin, which make them taste bad to predators and might even poison a predator that bites or swallows them (Amphibians 2005).

Some form of permanent or ephemeral water must be present to facilitate amphibian reproduction in the desert grassland. Livestock water developments and ponds are reliable water sources that are readily colonized by amphibians. Summer thunderstorms routinely fill small playas and pools with water. When this happens, there is a surge in amphibian reproduction and populations (Parmenter and Van Devender 1995).

When we think of frogs, we generally picture what are called "true frogs." These amphibians are members of the family *Ranidae*, containing more than 400 species. Frogs from this family can be found on every continent except Antarctica. These frogs are characterized by (1) bulging eyes, (2) strong, long, webbed hind feet that are adapted for leaping and swimming, (3) smooth or slimy skin, and (4) eggs in clusters (Frogs and Toads 2005). The term toad refers to "true toads," members of the family *Bufonidae*, containing more than 300 species. True toads can be found worldwide except in Australasia, polar regions, Madagascar, and Polynesia. These amphibians are characterized by (1) stubby bodies with short hind legs for walking instead of hopping like true frogs, (2) warty and dry skin, (3) paratoid, poison, glands behind the eyes, (4) eggs laid in long chains. Some toads (genera *Nectophrynoides*), however, are the only types of frogs and toads to bear live young (Frogs and Toads 2005).

The physical distinctions between frogs and toads can easily get blurred because sometimes the features appear mixed or less obvious, and certain species even legitimately fall into both categories. It is not uncommon, for example, to find a warty-skinned frog that is not a toad, or even a slimy toad. Even the more invisible morphological features such as cartilage structure has been found to sometimes fit both categories (Frogs and Toads 2005).

Desert grassland is not usually thought of as conducive habitat for amphibians. Certain toads, however, including Couch's (*Scaphiopus couchi*), plains (*S. bombifrons*), and western (*S. hammondi*) spadefoot toads, and green (*Bufo debilis*), Great Plains (*B. cognatus*), and southwestern Woodhouse's (*B. woodhousei australis*) toads, can be quite common. The true frogs, such as Chiricahua (*Rana chiricahuensis*), lowland (*R. yavapaiensis*), and plains (*R. blairi*) leopard frogs, and the introduced bullfrog (*R. catesbeiana*), are generally limited to permanent, often artificially developed water sources (Parmenter and Van Devender 1995).

The last group of amphibians that is addressed are salamanders. Salamanders are in the Order *Caudata*. These amphibians date back 150 million years ago to the Triassic period (Salamanders 2005b). They are divided into nine families, with some 400 species worldwide. More than half of these are found only in the New World, and the eastern and western regions of North America are centers of salamander diversity. Salamanders are tailed amphibians having four legs of more-or-less equal size. Most have vertical creases down their sides called costal grooves. They are easily distinguished from lizards by a lack of claws and scales (Salamanders 2005a).

There are three types of salamanders: totally aquatic, semiaquatic, and completely terrestrial (Kaplan 2002). Most salamander species are largely terrestrial as adults but lay their eggs in or near water. They undergo a gilled, aquatic larval stage before transforming into reproductive adults and dispersing to terrestrial habitats (Salamanders 2005a). However, some species retain their gills through their life. They are able to take up oxygen through the skin, and in addition the lungless salamander can also take up oxygen through the membrane of the mouth. They have mucus-forming glands that help to keep them moist, and the glands also expel toxic secretions when the animal fears danger. Whether aquatic or terrestrial, salamanders need moisture for survival and are found in only wet or damp environments (Salamanders 2005b).

The majority of salamanders and their larva are carnivorous, preying on insects, worms, and other small invertebrates. Large adults will eat fish, frogs, and other salamanders. Secretive, they are chiefly nocturnal, hiding under fallen logs and damp leaf litter during the daylight hours. The larvae begin feeding immediately after hatching, devouring tiny aquatic animals. Likely they perform important ecological roles in the communities where they live (Salamanders 2005a,b, Kaplan 2002).

Occasionally one finds tiger salamanders (*Ambystoma tigrinum*) in desert grassland water developments (Parmenter and Van Devender 1995). The tiger salamander covers a wide range of areas extending nearly coast to coast in North America. There are several subspecies within this complex. The tiger salamanders are large and robust, reaching average total lengths up to 8.5 inches (21.6 cm), though some individuals over 12 inches (30.5 cm) long have been found. Outside of the breeding season they are seldom seen, as they spend most of their time underground, often in mammal burrows (Salamanders 2002).

Tiger salamanders living in isolated ponds may exhibit a condition known as neoteny, in which the animal becomes mature at an earlier stage in life than usual. The salamanders reproduce as aquatic larvae and may never transform into terrestrial adults. Neoteny is a survival mechanism some species in arid climates have evolved to assure they can reproduce in stressed conditions (Parmenter and Van Devender 1995).

Conclusions

The biology, ecology, and management of several important grassland terrestrial and aquatic vertebrates have been presented. Some of these species, for example prairie dogs and gophers, have been and are considered pests and nuisances by ranchers, farmers, and many others. Voles, kangaroo rats, and other small rodents are often considered as little insignificant creatures that are not even considered in management planning, but as discussed above, each of the species are essential to the functioning of grassland ecosystems.

The roles each of the species play within the ecosystems are numerous and diverse. All of the species in this chapter are prey for different predators. Prairie dog and pocket gopher burrows provide habitat for large suites of other species. Prairie dogs are required as food for the most endangered species in the United States, black-footed ferret. Not only does the digging performed by voles, gophers, and other mammals provide habitats for many other species, their activities also aerate and turn the soil, recycle nutrients, and in so doing, expose new enriched soil. The new soil creates beds for vegetation that differ from the vegetation in the surrounding areas, and this consequently contributes to the diversity and heterogeneity of habitats.

Additional examples of species that are major players in ecosystems are bats. Bats play an important role in pollinating certain plants, and as such they assist in maintaining the species that have ecological relationships with those plants they pollinate. As insectivores, bats likely play a role in regulating insect populations and insect-related ecological processes. Bat guano supports entire ecosystems of unique organisms.

In summary, the interconnection and integration of the species in this chapter—and additional species, both animal and plant, that were not mentioned—indicate

66

USDA Forest Service Gen. Tech. Rep. RMRS-GTR-135-vol. 2. 2005

how crucial it is to manage grasslands and ecosystems, even including the so-called pests, nuisances, and obscure little insignificant creatures, in order to maintain healthy systems that will provide benefits now and in the future.

Acknowledgments

I thank Mark A. Rumble, Fred B. Samson, and John Sidle for reviewing this chapter and providing insightful comments. I express my appreciation to Deborah M. Finch for editing the chapter. Also great gratitude goes to Kerri Mich and Doug Paulson for their assistance in creating the distribution maps.

References

Amphibians. 2005. Animal Bytes: Amphibians. Available: URL http://sandiegozoo.org/animalbytes/a-amphibians.html

Andelt, W.F. and S. Ahmed. 2004. Managing voles in Colorado. Colorado State University. Available: URL http://www.ext.coloradostate.edu/pubs/natres/06507.html

Black-Footed Ferret. 1995. Feature Series. U.S. Fish and Wildlife Service. Vol. 1, No. 1. 2 p. Available: URL http://www.r6.fws.gov/feature/ferrets.html

Black-Footed Ferret. 1997. Wyoming Game and Fish Dept. Conservation Publication. Vol.13, No. 8. 4 p. Available: URL http://gf.state.wy.us/services/publications/wildtimes/ferret.htm

Black-Footed Ferret. 2004. Colorado Division of Wildlife. Available: URL http://wildlife. state.co.us/Educationlmammalsguide/black_footed_ferret.asp

Black-Footed Ferret. 2005a. The Mammals of Texas Available: URL http://gf.state.wy.us/services/publications/wildtimes/ferret.htm

Black-Footed Ferret. 2005b. National Parks Conservation Association. Available: URL
http://www.npca.org/wildlife_protection/wildlife_facts/ferret.asp

Black-Footed Ferret. 2005c. Wikipedia. Available: URL http://en.wikipedia.org/wiki/Black-Footed_Ferret

Brand, C.J. 2002. Landscape Ecology of Plague in the American Southwest, September 19-20, 2000, Fort Collins, Colorado, Proceedings of an American Southwest Workshop: Fleston, Virginia, U.S. Geological Survey Information and Technology Report 2002-0001, 24 p.

Bryan, H.D. 2005. Voles. The University of Tennessee, Agricultural Extension Service. Available: URL http://knox.tennessee.edu/voles.htm

Burgess, T. 1996. Desert Grasslands, mixed shrub, savanna, shrub, or semidesessrt scrub? The dilemma of coexisting growth forms. In: The desert grassland. M. P, McClaran and T. R. Van Devender (eds). The University of Arizona Press. Tucson, Arizona.

Cato, P. 2005. Deer mouse. San Diego Natural History Museum. Available: URL http://www.sdnhm.org/fieldguide/mammals/peroman.html

CBSG. 2004. Black-Footed ferret population management planning workshop. Final report. IUCN/SSC Conservation Breeding Specialist Group. Apple Valley, MN. 129 pp.

CDC. 2004. All about hantaviruses. Center for Disease Conrol. Available: URL http://www.cdc.gov/ncidod/diseases/hanta/noframes/rodents.html

Chung-McCoubrey, A.L. 1996. Grassland bats and management in the Southwest. In: D.M. Finch (ed). 1996 Ecosystem disturbance and wildlife conservation in western grasslands – A symposium preceedings, September 22-26, 1994; Albuquerque, NM. Gen. Tech. Rep. RM-GTR-285. Fort Collins, CO: USDA Forest Service, Rocky Mountain Forest and Range Experiment Station. 82 p.

Cook, T. 1997. The Eastern and Western Box Turtle. Available: URL http://boxturtlesite.org/eastern.html

Cully, J.F. and E.S. Williams. 2002. Interspecific Comparisons of Sylvatic Plague in Prairie Dogs. Page 6 In: Brand, C.J., 2002, Landscape Ecology of Plague in the American Southwest, September 19—20, 2000, Fort Collins, Colorado, Proceedings of an American Southwest Workshop: Fleston, Virginia, U.S. Geological Survey. Information and Technology Report 2002—0001, 24 p.

Deer Mouse. 2005. Deer mouse. Animal Fact. Available: URL http://wildwnc.org/af/deermouse.html

Desert Cottontail. 2005. Desert cottontail. Desert USA. Available: URL http://desertusa.com/mag00/apr/papr/rabbit.hrml

Desert USA. 2005. Botta's Pocket Gopher. Available: URL http://www.desertusa.com/mag01/jun/papr/gopher.html

Eastern Cottontail. 2005. Eastern cottontail. Available: URL http://www.iwr-online.org/kids/Facts/Mammals/cottontail.htm

Fagerstone, K.A. and C.A. Ramey. 1996. Rodents and lagomorphs. In:Range Wildlife, Kausmann, P.R., (ed). The Society of Range Management, Denver, Colorado. 440 p.

Ferret Facts. 2005. Black-Footed Ferret Recovery Implementation Team. Available: URL http://www.blackfootedferret.org/facts.html

Fields, M.J., D.P. Coffin, and J.R. Goez. 1999. Burrowing activities of kangaroo rats and patterns in plant species dominance at a shortgrass steppe-desert grassland ecotone. Journal of Vegetative Science. 10:123-130.

Findley, J.S.1989. Morphological patterns in rodent communities of southwestern North America. Pages 253-263 in D.W. Morris, Z. Abramsky, B.J. Fox, and M.R. Willig (ed). Patterns in the structure of mammalian communities. The Museum, Texas Tech. University Spec. Publ. 266 p.

Forest Preserve District of Cook County. 1973. The Pocket Gopher. Nature Bulletin No. 493-A. 2 p. Available: URL http://www.newton.dep.anl.gov/natbltn/400-499/nb493.htm

Forest Preserve District of Cook County. 1974. Deer mice and white-footed mice. Nature Bulletin No. 545-A. pp. 2. Available: URL http://www.newton.dep.anl.gov/natbltn/500-599/nb545.htm

Frogs and Toads. 2005. Frogs and toads. Available: URL http://allaboutfrogs.org/weird/general/frogtoad.html

Geiger, B. 2002. Mysterious Mounds. The mima mounds. Available: URL http://www.homestead.com/wintersteel/Mima_Mounds~ns4.html

Geomyidae. 2005. Available: URL hppt://www.chez.com/rodent/Geomyidae/Geomydae.html

Gila Monster.2005a. NatureServe Explorer Available:URL http://www.natureserve.org/explorer/servlet/NatureServe?init=Species

Gila Monster. 2005b. BISOM_M. Available: URL http://fwie.fw.vt.edu/states/nmex_main/species/030135.htm

Gila Monster. 2005c. Arizona Game and Fish Department Heritage Data Management System. Available: URL http://www.azgfd.gov/w_c/edits/documents/Helosuci.d_001.pdf

Gober, P. 2002. Dog 12-Month Finding the Significance of the Plague Threat in the U.S. Fish and Wildlife Service: Black-Tailed Prairie. Page 13 In Brand, C.J. (ed), 2002, Landscape Ecology of Plague in the American Southwest, September 19—20, 2000, Fort Collins, Colorado, Proceedings of an American Southwest Workshop: Fleston, Virginia, U.S. Geological Survey Information and Technology Report 2002—0001, 24 p.

Hatfield-Etchberger, L., B. Stroh, B. Bibles, and R. Etchberger. 2002. Investigating Epizootic Plague Transmission: Comparison of Flea/Host Relationships Within an Established Prairie Dog Colony to Adjacent Habitat. Page 8 In Brand, C.J., 2002, Landscape Ecology of Plague in the American Southwest, September 19—20, 2000, Fort Collins, Colorado, Proceedings of an American Southwest Workshop: Fleston, Virginia, U.S. Geological Survey Information and Technology Report 2002—0001, 24 p.

Heteromyidae. 2000. Heteromyidae: kangaroo rats and pocket mice. Arizona-Sonora Desert Museum. Available: URL http://www.desertmuseum.org/books/nhsd_heteromyidae.html

Heteromyidae. 2005. Heteromyidae. Wikipedia. Available: URL http://en.wikipedia.org/wiki/Hetermomyidae

Hof, J., M. Bevers, D.W. Uresk, 0.L. Sawtbeck. 2002. Population dependent dispersal: habitat placement for the black-tailed prairie dog. Spatial optimization in ecological applications. New York: Columbia University Press. 114-124 p.

Howard, V.W. Jr. 1994, Kangaroo rats. Prevention and Control of Wildlife Damage – 1994. Cooperative Extension Division. Institute

USDA Forest Service Gen. Tech. Rep. RMRS-GTR-135-vol. 2. 2005

67

of Agriculture and Natural Resources. University of Nebraska – Lincoln. 4 p.

Huntly, N. and R. Inouye. 1988. Pocket gophers in ecosystems: patterns and mechanisms. BioScience 38: 786-793.

Hygnstrom, S.E. and D.E. Virchow. 1994. Prairie Dogs. Prevention and Control of Wildlife Damage – 1994. Cooperative Extension Division, Institute of Agriculture and Natural Resources, University of Nebraska – Lincoln, 11 p.

Jones, C. and R.W. Manning. 1996. The mammals. In: Range Wildlife, Kausmann, P.R. (ed). The Society of Range Management, Denver, Colorado. 440 p.

Kangaroo Rat. 2005a. Available: URL http://www.discverseaz.com/Wildlife/Kangaroo_rat.html

Kangaroo Rat. 2005b. Kangaroo Rats. DesertUSA. Available: URL http://www.desertusa.com/aug96/du_krat.html

Kangaroo Rat. 2005c. Merriam's Kangaroo Rat. The Mammals of Texas – Online Edition. Available: URL http://www.nsrl.ttu.edu/tmotl/dipomerr.htm

Kaplan, M. 2002. Salamanders and newts. Available: URL http://www.anapsid.org/sallies.html

Knowles, C. 2002. Status of White-tailed and Gunnison's Prairie Dogs. National Wildlife Federation, Missoula, MT and Environmental Defense, Washington, DC. 30 p.

Kotliar, N.B. 2000. Application of the new keystone-species concept to prairie dogs: how well does it work? Conservation Biology. 14:1715-1721.

Lagomorphs. 2005a. Rabbits, Hares, and Pikas. Available: URL http://www.bobpickett.org/order_lagomorpha.htm

Lagomorphs. 2005b. Rabbits. Wikipedia. Available: URL http://www.snowspine.com/beastiary/rabbits.html

Mammals. 1997. Introduction to Mammals. Available: URL http://www.educationalimages.com/it110007.htm

Mammals. 2005. Deer mouse. eNature. National Wildlife Federation. Available: URL http://www.enature.com/fieldguide/showSpeciesFT.asp?fotogID=750andcurPageNum=5andrecnum=MA0093

Meadow Vole. 2005. Meadow vole. Available: URL http://www.fcps.k12.va.us/StratfordLandingES/Ecology/mpages/meadow_vole.htm

Mexican Beaded Lizard. 2005. Lizards. Available: URL http://www.corrystuart.net/child_lizards.html

Moodie, K.B. and T.R. Van Devender. 1979. Extinction and extirpation in the herpetofauna of the southern High Plains with emphasis on *Geochelone wilsoni* (Testudinidae). Herpetologica 35:198-206.

Mueggler, W.F. 1967. Voles damage big sagebrush in southwestern Montana. S. Range Manage. 20:88-90.

Naylor, V. 1994. Black-Footed Ferret. Badlands National Park. Available: URL http://www.northern.edu/natsource/ENDANG1/Bfferrl.htm

Order Lagomorpha. 2005. Order Lagomorpha: Hares and Rabbits. The Mammals of Texas - Online Edition. Available: URL http://www.nsrl.ttu.edu/tmot1/ordlagom.htm

Parmenter, R.R. and T.R. Van Devender. 1995. Diversty, spectial variability, and functional roles of vertebrates in the desert grasslands. In: The desert grassland. M.P, McClaran and T.R. Van Devender (eds). The University of Arizona Press, Tucson.

Parmley, D. 1990. Late Pleistocene snakes from Fowlkes Cave, Culberson County, Texas. Journal of Herpetology 24:266-274.

Pauli, J.N. 2005, Ecological studies of the black-tale prairie dog: implications for biology and conservation. Masters Thesis. University of Wyoming. Laramie. 77 p.

Payne, T. and W. Caire. 1999. Species diversity of small mammals in the tallgrass prairie preserve, Osage County, Oklahoma. Proc. Oklahoma Academy of Science. 79:51-59.

Payton, I.J., M. Fenner, and G.L. Williams. 2002. Keystone species: the concept and its relevance for conservation management in New Zealand. Science for Conservation 203. 29 p.

Pocket Gophers. 2005a. Arizona-Sonora Desert Museum. Available: URL http://www.desertmuseum.org/books/nhsd_gophers.html

Pocket Gophers. 2005b. Available: URL http://cecalaveras.ucdavis.edu/pocket.htm

Pocket Gopher. 2005c. Pocket Gopher. Available: URL http://www.holoweb.com/cannon/pocket.htm

Pocket Mice. 2005. Hispid Pocket Mouse. The Mammals of Taxas – Online Edition. Available: URL http://www.nsrt.ttu.eduu/tmit1/cheahisp.htm

Preston, S. D. and L. F Jacobs. 2001. Conspecific pilferage but not presence affects Merriam's kangaroo rat cache strategy. Behavioral Ecology. 12:517-523.

Reichman, J. 2004. Pocket gopher serves as 'Ecosystem Engineers.' Ascribe Science News Service. University of California, Santa Barbara. Available: URL http://www.highbeam.com

Reptiles. 2005. Animal Bytes: Reptiles. Avaibable: URL http://sandiegozoo.org/animalbytes/a-reptiles.html

Rogers, K.L. 1982. Herpetofaunas of the Courtland Canal and Hall Ash local faunas (Pleistocene: Early Kansas) of Jewell Co., Kansas. Journal of Herpetology 16:174-177.

Saimon, T.P. and W.P. Gorenzel. 2002. Voles. University of California. Available: URL http://www.imp.ucdavis.edu/PKG/PESTNOTES/pn7439.html

Salamanders. 2002. U.S. Department of the Interior, U.S. Geological Survey Northern Prairie Wildlife Research Center, 8711 37th St. SE, Jamestown, ND 58401 USA Available: URL http://www.npwrc.usgs.gov/narcam/idguide/atigrin.htm

Salamanders. 2005a. Order Caudata: Salamanders. Available: URL http://vernalpools.rtpi.org/guides/order.htm?order=Caudata

Salamanders. 2005b. Salamanders and newts. Maryland Department of Environmental Protection. Available: URL http://www.montgomerycountymd.gov/deptmpl.asp?url=/content/dep/herps/Newts.asp#top

Savage, J.M. 1960. Evolution of a peninsular herpetofauna. Systematic Zoology 9:184-212.

Saving a Species. 2005. Black-Footed Ferret Recovery Implementation Team. Available: URL http://www.blackfootedferret.org/saving-captive.html

Scott, N.J. Jr. 1996. Evolution and management of the North American grassland herpetofauna. In: D.M. Finch (ed). Ecosystem disturbance and wildlife conservation in western grasslands – A symposium preceedings, September 22-26, 1994; Albuquerque, NM. General Technical Report RM-GTR-285. Fort Collins, CO: USDA Forest Service, Rocky Mountain Forest and Range Experiment Station. 82 p.

Severe, D.S. 1977. Revegetation of black-tailed prairie dog mounds on short-grass prairie in Colorado. MS. Thesis, Colorado State Univ., Fort Collins. 92 p.

Sevilleta LTER: Data. 1998a. Data: Species : Mammal : Banner-tailed Kangaroo Rat - *Dipodomys spectabilis* Available: URL http://sevilleta.unm.edu/data/species/mammals/profile/banner-tailed-kanfaroo-rat.html

Sevilleta LTER: Data. 1998b. Data: Species : Mammal : Botta's Pocket Gopher – *Thomomys bottae*. Available: URL http://sevilleta.unm.edu/data/species/mammal/sevillet/profile/bottas-pocket-gopher.html

Sevilleta LTER: Data. 1998c. Data: Species : Mammal : Gunnison Prairie Dog. Available: URL http://sevilleta.unm.edu/data/species/mammal/sevillet/profile/gunnison-prairie-dog.html

Sevilleta LTER: Data. 1998d. Data: Species : Mammal : Merriam's Kangaroo Rat - *Dipodomys merriami* Available: URL http://sevilleta.unm.edu/data/species/mammal/sevillet/profile/merriams_kangaroo-rat.html

Sevilleta LTER: Research. 2001. Research: Local: Plants: Kangaroo Rats and Dominance Available: URL http://sevilleta.unm.edu/data/contents/SEV114/kratdominance/

Sullivan, L.M. 2005. Pocket Gophers. University of Arizona. Available: URL http://www.ag.arizona.edu/urbanipm/rodents/pocketgophers.html

Tracy, R.L. and G.E. Walsberg. 2002, Kangaroo rats revisited: re-evaluating a classic case of desert survival. Oecologia. 133:449-457.

Turtles. 2005. Testudines: Life History and Ecology Available: URL http://www.ucmp.berkeley.edu/anapsids/testudines/testudineslh.html

Uresk, D.W. and D.D. Paulson. 1988. Estimated carrying capacity for cattle competing with prairie dogs and forage utilization in western South Dakota. Pages 387-390 In R. C. Szaro, K.E. Severson, and D.R. Patton (eds). Proc. symposium management of amphibians, reptiles, and small mammals in North America. Fort Collins, CO: U.S. Department of Agriculture Rocky Mountain Forest and Range Experiment Station. Gen. Tech. Rep. RM-166.

68

USDA Forest Service Gen. Tech. Rep. RMRS-GTR-135-vol. 2. 2005

Wagner, D. and L.C. Drickamer. 2004. Abiotic habitat correlates of Gunnison's prairie dog in Arizona. Journal of Wildlife Management. 68:188-197.

Western Box Turtle. 2005a. Western box turtle (*Terrapene ornata*). Arizona-Sonora Desert Museum. . Available: URL http://www.desertmuseum.org/books/nhsd_terrapene.html

Western Box Turtle. 2005b. NatureServe Explorer Available: URL http://www.natureserve.org/explorer/servlet/NatureServe?init=Species

Wiscomb, G.W. and T.A. Messmer. 1988. Pocket Gophers. Resources Department of Fisheries and Wildlife Utah State University, Logan, Utah. pp. 10 Available: URL http://extension.usu.edu?files/natrpubs/gopher.html

USDA Forest Service Gen. Tech. Rep. RMRS-GTR-135-vol. 2. 2005

69

70

USDA Forest Service Gen. Tech. Rep. RMRS-GTR-135-vol. 2. 2005

Michele Merola-Zwartjes

Chapter 4:
Birds of Southwestern Grasslands: Status, Conservation, and Management

Status and Conservation: Introduction

In the Southwestern United States, the grassland avifauna is collectively composed of a mixture of species found primarily in desert grasslands, shortgrass steppe, wet meadows, and alpine tundra (as used here, desert grasslands incorporate both arid grasslands and desert shrub grasslands). Of these habitats, desert grasslands and shortgrass steppe are the most extensive and support the greatest number of grassland bird species. Desert grasslands are patchily distributed across the southern halves of New Mexico and Arizona, and shortgrass steppe is a component of the Great Plains system that in the Southwest region extends across the eastern half of New Mexico into the panhandles of Texas and Oklahoma. Alpine tundra and particularly wet meadows are limited in geographic extent and support relatively few species of grassland birds in this region (see chapter 2 for detailed maps of the distribution of grassland types). Though their geographic extent may vary, all of these grassland systems provide habitat for distinctive grassland bird species in the Southwest and are therefore worthy of management concern.

The grassland bird community of the Southwest has been shaped by a variety of forces. The challenge of surviving in the arid climate, as well as a history of coevolution with the effects of grazing and wildfire,

are some of the primary factors that have influenced the diversity of species found here. The relative lack of structural heterogeneity in grassland habitats has also played an important role in determining species composition, as the lack of shrubs or trees eliminates a variety of potential ecological niches for birds to exploit. This structural simplicity has resulted in an avifauna that tends to be characterized by specialists, species that have evolved within those few, specific niches available. Wilson's phalarope, for example, is a wetland species that occurs only locally where water is available in the grassland landscape. Some species, including burrowing owls, are highly dependent upon active prairie dog towns, while others such as Baird's sparrow coevolved with grazing ungulates and consequently seek out habitats with a mosaic of grass heights. Species such as horned larks are partial to grass cover so low that it is almost bare ground, while Botteri's sparrow prefers the towering bunchgrasses of big sacaton (*Sporobolus wrightii*) grasslands.

The end result of these collective processes is an avian community that is simple in terms of species richness (few different species), but high in numbers of individual species. For example, one survey of the Pawnee National Grasslands in Colorado found that just three birds (horned lark, McCown's longspur, and lark bunting) accounted for 87 percent of all 1,047 individuals recorded (14 native species total; Knopf 1996a); similar results have been reported in other

USDA Forest Service Gen. Tech. Rep. RMRS-GTR-135-vol. 2. 2005

71

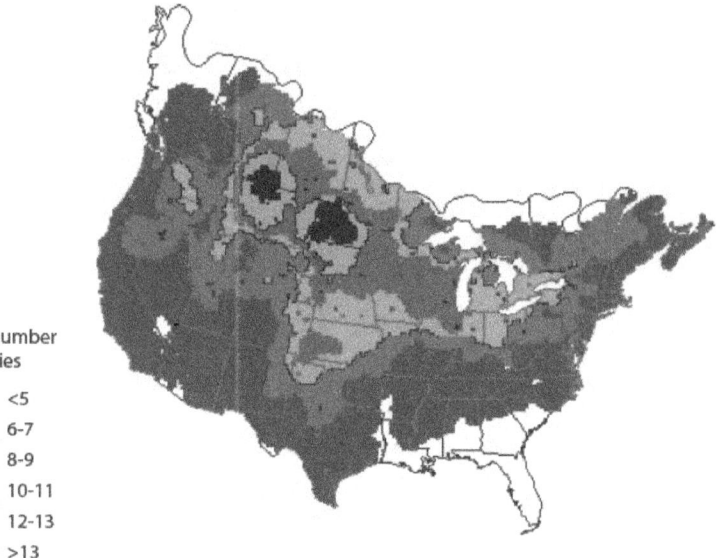

Figure 4-1. Species richness of grassland birds breeding in the United States and Canada. Numbers are average number of species detected per route on the Breeding Bird Survey, years 1982 to 1996 (from Sauer and others 1995).

Observed Number
of Species

- <5
- 6-7
- 8-9
- 10-11
- 12-13
- >13

grassland habitats as well (for example, Kantrud and Kologiski 1982). Figure 4-1 graphically illustrates the relatively low species diversity of grassland birds in the Southwest during the breeding season, based upon the results of the Breeding Bird Survey.[1] However, it is important to note that diversity in this region increases markedly during the winter, due to the influx of short distance migrants. For example, a comparison of the distribution of lark buntings during the breeding season and in the winter demonstrates how high numbers of these grassland breeding birds concentrate in the Southwest during the winter months (fig. 4-2 and 4-3). For the lark bunting and numerous other species of grassland birds that do not travel all the way to the neotropics for the winter, the grassland systems of the Southwest provide habitat that is critically important for overwinter survivorship.

With the possible exception of rodents, birds generally outnumber all other vertebrate groups in grassland ecosystems (C. Bock personal communication 2002, Parmenter and Van Devender 1995). The low number of species reflects a limited number of ecological niches,

resulting in a relatively specialized avifauna. While this specialization has allowed for the success of grassland endemics in the Southwest, this success has come at a price. Many species of grassland birds are apparently now in decline, due largely to the alteration or outright loss of the habitats that grassland specialists have historically depended upon.

The recent declines in numerous species of grassland birds have made them a high priority for conservation for both governmental agencies and nongovernmental organizations alike. Table 4-1 lists some of the bird species that characterize the grassland habitats of the Southwest and indicates their conservation status. Due to the relatively limited information available on birds of wet meadows and alpine tundra in the Southwestern region, the major focus of this review will be on birds inhabiting the desert grassland and shortgrass steppe ecosystems. Information specific to Southwestern grasslands is used whenever possible. However, as the majority of research on grassland birds of the United States has been focused on the habitats of the Great Plains region, in many cases data from Arizona and/or New Mexico are simply not available. Research from other regions may be used when data from the Southwest is lacking, and will be so noted.

Population Trends and Status

Concerns over apparent declines in populations of North American birds, particularly migratory songbirds, have been growing since the 1960s (for example, Aldrich and Robbins 1970, Ambuel and Temple 1982, Briggs and Criswell 1979, Carson 1962). At least initially, decreasing numbers of neotropical migrants in the Eastern U.S. forests were the primary focus of these worries (for example, Robbins and others

---

[1] The Breeding Bird Survey (BBS), begun under the auspices of the U.S. Fish and Wildlife Services in 1966, consists of nearly 3,700 randomly located permanent survey routes located along secondary roads throughout the continental United States and Canada; each route is surveyed annually during the breeding season (Sauer and others 1997). The total number of individuals of each species recorded along the route is used as an index of relative abundance; long-term trends are determined by a route-regression method. Although the BBS has been criticized for a variety of factors, such as observer variability (see DeSante and George 1994 for a brief review), it nonetheless remains highly valuable as the most comprehensive and long-running quantitative survey of any vertebrate group in North America.

72

USDA Forest Service Gen. Tech. Rep. RMRS-GTR-135-vol. 2. 2005

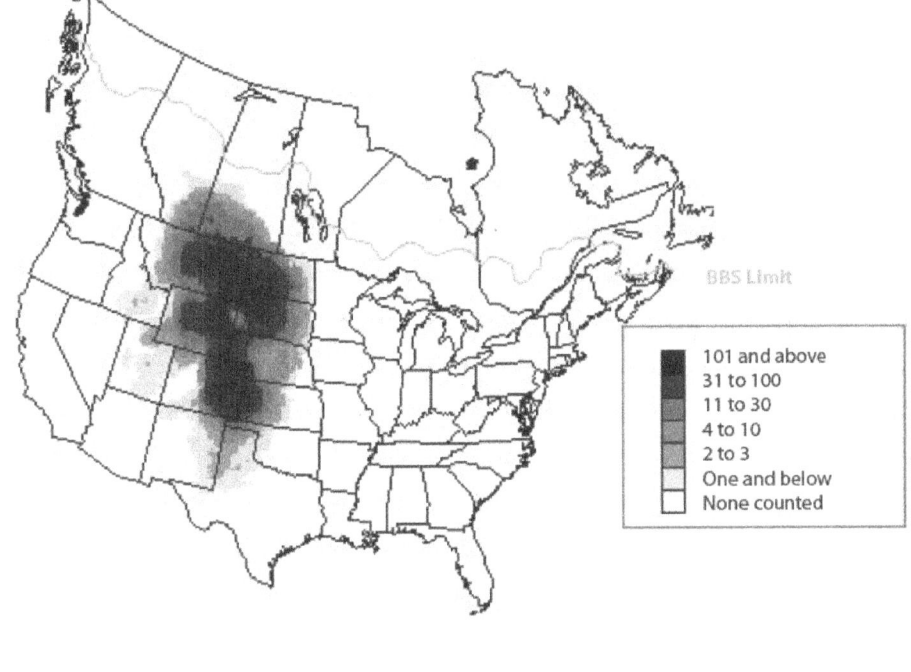

Figure 4-2. Distribution and densities of breeding lark buntings in the United States and Canada, as mean numbers of individuals detected per route per year. Data from Breeding Bird Surveys averaged over the years 1982 to 1996 (Sauer and others 2001).

101 and above
31 to 100
11 to 30
4 to 10
2 to 3
One and below
None counted

Average Count

< 1
1-3
3-10
10-30
30-100
> 100

Figure 4-3. Winter distribution and densities of lark buntings, based on Christmas Bird Count data. Counts are average number of birds detected per survey over the years 1982 to 1996 (from Sauer and others 2001). Like many short-distance migrants, this species concentrates in the grasslands of the Southwest for the winter months.

1989). More recent analyses, however, suggest that the negative population trends of North American birds are most apparent in the grassland habitats of the United States. Many researchers now believe that grassland bird populations have been declining across the continent for approximately the last 50 years (Askins 1993, Peterjohn and Sauer 1999). Grassland birds, it is claimed, have experienced "steeper, more consistent, and more geographically widespread declines than any other behavioral or ecological guild" (Knopf 1994:251). These declines have been largely due, it is believed, to the degradation and outright loss of grassland habitats (Collar and others 1992, DeSante and George 1994, Herkert and others 1996, Knopf 1994, Stotz and others 1996, Vickery and others 1999b). Habitat loss or alteration in these systems has occurred as the result of conversion of grasslands to agriculture, overgrazing or inappropriate grazing

USDA Forest Service Gen. Tech. Rep. RMRS-GTR-135-vol. 2. 2005

73

Table 4-1. Partial list of bird species typically found in the various grassland types of Arizona and/or New Mexico, with particular emphasis on those species that are of conservation concern. Common names in bold face type indicate that the species is listed as endangered or threatened under Federal and/or State law (see superscript for specific designation). This list is not meant to be exhaustive but rather presents some of the more characteristic species likely to be found in these vegetation types. Species are presented in taxonomic order.

Common name[a]	Desert grasslands	Shortgrass steppe (Great Plains)	Wet meadows	Alpine tundra	Season of use[b]	USFWS migratory nongame bird of management concern[c]	NM Partners in Flight priority ranking[d]	AZ Partners in Flight priority species[e]
Mountain plover		•			B	•	Highest priority	
Long-billed curlew		•			B		Highest priority	
Wilson's phalarope			•		B		Highest priority	
Common snipe			•		Y, W			
Golden eagle	•	•			Y			
Northern harrier	•	•	•		Y, W	•		
Swainson's hawk	•	•			B			•
Ferruginous hawk ST-AZ	•	•			Y, W	•	Highest priority	•
Prairie falcon	•	•			Y		Highest priority	
Northern Aplomado falcon E, SE-AZ, SE-NM	•				X			•
White-tailed ptarmigan SE-NM				•	Y		Highest priority	
Lesser prairie chicken C		•			Y			
Masked bobwhite E, SE-AZ	•				Y			
Scaled quail	•	•			Y		High responsibility	
Short-eared owl	•	•	•	•	M, W			
Burrowing owl	•	•			B, Y	•	High responsibility	•
Common nighthawk	•	•			B		High responsibility	
Lesser nighthawk	•				B		High responsibility	
Broad-tailed hummingbird			•		B		High responsibility	
Western kingbird	•	•			B			
Cassin's kingbird	•	•			B		High responsibility	
Scissor-tailed flycatcher	•	•			B		Highest priority	
Ash-throated flycatcher	•	•			B			
Say's Phoebe	•	•			B, Y		High responsibility	
Horned lark	•	•		•	Y			
Chihuahuan raven	•	•			B, Y		High responsibility	
Cactus wren	•				Y			
Mountain bluebird	•	•	•	•	Y, W		Priority	
Loggerhead shrike	•	•			Y	•	Priority	
Bendire's thrasher	•	•			B, Y	•	Highest priority	
American pipit				•	B			
Sprague's pipit SC-AZ	•				W		Highest priority	
Common yellowthroat			•		B			
Grasshopper sparrow (includes Arizona grasshopper sparrow ST-NM)	•	•	•		B, W	•	Highest priority	•
Baird's sparrow ST-AZ, ST-NM	•				W	•	Highest priority	•
Vesper sparrow	•	•			B, W			
Savannah sparrow			•		B, W		Priority	
Lark sparrow	•	•			B, Y	•		
Black-throated sparrow	•				B, Y	•		

Table 4-1. *Continued.*

Species	C1	C2	C3	C4	Season	C6	Priority	C8
Sage sparrow	•				W	•		•
Botteri's sparrow	•	•			B	•	Highest priority	•
Cassin's sparrow	•	•			B, Y	•	High responsibility	•
Rufous-winged sparrow	•				Y			•
McCown's longspur	•	•			W		Highest priority	
Chestnut-collared longspur	•	•			W			
Dickcissel*		•			B		Highest priority	
Lark bunting		•			B, Y, W		Highest priority	
Bobolink* SE-AZ			•		B		Highest priority	
Western meadowlark	•	•	•		Y			
Eastern meadowlark (includes southwestern subspecies lilianae)	•	•	•		Y		Priority	
Red-winged blackbird			•		Y			
Brewer's blackbird			•		Y, W			
Brown-headed cowbird	•	•			B, Y			
Brown-capped rosy finch				•	Y		Highest priority	

[a] Superscripts following name indicate the following Federal Endangered Species Act designations: E = Endangered, PT = Proposed Threatened, C = Candidate (USFWS 2002). State designations are as follows: SE = State endangered, ST = State threatened, SC = State candidate (AGFD 1988; NMDGF 2002). An asterisk * indicates highly localized breeding populations.

[b] B = breeding, W = wintering, Y = year-round, M = in migration. X = currently extirpated; accidental sightings may occur. More than one designation indicates that season of use differs depending upon geographic location.

[c] In Southwest Region (USFWS 1995).

[d] Based on New Mexico Partners in Flight Bird Conservation Plan (NMPIF 2001).

[e] Based on Arizona Partners in Flight Bird Conservation Plan (Latta and others 1999). Note that species in the Arizona plan are not broken down into separate ranking categories, as in the New Mexico plan. However, individual priority scores are given for each species in appendices B and D of the plan.

regimes, the introduction of exotic grasses, fire suppression, succession to shrublands, and fragmentation (Herkert 1994, Vickery and others 1994, 1999a,b).

In one of the first studies to specifically address declines in Western birds, DeSante and George (1994)

Lark bunting. (Photo by Gary Kramer, courtesy of USDA Natural Resources Conservation Service)

produced a list of 75 native species whose breeding populations had declined substantially in at least one Western State over the past 100 years. For Western birds, destruction of riparian habitats was the probable cause of decline for the greatest number of species (16), followed closely by destruction of grassland habitats (15), shooting (13), overgrazing (9), cowbird parasitism (7), logging and clearing of forests (7), and other causes. Table 4-2 presents a subset of this comprehensive list, highlighting those species of the Western United States for which destruction of grassland habitats, overgrazing, or cowbird parasitism—in other words, those factors most relevant to our discussion of Southwestern grasslands—have been implicated in the reported population declines.

These same authors also considered data collected from the Breeding Bird Survey over a period of 26 years, from 1966 to 1991 (DeSante and George 1994). In this population trend analysis, Western birds were divided into two groups: long-distance migrants that winter in the neotropics, and short-distance migrants that winter in the temperate zone of North America, primarily the Southwestern United States and Mexico. Of the short-distance migrants that displayed significant population trends, 79 percent were declining while only 21 percent showed increasing trends. In contrast, long-distance migrants did not undergo any significant population trends in the Western United States during this same

Table 4-2. Native species of landbirds that have decreased in the Western United States for reasons related to grassland habitat destruction, overgrazing, or cowbird parasitism, based on a review of major State-level literature. Listed are species that are known to have decreased in the last 100 years. The superscript [E] denotes species that have been extirpated; species with an asterisk * are those whose breeding populations have decreased by more than 50 percent. Modified from DeSante and George (1994).

Species	Western States where populations have declined	Probable cause
Sage grouse	WA*, OR*, CA*, NV*, ID, MT, UT*, NM[E]	Shooting, overgrazing, destruction of grasslands
Greater prairie-chicken	MT[E], CO*	Shooting, destruction of grasslands
Lesser prairie-chicken	CO*, NM*	Shooting, destruction of grasslands
Sharp-tailed grouse	WA*, OR[E], CA[E], NV*, ID*, MT*, WY*, UT*, CO*, NM[E]	Shooting, overgrazing, destruction of grasslands
Montezuma quail	AZ*, NM*	Overgrazing
Northern bobwhite	WY, AZ[E], NM*	Overgrazing, hunting
Scaled quail	AZ*, NM*	Overgrazing, destruction of grasslands
Burrowing owl	CA*, NV*, ID, MT, CO*, AZ, NM*	Destruction of grasslands, elimination of fossorial mammals, agricultural development, urbanization
Short-eared owl	CA*, NM*	Destruction of grasslands
Willow flycatcher	CA*, AZ*	Destruction of riparian habitat, cowbird parasitism
Horned lark	AZ	Destruction of grasslands
Bell's vireo	CA*, AZ*	Cowbird parasitism, destruction of riparian habitat
Gray vireo	CA*, AZ	Cowbird parasitism?
Yellow warbler	OR, CA*, AZ*	Cowbird parasitism, destruction of riparian habitat
Common yellowthroat	CA, AZ	Drainage of marshes and loss of riparian habitat, cowbird parasitism?
Yellow-breasted chat	CA, NV*	Destruction of riparian habitat, cowbird parasitism?
Botteri's sparrow	AZ*	Overgrazing, destruction of grasslands
Rufous-winged sparrow	AZ*	Overgrazing
Chipping sparrow	WA, OR	Unknown (cowbird parasitism?)
Vesper sparrow	WA, OR	Destruction of grasslands?
Lark bunting	CA, NV	Destruction of grasslands
Baird's sparrow	AZ*	Destruction of grasslands
McCown's longspur	AZ*, NM*	Destruction of grasslands
Chestnut-collared longspur	AZ, NM*	Destruction of grasslands

period. These striking results point up an interesting difference between migratory bird population trends in the Eastern and Western United States. In the East, we have evidence for accelerating declines in forest-dwelling, long-distance neotropical migrants (Askins and others 1990, Robbins and others 1989, Sauer and Droege 1992, Terborgh 1989). The West, by contrast, is witnessing declines in short-distance migrants, and especially those species associated with grasslands and shrublands (DeSante and George 1994). Several reasons are suggested for these declines in the West, including the destruction of grassland ecosystems, overgrazing, and increased levels of cowbird parasitism (DeSante and George 1994). There may also be a

connection between the declines in several species of Western short-distance migrants and the degradation of their wintering habitat (again primarily grasslands and shrublands) in the Southwestern United States and Northwestern Mexico (see table 4-3), although researchers warn of the lack of sound information on the wintering ecology of western migratory birds (for example, Knopf 1994).

Other approaches to analysis of population trends from BBS data have produced similar results, in which grassland birds in particular appear to be declining in numbers. In their analysis of 31 years of BBS data, covering the period from 1966 through 1996, Peterjohn and Sauer (1999) propose that approximately

Table 4-3. Short-distance migrants that winter primarily in grasslands of the Southwestern United States or Northwestern Mexico with decreasing population trends during either the Breeding Bird Survey census periods 1966 to 1991 (26 years) and 1979 to 1991 (13 years; last half of census period) based on the Population Trend Ranks of Carter and Barker (1993). D indicates a decreasing trend, I an increasing trend, ---- indicates a trend that was not significant in either direction. Modified from DeSante and George (1994).

Species	26 years of BBS 1966-1991		Last 13 years of BBS 1979-1991	
	Trend	# of States	Trend	# of States
Burrowing owl	D	5	D	5
Short-eared owl	D	1	D	4
Common poorwill	D	1	---	3
Say's phoebe	D	10	---	10
Horned lark	D	11	D	11
Sprague's pipit	D	1	D	1
Loggerhead shrike	---	9	D	9
Chipping sparrow	D	10	D	11
Brewer's sparrow	D	7	D	7
Black-chinned sparrow	D	1	D	1
Black-throated sparrow	D	5	---	5
Baird's sparrow*	I	1	D	1
Grasshopper sparrow	D	6	---	6
Fox Sparrow	D	1	---	2
Song sparrow	D	8	---	8
White-crowned sparrow	D	5	D	7
Eastern meadowlark	D	1	D	1
Western meadowlark	D	10	---	11
Brewer's blackbird	D	8	---	9

* Species that increased during one time period but decreased during the other.

three-quarters (77 percent) of our grassland bird species have been declining in numbers since at least the 1960s, nearly half of them (48 percent) significantly so (table 4-4).

In response to the growing concerns over grassland bird numbers, many species are now considered priority targets for conservation by Partners In Flight (a State, Federal, and private partnership working to conserve birds in the Western Hemisphere) and the U.S. Fish and Wildlife Service (see table 4-1). The northern aplomado falcon and masked bobwhite are officially listed as endangered, and the lesser prairie chicken is a candidate for listing under the Endangered Species Act. Several other grassland birds have been considered for listing as well (for example, Baird's sparrow, mountain plover). The reasons for the declines of these grassland birds are myriad, but several factors appear to be common across many of the species.

The sections that follow present a brief overview of some of the most prevalent threats to grassland birds in the Southwest today, including various agents contributing to habitat loss, alteration and fragmentation; the effect of declining prairie dog populations; pesticide impacts; cowbird parasitism; and the consequences of haying and mowing practices.

Habitat Loss, Alteration, and Fragmentation

Habitat loss or destruction has had a major impact on grassland birds across the continental United States. Much recent media attention has focused on the loss of the tallgrass prairie in the Eastern United States and central Great Plains region. Because of its suitability for conversion to agriculture, it is estimated that the tallgrass prairie has been reduced to less than 2 percent of its original extent, and even less than that remains in some States (Samson and Knopf 1994). Although they have not received the same degree of popular coverage, the desert grasslands of the Southwest have also experienced dramatic losses over the past century. One study of desert grasslands in southern New Mexico suggests that although about 75 percent of this region was covered in grasslands prior to the late 1800s, by the late 1960s only 5 percent grassland coverage remained (York and Dick-Peddie 1969). Areas that had formerly been characterized as supporting "heavy growth" or "excellent stands" of grama grass (*Bouteloua* spp.) are now shrublands dominated by creosotebush (*Larrea tridentata*), mesquite (*Prosopis* spp.), or juniper (*Juniperus* spp.) (York and Dick-Peddie 1969). Although debate continues over the mechanism(s) that may have promoted this conversion, there is little question that the historic grasslands of the Southwest have experienced a rapid and dramatic invasion of woody plants and cacti since Euro-American settlement (Bahre 1995, Humphrey 1958, York and Dick-Peddie 1969). In assessing human impacts on the grasslands of southeastern Arizona, Bahre (1995:231) concludes "the two most dramatic changes in the grasslands are the extensive increases in woody shrubs and trees and the landscape fragmentation resulting from localized urban and rural settlements."

Although more of the shortgrass prairie remains in Western States (approximately 60 percent; Weaver and others 1996), these Southwestern grasslands are also slowly but steadily being lost to urban sprawl and conversion to agriculture, among other causes. Dick-Peddie (1993) proposes that the primary reason for loss of the shortgrass prairie in eastern New Mexico is farming (both dryland and irrigation), and secondarily due to urbanization and livestock grazing. Studies show that, at least in other grassland regions,

USDA Forest Service Gen. Tech. Rep. RMRS-GTR-135-vol. 2. 2005

77

Table 4-4. Continental trend estimates for North American grassland birds, based on Breeding Bird Survey data over a 31-year period from 1966 to 1996. Species with significant declines are in **bold type**; ** denotes a p-value of 0.01<p<0.05; *** denotes a p-value of < 0.01. Species in *italics* are those with decreasing trends that are not statistically significant. N is the number of BBS routes for which each species has been recorded. Modified from Peterjohn and Sauer (1999).

Species	1966-1996 Mean % change per year	p	N	Mean # of individuals per route
Northern harrier	-0.6	---	891	0.49
Ferruginous hawk	5.2	***	186	0.25
Ring-necked pheasant [Introduced]	-1.0	**	1206	7.30
Sharp-tailed grouse	0.3	---	124	0.55
Mountain plover	-2.7	**	33	0.31
Upland sandpiper	1.3	***	581	2.22
Long-billed curlew	-1.4	---	202	1.45
Short-eared owl	-2.8	---	132	0.21
Horned lark	-1.3	***	1805	27.02
Sedge wren	2.2	**	307	1.15
Sprague's pipit	-4.7	***	108	1.41
Dickcissel	-1.6	***	783	16.29
Cassin's sparrow	-2.5	***	203	16.31
Vesper sparrow	-0.8	**	1462	7.84
Lark bunting	-0.9	---	332	42.97
Savannah sparrow	-0.6	**	1477	8.40
Baird's sparrow	-1.6	---	115	1.87
Grasshopper sparrow	-3.6	***	1404	3.97
Henslow's sparrow	-8.8	***	149	0.15
LeConte's sparrow	1.4	---	154	0.73
McCown's longspur	1.1	---	59	4.57
Chestnut-collared longspur	-0.1	---	145	9.27
Bobolink	-1.6	***	1134	5.35
Eastern meadowlark	-2.6	***	1921	20.29
Western meadowlark	-0.6	**	1480	44.48

some birds may continue to utilize agricultural fields, particularly those used for haycropping, as surrogate grasslands (Herkert 1994; although useful for forage, hay fields have potential negative impacts on nest success; see below). However, as these fields are converted to rowcropping—a trend that has been increasing over the past 50 years—their habitat value is lost (Herkert 1994). Haycropping and rowcropping are far more common in the Great Plains region than in the Southwest. Agricultural fields in the Southwest are more likely to be planted in chile or cotton rather than grains and grasslike crops, and therefore are not as likely to provide suitable habitat for grassland birds.

Like the Great Plains, the grasslands of the Southwest have suffered significant direct losses of cover through various agents. This destruction of grassland habitats is one of the most prevalent factors implicated in the declines of Western grassland birds (DeSante and George 1994). Even if the changes are not permanent but potentially reversible, grassland systems may be altered or degraded to the point that they no longer provide suitable habitat for some species of birds, and are thus essentially "lost." Altered fire regimes, shrub encroachment, grazing by domestic stock, and introduced grasses are some of the factors that contribute to habitat alteration and loss through changes in species composition and habitat structure.

Altered Fire Regimes and Shrub Encroachment—Fire plays a critically important role in most grassland systems. Without periodic fires, woody plants begin to take hold and invade grasslands, converting them to shrublands or woodlands. The grasslands of the Southwest are no exception. Many researchers agree that historically fires were both common and extensive in the desert grasslands, and that these fires were instrumental in maintaining the integrity of these systems (Bahre 1991, Humphrey 1958, but see Dick-Peddie 1993). The exception may be grasslands dominated by black grama (*Bouteloua* *eriopoda*). Black grama suffers severe negative impacts from burning, indicating that this species is not fire-adapted and probably did not evolve under a history of frequent burning (Buffington and Herbel 1965, Dick-Peddie 1993).

The natural frequency and extent of grassland fires in the Southwest are believed to have declined dramatically since Euro-American settlement of the region in the late 1800s (Bahre 1991, 1995, Humphrey 1958). A review of the role of fire in desert grasslands reveals that the natural frequency of fire in these systems was probably on the order of every 7 to 10 years (McPherson 1995 and references therein). Fires occurring on this cycle are believed to be sufficient to prevent the establishment of woody plants by killing seeds on the surface and preventing woody plants from reaching the age where resprouting is possible (McPherson 1995). Although fires eliminate grass cover in the short term, in the long term grasses are rejuvenated by the occurrence of fire and benefit from the elimination of woody plants. The timing of fires is also important. Fire in the early summer, when the growth of many perennials is just beginning, can negatively impact warm season grasses, whereas these same grasses are tolerant of fire during the dormant season (McPherson 1995).

Although many factors contribute to fire regimes, perhaps the most important change that has resulted in decreased fire frequency and intensity in the Southwest is the lack of fine fuels to carry the fires (Humphrey 1958, McPherson 1995). Historically, the timing of this change corresponded with the widespread increase in livestock grazing in the Southwest after 1880. At this time, stocking rates reached record levels, and overgrazing was actually encouraged to reduce the fire hazard and encourage the growth of trees (Bahre 1991, Leopold 1924, as cited in McPherson 1995). Today, fragmentation from roads and suburban developments also acts to contain the spread of extensive wildfires (Bahre 1995, McPherson 1995). These changes in the frequency and intensity of natural fire regimes have doubtless contributed to the widespread conversion of Southwestern grasslands to shrublands (Archer 1989, Brown 1982, Humphrey 1958). Grazing by livestock and the eradication of prairie dogs may also play a role in increasing woody plant cover, as discussed below.

The net result of the conversion of grasslands to shrublands is a loss of habitat for grassland birds such as grasshopper sparrows that avoid areas with woody plant cover. Changes in fire regimes also impact the physical structure and plant species composition of grasslands, thereby impacting the potential habitat or food resources utilized by grassland birds (McPherson 1995). Species that use areas of bare ground or short grass cover, such as horned larks or lark sparrows, are negatively impacted by a reduction in fire frequencies.

Vesper sparrows and other species that depend upon increases in seed-producing plants following fires also suffer negative consequences from fewer fires. Some grassland birds, such as Cassin's sparrows, do benefit from an increased shrub component in their habitat. However, as the invasion of woody plants has now become so extensive throughout the grasslands of the Southwest, it is the more specialized pure grassland endemics that will be suffering the negative impacts of this form of habitat loss.

To further complicate matters, McPherson (1995) notes that once woody plants come to dominate a grassland system, the reintroduction of fire alone is insufficient to return it to its original composition. The use of herbicides or mechanical controls must be introduced to restore grassland habitat after woody plants have become established. Also, some exotic grasses such as Lehmann lovegrass increase after fire, and such grasses provide more fine fuel to carry fires than native species of grasses (Cox and others 1984). This may result in a positive feedback loop, in which introduced grasses play a beneficial role in terms of increasing fire frequency, yet also have the negative consequences of extending the coverage of the less-desirable exotic grasses as well as increasing the intensity of fire (Anable and others 1992, see "Exotic Grasses," below).

Livestock Grazing—Livestock grazing is the predominant land use in the Western States. More than 70 percent of the land area in the West (11 States, from Montana, Wyoming, Colorado, and New Mexico westward) is grazed by livestock, predominantly cattle, including wilderness areas, wildlife refuges, National Forests, and some National Parks (Fleischner 1994 and references therein). Inappropriate livestock grazing is widely believed to be one of the greatest sources of habitat degradation in the West (for example, Noss and Cooperrider 1994), leading to widespread declines in the native wildlife of North American grasslands (Fleischner 1994). However, the impacts of grazing vary widely according to grazing intensity or stocking rates, season of grazing, the species of livestock involved, and the degree of active management, such as pasture rotation (Fleischner 1994, Jones 2000). Although much has been written about the overall ecological impacts of grazing (for example, Fleischner 1994, Hobbs and Huenneke 1992, Noss and Cooperrider 1994, Saab and others 1995, Jones 2000), this discussion will only briefly review the impacts of grazing with respect to grassland birds of the Southwestern States.

The response of grassland birds to livestock grazing varies widely according to the species of bird in question, the type of habitat being grazed, and the ecological history of the region. In general, birds are not directly affected by the presence of livestock per se, but rather experience the more indirect effects of

USDA Forest Service Gen. Tech. Rep. RMRS-GTR-135-vol. 2. 2005

79

grazing impacts on grassland vegetation and ecosystem dynamics (Bock and Webb 1984; the exception is ground-nesting birds, which may be directly impacted by livestock during the breeding season; see below). The shortgrass prairie region was historically grazed by large numbers of native herbivores, primarily bison, pronghorn, and prairie dogs. As bison and pronghorn preferentially graze near prairie dog towns, this resulted in concentrating areas of disturbance due to heavy grazing and trampling, resulting in a mosaic of microhabitats ranging from areas of bare ground to dense concentrations of grasses (Coppock and others 1983, Knopf 1996a, Krueger 1986). Native birds of the shortgrass prairie evolved within this grazed mosaic, and the various species adapted to different aspects of the landscape or evolved to utilize a mixture of micro-habitat types (for example, for nesting versus foraging). Birds such as mountain plovers or McCown's longspurs will use areas of excessive grazing pressure (Knopf and Miller 1994, Warner 1994), while species such as long-billed curlews, lark buntings, and Sprague's pipits use shortgrass landscapes that have been heavily grazed but require a mixture of interspersed taller grasses for nesting (Bicak and others 1982, Finch and others 1987, Kantrud 1981). Although historically grazing provided such a mixture of conditions, most current livestock grazing regimes do not result in the heterogeneous grassland structure that was produced by native herbivores. Bison were nomadic and grazed over large expanses of the landscape. As bison were eliminated and livestock came to dominate the Western range in the late 1800s, homesteaders began to fence the grasslands, reducing the natural variability in the grazing behavior of the livestock and resulting in standardized grazing intensities and relatively homogeneous structure of the grasslands, thereby eliminating the habitat heterogeneity required by many grassland birds (Knopf 1996b).

The blue grama (*Bouteloua gracilis*) and buffalo grass (*Buchloe dactyloides*) of the shortgrass prairie coevolved with bison and are adapted to heavy grazing pressure; these grasses thrive under such conditions by reproducing both sexually and by tillering (Knopf 1994). By contrast, the desert grasslands of the Southwest probably evolved in the absence of large herds of grazing ungulates. Most evidence points to an absence of large herds of bison west of the Rockies (Durrant 1970, Gustafson 1972, as cited in Mack and Thompson 1982). The arid grasslands of the Southwest tend to be dominated by caespitose bunchgrasses, which are highly susceptible to grazing by ungulates and which respond in a manner quite distinctive from the grasses of the shortgrass prairie (Daubenmire 1970, Dyer 1979, Tisdale 1961). Whereas grazed areas in the shortgrass prairie tend to be recolonized by predominantly native plants (Mack and Thompson 1982 and references

therein), the morphological and physiological features of bunch grasses render them incapable of recovering quickly from grazing. Continuous grazing in desert grasslands leads to changes in species composition, where bunch grasses are replaced by sod-forming grasses or annuals (Brown 1982), or invaded by Eurasian weeds (Mack and Thompson 1982, see also Milchunas and others 1988). Furthermore, the soils of these grasslands that evolved with few native grazers are protected by a cryptogamic crust of mosses, lichens, and liverworts; this crust can be permanently destroyed by the trampling of large ungulates, producing sites for the establishment of exotic species (Daubenmire 1970, Mack and Thompson 1982).

Grazing has also been implicated in the widespread increase in woody plant cover witnessed in Southwestern grasslands (Bahre 1995, Dick-Peddie 1993, Humphrey 1958, York and Dick-Peddie 1969). Grazing by livestock encourages invasion by woody plants by reducing the fine fuels available for fire and by facilitating the dispersal and establishment of propagules of woody invaders (Archer 1989, Bock and Bock 1987, 1988, Hobbs and Huenneke 1992, Humphrey 1987). Livestock may also promote the growth of woody vegetation by selectively grazing on the more palatable species of grasses and herbs, effectively reducing competition within the plant community for the less palatable woody plants (Humphrey 1958). Many Southwestern grasslands subjected to livestock grazing, in combination with drought, have thus been degraded and transformed to landscapes of desert scrub (Buffington and Herbel 1965, Neilson 1986, Schlesinger and others 1990). This change in vegetation composition and structure greatly affects the suitability of the habitat for native grassland birds, as well as for other animal species.

Birds that prefer excessively grazed areas, such as horned larks, tend to respond positively to grazing wherever they are found (Saab and others 1995). For other species, it depends on the region of interest. Grasshopper sparrows or lark buntings, for example, may respond positively to moderate levels of grazing in tallgrass prairies, but show negative effects when the grazing takes place in shortgrass prairies or desert grasslands (Saab and others 1995 and references therein). Ferruginous hawks respond differentially to grazing depending on the stage of life cycle in question; grazing benefits these hawks by opening up grasslands for foraging, but they prefer ungrazed areas with more substantial cover for nesting (Saab and others 1995). Several species of grassland birds have responded negatively to grazing wherever they have been studied; these include the common yellowthroat and Botteri's, Cassin's, savannah, Baird's, and Henslow's sparrows (Saab and others 1995). Ground-nesting species are especially vulnerable in areas that are grazed. Temple

80

USDA Forest Service Gen. Tech. Rep. RMRS-GTR-135-vol. 2. 2005

and others (1999) report that 64 percent of nests were lost when cattle were introduced into a pasture with good grass cover, and experiments with artificial ground nests have similarly demonstrated a high rate of nest loss from trampling and nest abandonment due to cattle disturbance (Koerth and others 1983, Paine and others 1996). Table 4-5 shows the observed responses of various species of neotropical migratory birds to cattle grazing in Southwestern grasslands.

Exotic Grasses—In Arizona, grasslands that have been seeded with Lehmann and Boer lovegrass (Eragrostis lehmanniana and E. curvula var. conferta), exotic grasses used for cattle forage, have been described as "biologically sterile" (Bock and others 1986:462). Twenty-six native species (10 plants, five birds, three rodents, and eight grasshoppers) were found to be significantly more abundant in native grasslands; only three native species (one bird, one rodent, and one grasshopper) were more common in the grasslands dominated by the African lovegrasses. Bock and others (1986:462) explain: "Indigenous animals appear to have evolved specific dependencies on the native flora and/or its associated fauna, insofar as most find the exotic grasslands far less inhabitable."

This is a mounting problem in the West, as exotic grasses that are either intentionally introduced or invade following disturbance (for example, cheatgrass

Bromus tectorum and crested wheatgrass *Agropyron cristatum*) may spread extremely quickly and displace native grasses (Mack 1981, Marlette and Anderson 1986). Exotics such as Lehmann lovegrass also increase in response to grazing, as livestock tend to preferentially forage on the native grasses, reducing competition for the lovegrasses (Bahre 1995 and references therein). The increase of such exotics may have further ramifications as well, as they alter the natural fire regimes and lead to further ecological changes in the system, as discussed above (for example, Anable and others 1992, Cox and others 1990). This issue is discussed in more detail in chapter 2 of this volume.

Habitat Fragmentation—Fragmentation of habitats has been called "one of the greatest threats to biodiversity worldwide" (Noss and Cooperrider 1994:51). There are essentially three components to habitat fragmentation. First, any fragmentation by processes such as the building of roads or urban development necessarily results in the outright loss of some portion of the original habitat. The second component is fragmentation per se, in which the remaining habitat is reduced to small, isolated patches across the landscape. "Edge effects" make up the third component of fragmentation. These effects refer to the alteration of physical processes and biotic interactions

Table 4-5. Response of neotropical migratory birds to grazing on grassland types found in the Western United States (semidesert, shortgrass, and mixed grassland types). Note that due to a paucity of data from the Southwest, many of the responses reported here are based on studies from different geographical regions. Modified from Saab and others (1995).

Species	Region	Grassland type	Grazing intensity[a]	Effect[b]	Reference
Northern harrier	S. Dakota	Mixed grass	Moderate	-	Duebbert and Lokemoen 1977
	N. Plains	Mixed grass	Variable	-	Kantrud and Kologiski 1982
Ferruginous hawk	N. Plains	Mixed grass	Variable	+	Kantrud and Kologiski 1982
	S. Dakota	Mixed grass		+	Lokemoen and Duebbert 1976
Killdeer	Colorado	Shortgrass	Heavy	+	Ryder 1980
	N. Plains	Mixed grass	Moderate, heavy	+	Kantrud and Kologiski 1982
Mountain plover	Colorado	Shortgrass	Heavy	+	Graul 1975
	Colorado	Shortgrass	Heavy	+	Ryder 1980
	N. Plains	Mixed grass	Moderate	0	Kantrud and Kologiski 1982
	N. Plains	Mixed grass	Heavy	+	Kantrud and Kologiski 1982
Long-billed curlew	Colorado	Shortgrass	Heavy	+	Ryder 1980
	N. Plains	Mixed grass	Moderate, heavy	0	Kantrud and Kologiski 1982
Mourning dove	S. Arizona	Semidesert	Moderate	+	Bock and others 1984
	Colorado	Shortgrass	Heavy	0	Ryder 1980
	N. Plains	Mixed grass	Heavy	Mixed	Kantrud and Kologiski 1982
Burrowing owl	N. Plains	Mixed grass	Moderate	0	Kantrud and Kologiski 1982
	N. Plains	Mixed grass	Heavy	+	Kantrud and Kologiski 1982
Short-eared owl	S. Dakota	Mixed grass	Moderate	-	Duebbert and Lokemoen 1977
	N. Plains	Mixed grass	Variable	-	Kantrud and Higgins 1992
Common nighthawk	Colorado	Shortgrass	Heavy	+	Ryder 1980
	N. Plains	Mixed grass	Moderate	0	Kantrud and Kologiski 1982
	N. Plains	Mixed grass	Heavy	+	Kantrud and Kologiski 1982

USDA Forest Service Gen. Tech. Rep. RMRS-GTR-135-vol. 2. 2005

81

Table 4-5. *Continued.*

Species	Region	Grassland type	Grazing intensity[a]	Effect[b]	Reference
Horned lark	S. Arizona	Semidesert	Moderate	+	Bock and others 1984
	Colorado	Shortgrass	Heavy	+	Ryder 1980
	Plains	Shortgrass	Heavy	+	Wiens 1973
	Saskatchewan	Mixed/short		+	Maher 1979
	Alberta	Mixed grass	Heavy	+	Owens and Myres 1973
	S. Dakota	Mixed grass	Heavy	+	Wiens 1973
	N. Plains	Mixed grass	Moderate, heavy	+	Kantrud and Kologiski 1982
Northern mockingbird	S. Arizona	Semidesert	Moderate	+	Bock and others 1984
Sprague's pipit	N. Plains	Mixed grass	Moderate	0	Kantrud and Kologiski 1982
	N. Plains	Mixed grass	Heavy	-	Kantrud and Kologiski 1982
	Saskatchewan	Mixed/short		-	Maher 1979
	Alberta	Mixed grass	Heavy	-	Owens and Myres 1973
Botteri's sparrow	S. Arizona	Semidesert	Moderate	-	Webb and Bock 1990
Cassin's sparrow	S. Arizona	Semidesert	Moderate	-	Bock and Bock 1988
Brewer's sparrow	S. Arizona	Semidesert	Moderate	+	Bock and others 1984
	Colorado	Shortgrass	Heavy	-	Ryder 1980
	N. Plains	Mixed grass	Moderate	0	Kantrud and Kologiski 1982
	N. Plains	Mixed grass	Heavy	-	Kantrud and Kologiski 1982
Vesper sparrow	S. Arizona	Semidesert	Moderate	0	Bock and others 1984
	Alberta	Mixed grass	Heavy	+	Owens and Myres 1973
	N. Plains	Mixed grass	Moderate	0	Kantrud and Kologiski 1982
Lark sparrow	S. Arizona	Semidesert	Moderate		Bock and others 1984
Black-throated sparrow	S. Arizona	Semidesert	Moderate	+	Bock and others 1984
Lark bunting	N. Texas	Shortgrass	Heavy	-	Wiens 1973
	Colorado	Shortgrass	Heavy	-	Ryder 1980
	N. Plains	Mixed grass	Moderate	0	Kantrud and Kologiski 1982
	N. Plains	Mixed grass	Heavy	0	Kantrud and Kologiski 1982
Savannah sparrow	Saskatchewan	Mixed/short		-	Maher 1979
	Alberta	Mixed grass	Heavy	-	Owen and Myres 1973
Baird's sparrow	Saskatchewan	Mixed/short		-	Maher 1979
	Alberta	Mixed grass	Heavy	-	Owen and Myres 1973
	N. Plains	Mixed grass	Moderate, Heavy	-	Kantrud and Kologiski 1982
Grasshopper sparrow	S. Arizona	Semidesert	Moderate	-	Bock and others 1984
	Colorado	Shortgrass	Heavy	-	Ryder 1980
	N. Texas	Shortgrass	Heavy	-	Wiens 1973
	S. Dakota	Mixed grass	Heavy	-	Wiens 1973
	N. Plains	Mixed grass	Moderate, Heavy	-	Kantrud and Kologiski 1982
Mccown's longspur	Colorado	Shortgrass	Heavy	+	Ryder 1980
	Saskatchewan	Mixed/short		+	Maher 1979
	N. Plains	Mixed grass	Moderate, Heavy	+	Kantrud and Kologiski 1982
Chestnut-collared longspur	S. Arizona	Semidesert	Moderate	+	Bock and Bock 1988
	Colorado	Shortgrass	Heavy	0	Ryder 1980
	Saskatchewan	Mixed/short		+	Maher 1979
	Alberta	Mixed grass	Heavy	-	Owens and Myres 1973
	N. Plains	Mixed grass	Moderate, Heavy	0	Kantrud and Kologiski 1982
Bobolink	N. Plains	Mixed grass	Moderate, Heavy	-	Kantrud and Kologiski 1982
Eastern meadowlark	S. Arizona	Semidesert	Moderate	0	Bock et al. 1984
Western meadowlark	Colorado	Shortgrass	Heavy	-	Ryder 1980
	N. Texas	Shortgrass	Heavy	-	Wiens 1973
	Saskatchewan	Mixed/short		-	Maher 1979
	Alberta	Mixed grass	Heavy	0	Owens and Myres 1973
	S. Dakota	Mixed grass	Heavy	-	Wiens 1973
	N. Plains	Mixed grass	Moderate	0	Kantrud and Kologiski 1982
	N. Plains	Mixed grass	Heavy	-	Kantrud and Kologiski 1982
Brown-headed cowbird	N. Plains	Mixed grass	Moderate, heavy	0	Kantrud and Kologiski 1982

[a] Grazing intensity as reported by original authors; where more than one level of intensity is reported, both were tested separately and found to have the same effect.
[b] Grazing effects on abundance: + = increase, - = decrease, 0 = no effect.

that result from the creation of habitat edges in an environment where there formerly were none.

Habitat fragmentation has been most thoroughly studied for forest-dwelling birds (for example, Lovejoy and others 1986, Robinson and others 1995b), but we are slowly accumulating information on the impacts of fragmentation on grassland birds (Bock and others 1999, Herkert 1994, Vickery and others 1994). Many grassland nesting species appear to have large area requirements, and simply are not found utilizing grasslands that are less than a particular area in extent; these are so called "area-sensitive" species. Such birds will not nest in habitat fragments below a certain threshold size, even if the fragment is large enough to hold several average-sized nesting territories and appears to be of suitable quality (Herkert 1994, O'Leary and Nyberg 2000, Samson 1980, Vickery and others 1994). The minimum area requirements vary widely among species: eastern meadowlarks may require only 5 ha, savannah sparrows are not found in fragments less than 40 ha, and greater prairie-chickens regularly breed in fragments of at least 160 ha (Herkert 1994, Samson 1980, Westemeier 1985).

Grassland birds also appear to avoid nesting close to habitat edges; such edges may be created by roads, treelines, fences, or urban development. Of the eight grassland nesting birds they studied, Bock and others (1999) found that five were significantly more abundant in interior plots (greater than 200 m from the suburban edge) than in edge plots adjacent to suburban areas, and two others were more abundant in the interior plots, although not significantly so. The five species that avoided nesting in the edge are all declining grassland species: vesper sparrow, savannah sparrow, grasshopper sparrow, bobolink, and western meadowlark. In contrast, the edge plots held nearly five times the abundance of common and/or exotic bird species: robins, starlings, grackles, house finches, and house sparrows (Bock and others 1999). This demonstrates a common trend witnessed along habitat edges: native grassland endemics have declined, while introduced and "weedy" or more cosmopolitan species have dramatically increased (Knopf 1994). As an example, Yahner (1983) found that of 47 bird species observed using shelterbelts in western Minnesota, only three were species that were typical of the historical grasslands found in that area.

In addition to opening up grasslands to potential invasion by opportunistic species, the creation of edges results in increased levels of predation and parasitism for nesting birds. The addition of trees, fences, telephone poles, and other vertical structures in a grassland landscape provide cover and perches for predators, leading to increased rates of predation along edges (Burger and others 1994, Gates and Gysel 1978, Johnson and Temple 1990, Møller 1989, Ratti and

Reese 1988, Winter and others 2000). Urban development leads to the introduction of associated "urban" predators, such as skunks, raccoons, and cats (Wilcove 1985). Perches along edges also serve as "lookout sites" for brown-headed cowbirds, a critical habitat feature required by this nest parasite to successfully locate potential host nests in grasslands (Norman and Robertson 1975). Levels of cowbird parasitism are significantly greater for grassland birds nesting near edges, resulting in reduced nest productivity or even complete nest failure (Best 1978, Johnson and Temple 1986, 1990, Wray and others 1982). Dickcissels, for example, are known to suffer negative consequences from brown-headed cowbird parasitism (Zimmerman 1983). In areas of urban or surburban development, human disturbance may also play a role in the reduced density of grassland nesting birds in fragmented edge habitats (Knight and Gutzwiller 1995). Meadowlarks are an example of grassland breeding birds that are sensitive to disturbance at the nest (Lanyon 1995).

Haying and Mowing

The production and harvesting of hay is another land use that has increased with the development of the livestock industry. The harvesting of wild hay was once a common and economically viable practice in some Southwestern grasslands (Bahre 1987) but is now relatively limited in this region. A brief discussion of the effects of haying and mowing is included here to address those areas of the Southwest that may still engage in these practices.

As native grasslands have disappeared, many grassland birds have been forced to utilize "artificial" grassland habitats for nesting and for foraging; lands managed to produce forage for livestock are often attractive to grassland nesting birds (Sample 1989, as cited in Temple and others 1999). In hayfields that are mowed, birds are rarely successful in raising young. Birds are attracted to these hayfields and initiate nesting, but particularly due to trends toward earlier, more frequent mowing (Ratti and Scott 1991, Rodenhouse and others 1993, Ryan 1986), nests are destroyed or territories abandoned before the young birds fledge (Beintema and Muskens 1987, Bollinger and others 1990, Bryan and Best 1994, Frawley and Best 1991, Warner and Etter 1989). If forage crops are being raised, nests may be trampled or abandoned by the parents due to excessive disturbance when cattle densities are too high (Koerth and others 1983, Paine and others 1996). Pastures or hayfields thus often tend to act as population "sinks," because breeding birds are attracted to them but are doomed to failure in their reproductive efforts (Temple and others 1999).

The impact of haying and mowing on grassland nesting birds is determined by the timing and frequency

USDA Forest Service Gen. Tech. Rep. RMRS-GTR-135-vol. 2. 2005

83

of such practices, and upon the habitat preference of the species in question. Bobolinks and savannah sparrows are negatively impacted in areas that are mowed (Bollinger and others 1990, Warner 1992), whereas those that prefer areas of short vegetation for nesting, such as horned larks or vesper sparrows, may increase as long as the mowing does not coincide with the nesting cycle (Laursen 1981).

Hayfields are typically cut at least once per year, with two to four cuts over the season being common. Harvests during May and June, the peak breeding season for most grassland nesting birds, are particularly harmful. In one study in New York, the production of bobolink fledglings in a hayfield was estimated to be reduced by 40 percent by mowing practices (Bollinger and others 1990). Mowing is increasingly being considered one of the most probable factors contributing to the decline of grassland nesting birds, at least in some areas (Bollinger and others 1990, Frawley and Best 1991).

Direct Mortality and Indirect Effects of Pesticides

As more of the nation's grasslands are converted to agriculture, increasing numbers of our grassland birds that use agricultural fields are exposed to potentially harmful chemicals. Concerns over the possibly lethal effects of pesticides first came to light in the early 1960s, when populations of birds such as brown pelicans and peregrine falcons were plummeting as a result of eggshell thinning caused by DDE, a byproduct of the popular organochlorine pesticide DDT (Anderson and Hickey 1972). Although the use of DDT was banned in the United States in 1972, as were most chlorinated insecticides, many of these compounds continue to be used in Latin America and South America, and elevated contaminant burdens continue to be found in North American birds that migrate to the neotropics for the winter (DeWeese and others 1986, Henny and others 1982, Johnston 1975, White and others 1981). In addition, "hot spots" of contamination persist. In New Mexico and Texas, for example, contamination from DDE residues continues to negatively impact reproduction in birds (White and Krynitsky 1986). Today most of the pesticides used in the United States are organophosphates and carbamates (Szmedra 1991). Despite the near extinctions of some species of birds from DDT, pesticide usage has increased dramatically since the 1960s. In 1964, 366 million lb of pesticides were used in agricultural applications in the United States; by 1997, that figure had more than doubled to 770 million lb a year (Aspelin and Grube 1999). Table 4-6 lists the leading pesticides causing avian mortalities in the United States.

Pesticides may affect birds in many ways. Acute mortality is, of course, the most obvious negative impact (Grue and others 1983). The pesticide carbofuran, for example, is estimated to kill between 1 and 2 million birds a year in the United States (EPA 1989). The toxicity of a pesticide may vary according to its form; birds have been found to be particularly susceptible to the ingestion of insecticide-treated seed and insecticide granules (Pimentel and others 1992). Direct mortality is often difficult to assess, however, as the bodies of birds that have died from poisoning or other causes are generally not found. Studies have shown that, in general, most bird carcasses (62 to 92 percent) are scavenged and disappear within 24 hours of death (Balcomb 1986, Wobeser and Wobeser 1992). In addition, birds that have been poisoned often do not die immediately but will move from the site of poisoning to take cover (Vyas 1999 and references therein); therefore, the deaths—if noticed—are not necessarily associated with any particular pesticide application event. However, there are many documented incidents in which grassland birds have been found accidentally poisoned by pesticides (for example, Grue and others 1983, Hill and Fleming 1982, McLeod 1967). Horned larks—one of the most common grassland birds in the United States—have been found killed by both carbamate pesticides (Stone 1979) and organophosphorous compounds (Beason 1995, DeWeese and others 1983). Although acute mortality has not been observed, some researchers have expressed concern over the possible negative impacts of the endangered aplomado falcon preying on bird species in the Lower Rio Grande Valley that have elevated levels of DDE and other contaminants (Mora and others 1997). And of course, the impacts of pesticides on migratory birds are not restricted to events that occur in the United States. From 1995 to 1996, nearly 6,000 wintering Swainson's hawks perished in Argentina as the result of ingesting monocrotophos, an organophosphate insecticide used to control grasshoppers, a favorite prey item of the hawk (DiSilvestro 1996). In addition, some North American grassland birds are intentionally poisoned while on their wintering grounds in South America, where they are considered to be agricultural pests (for example, dickcissels; Basili and Temple 1999).

Far exceeding the direct effects of acute mortality from pesticide exposure are the sublethal effects that are more likely to contribute to long-term population declines in grassland birds and other species (Grue and others 1997). Avian exposure to organophosphates and carbamate insecticides have been found to produce a variety of physiological and behavioral deficiencies, including decreased body weight (Grue and Shipley 1984), lethargic behavior (Hart 1993), reduced territorial maintenance (Busby and others 1990), decreased clutch size (Grue and others 1997 and references therein), reduced parental attentiveness (Busby and others 1990), decreased nestling growth

84

USDA Forest Service Gen. Tech. Rep. RMRS-GTR-135-vol. 2. 2005

Table 4-6. Leading pesticides causing avian mortalities in the United States. Fifty-five percent of all incidents reported are associated with two insecticides, Carbofuran and Diazinon. Based on the Ecological Incident Information System (EIIS) as of 1999, as reported by the American Bird Conservancy (2001). See also Mastrota (1999).

Active ingredient	Trade name	# of avian incidents in EIIS		# of carcasses	Common uses	Notes
		Total	Probable[a]			
Carbofuran	Furadan	352	241	12,341	Grapes, corn, alfalfa	Most granular uses cancelled in 1991
Diazinon	Diazinon, Spectracide	267	165	4,434	Lawns and turf	Uses cancelled on golf courses in 1989
Chlordane	Chlordane, Termide	70			Termiticide	Cancelled in 1987
Fenthion	Baytex, Baycide	58	47	5,545	Avicide, mosquito control	Use as avicide cancelled in 1999
Chlorpyrifos	Dursban, Lorsban	57	37		Termiticide, lawn and turf	
Brodifacoum	Havoc, Talon	47	47		Rodent control	
Parathion	Parathion, Folidol	45		2,457	Small grains, sunflower, alfalfa	
Famphur	Warbex	31			Livestock	

[a] includes those incidents that were convincingly linked to pesticide use, and not linked to pesticide misuse.

rates (Patnode and White 1991), increased postfledging mortality (Hooper and others 1990), reduced return rates to breeding grounds (Millikin and Smith 1990), and an inability to thermoregulate properly, resulting in hypothermia (Grue and others 1997). There are also more indirect effects on bird populations, such as a reduction in prey abundance for insectivorous species (DeWeese and others 1979, Hunter and Witham 1985, Moulding 1976).

Although pesticide usage on agricultural fields may be contributing to the observed declines in North American grassland birds, we do not currently have adequate data to say so definitively (Gard and Hooper 1995). However, one estimate proposes that as many as 67 million birds are killed by pesticides on farmlands in the United States every year (Pimentel and others 1992); that estimate recently increased to 72 million annually (Pimentel 2001). Birds are more sensitive to contaminants than other wildlife (Grue and others 1983), and as the breeding season for most birds is during the time of peak insect abundance to provide food for their chicks, it also unfortunately coincides with the time of greatest pesticide usage (Gard and Hooper 1995). Some crops, such as apples and cotton, may be sprayed as many as 20 times per growing season (Pimentel and others 1991). From these facts and the known negative impacts of pesticides on birds, both in terms of acute mortality and long-term sublethal effects, we can infer that grassland birds nesting in agricultural areas are at high risk. More research is badly needed to more exactly assess any possible link between agricultural pesticide use and declines in grassland birds.

Loss of Prairie Dog Colonies

The prairie dog is considered a "keystone" species, a species that has a large overall effect on a community or ecosystem disproportionate to its abundance (Kotliar and others 1999, Power and others 1996). The activities of these burrowing animals have a dramatic impact on the patch dynamics and ecosystem function of the Western grasslands that they inhabit. Prairie dog disturbances impact the physical and chemical properties of the soil, alter vegetational structure, affect plant species composition, and improve the nutrient value of plants growing in the vicinity of their colonies (O'Meilia and others 1982 and references therein, Whicker and Detling 1988). Active prairie dog towns contribute to increased biological diversity by supporting a different complement of species compared to areas unoccupied by prairie dogs (Agnew and others 1986, Mellink and Madrigal 1993, O'Meilia and others 1982). Furthermore, several vertebrate species are considered highly dependent upon prairie dogs either as prey or for the habitat provided by their colonies, including the endangered black-footed ferret *Mustela nigripes* (see Kotliar and others 1999 for an excellent review).

Once a dominant force in the grasslands of the Western United States, the ecological impact of the prairie dog on these systems has nearly been extinguished. Up until the early 1900s, prairie dog colonies were estimated to cover hundreds of millions of acres

USDA Forest Service Gen. Tech. Rep. RMRS-GTR-135-vol. 2. 2005

85

of shortgrass prairie and desert grasslands west of the Great Plains (Anderson and others 1986). Today prairie dogs are estimated to persist on a mere 2 percent of their former range (Anderson and others 1986, Miller and others 1994). One species, the Utah prairie dog (*Cynomys parvidens*) is listed as threatened, and the black-tailed prairie dog *C. ludovicianus*, formerly the most abundant and widespread of the five species of prairie dogs in North America, has been considered for listing (USFWS 2000). The population numbers of the black-tailed prairie dog are estimated to have been reduced by 98 percent, and the species may occupy as little as 0.5 percent of its original range (Mac and others 1998, as cited in USFWS 2000). Although the conversion of native prairie habitat to other land uses may have contributed to some degree, undoubtedly the greatest single factor in the loss of prairie dogs has been the concerted effort by both Federal and State government agencies to exterminate these animals for the benefit of the livestock industry (Mulhern and Knowles 1996, Parmenter and Van Devender 1995).

The campaign to eradicate prairie dogs from Western grasslands began in earnest following the release of a Department of Agriculture report suggesting that the presence of prairie dogs may reduce range productivity by 50 to 75 percent (Merriam 1902). The U.S. Biological Survey responded with a massive poisoning campaign under the auspices of its Predator and Rodent Control program. Aiming to reduce competition with livestock, millions of acres of prairie dog colonies were poisoned, and shooting of prairie dogs was encouraged across their range (Bell 1921, Mulhern and Knowles 1996, Parmenter and Van Devender 1995, Van Pelt 1999). Fear of sylvatic plague buoyed these efforts after the bacterium was discovered in black-tailed prairie dogs in Texas in the 1940s (Cully 1989, Mulhern and Knowles 1996). In some States, annual extermination of prairie dogs on State and privately owned lands was a legal requirement. Nebraska, for example, only recently repealed this mandate in 1995 (Van Pelt 1999).

The black-tailed prairie dog and the Gunnison's prairie dog *C. gunnisoni* are the two species that inhabit the grasslands of Arizona and New Mexico. Described as occurring in "immense colonies" in Arizona in 1885 (Mearns 1907), the Arizona prairie dog *C.l. arizonensis*, a subspecies of the black-tailed prairie dog, was largely extirpated from that State by 1938; one small single colony survived until 1960 (Van Pelt 1999). In New Mexico, the range of the black-tailed prairie dog has been reduced by at least 25 percent (Hubbard and Schmitt 1984). In the Animas Valley, for example, biologists from the Museum of Southwestern Biology did not observe one single prairie dog between the years 1955 and 1972 (Findley 1987). Yet in 1908 Vernon Bailey had described this same area as an almost continuous prairie dog town for its length and breadth, estimating that over 6 million prairie dogs inhabited the valley (Bailey 1932).

As a keystone species, the elimination of the prairie dog has had far-reaching repercussions, including declines in several species of grassland birds. In a critical review of the evidence, Kotliar and others (1999) propose that nine vertebrate species may be considered to be truly dependent upon prairie dogs. Five of these nine species are grassland birds: the mountain plover, burrowing owl, ferruginous hawk, golden eagle, and horned lark (the others are the black-footed ferret, swift fox *Vulpes velox*, deer mouse *Peromyscus maniculatus*, and northern grasshopper mouse *Onychomys leucogaster*). For all of these species except the horned lark, evidence shows that local or landscape-level declines have closely corresponded with declines in prairie dog populations (Kotliar and others 1999 and references therein). For these birds, prairie dogs may serve as primary prey items (ferruginous hawks and golden eagles) or their activities may provide critical habitat (nest burrows for burrowing owls, preferred areas of short vegetation and/or bare ground for mountain plovers and horned larks). The decline of prairie dog populations was one of the key factors mentioned in the proposal to list the mountain plover as a threatened species (USFWS 1999a) and has been clearly linked with local declines in burrowing owls and ferruginous hawks (Cully 1991, Desmond and others 2000).

Many other species of grassland birds have been reported in association with prairie dog colonies as well. In the largest complex of prairie dog colonies remaining in Mexico, Manzano-Fischer and others (1999) report that 31 percent of the birds observed on the colonies are grassland specialists; this includes a new record for wintering mountain plovers in the State of Chihuahua. Numerous avian species have been recorded as prairie dog associates, well beyond the five birds named earlier (for example, Agnew and others 1986, Sharps and Uresk 1990), but at present there is not enough evidence to determine the degree of their dependence and the potential impact of the elimination of prairie dogs on their populations (Kotliar and others 1999).

Notwithstanding the drastic declines already witnessed in prairie dog numbers and the evidence of a cascade effect on other species, prairie dogs today are still widely considered to be vermin and enjoy little in the way of legal safeguards (Van Pelt 1999). This is in spite of more recent evidence that the level of competition between prairie dogs and livestock is more likely on the order of 4 to 7 percent (Uresk and Paulson 1988, as cited in Miller and others 1994), and that there is no significant difference in the market weight of steers whether they graze in conjunction with prairie dogs or not (O'Meilia and others 1982), although it should be noted that the statistically insignificant weight difference did result in an economic loss. Forage on prairie dog colonies is of higher quality, and the increased nutritional value of herbage on colonies may act to offset any decrease in biomass as a result of clipping by prairie dogs (Holland and Detling 1990, O'Meilia and others 1982 and references therein). Bison, elk, pronghorn, and livestock preferentially graze on prairie dog colonies, presumably because of the increased value and palatability of the herbage there (Coppock and others 1983, Knowles 1986, Krueger 1986, Wydeven and Dahlgren 1985). Prairie dogs also play an important role in inhibiting the growth of woody invaders such as mesquite *Prosopis* spp. (Koford 1958, Weltzin and others 1997). The elimination of prairie dogs may be partially responsible for the widespread encroachment of mesquite into Southwestern grasslands in recent years (Parmenter and Van Devender 1995).

Following their comprehensive review, Kotliar and others (1999:186) conclude prairie dogs are "crucial to the structure and function of native prairie systems." Further elimination of prairie dog colonies will almost certainly have negative effects on many species of grassland birds as well as grassland ecosystems as a whole in the Southwest. Not only are scientists today stressing the importance of preserving remaining prairie dog colonies (for example, Miller and others 1994), some are going further and calling for the reintroduction of prairie dogs to restore ecosystem function (for example, Manzano-Fischer and others 1999).

Cowbird Parasitism

Cowbirds of the genus *Molothrus* are brood parasites; these birds do not raise their own young but instead lay their eggs in the nests of host species. The brown-headed cowbird *Molothrus ater* is the species commonly found throughout the United States, although recently the bronzed cowbird *M. aeneus* has begun expanding its range northward from Mexico into Texas, New Mexico, and Arizona. As grassland birds are one of the guilds least likely to be impacted by cowbird parasitism, this discussion will be relatively brief and will focus on the brown-headed cowbird, as we have the most information on that species.

The brown-headed cowbird is native to the shortgrass prairie west of the Mississippi (Friedmann 1929, Mayfield 1965). This species was originally known as the "buffalo bird" because it was found in association with the great herds of bison on the plains. Cowbirds forage for grain in short grass and on bare ground, and they follow herd animals to catch the insects stirred up by their motion through the grass. Several aspects to the life history of the brown-headed cowbird (hereafter just "cowbird") make this species a particularly formidable threat to many bird species. The cowbird is a generalist parasite; that is, it does not specialize on any particular host species. Cowbirds are now known to parasitize at least 240 species of birds in North America (Friedmann and Kiff 1985). In addition, female cowbirds may lay from 30 to 40 eggs a year; some females in captivity have produced nearly 80 eggs in a single season (Robinson and others 1995b), thus giving each individual the capacity to parasitize numerous host nests. Cowbirds are not restricted by specific habitat needs because they can utilize foraging areas quite distant and different from the areas that they use to search for host nests, allowing them to be found in a tremendous range of breeding habitats. Finally, cowbirds are highly successful by producing eggs with a short incubation period. Their eggs will hatch before that of the host species, and as cowbirds generally parasitize species smaller than themselves and cowbird nestlings have extremely high growth rates, the young cowbirds soon outcompete their nestmates, leading to decreased success of the host or even complete nest failure (Robinson and others 1995b). Additionally, most females will remove a host egg before laying their own, further decreasing the reproductive success of the host (Friedmann 1963, Sealy 1992, Weatherhead 1989). If there are two or more cowbird eggs in a nest, even a species that might normally be capable of raising one cowbird chick in addition to its own will most likely fail to raise any of its own nestlings to maturity (Robinson and others 1995b). High levels of cowbird parasitism have been associated with the eradication of entire populations of some bird species, such as the black-capped vireo (Gryzbowski 1991).

Birds that evolved in the historical range of the cowbird in the Midwest have for the most part developed the ability to recognize and eject cowbird eggs, or to abandon parasitized nests (Rothstein 1975, 1977, 1982, Scott 1977). Other birds, such as the Southwestern willow flycatcher, have not (Robinson and others 1995b). Cowbirds have become a problem because human alteration of the environment has allowed them to vastly expand their range, giving them access to any number of naïve host species. The combination of human settlements, clearing of forests, and introduction of livestock has allowed the cowbird population in North America to virtually explode since the early 1900s (fig. 4-4).

Although grassland birds face many challenges, parasitism by cowbirds is currently one of the lesser threats. In general, ground-nesting grassland species are only rarely parasitized. Out of 98 neotropical migratory birds, Robinson and others (1995a) classify only two grassland nesting species as common cowbird hosts and five as uncommon hosts. The highest rates of nest parasitism occur in areas with an open subcanopy, which presumably provides a vantage point for female cowbirds searching for nests (Robinson and others 1995b). Because true grassland habitats lack

USDA Forest Service Gen. Tech. Rep. RMRS-GTR-135-vol. 2. 2005

87

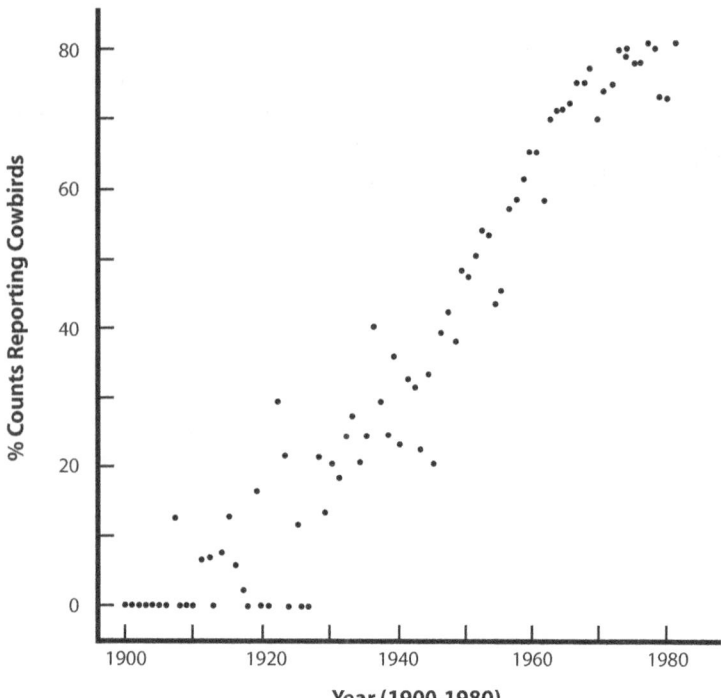

Figure 4-4. The percent of Audubon Christmas bird counts reporting cowbirds, from 1900 to 1980 ($r = 0.96$, $p < 0.01$) (from Brittingham and Temple 1983).

such potential perches, cowbirds are hampered by the inability to locate and monitor host nests on the ground. However, this fact also points to the importance of minimizing edge habitats in grasslands and illustrates how the introduction of vertical structures such as fences or telephone poles can alter this situation. If woody corridors or edges are available within a grassland habitat, rates of cowbird parasitism on grassland birds nesting close to that edge increase dramatically (Johnson and Temple 1990). To keep levels of cowbird parasitism on grassland birds low, the creation of woody edge habitats such as treelines or the establishment of livestock corrals and other structures must be kept to an absolute minimum within the remaining native grassland habitat.

Management for Grassland Birds in the Southwest_____

General Recommendations and Resources

Most of the published literature on managing for grassland birds has focused on the prairies of the Midwest and therefore has dealt primarily with birds inhabiting mixed-grass and tallgrass habitats. Unfortunately there has been little guidance available for managing birds that inhabit the more arid grasslands of the Southwest, but a few recent publications should serve as excellent resources for land managers in this region. For those working primarily in shortgrass steppe, the Rocky Mountain Bird Observatory has published a landowner's guide to best management practices for birds of the shortgrass prairie (Gillihan and others 2001); the Observatory also hosts a website that provides numerous resources for conservation of shortgrass prairie birds: http://www.rmbo.org. The Bird Conservation Plans produced by Partners in Flight of both Arizona and New Mexico provide management recommendations for all of the major habitat types in these States, and the plans should be a highly valuable resource for land managers in these States (Latta and others 1999, NMPIF 2001). Much of what follows in this introduction is based upon the information from these three sources. In addition, Partners in Flight has recently constructed a Web site that is an outstanding resource for best management practices to benefit birds in a variety of ecosystems, including grasslands. It is available online at http://www.partnersinflight.org/pubs/BMPs.htm.

In general, it is important to keep in mind that desert grasslands are even more arid and fragile than shortgrass prairie, and that desert grasslands are much more sensitive to livestock pressures because they did not evolve in concert with large numbers of native grazers, as did the flora of the shortgrass prairie. Desert grasslands should therefore be treated more conservatively than the grasslands of the shortgrass steppe. Management practices that have been developed based on climatic conditions in other regions must be adapted according to the local soil, precipitation, and plant composition characteristics, with careful, ongoing monitoring of management practices to ensure the continued viability of the system. Fire, for example, is a common management tool in grassland systems. However, as already noted, historically fires were more infrequent in desert grasslands than in mixed-grass or tallgrass prairies and may have negative impacts on grasslands composed primarily of black grama (see also chapter 3 of this volume). The U.S. Geological Survey in Tucson, AZ, the U.S. Natural Resources Conservation Service, U.S. Bureau of Land Management, and land stewards for The Nature Conservancy are good resources for information on the recommended frequency and timing of fires for the grasslands in your area.

In managing for grassland birds, it is necessary to first determine which species are currently present on the land in question, as well as which species could potentially inhabit the property if the right conditions were available. For assistance in this regard, wildlife biologists from the USDA Forest Service and USDI Fish and Wildlife Service should be able to help, and your local representatives of Partners in Flight or the National Audubon Society are also good sources of information.

A common confounding factor is that management practices for one species may conflict with those of another species that is present or could potentially occur in the area. For example, management to improve habitat for Sprague's pipits, which avoid woody vegetation, would be at odds with management for Cassin's sparrows or loggerhead shrikes, both of which require some degree of shrub cover. In these cases a choice must be made. If the property is extensive enough to divide into large separate management units, one may choose to manage for both species separately on different parts of the landscape. In these circumstances, researching the minimum area requirements for the species in question is important, if such information is available. Alternatively, one could opt to manage the land for the species that is of greater conservation concern in the area (Gillihan and Hutchings 2000). Again, the Arizona and New Mexico Partners in Flight Bird Conservation Plans are good resources for this information, as the plans clearly outline groups of bird species that will benefit from similar management practices and highlight those species of conservation concern.

Some general management recommendations for grassland habitats of the Southwestern United States include:

- Whenever possible, preserve native grasslands and the plant and animal species found there; expansive areas of contiguous grasslands are especially important for conservation.
- As a general rule, managers should strive to maintain grass canopy at 50 to 65 percent coverage and keep areas of bare ground to a minimum. Shrub cover should not exceed 20 percent. In desert grasslands, tall shrubs (including yuccas) of 3 m (9 ft) or more in height should be encouraged for use as nest sites.
- Restore and/or preserve natural water sources in grassland systems, such as cienegas, springs, playas, lakes, and so forth. For wet meadows, restore areas drained for agriculture.
- Minimize use of alpine tundra areas for recreation and livestock use to protect these fragile systems from trampling and erosion.
- Determine appropriate grazing systems for the land according to local climatic conditions and the type of habitat preferred by birds of management concern in your area. Appropriate systems may include deferred rotation or rest rotation; continuous grazing is not recommended. In the Midwest, a "bird friendly" rotation system was developed

that includes setting aside approximately one-third of the total pasture (a minimum of 8 ha) as a "refuge" for grassland nesting birds. This area is excluded from grazing and other disturbances for 6 weeks during the peak breeding season, to allow birds time to complete their nesting cycle (Bartelt 1997).

- Set aside large areas of land from grazing. Permanent grazing exclosures of at least 1,000 ha are recommended to create a mosaic of habitats within more heavily grazed areas and to provide appropriate habitat for grassland birds that are intolerant of grazing (Saab and others 1995). If permanent exclusion is not possible, the area should be rested from grazing for a minimum of 25 to 50 years (Bock and others 1993).
- Limit forage utilization to 35 to 40 percent in years of good rainfall and reduce stocking rates in drought years (Paulesen and Ares 1962, as cited in Loftin and others 2000).
- Manage grassland parcels as large units rather than as many small ones, as many grassland bird species exhibit a preference for extensive areas of grasslands.
- Schedule management activities (haying, burning, and such) to avoid the breeding season (early spring through mid-July for most species). High stocking rates should also be avoided during this time, when nests of ground-nesting birds have a high likelihood of being trampled.
- Mow or burn uncultivated areas in rotation, to create a patchwork of habitat types available for birds (working in large units of land). Use a flush bar on mowing devices and mow slowly in a back-and-forth pattern to give birds time to escape (see Gillihan and others 2001).
- If using fire as a management tool, research the natural (that is, historical) frequency of fires for the area in question and time burns to avoid the nesting and fledging times of local grassland birds.
- Use Integrated Pest Management Practices whenever possible; if chemical controls are necessary, use those that degrade rapidly.
- Preserve and/or restore colonies of small rodents, such as prairie dogs, that serve as important food sources for species of grassland birds such as golden eagles and ferruginous hawks and provide habitat for numerous other species such as burrowing owls and mountain plovers.
- Restore and reseed grasslands with native species of grasses.
- In all cases, bird populations should be monitored and management practices altered accordingly, if need be, to maintain or increase populations of the target species.

USDA Forest Service Gen. Tech. Rep. RMRS-GTR-135-vol. 2. 2005

89

A good starting point for gathering information on many general grassland management issues in the Southwest is *The Future of Arid Grasslands: Identifying Issues, Seeking Solutions*, available from the USDA Forest Service (Tellman and others 1998).

Management Reviews for Select Species of Grassland Birds

This section contains some brief reviews and specific management recommendations for selected representative species of Southwestern grassland birds. These particular species represent various examples of the broad variety of birds typical of the grasslands of the Southwest, including both resident and migratory species and birds of various ecological guilds and grassland habitat preferences, with an emphasis on species believed to be in decline. These summaries are not intended to represent an exhaustive accounting of all Southwestern grassland birds; such a review is beyond the scope of this document. Furthermore, some typical grassland species of the Southwest with limited distributions, such as the northern aplomado falcon and masked bobwhite, have not been included. Although these species certainly rank highly in terms of conservation concern, both being endangered, they were excluded from the discussion here because of the limited relevance of the information for most land managers in the region (northern aplomado falcons having been extirpated from New Mexico and Arizona, and the masked bobwhite occurring only on the Buenos Aires National Wildlife Refuge in Arizona). In addition, these species already have comprehensive recovery plans in place, managers can access through the USDI Fish and Wildlife Service's Environmental Conservation Online System at http://ecos.fws.gov.

Additional management recommendations for other grassland bird species not covered here may be found in the Partners in Flight Bird Conservation Plans for New Mexico and Arizona and the Rocky Mountain Bird Observatory's publication *Sharing Your Land with Shortgrass Prairie Birds*, referred to in the preceding section. Another potential resource is *Effects of Management Practices on Grassland Birds*, a series of species accounts compiled by the Northern Prairie Wildlife Research Center (Johnson and Igl 2001). Although their emphasis is on grassland birds of the northern Great Plains, management recommendations for many species that also occur in the Southwest may be found in these comprehensive accounts available online at http://www.npwrc.usgs.gov/resource/literatr/grasbird/grasbird.htm. See also the best management practices for grassland birds available from the Partners in Flight Web site at http://www.partnersinflight.org/pubs/BMPs.htm.

All of the species accounts that follow end with a list of associated species. The birds listed are those that may typically be found in habitats similar to that of the species detailed and that may also benefit from some of the recommended habitat management practices. However, not all of the species listed will necessarily respond in the same manner. If management for a particular group of species is the goal, the manager should further research the recommendations for each of those species individually. In the interest of saving space, multiple references that are cited within a single review document are cited as "and references therein" rather than listing each citation individually.

Ferruginous Hawk *Buteo regalis*

Distribution and Population Trends—During the breeding season, ferruginous hawks are found in appropriate grassland or shrubland habitats across the Intermountain West and Western Great Plains from Southwestern Canada south to northern Arizona, New Mexico, and Texas (fig. 4-5). In the central portion of its range, including Colorado, eastern Utah, northern Arizona, and New Mexico, this hawk is a year-round resident. In New Mexico, the ferruginous hawk is a regular resident on the Eastern Plains and the Plains of San Agustin; migratory individuals and wintering populations are also found across the State (Hubbard 1978). In Arizona, the ferruginous hawk is a year-round resident in the northern half of the State, with many migratory birds moving into the southern part of the State to winter (Glinski 1998).

In the winter, the more northerly breeding populations migrate southward. Wintering ferruginous hawks are most common in California, Colorado, Arizona, New Mexico, and northern Texas; smaller numbers are found throughout their range from southern Wyoming and Nebraska southward into Baja California and north-central Mexico (fig. 4-6).

For the most part, this species appears to still occupy most of its historic range; the primary exception is a reported range contraction in south-central Canada in the early 1900s due to conversion of native grassland habitats to agricultural uses (Bechard and Schmutz 1995). Numbers of wintering birds are reported to have increased in California and in the eastern portion of the hawk's range since the 1980s due to loss of wintering habitat in the Great Plains (Bechard and Schmutz 1995). Bechard and Schmutz (1995, and references therein) state that the ferruginous hawk is considered to be declining in several areas, and recent declines have been documented in northern Utah and eastern Nevada (Olendorff 1993). Populations in Arizona also appear to be decreasing in size as well as range (Glinski 1998).

There is much conflicting information on the population status of this species. A petition to list

90

USDA Forest Service Gen. Tech. Rep. RMRS-GTR-135-vol. 2. 2005

Figure 4-5. Distribution and densities of breeding ferruginous hawks in the United States and Canada, as mean numbers of individuals detected per route per year. Data averaged from Breeding Bird Surveys over the years 1982 to 1996 (Sauer and others 2001).

101 and above
31 to 100
11 to 30
4 to 10
2 to 3
One and above
None counted

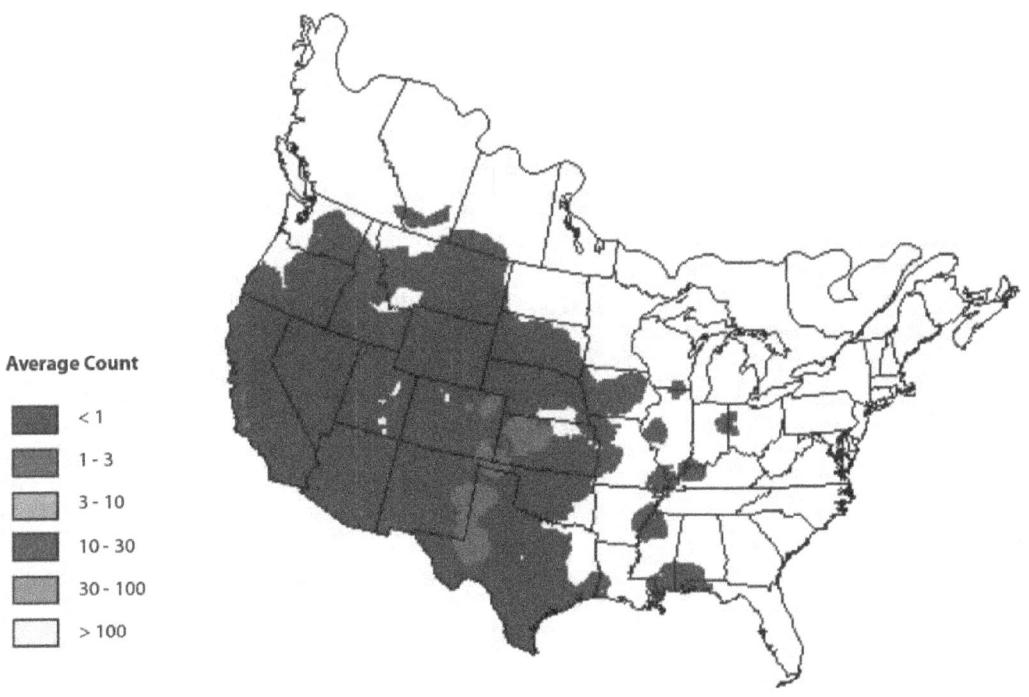

Figure 4-6. Winter distribution and densities of ferruginous hawks, based on Christmas Bird Count data. Counts are average number of birds detected per survey over the years 1982-1996 (from Sauer and others 2001).

Average Count

< 1
1 - 3
3 - 10
10 - 30
30 - 100
> 100

the ferruginous hawk under the Federal Endangered Species Act in 1991 (Ure and others 1991) was denied (USFWS 1992). In contrast to the declines proposed by several researchers (cited above), Peterjohn and Sauer (1999), in their analysis of Breeding Bird Survey (BBS) data from 1966 to 1999, reported that the ferruginous hawk was one of only three species of grassland birds demonstrating a positive population trend. During this period, BBS data reflects an annual increase in ferruginous hawk numbers of 5.2 percent (p < 0.01, n = 186); the rate of increase was even greater in more recent years, demonstrating a 7.2 percent annual increase from 1980 to 1996 (0.01 < p < 0.05, n = 170). Some of the inconsistencies come, no doubt, from the small numbers of raptors that tend to be detected on BBS routes and the resulting tenuous validity of any

USDA Forest Service Gen. Tech. Rep. RMRS-GTR-135-vol. 2. 2005

91

statistical analysis attempted to identify trends based on that data (Sauer and others 2001). Furthermore, ferruginous hawk populations are known to fluctuate in concert with cycles in prey abundance (Dechant and others 2001a and references therein), so it may be natural for their numbers to oscillate over time (Bechard and Schmutz 1995). Regardless of population fluctuations, the continental population of ferruginous hawks is relatively small and therefore worthy of conservation concern; a 1993 estimate placed the number of individuals in North America at somewhere between 6,000 and 11,000 birds (Olendorff 1993). The ferruginous hawk is a USFWS Migratory Nongame Bird of Management Concern, is designated as a Highest Priority species by New Mexico Partners in Flight, and is a priority species in the Arizona Bird Conservation Plan. The ferruginous hawk is considered Threatened by the State of Arizona (table 4-1).

Preferred Habitat and Nest Site Characteristics—Preferred breeding habitat includes flat, rolling grasslands, deserts, and shrubsteppe regions; ferruginous hawks avoid high elevations, interior forests, and narrow canyons (Bechard and Schmutz 1995). Ferruginous hawks will also use woodland edges (Olendorff 1993). Although they utilize pastures and croplands to some extent for nesting and foraging, these hawks tend to avoid areas where more than 50 percent of the landscape has been converted to such uses (Dechant and others 2001a and references therein). They are also sensitive to human disturbance and prefer to nest far from human activities (Dechant and others 2001a and references therein).

One of the key criteria for breeding habitat is an abundance of prey. Ferruginous hawks specialize on small mammals, and their diet is largely based on prairie dogs (*Cynonmys* spp.), ground squirrels (*Spermophilus* spp.), and rabbits (*Lepus* spp.) (Bechard and Schmutz 1995 and references therein). These hawks will avoid areas of dense vegetation that interfere with their ability to see prey (Dechant and others 2001a).

Winter habitat is similar to that used in the breeding season—extensive, open areas of grassland, desert, or shrubland—except that in the winter there is an even greater dependence of this hawk upon prairie dogs and ground squirrels, and they tend to congregate in the vicinity of prairie dog towns (Bechard and Schmutz 1995, Berry and others 1998, Plumpton and Andersen 1998). In Arizona and New Mexico, pocket gophers (*Thomomys* spp.) are also important prey (Bechard and Schmutz 1995). Wintering ferruginous hawks in Colorado avoided landscapes that were more than 5 to 7 percent urbanized (Berry and others 1998).

Ferruginous hawk nests are large, bulky structures that may be added to and used year after year (Bechard and Schmutz 1995). Most often ferruginous hawks will nest in a lone tree or artificial structure,

such as a utility pole, but they will also nest directly on the ground (Bechard and Schmutz 1995). Trees appear to be the preferred site if they are available (Bent 1937, Bechard and Schmutz 1995). In a sample of more than 2,000 ferruginous hawk nests, Olendorff (1993) found that 49 percent were placed in trees or shrubs, 21 percent were on cliffs, 12 percent on utility structures, and 10 percent on ground outcrops. When nesting on the ground, nests are usually placed on a slope, knoll, ridgecrest, or rock pinnacle rather than on level ground (Palmer 1988). In New Mexico, nests are often found near the edge of open grasslands in juniper savannas or pinyon-juniper woodlands (Hawks Aloft 1998).

Timing of Breeding and Migration—In the Southwest, breeding ferruginous hawks are believed to be resident year-round (Bechard and Schmutz 1995). Wintering individuals from more northerly breeding populations begin migrating south from August through October (Schmutz and Fyfe 1987), and return to their breeding grounds from February through April (Lokemoen and Duebbert 1976).

Breeding pairs begin forming in February or March, and in the Southwest most nest building activity occurs in March (Bechard and Schmutz 1995). Ferruginous hawks generally raise only a single brood a year (Bechard and Schmutz 1995). Incubation is estimated to be 32 to 33 days (Palmer 1988), and the young hawks typically leave the nest between 38 and 50 days after hatching (Bechard and Schmutz 1995). Ferruginous hawks are highly sensitive to disturbance during the breeding season and are particularly likely to abandon nests in the early stages of nesting, during the incubation period (Dechant and others 2001a and references therein). Reproductive success is closely linked with the local abundance of major prey species (Schmutz and Hungle 1989, Woffinden and Murphy 1989).

Area Requirements— In a study of several breeding areas, the average nearest neighbor distance between ferruginous hawk nests was 13.4 km (Olendorff 1993). Home range sizes vary widely, from 3 to 8 km^2 in the Great Basin (Janes 1985) up to 90 km^2 in Washington (Leary and others 1998). In Idaho, Wakely (1978) estimated that approximately 22 km^2 may be required to support one pair of ferruginous hawks. Wintering ferruginous hawks in Colorado used average home ranges of between 2.3 km^2 and 4.7 km^2; habitat suitability was highly dependent upon the presence of black-tailed prairie dog colonies (Plumpton and Andersen 1998).

Management Issues and Recommendations—Ferruginous hawks will avoid areas that have been largely converted to agriculture but appear to be relatively tolerant of grazing (for example, Kantrud and Kologiski 1982, Wakely 1978). A key management recommendation is therefore the protection of large

92

USDA Forest Service Gen. Tech. Rep. RMRS-GTR-135-vol. 2. 2005

tracts of native grassland from conversion to cropland or urbanization (Dechant and others 2001a).

Ranching operations appear to be largely consistent with ferruginous hawk conservation (Bechard and Schmutz 1995). The provision of abundant prey populations is also a critical consideration for this hawk (Dechant and others 2001a). Any land uses should be managed so as to maintain large numbers of small mammals, particularly ground squirrels and prairie dogs. Reintroduction of prairie dogs into areas formerly occupied will also benefit the ferruginous hawk, as well as other bird species that occur in association with prairie dogs (for example, burrowing owls; Latta and others 1999). Although it has been proposed that grazing may benefit ferruginous hawks by decreasing vegetative cover and thereby increasing the visibility of potential prey (Wakely 1978), Bock and others (1993) warn that reduction of ground cover in shrubsteppe habitats may result in decreased numbers of small mammals, therefore lowering the quality of the habitat for foraging ferruginous hawks. Increasing quality habitat for small mammals may also be achieved through creating a mosaic of habitats when converting land; for example, by leaving patches of untreated areas when clearing sagebrush steppe for conversion to grassland (Howard and Wolfe 1976). Attempts to eliminate populations of small mammals will negatively impact ferruginous hawks by removing their prey base. It is recommended that such control be exercised only to reduce high points in the cyclic populations of small mammals rather than trying to eliminate them altogether (Olendorff 1993). In addition, use of poisons such as strychnine on rodents may secondarily poison ferruginous hawks (Bechard and Schmutz 1995).

The provision of suitable nesting substrates is often successful in encouraging the reoccupation of formerly utilized areas, such as where woodlands have been converted to grasslands or natural nest areas have been lost through other means. This may be achieved by leaving individual trees or patches of trees when converting wooded areas to grasslands (Olendorff 1993), by protecting existing trees or nest structures such as old utility poles through fencing or by other means (Olendorff 1993), or by the provision of artificial nest platforms. Schmutz and others (1984) describe platform designs that have been used successfully in Canada. Scattered trees and utility poles may also be useful as hunting perches.

One of the most important management tools for this species is to avoid disturbance at the nest sites from roughly March through July or August (Bechard and Schmutz 1995, Howard and Wolfe 1976). As these hawks are most likely to abandon their nests during the incubation period, protection of these nests from March through May is of the utmost importance. It is recommended that any treatments of the land, such as plowing, burning, chaining, or discing, be performed during the nonnesting season (Olendorff 1993). Olendorff (1993) suggests creating buffer zones of 0.25 km radius around active ferruginous hawk nests for any brief disturbances, 0.5 km for intermittent activities, 0.8 km for more prolonged activities, and approximately 1.0 km for construction or other activities that will continue over several months or more.

Associated Species—Golden eagle, northern harrier, American kestrel, prairie falcon, scaled quail, mountain plover, burrowing owl (if burrows present), mourning dove, common nighthawk, ladder-backed woodpecker, Say's phoebe, horned lark, loggerhead shrike, Bendire's thrasher, vesper sparrow, lark sparrow, Eastern meadowlark, Western meadowlark, common raven (Latta and others 1999, NMPIF 2001).

Lesser Prairie-Chicken *Tympanuchus pallidicinctus*

Distribution and Population Trends—The range of the lesser prairie-chicken has always been restricted to five States within the Southern Great Plains: Kansas, Oklahoma, Colorado, Texas, and New Mexico. In New Mexico, the greatest concentration of lesser prairie-chickens occurs within just 21 percent of its former range within the State, in southern Roosevelt, northern Lea, and eastern Chaves Counties (Bailey and Williams 2000). Small and/or isolated populations may also be found in Curry, extreme southern Quay, southern Guadalupe, central DeBaca, and northern Roosevelt Counties, an area comprising approximately 23 percent of its former distribution; the lesser prairie-chicken is presumed to have been extirpated from the remaining 56 percent of its historical range in the northeastern and southeastern portions of the State (Bailey and Williams 2000).

The estimated current distribution of lesser prairie-chickens is presented in figure 4-7. Although technically still found throughout this range, since the 1900s the numbers of lesser prairie-chickens have been drastically reduced, and the populations within this range have become highly fragmented and isolated from one another (Giesen 1998). Overall the range covered by lesser prairie-chickens within the boundaries of their historical distribution is estimated to have declined by 92 percent since the 1800s; between the years 1963 and 1980 this species disappeared from 78 percent of its remaining range (Taylor and Guthery 1980). The extirpation of the lesser prairie-chicken from much of its former habitat reflects an estimated 97 percent decrease in the population of this species since the 1800s (Crawford 1980, Taylor and Guthery 1980). Formerly a highly abundant bird, in 1914 Walter Colvin reported

USDA Forest Service Gen. Tech. Rep. RMRS-GTR-135-vol. 2. 2005

93

Figure 4-7. Approximate current range boundaries of the lesser prairie chicken (from National Geographic Society 1999).

Lesser prairie chicken. (Photo by Gary Kramer, USDA Natural Resources Conservation Service)

seeing "flocks of fifty to five hundred . . . there were from thirty-five hundred to four thousand chickens in this one field, a sight never to be forgotten" (Colvin 1914, as cited in Bent 1932:283). Yet within only a few years, Colvin found that the numbers of lesser prairie-chickens had already noticeably diminished in this same area; he proposed that it was not the result of hunting, as hunters were so few in the area, but that rather it was "due largely to the cutting up of this vast wilderness into small farms . . . with the advancement of civilization the flocks scatter and become depleted" (Colvin 1914, as cited in Bent 1932:284).

The lesser prairie-chicken has continued its precipitous decline since that time, an apparent victim of habitat loss and fragmentation due to recurrent droughts exacerbated by overgrazing of rangelands, conversion of rangelands to croplands, chemical control of sand sage and shinnery oak; hunting may have played some role after populations had already been reduced to vulnerable levels (Bent 1932, Crawford 1980, Hoffman 1963, Jackson and DeArment 1963, Mote and others 1999, Taylor and Guthery 1980). In New Mexico, dramatic reductions in the population were noticeable as early as 1926 (Ligon 1927). The historical population of lesser prairie-chickens in New Mexico was estimated at 125,000, by 1968, and that number is estimated to have fallen to 8,000 to 10,000 birds (Sands 1968). Additional factors cited in the decline of the lesser prairie-chicken in New Mexico include oil and gas development and small population effects, such as inbreeding depression and increased vulnerability to stochastic environmental events that often occur in reduced, isolated populations (Bailey and Williams 2000). In addition, Bailey and others (2000) found that within the remaining core distribution of the lesser prairie-chicken in New Mexico, only 4 percent of the potential nesting habitat could be rated as in good condition; the remainder was only fair (16 percent) or poor (80 percent). The quality of nesting habitat is therefore also a likely limiting factor for lesser prairie-chickens in New Mexico.

The lesser prairie-chicken is listed as a threatened species in Colorado (Giesen 2000), and it has been recommended for listing as such in New Mexico (Bailey 1999). In 1995 it was proposed that the lesser prairie-chicken be listed as threatened under the Endangered Species Act. In 1998, the USDI Fish and Wildlife Service issued a "warranted but precluded" finding, indicating that although the data support the listing, other priorities currently take precedence (USFWS 1998). All attempts at translocating lesser prairie-chickens for reintroduction or augmentation of existing populations have failed to date (Giesen 1998 and references therein, Horton 2000). Despite the recognition that it is likely to become an endangered species within the foreseeable future (the definition of "threatened"), the States of Kansas and Texas continue to allow hunting of the lesser prairie-chicken during limited open seasons (Giesen 1998).

Preferred Habitat and Nest Placement Characteristics—The original distribution of the lesser prairie-chicken coincided with the distribution of sand sage-bluestem (*Artemisia filifolia-Schizachyrium* spp.) and shinnery oak-bluestem (*Quercus havardii-Schizachyrium* spp.) vegetation types. In the southwestern portion of its range (New Mexico, Texas, Oklahoma), the lesser prairie-chicken is found in sand-shinnery oak grasslands dominated by sand bluestem *Andropogon hallii*, little bluestem *Schizachyrium scoparium*, sand dropseed *Sporobolus cryptandrus*, three-awn *Aristida* spp., and blue grama; sideoats grama *B. curtipendula*, hairy grama *B. hirsuta* and buffalograss may also occur (Copelin 1963, Giesen 1998 and references therein).

94

USDA Forest Service Gen. Tech. Rep. RMRS-GTR-135-vol. 2. 2005

The lesser prairie-chicken is not migratory and requires a complex of habitats within a relatively limited area to meet its needs across seasons. It is a lekking species, meaning that males congregate on special display grounds called "leks" to perform their communal courtship displays; females attend leks to select a mate but otherwise are entirely responsible for raising the young on their own. The lek forms the center of all other habitats for the lesser prairie-chicken; most birds will spend their entire life within a 5 km radius of the lek site (Applegate and Riley 1998). Lek sites are characterized by short, sparse vegetation that allows for excellent visibility, and the sites are often on elevated knolls or ridges (Copelin 1963, Jones 1963, Taylor and Guthery 1980). Disturbed areas created by human activities, such as oil pads, roads, burning, or herbicide treatment, may be used as display sites (Giesen 1998 and references therein). Usually, though, populations have traditional lek sites that may be used continuously for decades (Copelin 1963, Giesen 1998); males display a high degree of fidelity to their traditional display grounds (Campbell 1972).

Because hens usually nest within 3 km of the lek site, they require appropriate habitat for nesting and brood-rearing within this range (Giesen 1994). High quality nesting habitat is characterized by dense clumps of tall grasses with scattered forbs and shrubs. Tall bunchgrasses (43 to 81 cm height) in dense clumps (1 to 3.3 m diameter) are typical in quality habitats; nests may be placed either at the base of such grasses or under sand sage or shinnery oak (Applegate and Riley 1998, Giesen 1998). Good nesting habitat is composed of approximately 65 percent tallgrass cover and 30 percent shrubs, with some additional forbs (Riley and others 1992). In New Mexico, female prairie-chickens used bluestem grasses most frequently as nesting cover. Greater nest success was associated with higher basal composition of sand bluestem (greater than 25 percent) and vegetation at a mean height of 66.6 cm (as opposed to a mean of 34.9 cm at unsuccessful nests; Riley and others 1992). Nest success is positively correlated with the height, density, and abundance of residual grasses (dead, standing vegetation from the previous year); nesting habitat is therefore particularly vulnerable to degradation through overgrazing, which diminishes the height and density of residual grasses (Bailey and others 2000, Giesen 1998).

Lesser prairie-chicken chicks are highly precocious and leave the nest within hours of hatching (Giesen 1998). The chicks cannot move through extremely dense grasses, and so broods are reared in habitats that are more open at the ground level than those used for nesting (Applegate and Riley 1998). Unlike adults, chicks are almost entirely insectivorous and require habitats that will supply an abundance of grasshoppers, treehoppers, and beetles, their preferred prey items

(Applegate and Riley 1998, Davis and others 1979). Good brood-rearing habitat is composed of 40 to 45 percent grasses with an equal quantity of shrubs and the remainder composed of forbs; bare ground coverage should be about 60 percent, with the rest live and residual plants to provide food and cover (Riley and Davis 1993). The requirement for more open vegetation and increased forbs makes brood habitat less vulnerable to disturbance. In fact, moderate levels of grazing, burning, or other disturbances may improve dense grassland habitats by creating an open mosaic of vegetation that is more suitable for foraging by prairie-chicken adults and chicks alike (Applegate and Riley 1998, Bailey and others 2000, Davis and others 1979).

The diet of the lesser prairie-chicken changes with the season, and consequently so does its foraging habitat. In the spring and summer, birds in New Mexico feed on approximately 55 percent animal foods, 23 percent vegetative material (leaves and flowers), and 22 percent mast and seeds (Davis and others 1979). In the fall, the vegetable portion of the diet increases to include 43 percent seeds, 39 percent leaves and flowers, and 15 percent insects; winter birds subsist primarily upon the acorns of shinnery oak (69 percent of diet) and the seeds of wild buckwheat (*Eriogonum* spp.) (Riley and others 1993a). Shinnery oaks are a particularly important food source for this species in the fall and winter, when they provide more than 50 percent of the bird's diet in the form of either acorns or other vegetative matter (Riley and others 1993a). Good foraging habitat in the fall and winter comprises approximately 60 to 65 percent grasses and 35 to 40 percent shinnery oak or sand sage (Riley and others 1993b). In addition, lesser prairie-chickens commonly make use of cultivated grain fields in the winter where these are available (Applegate and Riley 1998, Campbell 1972, Giesen 1998). The availability of free water does not appear to be a requirement at any time of year (Giesen 1998).

Timing of Breeding and Migration—Hens attend leks from late March through May. In Colorado, New Mexico, and Texas, the peak of breeding activity is usually during the second and third weeks of April. Nests are initiated in mid-April through late May, and hatching peaks from late May to mid-June. If the first nest fails, the hens may renest, extending the hatching period through early July. Broods of chicks break up at 12 to 15 weeks of age, coinciding with fall dispersal (Giesen 1998).

Lesser prairie-chickens are not migratory; their seasonal movements and home ranges are restricted to the suitable habitats adjacent to their lek sites (Giesen 1998). Males may be present at lek sites from January through June and then again from September through

USDA Forest Service Gen. Tech. Rep. RMRS-GTR-135-vol. 2. 2005

95

November; most display activity is restricted to mid-February through early May (Giesen 1998).

Area Requirements—In New Mexico, the home range of hens during the nesting season ranges from 8.5 to 92 ha; outside of the nesting season, home ranges may range from 62 to 240 ha (Giesen 1998 and references therein). Home range requirements tend to increase in drought years due to the reduction in cover and increased scarcity of food (Copelin 1963, Merchant 1982, as cited in Giesen 1998). An area estimated at at least 32 km^2 and composed of a minimum of 63 percent good quality shrub/grassland habitat is required to support a population of lesser prairie-chickens over the long term (Mote and others 1999).

Management Issues and Recommendations—Lesser prairie-chickens require extensive areas of sand sage or shinnery oak grasslands with a mosaic of habitats that provide adequate nesting habitat, brood habitat, and fall-winter habitat all within range of a central lek site (Applegate and Riley 1998, Davis and others 1979). In addition to maintaining and preserving high quality habitats where they still occur, such a mosaic of habitats may be created through the controlled use of proper grazing, prescribed fire, and brush control techniques in sand sage or shinnery oak grassland landscapes.

Excessive livestock grazing of grasslands, particularly during drought years, is highly detrimental to successful reproduction in lesser prairie-chickens (Merchant 1982, as cited in Giesen 1998). Long recognized as one of the primary threats to the lesser prairie-chicken (Bent 1932), intensive long-term grazing can alter plant species composition, reduce the abundance of preferred tall grass species, and dramatically reduce the residual vegetative cover required by this species (Applegate and Riley 1998, Bailey and Williams 2000, Bailey and others 2000).

To improve or maintain optimum nesting cover, grazing utilization levels should be less than 25 to 35 percent of the annual growth of forage species (Holochek and others 1989, Riley and others 1992, 1993b). Deferred and rest-rotation systems may also be used if high quality nesting and brood rearing habitat with residual grass cover is available in deferred and rested pastures (Applegate and Riley 1998). Cattle exclosures may be used in areas likely to be used for nesting; these areas should receive little if any grazing pressure (Taylor and Guthery 1980). The negative impacts of grazing on prairie-chicken habitat during drought years may be mitigated by promptly reducing livestock numbers during low precipitation years (Bailey and Williams 2000).

Shrubs are an important component of lesser prairie-chicken habitat, providing shade, cover from predators, and food (Cannon and Knopf 1981, Davis and others 1979, Giesen 1998, Taylor and Guthery 1980). Brush control programs that have resulted in the eradication of sand sage and/or shinnery oak have negatively impacted lesser prairie-chickens (Cannon and Knopf 1981, Haukos and Smith 1989, Jackson and DeArment 1963). If more than 40 to 50 percent of the landscape coverage is shinnery oak, limited reduction of the shrub may benefit the lesser prairie-chicken, provided that subsequent management allows for an increase in tall bunchgrasses (Davis and others 1979, Doerr and Guthery 1980, Mote and others 1999). However, any reduction in shinnery oak simultaneously reduces an important source of winter food (Jackson and DeArment 1963), and as this species reproduces vegetatively, any eradication is essentially permanent (Bailey and Williams 2000). If adequate food and cover remain, chemical control of shinnery oak and sand sage should not have a negative impact (Donaldson 1969, as cited in Giesen 1998, Olawsky and Smith 1991).

If shrub control is desirable, no more than 50 to 70 percent of the shrub cover should be eliminated to maintain appropriate habitat for lesser prairie-chickens (Doerr and Guthery 1980). Applying chemical controls so as to create a mosaic of treated and untreated areas is one option (Olawsky and Smith 1991). Pesticide (herbicide and insecticide) use should always be kept to a minimum because it not only reduces the shrubs and forbs that support the insects that are an important food source for the prairie-chickens, but it may also directly reduce insect populations (Applegate and Riley 1998).

Prescribed burning can be used to improve habitat by increasing vegetative growth and insect abundance; burns should be limited to 20 to 33 percent of the management unit to ensure the preservation of residual nesting cover (Bidwell and others 1995, cited in Mote and others 1999). Burned areas may not recover to the point of providing adequate cover for nesting until 2 to 3 years after the fire (Boyd and Bidwell 2001). Applegate and Riley (1998) suggest burning in the late winter or early spring every 3 to 4 years over 20 to 33 percent of rangeland to rejuvenate grasses.

Burns, herbicides, or mowing may also be used to create artificial leks of short, sparse vegetation in areas of extensive but relatively homogeneous habitat where natural lek sites are lacking. Lek sites should be placed in elevated areas where possible and should be placed at least 1.2 km apart (Taylor 1980). Applegate and Riley (1998) suggest that a habitat complex should contain at least six and preferably 10 or more lek sites with a distance between leks of about 2 km. During the breeding season (April through July), activities should be restricted within a 3 km radius of any lek site, whether natural or artificially created, in order to minimize disturbance of nests and chicks (Giesen 1998, USFWS 1998).

As fragmentation and isolation of populations is one of the greatest threats to the lesser prairie-chicken, extensive, contiguous expanses of native shrub-grass-

96

USDA Forest Service Gen. Tech. Rep. RMRS-GTR-135-vol. 2. 2005

land habitats should be preserved whenever possible to maintain connectivity between the remaining populations. In areas dominated by trees or exotic grasses, lesser prairie-chickens would benefit from the conversion of these areas to native shinnery oak, sand sage, and native, warm season grasses (Applegate and Riley 1998). The provision of small grainfields within the general area may help to sustain lesser prairie-chickens in the winter by augmenting their food supply (Applegate and Riley 1998).

Associated Species—Swainson's hawk, ferruginous hawk, scaled quail, northern bobwhite, mourning dove, common nighthawk, scissor-tailed flycatcher, western kingbird, loggerhead shrike, Chihuahuan raven, northern mockingbird, Cassin's sparrow, lark bunting, chestnut-collared longspur (C. Rustay, personal communication 2002, S.O. Williams, personal communication 2002).

Scaled Quail *Callipepla squamata*

Distribution and Population Trends—The scaled quail or "cottontop" is a common bird in the desert grasslands and sparse scrublands of the Southwest. Although primarily a Mexican species, the range of the scaled quail extends northward from Central Mexico into southwestern Kansas, southeastern Colorado, the Oklahoma Panhandle and southwestern Oklahoma, western and southern Texas, and throughout most of New Mexico and southeastern Arizona (American Ornithologists' Union 1998). In Arizona, the scaled quail is found in southeastern and south-central areas, west to the Baboquivari Mountains, north to the Gila River Valley and to the Arizona New Mexico border. The species also occurs locally in the upper Colorado River drainage, possibly through introductions (Phillips

and others 1964). In New Mexico, the scaled quail is found almost Statewide below elevations of approximately 2,100 m (Hubbard 1978). The scaled quail is a nonmigratory resident; the breeding and wintering distributions and densities of this species in the United States are shown in figures 4-8 and 4-9.

Recent literature on the scaled quail refers to declines in the abundance of this species over its range in the United States (for example, Schemnitz 1994). Inspection of Breeding Bird Survey data, however, reveals that the reported surveywide decline (-3.7 percent annually, $p = 0.05$, $n = 147$) appears to be primarily driven by significant declines in Texas. During the years 1966 to 2000, there were no significant trends in the numbers of scaled quail in any other State (Sauer and others 2001). Natural variability in the abundance of scaled quail makes population trend analysis a challenge for this species. Researchers refer to the characteristic "boom and bust" cycles of scaled quail populations, when periods of abundance are interrupted by widespread reproductive failure in the species (Payne and Bryant 1994, Schemnitz 1994). The cycling of scaled quail populations is thought to be in part driven by patterns in rainfall, with widespread reproductive failure occurring as the result of drought and an inadequate supply of succulent green vegetation (Campbell and others 1973, Schemnitz 1994). High mortality may also follow severe winters with deep snows (Schemnitz 1994). Several authors have speculated that excessive grazing by livestock has degraded habitat for the scaled quail by altering the composition and structure of the plant communities used for both food and cover, leading to at least localized declines (Brennan 1993, as cited in Schemnitz 1994, Ligon 1937, Schemnitz 1994). The scaled quail is a High Responsibility species for New Mexico Partners in Flight (NMPIF 2001).

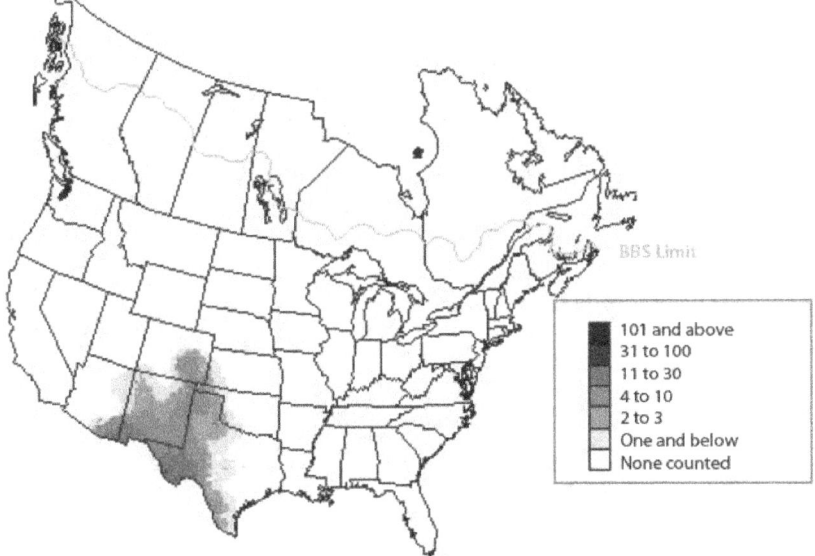

Figure 4-8. Distribution and densities of breeding scaled quail in the United States and Canada, as mean numbers of individuals detected per route per year. Data averaged from Breeding Bird Surveys over the years 1982 to 1996 (Sauer and others 2001).

101 and above
31 to 100
11 to 30
4 to 10
2 to 3
One and below
None counted

Average Count

■ < 1
■ 1 - 3
□ 3 - 10
■ 10 - 30
■ 30 - 100
□ > 100

Figure 4-9. Winter distribution and densities of scaled quail, based on Christmas Bird Count data. Counts are average number of birds detected per survey over the years 1982 to 1996 (from Sauer and others 2001).

Preferred Habitat and Nest Site Selection— There have been surprisingly few studies of habitat requirements for the scaled quail, especially considering its status as a gamebird. In general, desert grasslands with scattered shrubs and seed-producing forbs appear to provide high quality habitat for scaled quail. Breeding and nonbreeding habitat are believed to be essentially the same (Schemnitz 1994). In New Mexico, scaled quail are common in areas dominated by bunchgrasses such as mesa dropseed *Sporobolus flexuosus* with a scattered shrub component (Saiwana and others 1998). Bunchgrasses tend to have a relatively large amount of bare ground in the interstitial spaces, providing for easy passage by quail that typically walk rather than fly for casual movements. Such openings between the grasses are particularly important for the movements of chicks. Probably for the same reason, scaled quail are generally not found in grasslands of dense, stoloniferous grasses such as black grama (Saiwana and others 1998, Smith and others 1996). In northern New Mexico, scaled quail are found in blue grama grasslands with scattered shrubs (Zwartjes and others 2005). In southern Arizona, a combination of low-growing grasses, forbs, and shrubs with a ground cover between 10 and 50 percent has been described as optimum habitat for the scaled quail (Goodwin and Hungerford 1977).

The species composition and structure of vegetation are key components of scaled quail habitat for many reasons. For one, unlike most birds, green foliage actually makes up a significant percentage of the diet. This is particularly true in the critical winter months when herbage comprises 30 percent of the food intake (Schemnitz 1994). In addition, the seeds of forbs and woody plants make up most of the scaled quail's diet (insects are also an important diet item, but grass seeds are relatively unimportant; Medina

1988, Schemnitz 1994). Certain plants are therefore key to providing favored food items. Mesquite seeds, for example, are considered important food items for scaled quail (Best and Smartt 1985, Davis and others 1975). In New Mexico, seeds of snakeweed *Gutierrezia sarothrae* are a staple during the winter months (Davis and others 1975).

Besides providing the required food items, plants play a role for scaled quail in terms of providing cover for nesting, roosting, escaping from predators, and for shade and rest (Schemnitz 1994). Because scaled quail use a variety of plants for many different reasons, they are most often found in habitats that provide diversity in terms of plant species composition, structure, and density (for example, Saiwana and others 1998, Schemnitz 1994). According to Schemnitz (1994), quality habitat for the scaled quail includes a diverse

Scaled quail.

mix of grasses and forbs, accompanied by scattered shrubs such as yucca (*Yucca* spp.), fourwing saltbush (*Atriplex canescens*), littleleaf and/or skunkbush sumac (*Rhus microphylla* and *R. trilobata*), and various cacti (*Opuntia* spp.).

Scaled quail roost on the ground and therefore require roosting cover. In New Mexico, Sawyer (1973) found that scaled quail preferred grasses for roosting cover when they were available. Stormer (1984) proposes that overall 35 percent shrub cover mixed with 45 percent ground cover of grasses 0.1 to 0.4 m tall should be adequate, if at least 1 percent of the shrubs provide suitable roosting cover (such as yucca about 0.4 m tall). Shrubs and grasses are also important for providing overhead cover for resting, shade, and protection from avian predators. In southern Arizona, mesquite and wolfberry (*Lycium* spp.) were important for these purposes (Goodwin and Hungerford 1977); mesquite provided important loafing and escape cover in southern New Mexico as well (Sawyer 1973). Scaled quail will avoid areas that are overly shrubby, however, presumably because such a condition interferes with escape flight (Sawyer 1973, Schemnitz 1994, Wallmo 1957). If natural cover is not available, scaled quail will readily make use of artificial cover such as lumber piles, old machinery, and so forth for both resting and escape purposes (for example, Schemnitz 1994).

The ground nest of the scaled quail is a shallow scrape sparsely lined with grasses, most often sheltered under a shrub or other plant (Baicich and Harrison 1997). In southern New Mexico, scaled quail nests were found well concealed beneath mesquite or small soapweed yuccas (*Y. glauca*) (Sawyer 1973). Scaled quail nests have also been found in scrap piles (Schemnitz 1994).

Area Requirements—Little information is available on the area requirements of scaled quail. In the nonbreeding season (September through March or April) scaled quail form large coveys. Average home range sizes during the winter vary greatly: In Oklahoma, mean winter home range size was 21.1 ha, whereas in western Texas it was 145.7 ha (Schemnitz 1994 and references therein).

Timing of Breeding and Migration—Pair formation usually begins in mid-March. The earliest nests with eggs are documented on April 15, and the latest clutch hatched on September 22 in New Mexico (Jensen 1925). The incubation period is 22 to 23 days (Schemnitz 1994). True second broods are rare, but renesting after nest failure is common (Schemnitz 1994). In New Mexico, most chicks hatch between June and August (Campbell 1968). Reproductive success appears to be positively correlated with rainfall during the breeding season (Campbell 1968, Wallmo and Uzell 1958). This relationship is probably based upon the effects of rain on vegetative growth and also on the supply of insects and seeds for successfully raising chicks. Vitamin A is important to quail reproduction, and vitamin A levels increase in green plants as a function of rainfall (Hungerford 1964, Lehmann 1953, Wallmo 1956, as cited in Campbell 1968).

The scaled quail is a resident nonmigrant. Movements between summer and winter ranges have been reported as less than 4 km in distance (Schemnitz 1961).

Management Issues and Recommendations—Scaled quail prefer an intermediate seral stage of grassland that contains sufficient shrubs for roosting and resting, enough herbaceous vegetation to provide seeds and insects, and good cover of bunchgrasses (for example, Saiwana and others 1998). Light to moderate grazing may be beneficial for scaled quail by maintaining this preferred habitat (Campbell and others 1973, Medina 1988). However, grazing that promotes high shrub density will have a negative impact on scaled quail, as will heavy levels of grazing that reduces the vegetative cover this species requires for food, loafing cover, and nesting cover (Schemnitz 1994). Heavy grazing that results in the elimination of bunchgrasses favored by this species will also have a detrimental effect. Saiwana (1990, as cited in Schemnitz 1994) suggests that moderate grazing levels utilizing 30 to 40 percent of grasses should provide good food and cover conditions for scaled quail. Grazing levels should be reduced in drought years to maintain quality habitat (Holochek and others 1989). During drought conditions in Texas, habitat quality was better and scaled quail abundance greater in pastures that were subjected to high intensity, short duration grazing when compared to pastures that were grazed continuously year-round (Campbell-Kissock and others 1984).

In grassland areas lacking sufficient natural occurrences of loafing, nesting, or escape cover, provision of human-made cover may enhance habitat for scaled quail (Schemnitz 1994 and references therein). In New Mexico, Campbell (1952) suggested placing brush piles near water sources to improve habitat. Although water is attractive to scaled quail, it is considered the least important feature of the habitat for this species (Snyder 1967, as cited in Schemnitz 1994) and scaled quail are often found far from permanent water sources (for example, Brown 1989).

Because scaled quail use woody plants for many purposes, overly aggressive shrub control efforts can have detrimental impacts on their populations. Thinning of shrubs, however, can improve habitat by providing the more open, scattered woody cover preferred by scaled quail, particularly if such thinning results in increased coverage of understory grasses and forbs (Sawyer 1973).

USDA Forest Service Gen. Tech. Rep. RMRS-GTR-135-vol. 2. 2005

99

Associated Species—Ferruginous hawk, long-billed curlew, scissor-tailed flycatcher, Bendire's thrasher, Cassin's sparrow (NMPIF 2001).

Mountain Plover *Charadrius montanus*

Distribution and Population Trends—Despite its common name, the mountain plover is not found in montane regions at all but is most commonly a denizen of flat, arid expanses of shortgrass prairie. In 1929, Bent (1962) described the breeding range of the mountain plover as extending along the eastern edge of the Rockies, from New Mexico into southern Canada, and eastward into the Dakotas down through Nebraska, Kansas, and Oklahoma into Texas. Within this range, the species was considered a common breeding resident and was abundant enough to be a common game bird for market hunters (Coues 1874, as cited in Graul and Webster 1976, Sandoz 1954). Concerns over the apparent decrease in numbers of mountain plovers were expressed as early as 1915. While admitting that some of this decline in abundance may have been attributable to market hunting, Cooke (1915) speculated that the major threat to the species was the loss of suitable breeding habitat to agriculture and livestock. In 1957, Laun (as cited in Graul and Webster 1976) conjectured that the majority of the breeding population of mountain plovers was restricted primarily to Montana, Wyoming, and Colorado. These States still support the greatest numbers of breeding mountain plovers, with additional populations in northeastern to west-central New Mexico and the Oklahoma and Texas Panhandle regions (fig. 4-10). There is an isolated population in the Davis Mountains of Texas, and evidence of breeding mountain plovers has recently been reported in both Utah and Nuevo Leon, Mexico

(Ellison-Manning and White 2001, Knopf 1996c and references therein, Knopf and Rupert 1999). Mountain plovers were not documented nesting in Canada until 1981 (Wallis and Wershler 1981), and there is only one documented breeding record for Arizona, from 1996 (McCarthey and Corman 1996). Currently, the two primary strongholds for breeding populations of mountain plovers are the Pawnee National Grassland in Colorado (Graul and Webster 1976) and the Charles M. Russell National Wildlife Refuge in Montana (Knopf and Miller 1994). Between them, these two areas are believed to support approximately half of the present continental population of nesting mountain plovers (Knopf and Miller 1994).

Mountain plovers winter in north-central California south to Baja and the northern mainland of Mexico, as well as southern Arizona and the southern coast of Texas (Knopf 1996c and references therein). By far the greatest concentration of wintering birds appears to be in the Sacramento, San Joaquin, and Imperial Valleys of central California (Knopf and Rupert 1995).

The mountain plover evolved in a grassland environment strongly influenced by the disturbance activities of vast numbers of dominant herbivores, including bison (*Bison bison*), prairie dogs (*Cynomys* spp.), and pronghorn (*Antilocapra americana*). The large-scale disappearance of these prairie animals, along with early market hunting practices and increased agricultural operations, have apparently contributed to the marked contraction witnessed in the breeding range of this species, as well as its significant decline in numbers. Knopf (1996c) estimates that the breeding population of mountain plovers may have decreased by nearly two-thirds between the years 1966 and 1993. As of 1995, the estimated North American population of mountain plovers totaled 8,000 to 10,000 birds (Knopf

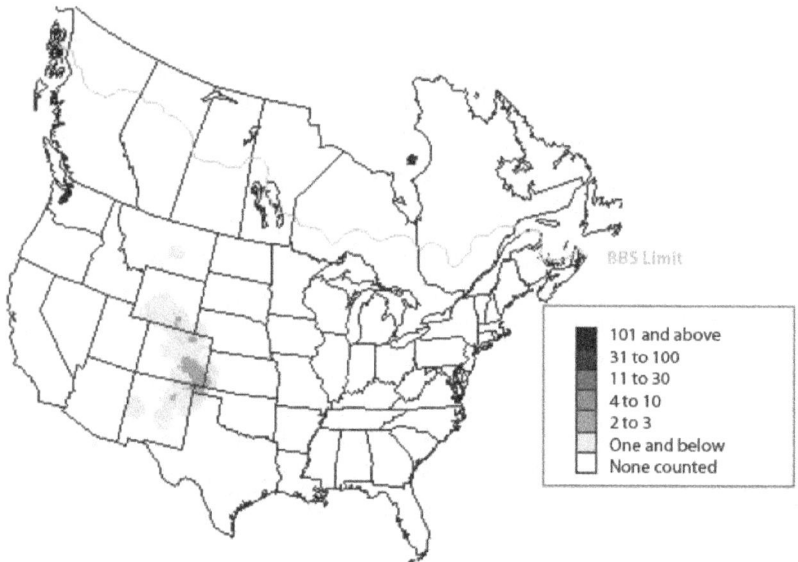

Figure 4-10. Distribution and densities of breeding mountain plovers in the United States and Canada, as mean numbers of individuals detected per route per year. Data from Breeding Bird Surveys averaged over the years 1982 to 1996 (Sauer and others 2001).

	101 and above
	31 to 100
	11 to 30
	4 to 10
	2 to 3
	One and below
	None counted

1996c). This is down from an estimated 214,200 to 319,200 breeding birds in 1975 (Graul and Webster 1976), although one of the authors acknowledges that estimate may have been off by as much as an order of magnitude (Knopf 1996c).

The mountain plover is a USFWS Migratory Nongame Bird of Management Concern and is a species designated Highest Priority by New Mexico Partners in Flight (table 4-1).

Preferred Habitat and Nest Placement Characteristics—The mountain plover both breeds and winters in open, flat arid country. In the breeding season, mountain plovers are most closely associated with expansive areas of short, sparse grasslands—most often blue grama *Bouteloua gracilis* and buffalo grass *Buchloe dactyloides*—with significant areas of bare ground (Finzel 1964, Graul 1975, Graul and Webster 1976, Knopf 1996c; Wallis and Wershler 1981). Vegetation height in preferred habitats tends to be approximately 10 cm (Graul 1975, Kantrud and Kologiski 1982, Parrish and others 1993, Wallis and Wershler 1981), and most often the area is flat, with less than 2 or 3 percent slope (Graul 1975, Knopf 1996c, Parrish and others 1993, Shackford 1991). Although sites used are primarily grasslands of short stature, mountain plovers will tolerate sparse amounts of taller vegetation, such as occasional shrubs or scattered clumps of cacti and bunchgrasses (Graul 1975).

On the Pawnee National Grassland in Colorado, an area of shortgrass prairie, sites used for nesting were composed of 68 percent grass cover (blue grama and buffalo grass) and 32 percent bare ground; prickly pear (*Opuntia* spp.) occurred on only 7 percent of the plots (Knopf and Miller 1994). By contrast, control plots ranged from 85 to 88 percent grass cover, and the number of plots with prickly pear on them ranged from 22 to 33 percent. When nesting in mixed grass prairie or sparse, semidesert shrublands, mountain plovers tend to use highly disturbed areas that offer shorter vegetation and more bare ground (Knopf 1996c). At the Charles M. Russell National Wildlife Refuge in Montana, mountain plovers nest in prairie dog colonies, in areas of approximately 27 percent bare ground (Olson and Edge 1985). Nest sites in blue grama grasslands in southern Canada ranged from 45 to 55 percent bare soil (Wallis and Wershler 1981) and were nearly 72 percent bare ground in Wyoming (Parrish and others 1993). This plover's strong preference for extensive areas of bare ground led Knopf and Miller (1994) to propose that 30 percent bare ground may not necessarily represent an optimum, but is more likely a minimum habitat requirement.

Their liking for bare ground explains why nesting mountain plovers are so frequently associated with highly disturbed areas, such as prairie dog towns (Ellison-Manning and White 2001, Knowles and Knowles 1984, Knowles and others 1982, Olson and Edge 1985, Olson-Edge and Edge 1987) and areas that have been subjected to heavy grazing (Dechant and others 2001b, Graul and Webster 1976, Kantrud and Kologiski 1982, Knowles and Knowles 1984, Knowles and others 1982, Wallis and Wershler 1981). Intensive summer grazing appears to create particularly favorable habitat for the mountain plover (Graul and Webster 1976, Wallis and Wershler 1981). Mountain plovers are associated with an intensity of grazing that is described by Knopf (1996a: 141) as "heavy grazing pressure to the point of excessive surface disturbance."

The nest of the mountain plover is a simple scrape in the ground, usually placed in a flat area of short grass (blue grama, sometimes mixed with buffalo grass), or in an area of entirely bare ground (Knopf 1996c). Mountain plovers also demonstrate a clear tendency to construct their nests near some conspicuous object in the environment; usually this is a pile of dried cow manure or a rock (Graul 1975, Knopf and Miller 1994, Olson and Edge 1985, Wallis and Wershler 1981). Mountain plovers are also found nesting in cultivated fields, either on plowed, barren ground, in early, low-growing croplands, or in stubble fields (Shackford 1991, Shackford and others 1999), although productivity in these habitats is probably low due to agricultural operations (see discussion below). After the chicks hatch, broods are immediately moved to areas with greater densities of forbs or with structures such as fence posts or watering tanks that serve to provide shade (Graul 1975).

In migration and during the winter, mountain plovers occupy habitats that are generally similar to those used in the breeding range. Particularly on the winter range, these plovers spend much of their time on plowed fields, but this is more likely due to the dominance of these habitats in the landscape than to choice; mountain plovers will preferentially use heavily grazed native grasslands or burned fields if they are available (Knopf and Rupert 1995). In New Mexico, mountain plovers are often located on commercial sod farms in the winter (Knopf 1996c). Alkali flats are used when available (Knopf and Rupert 1995).

Area Requirements—At the Pawnee National Grassland site in Colorado, Knopf and Rupert (1996) studied the minimum area required by mountain plovers to successfully raise chicks. They found that the absolute minimum area required was 28 ha, but the average was closer to 57 ha (range 28 to 91 ha). However, it should be noted that these plovers raised their chicks in broadly overlapping territories; therefore, a suitable area of habitat may provide the potential for two or three individuals to produce successful broods.

In areas where mountain plovers depend on prairie dog colonies to provide the appropriate habitat, this

USDA Forest Service Gen. Tech. Rep. RMRS-GTR-135-vol. 2. 2005

101

species demonstrates a clear preference for large colonies. In Montana, the average size of prairie dog towns this plover used was 57.5 ha (Knowles and Knowles 1984); towns less than 10 ha were considered to be of marginal habitat quality (Dechant and others 2001b).

Timing of Breeding and Migration—Mountain plovers arrive on the breeding grounds from early March to mid-April and depart for their winter range from early July through August (Knopf 1996c). Mountain plovers become more gregarious in migration and in winter and may start to be seen forming small flocks in June or July on the breeding grounds (Graul 1975).

In Colorado, the earliest clutches were laid in mid April, and the latest clutches were started in mid-June (Graul 1975). Although only one brood is raised per individual per season, mountain plovers may increase their productivity by double-clutching. The female first lays a complete clutch that the male incubates, and then lays a second complete clutch that she incubates herself (Graul 1975, Knopf 1996c). Mountain plovers may renest after the loss of a clutch or brood if it is early in the season, usually before June (Knopf 1996c). Incubation is 29 days, and chicks are led away from the nest within hours of hatching—generally as soon as they are dry (Graul 1975).

Management Issues and Recommendations—One of the greatest problems facing mountain plovers today is their affinity for bare ground, and therefore their tendency to nest on plowed or cultivated fields (Knopf 1996c, Shackford and others 1999). Much of the grassland historically used by these plovers for breeding has been converted to agriculture, and these areas often end up serving as population sinks for the species. Early in the season, when the ground is bare or vegetation is short, plovers will nest in these fields, only to have their nests destroyed by farm equipment working the fields later in the spring (Knopf and Rupert 1999). They will also abandon their nests once the vegetation grows too tall, at about 20 cm in height (Knopf and Rupert 1999). Knopf and Rupert (1999) speculate that the decline in productivity of mountain plovers now relegated to nesting in agricultural fields may largely explain their more recent population declines. To reduce nest and chick losses, they advise not preparing fields for later sowing months in advance, so as not to attract nesting plovers early in the season when their nests are certain to be destroyed by later activities. Protection of extensive areas of native grasslands from conversion to tillage is an obvious and important strategy for protection of this and other grassland bird species (Dechant and others 2001b and references therein).

Management for the mountain plover hinges on providing extensive areas of flat grassland dominated by short, sparse vegetation, which may be achieved through a variety of means (Dechant and others 2001b). Recommendations to provide the short vegetation required by mountain plovers include grazing at heavy intensities in summer or late winter (Wallis and Wershler 1981). Heavy grazing is particularly important to provide short vegetation in mixed-grass landscapes (Knowles and others 1982, Wallis and Wershler 1981). The wisdom of intensively grazing desert grasslands to manage for mountain plovers is questionable and in need of further evaluation.

To more closely mimic the historic conditions experienced by mountain plovers, Wallis and Wershler (1981) suggest that grazing pressures be varied to provide a mosaic of areas that are intensively grazed, lightly grazed, and not grazed at all. This approach should provide more structural heterogeneity than is present in the evenly grazed grasslands we see today (Knopf and Rupert 1999); grasslands of such even structure do not provide appropriate habitat for mountain plovers (NMPIF 2001).

In the Southwest, historically the disturbed nest sites used by mountain plovers in desert grasslands would have been provided by the activities of prairie dogs, not bison (Mack and Thompson 1982). As prairie dog towns have declined in landscape coverage by 98 percent since 1900 (Miller and others 1994, Parmenter and Van Devender 1995), this has no doubt had a negative impact on mountain plover populations in the Southwest. Protection of existing prairie dog colonies is therefore an important management strategy for this species (NMPIF 2001).

Prescribed burning can also be used to maintain mountain plover breeding habitat (Dechant and others 2001b, Knopf 1996c). In shortgrass prairie, early spring burns are used to attract mountain plovers (NatureServe 2001), a strategy that has thus far been successful (Knopf 1996c).

Mountain plovers do not appear to be adversely impacted by oil and gas extraction activities, and may even be attracted to the disturbed, open areas of bare ground created around oil well pads (Day 1994, Dechant and others 2001b). It is advisable to limit any disturbance in the area during the breeding season, however (April through July; Ball 1996, as cited in Dechant and others 2001b).

Associated Species—Burrowing owl (if burrows present), horned lark, vesper sparrow (NMPIF 2001).

Long-Billed Curlew *Numenius americanus*

Distribution and Population Trends—The long-billed curlew was once common as a breeding bird throughout the Western United States as far east as Illinois and Wisconsin, and possibly Ohio (Bent 1962), and large migratory and wintering populations were found along the Eastern shores. In the 1800s, fall

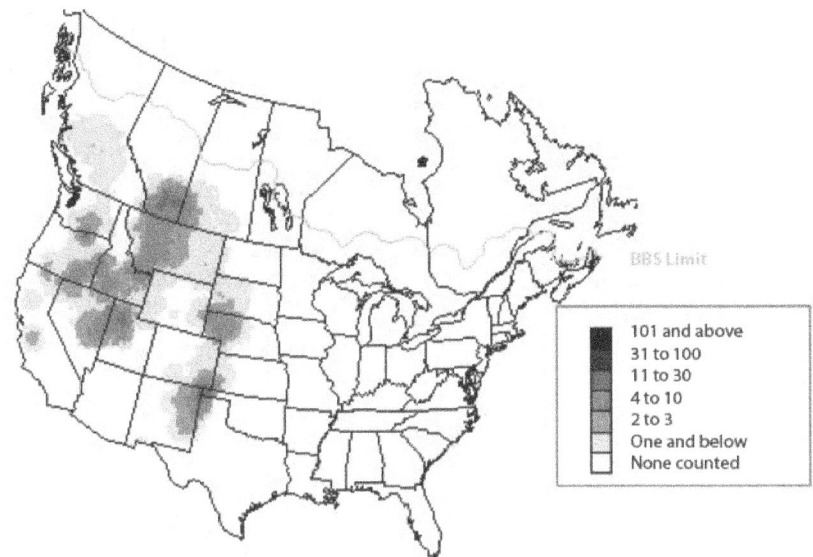

Figure 4-11. Distribution and densities of breeding long-billed curlews in the United States and Canada, as mean numbers of individuals detected per route per year. Data averaged from Breeding Bird Surveys over the years 1982 to 1996 (Sauer and others 2001).

BBS Limit

101 and above
31 to 100
11 to 30
4 to 10
2 to 3
One and below
None counted

market hunting took a heavy toll on wintering curlew populations along the Atlantic shore (Forbush 1912), and the long-billed curlew quickly became "only a rare straggler anywhere on the Atlantic coast" (Bent 1962:98). Curlews began to disappear simultaneously on their more easterly breeding grounds as human populations expanded westward and native prairies were lost to agricultural and livestock uses (Bent 1962, Pampush and Anthony 1993 and references therein, Sugden 1933). As early as 1873, the last breeding curlew was reported in Illinois (Bent 1962). The breeding range of the long-billed curlew is now restricted to localized areas in the grasslands of the Western United States and Southwestern Canada (fig. 4-11), but within these areas populations are not exhibiting any significant declines (Sauer and others 2001). In the Southwest, the greatest numbers of breeding long-billed curlews are found in the shortgrass plains of eastern and northeastern New Mexico, extending into the Panhandles of Texas and Oklahoma. Although this species does not breed regularly in Arizona, there is one recent record of long-billed curlews nesting just west of Springerville, with some indication that this may not have been an isolated occurrence (T. Corman, personal communication 2002). The long-billed curlew is occasionally found in the southern part of Arizona as a wintering migrant (American Ornithologists' Union 1998). Wintering curlews are also found in good numbers in eastern New Mexico and western Texas, particularly in the playa lakes region, although the greatest concentrations of winter birds are along the Gulf Coast of Texas and in the central valley of California (fig. 4-12). The long-billed curlew is a Highest Priority species for New Mexico Partners in Flight (table 4-1).

Preferred Habitat and Nest Placement Characteristics—Preferred habitat for the long-billed curlew in the breeding season consists of open, extensive areas of level to gently sloping grasslands such as shortgrass prairie or recently grazed or burned mixed-grass prairie (Dechant and others 2001c and references therein), often in the vicinity of a water source (Cochran and Anderson 1987, McCallum and others 1977). Vegetation is generally less than 10 cm tall with relatively little barren ground (Allen 1980, Bicak and others 1982, Cochran and Anderson 1987, Paton and Dalton 1994). A study at Great Salt Lake, Utah, reported a mean vegetation height ranging from 4.9 to 6.5 cm (Paton and Dalton 1994), and Redmond (1986) found that plant growth exceeding a height of 12 cm in the prebreeding season forced adults to forage away from their breeding territories and resulted in delayed egg laying. Curlews avoid areas with tall, dense shrubs and weedy vegetation (Pampush and Anthony 1993).

Although relatively short, even grasses characterize the breeding territory of the curlew, the nest itself is generally placed within a microsite of taller, denser grasses (Cochran and Anderson 1987, Pampush and Anthony 1993). In Utah, vegetation within 3 to 6 m of the nest was taller than that in the surrounding area, and there was less bare ground within 3 m of the nest itself (Paton and Dalton 1994). Although curlews nest on dry prairie or upland areas (for example, Silloway 1900), these sites are usually in proximity to wet meadows or some other water source (Johnsgard 1980). The proximity of mixed-grass uplands to wet meadows was considered the most important criterion for nest-site selection in Nebraska (Bicak 1977, as cited in Dechant and others 2001c), and dependence upon

USDA Forest Service Gen. Tech. Rep. RMRS-GTR-135-vol. 2. 2005

103

Figure 4-12. Winter distribution and densities of long-billed curlews, based on Christmas Bird Count data. Counts are average number of birds detected per survey over the years 1982 to 1996 (from Sauer and others 2001).

Average Count

- < 1
- 1 - 3
- 3 - 10
- 10 - 30
- 30 - 100
- > 100

moist grasslands or proximity to wetlands or some other water source (stock ponds, irrigation facilities) is seen as a key characteristic of habitat selection across the curlew's breeding range (Cochran and Anderson 1987, Ligon 1961, McCallum and others 1977, Paton and Dalton 1994). In some cases, however, curlews may be found nesting far from water because curlews tend to return to the same location to nest each year, regardless of whether the water source that originally attracted them to the area is still available or not (McCallum and others 1977).

The nest of the long-billed curlew is a simple scrape or hollow, thinly lined with grasses or other materials, although occasionally they will build a substantial platform of grasses to hold the eggs (Bent 1962). Curlews appear to choose nest sites near some conspicuous component of the environment, such as a shrub, mound of dirt, rocks, or discarded metal can, and nests are frequently reported next to piles of horse manure or cow dung (Dechant and others 2001c and references therein). Nests are also often placed on small hummocks or raised areas, presumably to aid with predator detection and/or to avoid moisture or flooding when nesting in wet areas (Cochran and Anderson 1987).

Long-billed curlews only rarely utilize agricultural lands such as hay fields, croplands, fallow fields, or stubble fields for nesting (Bent 1962, Cochran and Anderson 1987, McCallum and others 1977, Renaud 1980, Salt and Wilk 1958, Shackford 1994), although these areas are used for foraging during incubation, and birds will move into these areas with their young to loaf and feed once the young have left the nest (Johnsgard 1980, Salt and Wilk 1958). In the breeding season and winter, curlews forage primarily in upland grasslands, often in prairie dog colonies, if available, feeding on insects, worms, caterpillars, and occasinally berries

or the eggs and nestlings of other birds (Dechant and others 2001c, Ehrlich and others 1988, Terres 1991). Their ability to detect prey may be one reason that curlews prefer short vegetation. Even though prey density may be higher in areas of tall grass, prey capture rates have been observed to be higher in short grass (Bicak 1983, Bicak and others 1982).

During migration and winter, curlews are often found in small groups, foraging in areas of shortgrass similar to that used for breeding. In these seasons they will also use grasslands that are even more sparse in terms of vegetation height and cover; however, they consistently eschew thick or brushy vegetation.

Area Requirements—Studies in Idaho found that long-billed curlew density during the breeding season was positively correlated with the amount of area providing suitable habitat, defined as vegetation less than 10 cm in height (Bicak and others 1982). In the most densely populated areas, territory sizes averaged 14 ha, with an unoccupied buffer zone of 300 to 500 m around the edge of suitable habitat (Redmond and others 1981). In Washington State, territories were larger (20 ha) in flat, more homogenous grassland vegetation as compared to areas with more rolling hills and shrubs near the nesting sites (6 to 8 ha territory size) (Allen 1980).

The New Mexico Partners in Flight Bird Conservation Plan recommends a minimum of 2 ha per breeding pair and notes that nests can be as little as 229 m apart (NMPIF 2001).

Timing of Breeding and Migration—Long-billed curlews arrive on the breeding grounds quite early. In New Mexico most birds arrive in March, territories are established and nests initiated by April, and nests with eggs may be found from May through June (S.O. Williams, personal communication 2002). In some areas, eggs have been found in nests as late as July (Bent 1962, Redmond 1986). Incubation takes from 27 to 30 days, and the precocial young fledge in 32 to 45 days (Ehrlich and others 1988). In New Mexico, curlews generally begin to depart on their fall migration in July (S.O. Williams, personal communication 2002). Birds that have not successfully raised broods generally are the first to leave (Allen 1980, Paton and Dalton 1994). Long-billed curlews are single-brooded, and as a rule will not renest if the first attempt fails (Allen 1980), therefore the success of the first nest attempt is critical to the productivity in this species. Curlews tend to return to the same location to nest every year, and individual birds may even reuse the same territories (Allen 1980, McCallum and others 1977, Redmond and Jenni 1982, 1986).

Management Issues and Recommendations—Studies in western North America have consistently demonstrated that short vegetation (grasses less than 10 cm) is one of the key components in habitat mangagement for the long-billed curlew (Allen 1980, Bicak and others 1982, Cochran and Anderson 1987, Paton and Dalton 1994). Because of this preference, there are several measures that can be taken to enhance habitat suitability for the curlew. Actions that clear out areas of tall, dense residual vegetation prior to the onset of the nesting period, particularly following years of high rainfall, are especially important. Prescribed burning helps to clear out woody vegetation, increase habitat openness, and maintain grasses at a shorter height. Redmond and Jenni (1986) noted a 30 percent increase in the density of nesting curlews in western Idaho following a fall range fire. In New Mexico, late summer burning may improve grassland condition for the following breeding season (NMPIF 2001).

Mowing or haying also has the potential to maintain the short grass preferred by curlews, but in utilizing this method on the breeding grounds timing is critically important. Mowing must be accomplished so that short vegetation is available early in the season, when curlews first arrive to establish territories, and must be carried out when there is no danger of damaging active nests (essentially avoiding the months of April through July).

Grazing is another avenue for providing short grassland vegetation, although again timing is an important factor. Grazing must be accomplished such that short vegetation is available to the curlews prior to their arrival on the breeding grounds (mid-to-late March) (Bicak and others 1982, Cochran and Anderson 1987). Moderate grazing in known nesting areas just prior to nest initiation activities (usually March) may be beneficial (NMPIF 2001). Grazing during the nesting season should be avoided to prevent trampling of nests and young; nest studies in Wyoming and Idaho have demonstrated that curlew nests may be lost to trampling by livestock, and that nests in areas that were grazed during the incubation period had lower success rates than nests in ungrazed areas (Cochran and Anderson 1987, Redmond and Jenni 1986). Sheep appear to cause more damage through trampling than cattle (Sugden 1933). In South Dakota, curlews were observed to utilize unoccupied pastures, or pastures occupied by cattle, but did not use pastures with sheep present (Timken 1969).

Conversion of native prairie to agriculture has been indicated as one of the primary reasons for the extirpation of the long-billed curlew from many of its former breeding grounds (Bent 1962, Jewett 1936, Sugden 1933, Wickersham 1902). Hence, prevention of further losses of shortgrass prairie to agriculture is an important management goal, as is shortgrass steppe restoration. Maintenance of large areas of shortgrass is also important. Some researchers suggest that areas of suitable habitat need to be at least three times larger than the average long-billed curlew territory (14 ha) since curlews generally do not occupy a large buffer strip surrounding suitable habitat, bringing the minimum habitat area to 42 ha (Dechant and others 2001c, Redmond and others 1981).

Because long-billed curlews often show a preference for moist grasslands or at least proximity to wetlands (Ligon 1961, Dechant and others 2001c), any action that would result in a lowering of the water table, otherwise dry out the soil substrate, or eliminate available water sources should be avoided.

Associated Species—American kestrel, prairie falcon, scaled quail, western kingbird, lark bunting, vesper sparrow, Say's phoebe, western meadowlark (NMPIF 2001).

Burrowing Owl *Athene cunicularia*

Distribution and Population Trends—In the United States, breeding burrowing owls may be found in areas of open shortgrass prairie, desert grasslands, agricultural lands, and urban environments such as airports and vacant lots throughout the West (fig. 4-13; there is a separate subspecies of burrowing owl in Florida). Northerly breeding populations are migratory and will vacate the breeding grounds as far south as central California, New Mexico, Arizona, and northern Texas (fig. 4-14). California, New Mexico, and Arizona are considered important wintering areas for this species in the United States (James and Ethier 1989). In the Southwest, populations in the southern portions of New Mexico and Arizona are resident year-round.

In the United States, the burrowing owl is considered either endangered or a species of special concern in several States (Haug and others 1993 and references therein). Although reported as declining across its range (Haug and others 1993), Breeding Bird Survey

USDA Forest Service Gen. Tech. Rep. RMRS-GTR-135-vol. 2. 2005

105

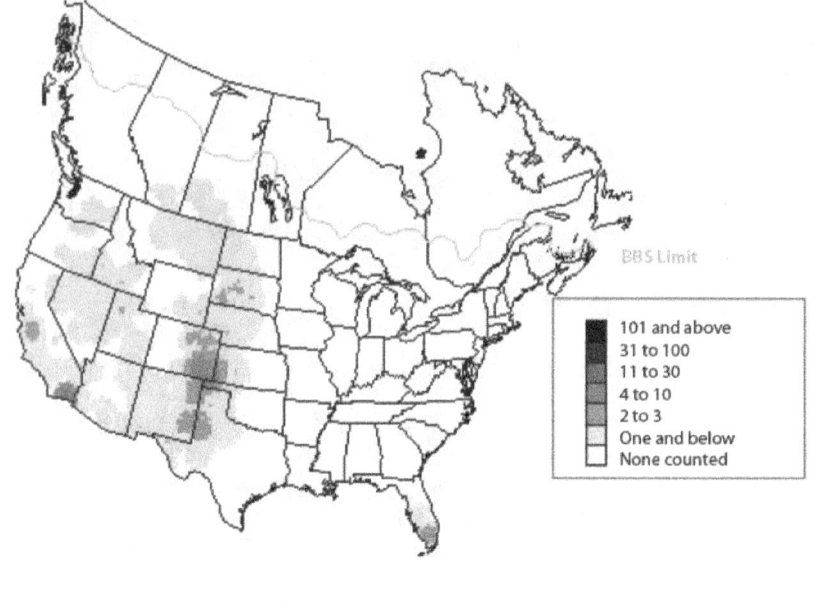

Figure 4-13. Distribution and densities of breeding burrowing owls in the United States and Canada, as mean numbers of individuals detected per route per year. Data averaged from Breeding Bird Surveys over the years 1982 to 1996 (Sauer and others 2001).

■	101 and above
	31 to 100
	11 to 30
	4 to 10
	2 to 3
	One and below
□	None counted

Figure 4-14. Winter distribution and densities of burrowing owls in the United States and Canada, based on Christmas Bird Count data. Counts are average number of birds detected per survey over the years 1982 to 1996 (from Sauer and others 2001).

Average Count

■	< 1
	1 - 3
	3 - 10
	10 - 30
	30 - 100
□	> 100

data do not show a significant downward trend over the years 1966 to 2000 (-1.6 percent annually, p = 0.56, n = 288; Sauer and others 2001). The greatest cause for concern is the Canadian population, which has shown dramatic and significant declines on the order of 11.6 percent a year (p = 0.02, n = 8) over the same 35 years (Sauer and others 2001). The burrowing owl has been extirpated from British Columbia, and the species is listed as threatened by the Committee on the Status of Endangered Wildlife in Canada (Haug and others 1993). This species is a USFWS Migratory Nongame Bird of Management Concern, is a High Responsibility species for New Mexico Partners in Flight, and is a priority species in the Arizona Partners in Flight Bird Conservation Plan (table 4-1).

In areas where numbers of burrowing owls are decreasing, these declines have been attributed primarily to habitat loss and fragmentation through agricultural and urban land conversion and extermination of burrowing mammal colonies (Bent 1938, Dundas and Jensen 1995, Haug and others 1993, Rodriguez Estrella and others 1998). Other factors cited in declines include a combination of pesticide usage, increased predation, and vehicle collisions (Clayton and Schmutz 1999, Haug and Didiuk 1991, James and Espie 1997, Sheffield 1997, Wellicome 1997). Vehicle collisions are a major source of mortality, particularly in fragmented habitats, as these owls will sit or hunt along roads at night, or attempt to feed on roadkill prey items (Bent 1938, Haug and Oliphant 1987, Haug and others 1993, Konrad and Gilmer 1984). Pesticides used in the vicinity of owl burrows or used for control of prairie dogs or ground squirrels may result in direct mortality to the owls or indirect mortality through the loss of their prey

Burrowing owl. (Photo © Courtney Conway, used with permission)

base (Baril 1993, Berkey and others 1993, James and Fox 1987, James and others 1990, Wellicome 1997). These small owls are already vulnerable to predators, and in fragmented habitats predation rates may be particularly high. Burrowing owls fall prey to a variety of predators, especially badgers, but also to domestic cats, opossums, weasels, skunks, and dogs (Bent 1938, Butts 1973, Green 1983 as cited in Haug and others 1993, Haug 1985).

Perhaps the greatest threat to this owl is the lost of nest burrows, the most critical component of its required breeding habitat (Haug 1985, Martin 1973, Thomsen 1971, Wedgwood 1978). Programs dedicated to the eradication of burrowing mammals such as prairie dogs have effectively eliminated most of the prime breeding habitat for burrowing owls, and this eradication is widely believed to be the primary reason for their decline (Butts 1973, Butts and Lewis 1982, Desmond and Savidge 1998, Faanes and Lingle 1995, Grant 1965). Activities such as intensive agriculture and urbanization have also been harmful in destroying the burrows used by these owls, as well as eliminating foraging habitat (Bent 1938, Faanes and Lingle 1995, Haug 1985, Konrad and Gilmer 1984).

Preferred Habitat and Nest Placement Characteristics—Burrowing owls are found in treeless, dry, open flat areas of shortgrass such as shortgrass prairie, deserts, or shrubsteppe, and are usually associated with colonies of burrowing mammals, most often prairie dogs or ground squirrels (for example, Bent 1938, Desmond and others 1995, Faanes and Lingle 1995, Konrad and Gilmer 1984, Plumpton and Lutz 1993). Burrowing owls may occasionally be found using old dens and burrows of badgers, marmots, skunks, armadillos, kangaroo rats, tortoises, foxes, and coyotes (Dechant and others 2001d, Haug and others 1993). Vegetation is short and sparse, and there is often a fair amount of bare ground. The availability of appropriate burrows for nesting is the critical limiting habitat factor for this owl, as the Western burrowing owl does not excavate its own burrows (Haug 1985, Martin 1973, Thomsen 1971). These owls will also occasionally use natural cavities in rocks if mammal burrows are not available (Gleason and Johnson 1985, Rich 1986). Burrowing owls often line their burrows with manure, speculated to be a predator avoidance mechanism by masking the smell of the burrow (Green and Anthony 1989, Martin 1973).

Burrowing owls appear to prefer areas of native grassland (for example, Clayton and Schmutz 1999), but also use pastures, fields, road right-of-ways, and a variety of urban habitats such as golf courses, cemeteries, and airports as long as the required nesting burrows are present (Botelho and Arrowood 1996, Dechant and others 2001d, Haug and others 1993). These owls are occasionally found nesting in croplands, but most of these nests probably fail when the land is cultivated (Dechant and others 2001d and references therein).

Burrowing owls prefer areas of short vegetation for nesting, most often areas of grasses approximately 10 cm in height (Butts 1973, Butts and Lewis 1982, Clayton and Schmutz 1999, Plumpton and Lutz 1993). Burrowing owls may be more closely associated with black-tailed prairie dogs than with white-tailed prairie dogs because the former keep the vegetation shorter and more open around their colonies (Martin 1983). Although these areas of short stature are used for nesting, burrowing owls often use nearby areas of taller vegetation for foraging, as they hunt for insects and small mammals, their primary prey items (Dechant and others 2001d, Haug and others 1993). Prey species for this owl tend to be more abundant in areas with taller vegetation (Wellicome 1994, Wellicome and Haug 1995), although vegetation more than 1m tall appears to be too tall for them to forage successfully (Dechant and others 2001d). Burrowing owls also appear to benefit from the presence of scattered observation perches such as shrubs or fence posts for hunting and detection of potential predators, although this practice is not as common in areas of quite short vegetation (for example, less than 5 to 8 cm; Grant 1965, Green and Anthony 1989, Haug and others 1993).

Large, densely populated prairie dog towns appear to provide the best nesting habitat for burrowing owls. Owls in larger colonies (some 35 ha) have higher rates of nesting success, experience lower rates of predation, and are more likely to return to nest at the same site in subsequent years than are owls that use smaller colonies or colonies with fewer prairie dogs (Butts 1973, Desmond and Savidge 1996, 1998, 1999). The abundance and density of nesting burrowing owls increase as a function of the number of active prairie dog burrows in a colony (Desmond and others 2000). Burrowing owls are only infrequently found in abandoned prairie dog colonies (Bent 1938, MacCracken and others 1984) as the structural integrity of the burrows deteriorates rapidly once the prairie dogs are absent, and the area is soon invaded by taller, denser vegetation (Butts 1973, Grant 1965).

USDA Forest Service Gen. Tech. Rep. RMRS-GTR-135-vol. 2. 2005

107

In Oklahoma, colonies became unsuitable for occupation by burrowing owls between 1 and 3 years after prairie dogs were removed (Butts 1973).

Area Requirements—Burrowing owls tend to cluster their nests within prairie dog colonies (Butts 1973, Desmond and Savidge 1996, Desmond and others 2000). Colonies of some 35 ha appear to provide adequate space requirements for these owls; mean nearest neighbor distances in these larger colonies was 125 m in Nebraska (Desmond 1991, Desmond and Savidge 1996, Desmond and others 1995). In Oregon, successful nests were generally more than 110 m apart (Green and Anthony 1989), and in Colorado mean nearest neighbor distances within prairie dog colonies were 101 m (Plumpton 1992, as cited in Dechant and others 2001d). Minimum nesting area requirements are estimated to range from 3.5 ha (Thompson 1984, as cited in Dechant and others 2001d) to 7.3 ha (Grant 1965). Foraging area requirements are considerably greater, although there are few quantitative studies. In Saskatchewan, mean foraging areas ranged from 35 ha (Sissons and others 1998) to 241 ha (Haug 1985, Haug and Oliphant 1990). As might be expected, foraging areas tend to be larger in areas with lower densities of potential prey (Haug 1985).

Timing of Migration and Breeding—Little is known of the migration and wintering ecology of this species. Northern migratory populations are believed to migrate southward in September and October and to return to their breeding grounds in March and April (Haug and others 1993). In the Southwest, more southerly populations in New Mexico and Arizona are believed to be permanent residents.

In New Mexico, egg laying commences in mid to late March (Martin 1973). Burrowing owls normally produce only one brood per season but will attempt to renest if the first nest fails early in the breeding season (Butts 1973, Wedgwood 1976). Incubation is 28 to 30 days, and the young leave the nest at about 44 days (Haug and others 1993). After hatching, the parents may divide the brood and move them between several nearby satellite burrows, possibly to reduce the risk of predation or to avoid nest parasites (Butts 1973, Butts and Lewis 1982, Desmond and Savidge 1998, 1999, Konrad and Gilmer 1984, Plumpton and Lutz 1993). For the most part, these owls may be able to nest successfully in areas subject to moderate levels of human disturbance (for example, on golf courses, college campuses; Botelho and Arrowood 1996, Haug and others 1993); they are most vulnerable during the egg laying and incubation stages (Olenick 1990, as cited in Haug and others 1993).

Although some migratory birds may return and use the same burrow in following years, more often burrowing owls will return to the same traditional nesting areas but not use the same burrow (Dechant and others 2001d and references therein). Resident birds use and maintain their burrows year-round (Haug and others 1993).

Management Issues and Recommendations—Eradication of fossorial mammal colonies quickly eliminates breeding populations of burrowing owls (Butts and Lewis 1982, Haug and others 1993). The protection, maintenance, and restoration of burrowing mammal populations, especially black-tailed prairie dogs in the Southwest, is one of the most important steps that can be taken to conserve this owl (Dechant and others 2001d, Haug and others 1993, Latta and others 1999, NatureServe 2001). Protection or expansion of large prairie dog colonies (approximatley 35 ha) may be especially beneficial (Dechant and others 2001d, Desmond and others 1995). If control measures against burrowing mammals are deemed absolutely necessary, these should be timed to avoid the breeding activities of burrowing owls (Butts 1973).

Traditional nesting sites should be preserved whenever possible. Where natural burrows are not available, artificial burrows may be installed to encourage occupation by burrowing owls; such burrows have been used successfully in the past (Collins and Landry 1977, Olenick 1990 as cited in Haug 1993, Thomson 1988 as cited in Dechant and others 2001d, Trulio 1997). Some researchers suggest providing horse or cow manure to burrowing owls if it is not otherwise available (Green and Anthony 1997).

Because burrowing owls are sensitive to the effects of habitat fragmentation, large, contiguous areas of native grasslands, especially treeless shortgrass plains, should be conserved to the extent possible (Clayton and Schmutz 1999, Warnock 1997, Warnock and James 1997, Wellicome and Haug 1995). The short vegetation required by the owls may be maintained through grazing, mowing, or periodic burning (Dechant and others 2001d). Although burrowing owls prefer to nest in grasslands that have been heavily grazed (Butts 1973, Bock and others 1993, James and Seabloom 1968, Kantrud and Kologiski 1982, MacCracken and others 1985, Wedgwood 1976), it may be important to provide a mosaic of grassland habitats that includes some areas of taller grass that support a greater abundance of prey for the owls while foraging (Dechant and others 2001d, NatureServe 2001). Extensive areas of overgrazed grassland may not provide the prey base required to support these owls (Dechant and others 2001d); rotational grazing will help to maintain adequate prey populations (Wellicome and others 1997). Note, however, that although measures such as grazing, mowing, or burning will provide the grasses of short stature used by these owls, these methods alone are not sufficient to provide the necessary habitat in the absence of fossorial mammals to construct and maintain the burrows used by the owls.

Burrowing owls are sensitive to pesticide use. Spraying carbofuran within 50 m of a nest burrow caused a 54 percent reduction in the number of young per nest (James and Fox 1987). In Oklahoma, application of sodium fluoroacetate to a prairie dog colony resulted in the eradication of burrowing owls nesting at the site (Butts 1973 as cited in Dechant and others 2001d). In addition to being potentially toxic to the owl itself, the use of pesticides may indirectly impact the owls by reducing their prey base (James and Fox 1987, James and others 1990). If the use of pesticides is absolutely necessary in an area where burrowing owls are nesting, those compounds with the lowest possible toxicity to nontarget animals should be used (Fox and others 1989, James and Fox 1987). Pesticides should not be sprayed within 600 m of nest burrows during the breeding season (Dechant and others 2001d and references therein).

Associated Species—Ferruginous hawk, golden eagle, prairie falcon, mountain plover, horned lark, common raven, loggerhead shrike, lark sparrow, black-throated sparrow, sage sparrow, McCown's longspur, eastern meadowlark, western meadowlark (Latta and others 1999, NMPIF 2001).

Loggerhead Shrike *Lanius ludovicianus*

Distribution and Population Trends—The loggerhead shrike is a breeding bird across most of the United States and south-central Canada; although it once occurred in the New England States, it is no longer found there. Historically, the core of its range is thought to have been deserts, shrub steppes, and southern savannas (Cade and Woods 1994), but clearing of forests in central and eastern North America in the 1800s allowed this species to greatly expand its range (Yosef 1996). However, this expanded range again contracted beginning in the latter half of the 20th century due to loss of appropriate habitat through succession, urbanization, and other causes (Yosef 1996). The current breeding distribution of the loggerhead shrike is shown in figure 4-15.

Loggerhead shrikes are migratory in the northern portion of their breeding range. In the more southerly area of its range (approximately northern California eastward across central Colorado, Kansas, and other Central States to northern Virginia, south to Chiapas, Mexico), the shrike is a permanent resident. The abundance and distribution of wintering loggerhead shrikes is shown in figure 4-16.

Although numerous grassland birds have been in decline across the United States in recent years, the loggerhead shrike is one of the few species that has shown consistently negative population trends across every region. Between the years 1966 and 2000, Breeding Bird Survey data indicate significant annual declines averaging 4.3 percent (p = 0.00, n = 407) in the East,

Loggerhead shrike. (Photo © Bill Schmoker, www.schmoker. org/BirdPics, used with permission)

3.0 percent (p = 0.00, n = 5.81) in the Central States, and 4.0 percent (p = 0.00, n = 421) in the West (Sauer and others 2001). In the Southwest, Arizona populations have declined 4.7 percent annually (p = 0.01, n = 50), and New Mexico populations have decreased on average by 5.7 percent a year (p = 0.00, n = 53) during the same period.

Much speculation exists on the underlying causes of these declines, but there is little hard evidence to support any one theory. In general it is thought that changes in land use practices and use of pesticides may be largely responsible (Yosef 1996). Graber and others (1973) suggested that early declines in Illinois, from roughly 1900 to the 1950s, were due to habitat loss, and then more rapid declines between 1957 and 1965 may have been a response to pesticide use during that period. Because of its carnivorous habits and especially its dependence upon grasshoppers, viewed as pests by most in the agricultural business, shrikes may be exposed to high levels of toxic chemicals. Shrikes have been found to have elevated levels of organochlorines in their tissues and eggs (Yosef 1996 and references therein), and may be ingesting pesticides through consumption of prey in areas that have been sprayed (Anderson and Duzan 1978, Korschgen 1970). Sharp declines in shrike abundance were noted in areas that had been treated with the pesticide dieldrin, intended to kill the grasshoppers that make up 30 to 75 percent of the shrike's diet (Yosef 1996). Because shrikes frequent shrubs and fencelines along roadways, they are also exposed to herbicide treatments used for roadside vegetation management (Yosef 1996). Other potential causes of decline include habitat loss or degradation due to urbanization, shrub removal, surface mining

USDA Forest Service Gen. Tech. Rep. RMRS-GTR-135-vol. 2. 2005

109

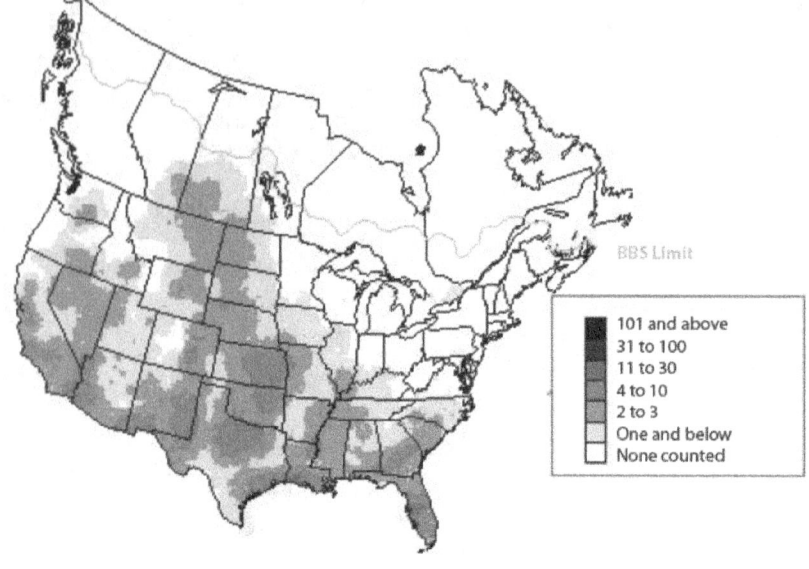

Figure 4-15. Distribution and densities of breeding loggerhead shrikes in the United States and Canada, as mean numbers of individuals detected per route per year. Data averaged from Breeding Bird Surveys over the years 1982 to 1996 (Sauer and others 2001).

101 and above
31 to 100
11 to 30
4 to 10
2 to 3
One and below
None counted

BBS Limit

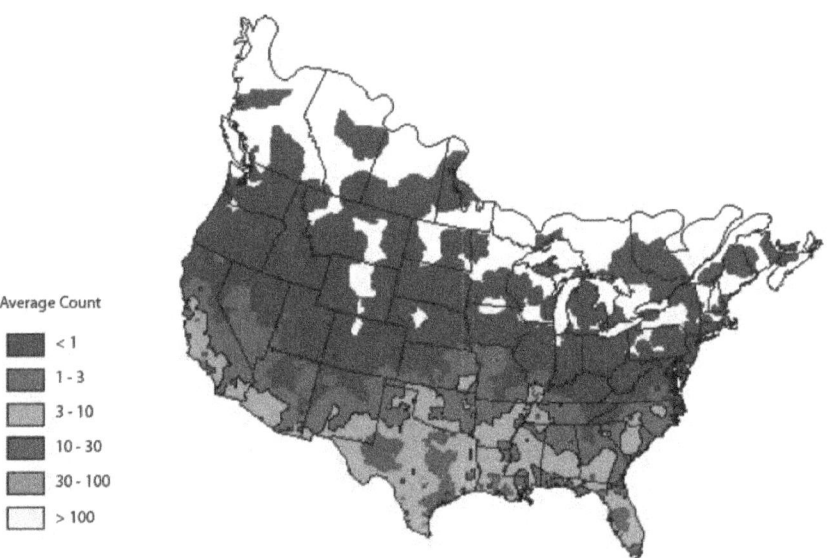

Average Count

< 1
1 - 3
3 - 10
10 - 30
30 - 100
> 100

Figure 4-16. Winter distribution and densities of loggerhead shrikes in the United States and Canada, based on Christmas Bird Count data. Counts are average number of birds detected per survey over the years 1982 to 1996 (from Sauer and others 2001).

operations, and overgrazing. The loggerhead shrike is listed as a Migratory Nongame Bird of Management Concern by the USDI Fish and Wildlife Service and is a Priority species for New Mexico Partners in Flight (table 4-1).

Preferred Habitat and Nest Placement Characteristics—Loggerhead shrikes use the same type of habitat year-round, and in areas such as the Southwest where they are resident, they are highly territorial, and pairs will defend the same territory permanently (Yosef 1996). Preferred habitat is open areas of short grass interspersed with areas of bare ground and widely scattered trees or shrubs (Dechant and others 2001e, Yosef 1996). These shrikes are found in deserts, prairies, pastures, sagebrush steppe, and open woodlands, as well as more suburban areas, golf courses, and cemeteries (Dechant and others 2001e, Yosef 1996). In any open country, the critical component of the habitat is the availability of elevated perches for hunting and appropriate shrubs or trees for nest sites (Brooks and Temple 1990, Craig 1978, Dechant and others 2001e, Yosef 1996, Yosef and Grubb 1994). Shrikes demonstrate a particular fondness for dense, thorny, woody vegetation, which they use both for nesting and for their peculiar habitat of impaling prey items for storage (Porter and others 1975, Yosef 1996); barbed wire fences are also frequently used for caching prey. Loggerhead shrikes are entirely carnivorous and spend much of the day hunting for grasshoppers, lizards, amphibians, small mammals, and even some small birds in open areas of short grass (Yosef 1996). Their hunting style requires elevated perches for sighting their prey; these perches may be shrubs or trees but are also often fences, utility lines or poles, leading to a high density of loggerhead shrikes along roadways (Yosef 1996). Fencerows or windbreaks between pastures also serve as popular nest and perch sites (Yosef 1996). In shrubsteppe habitats, loggerhead shrikes prefer a mosaic of shrubs and openings, with little slope and high horizontal and vertical structural diversity (Poole 1992, as cited in Dechant and others 2001e). Although shrikes forage in areas of short grass, presumably because of increased prey visibility, it appears that the best habitats also offer nearby patches of taller grasses that may harbor a greater reservoir of vertebrate prey species (Dechant and others 2001e).

Area Requirements—Territories generally range from 4 to 9 ha (Yosef 1996 and references therein); in semidesert habitats, territories tend to be larger, from 10 to 16 ha (NatureServe 2001). Territory size may vary both as a function of vegetation and perch density. Miller (1951) found that shrikes nesting in barren, sparsely vegetated dunes had territories two to three times as large as those nesting in more wooded sites. On agricultural lands, territory size decreased as the number of available perches increased (Yosef 1996).

Timing of Breeding and Migration—Loggerhead shrikes are early nesters. Nest construction may begin as early as February; in Arizona, eggs have been reported from March through June (Terres 1991, Yosef 1996). In several regions, the peak of nest initiation appears to be in mid-April (Yosef 1996 and references therein). The incubation period is 16 days, and the young leave the nest 17 to 20 days after hatching (Terres 1991, Yosef 1996). Loggerhead shrikes usually raise only a single brood a year, although they will attempt to renest following a failed attempt (Yosef 1996). In the Southwest, breeding pairs are resident on their territories year-round.

Management Issues and Recommendations— As nest sites and hunting perches are critical habitat elements for the loggerhead shrike, much of the management focus is on providing these key components in the grassland and shrubsteppe communities of the Southwest. Scattered trees or shrubs, fencerows, and shelterbelts should be maintained or planted in otherwise open pastures and grasslands to provide suitable nest sites and perches (Dechant and others 2001e, Hands and others 1989, Yosef 1996). Thorny shrubs and barbed wire fences are especially valuable components of shrike habitat that should be maintained whenever possible (NatureServe 2001). Augmenting existing fencerows by adding native, thorny trees or shrubs may enhance shrike habitat (Hellman 1994, as cited in Dechant and others 2001e). Shrikes do not appear to be particularly sensitive to human activities, so buildings or roadways near

nest sites is most likely not an issue for this species (NatureServe 2001).

As loggerhead shrikes seem to do best in grasslands that provide a mix of short and taller grasses (Gillihan and Hutchings 2000), activities such as grazing and mowing should be closely controlled to provide areas of taller grasses (20 cm or greater) that provide a greater abundance of vertebrate prey in addition to expanses of shorter vegetation (Dechant and others 2001e). When possible, trees and shrubs used for nesting and perching should be protected from cattle grazing and rubbing by fencing or other means (Dechant and others 2001e, Yosef 1996).

Whenever possible, use of herbicides or insecticides should be avoided in loggerhead shrike habitat (Dechant and others 2001e, Yosef 1996). To maintain roadside nesting habitats, Yosef (1996) suggests manual trimming or selective removal of shrubs or trees instead of frequent mowing or the use of herbicides.

Prescribed burning may be used sparingly to maintain shrike habitat by preventing the domination of woody vegetation, but if burning is conducted too frequently it may eliminate the trees and shrubs the shrike requires for quality habitat (Dechant and others 2001e).

Whenever possible, large tracts of native grasslands and sagebrush/scrub habitat should be preserved, and conversion of prairies to croplands should be avoided. To be of adequate size, protected areas should be large enough to support several average-sized territories of asymmetrical shape (Dechant and others 2001e), or about 30 to 48 ha minimum in semidesert habitats.

Associated Species—Ferruginous hawk, American kestrel, scaled quail, common nighthawk, ladder-backed woodpecker, Say's phoebe, scissor-tailed flycatcher, Bendire's thrasher, Cassin's sparrow, lark sparrow, black-throated sparrow, western meadowlark

Horned Lark *Eremophila alpestris*

Distribution and Population Trends—The horned lark is holarctic in distribution—that is, it is found throughout most of the northern hemisphere. In North America, breeding populations are found from the Arctic coast of northern Canada southward to Baja California and Central Mexico; portions of Central Canada and the Southeastern United States are excluded from the breeding range (fig. 4-17). Most birds are resident across their breeding ranges, but more northerly populations are migratory and will move southward in the winter months (fig. 4-18). Birds breeding at high elevations (for example, in tundra habitats) will move to lower elevations.

USDA Forest Service Gen. Tech. Rep. RMRS-GTR-135-vol. 2. 2005

111

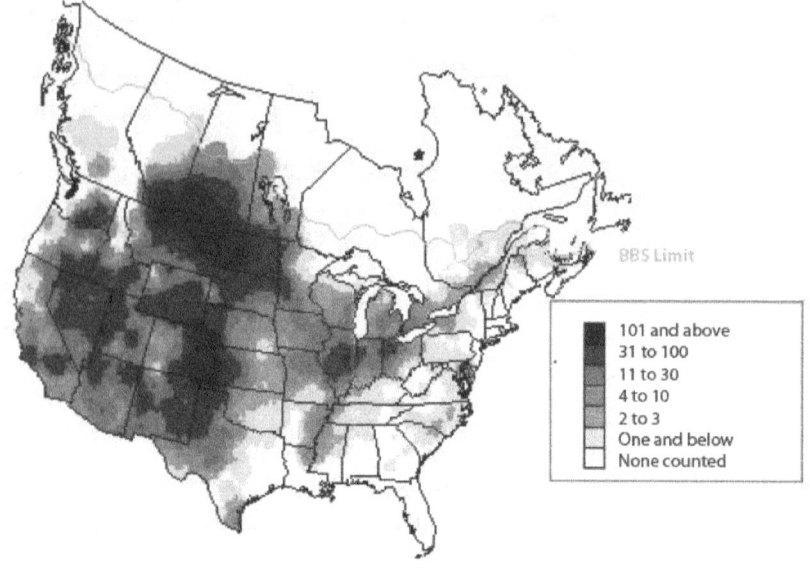

Figure 4-17. Distribution and densities of breeding horned larks in the United States and Canada, as mean numbers of individuals detected per route per year. Data averaged from Breeding Bird Surveys over the years 1982 to 1996 (Sauer and others 2001).

101 and above
31 to 100
11 to 30
4 to 10
2 to 3
One and below
None counted

Figure 4-18. Winter distribution and densities of horned larks in the United States and Canada, based on Christmas Bird Count data. Counts are average number of birds detected per survey over the years 1982 to 1996 (from Sauer and others 2001).

Average Count

< 1
1 - 3
3 - 10
10 - 30
30 - 100
> 100

This species is one of the few grassland birds that actually increased its range and numbers following Euro-American settlement of North America. Historically more restricted to the West, horned larks began a rapid expansion into the Midwest and Eastern States in the late 1800s. This range expansion coincided with the clearing of dense eastern forests and replacement of tallgrass prairie with agricultural fields, creating the types of open, short-statured herbaceous habitats preferred by this species (Hurley and Franks 1976). Horned larks will even colonize quite small, localized areas of suitable habitat, such as the mowed areas surrounding airplane landing strips; this has allowed them to expand into regions that are otherwise thickly forested and would not otherwise support this species.

Horned lark populations have declined in recent years, however, averaging a 2.7 percent negative trend annually across the continent (p = 0.00, n = 1,681; Sauer and others 2001) and dropping at an even higher rate in the Southwest. In New Mexico, Breeding Bird Survey data demonstrate an average 5.1 percent annual decrease in horned lark numbers between 1980 and 2000 (p = 0.00, n = 55); during that same period Arizona populations have declined by 6.2 percent a year on average (p = 0.001, n = 42; Sauer and others 2001). Although no precise cause has been pinpointed for these decreases, the recent increases in shrub cover in Southwestern grasslands in response to years of fire suppression and overgrazing have almost certainly played some role in eliminating suitable habitat for the horned lark in this region (Archer 1989, Bahre 1995, Glendening 1952, Humphrey 1958).

Preferred Habitat and Nest Placement Characteristics—The horned lark occurs in habitats covering a great variety of moisture regimes and elevations, as long as they share certain common characteristics: areas of short, sparse grassland with few to no woody plants and preferably at least some bare ground (Dinkins and others 2000 and references therein). Areas utilized include desert grasslands, shortgrass prairies, open, low-growing shrubsteppe habitats, and alpine meadows (Cannings and Threlfall 1981, Rotenberry and Wiens 1980, Verbeek 1967). Horned larks also readily make use of agricultural areas and are found in croplands, pastures, stubblefields, and roadsides (Beason 1995, Dinkins and others 2000 and references therein).

Numerous studies have reported that grass height in nesting habitat is approximately 10 cm (Dinkins and others 2000 and references therein). Areas used by horned larks in early spring will be abandoned later in spring or early summer when the vegetation reaches unsuitable heights (approximately 30 to 40 cm; Dinkins and others 2000). The highest population densities are often correlated with the amount of bare ground at the site (Beason 1995). Ranges reported are from 10 to 37 percent bare ground cover at occupied sites; shrub cover most often ranges from 0 to 7 percent (Dinkins and others 2000 and references therein). As an example of typical breeding habitat in the Western United States, in north-central Colorado Creighton (1974, as cited in Dinkins and others 2000) reported mean vegetation measurements of 65 percent shortgrass cover (blue grama and buffalo grass), 2 percent cover of mid-height grasses (for example, little bluestem), 6 percent sedge cover, 7 percent forb cover, 2 percent cactus cover, 0.8 percent shrub cover, 17 percent bare ground, 1 percent rock cover, and vegetation height of 7.2 cm. Horned larks consistently prefer open areas of short, sparse vegetation and tend to increase in abundance as the amount of forb and shrub cover decreases (Beason 1995 and references therein, Dinkins and others 2000 and references therein); they avoid forests and wetlands (Beason 1995, Dinkins and others 2000).

In the short term, horned larks consistently respond positively to heavy levels of grazing, most likely due to the resultant reduction in vegetation height and cover that this species seems to prefer (Anstey and others 1995 as cited in Dinkins and others 2000, Bock and Bock 1988). Horned larks have also been found to use the bare areas of ground created by cattle or bison disturbances (Skinner 1975). In Saskatchewan, Maher (1973) found horned lark densities to be three times greater on grazed as opposed to ungrazed grasslands. In assessing grazing regimes classified as light, moderate, or heavy, it is the moderate to heavy grazing regimes that create habitat most favored by horned larks (for example, Bock and Webb 1984, Kantrud and Kologiski 1982, Porter and Ryder 1974, Ryder 1980). Over the long term, however, continuous heavy grazing that leads to shrub encroachment will result in the ultimate loss of suitable habitat for the horned lark as this species avoids areas of woody vegetation.

Although several studies have reported finding horned larks to be more common in native pasture than in pastures of exotic grasses (Anstey and others 1995 as cited in Dinkins and others 2000, Dale and others 1997, Johnson and Schwartz 1993, Prescott and Murphy 1996 as cited in Dinkins and others 2000), some have found no difference (Davis and Duncan 1999, Sutter and Brigham 1998), and numerous studies have found high densities of horned larks in cultivated croplands (for example, Best and others 1997, Johnson and Igl 1995, King and Savidge 1995, Patterson and Best 1996, Prescott and Murphy 1999). Because they occupy areas with few shrubs and low vegetative cover, horned larks respond positively to burning. In Arizona, horned larks increased in numbers on burned plots for 2 to 3 years after the burn occurred (Bock and Bock 1992); the increased seed set observed in grasslands postburn (Bock and others 1976) would be a benefit to horned larks in addition to the vegetative changes that result from a burn. On mixed-grass prairie in Saskatchewan, the greatest densities of horned larks were recorded 2 years after a late summer burn (Maher 1973).

Nests are built in a small hollow or depression on the ground in areas of sparse grasses or barren ground (Baicich and Harrison 1997). Although natural depressions may be used, the female usually excavates the nest site herself (Beason and Franks 1973, Sutton 1927), then constructs a nest of fine plant materials within the depression. Nests are often placed out of the wind adjacent to a tuft of grass, cowpie, or other object (Baicich and Harrison 1997, Porter and Ryder 1974, With and Webb 1993).

Timing of Breeding and Migration—Resident horned larks are early breeders; pair formation may start as early as January, and nests are generally constructed from mid-March to mid-July. Horned larks usually raise from two to three broods a season and will renest if a nest attempt fails. Incubation generally lasts 11 days, and the young leave the nest about 10 days after hatching (Beason 1995).

In Southwestern grasslands, horned larks are permanent residents year-round (with the exception of high-altitude populations, which move to lower elevations during the nonbreeding season). These grasslands may support additional wintering

USDA Forest Service Gen. Tech. Rep. RMRS-GTR-135-vol. 2. 2005

113

migratory individuals as well, but where the more northerly populations winter is not known.

Area Requirements—Horned larks do not appear to be an area-sensitive species. In tallgrass prairies fragments in Illinois, Herkert (1991) found them in patches less than 10 ha. In shortgrass habitats of the West, breeding territory sizes ranged from 0.3 to 1.5 ha on lightly grazed pastures (average 0.7 ha; Boyd 1976, as cited in Dinkins and others 2000) to 1.0 to 1.7 ha on heavily summer and winter-grazed pastures (average 1.5 ha; Wiens 1970, 1971). In mixed-grass habitats, territories in pasture averaged 1.1 ha, and those in undisturbed areas averaged 1.6 ha (Wiens 1971).

Management Issues and Recommendations—The horned lark is tolerant of a wide range of disturbances. The most limiting factor for this species appears to be a reduction in suitable nesting habitat due to increased vegetation height and/or density, and particularly increases in woody plants. The horned lark therefore generally benefits from management practices such as burning, mowing, or grazing to reduce woody species and maintain vegetation at the preferred short, sparse levels (Dinkins and others 2000 and references therein). Skinner and others (1984) recommend prescribed burning in the spring to reduce woody species. As discussed above, horned larks respond positively to the reduction in grass height accompanying moderate or high levels of grazing. However, if grazing begins to promote woody plant establishment this will offset the benefits of grazing for horned lark habitat. Horned larks are somewhat more vulnerable to disturbance when nesting on croplands; frequent cultivation of these lands may destroy nests or young.

Due to their frequent use of agricultural lands, horned larks tend to be exposed to high levels of pesticide use, and there have been many documented cases of direct mortality or reduced densities of this species in response to such use (see Dinkins and others 2000 for detailed discussion and references). If pesticide applications are required, it is recommended that only rapidly degrading chemicals be used, and that they are applied at the lowest application rates possible (McEwen and others 1972).

Associated Species—Prairie falcon, mountain plover, burrowing owl (if burrows present), mourning dove, eastern meadowlark, western meadowlark.

Sprague's Pipit *Anthus spragueii* (Winter Only)

Distribution and Population Trends—Historically, Sprague's pipit was considered widespread and abundant (Robbins and Dale 1999 and references therein). This pipit has entirely disjunct breeding and wintering grounds, breeding in northern native prairies from southern Alberta, Saskatchewan, and Manitoba southward into Eastern Montana, western South Dakota, and northwestern Minnesota (fig. 4-19). Wintering birds are found from grasslands of southern Arizona and New Mexico east to Arkansas and Louisiana and south to central Mexico (American Ornithologists' Union 1998, Robbins and Dale 1999) (fig. 4-20). The species began to decline rapidly as Euro-American settlers in the 1800s converted the native prairie to agriculture (Robbins and Dale 1999). Thompson (1893) reported that as early as 1892, Sprague's pipit had entirely disappeared as a breeding bird from areas of Manitoba where it had been considered abundant only 10 years earlier. In the northern Great Plains of the United States, Roberts (1932, as cited in Bent 1950:53) described Sprague's pipit as being "one of the common birds of the valley" (referring to Minnesota's Red River Valley), but by 1939 Youngworth (as cited in Bent 1950:54) reported being able to "drive now for hundreds of miles in North and South Dakota and never hear or see a pipit."

Sprague's pipit continues to experience severe population declines, attributed to a combination of habitat loss through conversion of prairie to agriculture, overgrazing of native grasslands, shrub encroachment, and the introduction of exotic grasses and other plants (Bent 1950, Robbins and Dale 1999, Samson and Knopf 1994, Stewart 1975). Breeding Bird Survey data for the years 1966 through 2000 indicate significant negative trends surveywide, with populations declining at a rate of 4.7 percent a year (p < 0.01, n = 126, Sauer and others 2000). Sprague's pipit has been classified as Threatened by the Committee on the Status of Endangered Wildlife in Canada, is listed as a Species of Special Concern in Arizona, and is a Highest Priority species for New Mexico Partners in Flight; it is a candidate for State listing in Arizona (table 4-1).

Preferred Habitat—Little information has been published on the ecology of wintering Sprague's pipits. This account therefore presents data based on studies of wintering birds when it is available but will of necessity be supplemented with information from research on breeding pipits when deemed appropriate and will be so noted.

Sprague's pipit is one of the few bird species considered to be truly endemic to North American grasslands, in particular the shortgrass and mixed-grass prairies (Knopf 1996a, Robbins and Dale 1999). This pipit uses Southwestern grasslands solely as a migrant or winter resident, but winter habitat preferences of the species are virtually unstudied. Although it has generally been assumed that the pipit's winter habitat is similar to those observed on the breeding grounds (for example, Robbins and Dale 1999), the New Mexico Partners in Flight Bird Conservation Plan proposes that wintering habitat is somewhat different from summering habitat

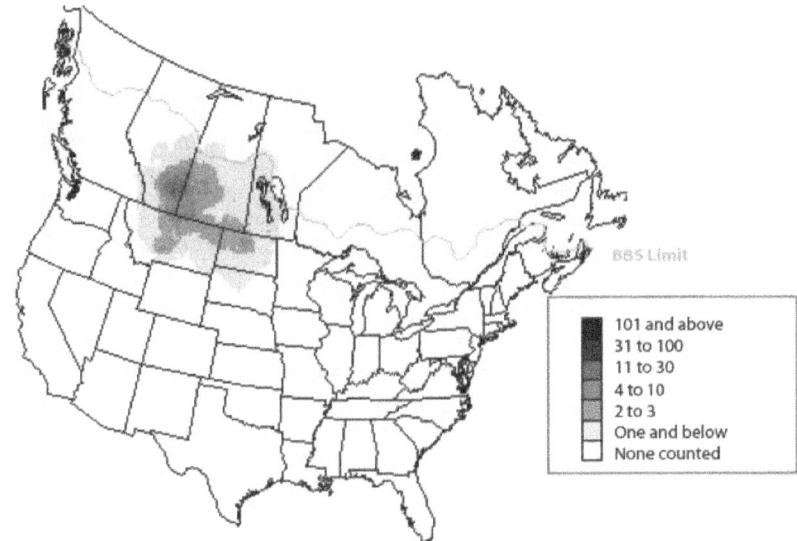

Figure 4-19. Distribution and densities of breeding Sprague's pipits in the United States and Canada, as mean numbers of individuals detected per route per year. Data averaged from Breeding Bird Surveys over the years 1982 to 1996 (Sauer and others 2001).

101 and above
31 to 100
11 to 30
4 to 10
2 to 3
One and below
None counted

(B. Howe, R. Meyer, personal communication as cited in NMPIF 2001). According to this plan, wintering pipits use areas with grasses greater than 0.3 m in height and with more than 60 percent grass canopy cover. Assuming that other aspects of habitat used between seasons may be similar, some particulars regarding pipit breeding habitat are presented here.

Nesting pipits demonstrate a preference for grasses of intermediate height and density with moderate to low levels of litter, low visual obstruction, and few or no woody plants; even grasslands with low shrub density are avoided (Robbins and Dale 1999 and references therein). Sutter (1996, 1997, as cited in Dechant and others 2001f) reports average vegetation characteristics at nest sites in Saskatchewan as 52.7 percent grass and sedge cover, 10.5 percent forb and shrub cover, 15.2 percent litter cover, 16.8 percent bare ground cover, 55.6 forb contacts per m^2, 27.7 cm maximum vegetation height, 2.4 cm litter depth, and vegetation density of 1.1 contacts above 10 cm and 3 contacts below 10 cm. Another Saskatchewan study found abundance to be positively associated with the cover of narrow-leaved grasses approximately 10 cm in height (Anstey and others 1995). Vegetation in alkaline meadows along lake borders and in dry lake bottoms has also been found to support Sprague's pipits (Saunders 1914, Stewart 1975, Wershler and others 1991).

Although preferred breeding habitat descriptions range broadly from lush grasslands (for example, Wershler and others 1991) to areas of sparse grass (for example, Kantrud 1981), one characteristic that is mentioned with remarkable consistency is a preference for native grasses over exotics. Numerous studies have reported significantly greater numbers of Sprague's pipits in native prairie when compared to pastures of introduced grasses such as smooth brome *Bromus inermis* or crested wheatgrass *Agropyron cristatum*

(Dechant and others 2001f and references therein). In Saskatchewan, Dale (1990, 1992, as cited in Robbins and Dale 1999) found that singing males were two to three times more abundant in native grasslands than in grasslands dominated by brome. Another study reports even more dramatic differences, with from four to 25 times as many singing males in native grassland when compared to crested wheatgrass at one site, and a complete absence of pipits from other crested wheatgrass sites in Alberta (Prescott and Wagner 1996, as cited in Dinkins and others 2000). Pipits are almost entirely absent from croplands during the breeding season (DeSmet and Conrad 1991, Owens and Myres 1973). Although not yet documented, Robbins and Dale (1999) speculate that conversion of native grasslands to croplands or exotic grasses on the wintering grounds may have had a significant negative impact on Sprague's pipits.

For the most part, Sprague's pipits appear to prefer undisturbed native grasslands, or if grazed, then only lightly to moderately so (Dale and others 1997, Faanes 1983, Maher 1973, Owens and Myres 1973, Stewart 1975, but see Kantrud 1981). Sprague's pipits tend to decrease in abundance as a function of increased grazing intensity (Dale 1984) and avoid heavily grazed grasslands (Anstey and others 1995, Kantrud and Kologiski 1982, Wershler and others 1991). Many variables come to play in determining the ultimate impact of grazing on pipits, including the timing and intensity of grazing, plant species composition, moisture regime, and soil type (Robbins and Dale 1999 and references therein). In the short term, heavy grazing probably reduces the grass height and density below the threshold preferred by pipits. In the long term, overgrazing would have a detrimental impact by promoting shrub encroachment and invasion by exotic plants, rendering grassland habitats unsuitable for Sprague's pipits.

Figure 4-20. Winter distribution and densities of Sprague's pipits in the United States and Canada, based on Christmas Bird Count data. Counts are average number of birds detected per survey over the years 1982 to 1996 (from Sauer and others 2001).

Average Count

▪	< 1
▪	1 - 3
▪	3 - 10
▪	10 - 30
▪	30 - 100
▫	> 100

Shrub and tree encroachment due to overgrazing on the wintering grounds of the pipit has been implicated in the loss of suitable habitat for this species (Robbins and Dale 1999, Stotz and others 1996).

Migratory and wintering habitat for the Sprague's pipit can include stubble and fallow agricultural fields, as well as weedy fields or pastures (American Ornithologists' Union 1998, Robbins and Dale 1999, Terres 1991). In the Southwest (Arizona and New Mexico), Sprague's pipits are found wintering primarily in extensive areas of well-developed desert grasslands (Hubbard 1978, Monson and Phillips 1981, Zwartjes and others 2005).

Area Requirements—The greatest densities of breeding Sprague's pipits are found in areas of extensive grasslands, suggesting that the species is area sensitive (Dechant and others 2001f and references therein). The area requirements of Sprague's pipits on their wintering grounds are as yet undocumented. We do know, however, that in the Southwest, wintering Sprague's pipits are known primarily from extensive areas of desert grasslands (Zwartjes and others 2005), and tend not to occur in areas of appropriate habitat less than 1 ha (NMPIF 2001).

Timing of Migration—Sprague's pipits are generally on their breeding grounds from April through September or October (Dechant and others 2001f). On the wintering grounds in the Southwest, pipits begin arriving in late September and continue through November (Phillips and others 1964). In New Mexico, the last migrants finish passing through by early December (Zwartjes and others 2005). Sprague's pipits may thus be expected in Arizona and New Mexico anytime from September through April.

Management Issues and Recommendations— Given the preference of Sprague's pipits for grasslands devoid of shrubs or trees, periodic burning of grassland habitats may be an appropriate management strategy (Dechant and others 2001f, NatureServe 2001). In Saskatchewan, Sprague's pipit numbers declined for the first 2 or 3 years following a burn but then recovered to densities similar to or greater than those of unburned control areas (Maher 1973, Pylypec 1991). Madden (1996, as cited in Robbins and Dale 1999) found that in North Dakota, pipits were most abundant 2 to 3 years after the occurrence of fire and up to 7 years afterward, but that none were present on native prairie that had not been burned or grazed in more than 8 years. Some researchers suggest grasslands should be burned every 2 to 4 years to provide suitable habitat for pipits on the breeding grounds (Madden 1996 as cited in Robbins and Dale 1999, Madden and others 1999). The recommended frequency for winter habitat, particularly in the desert grasslands of the Southwest, must be gauged according to local conditions (for example, moisture regimes, species composition of grassland). It should be noted that although relatively frequent burning may be appropriate in some portions of the pipit's breeding range, studies conducted in drier areas report that pipit abundance may remain high in undisturbed (unburned) native grasslands for 15 to 32 years (for example, Dale and others 1997). Thus, the required frequency of burning of winter habitat in the Southwest is most likely far lower than that suggested on many parts of its breeding grounds. Following a burn, pipit densities should initially decline as it requires a year or two for the vegetation to recover to the desired density and height, but burning should be beneficial in the long run to prevent the establishment of woody plants and clear out excessive litter and dead vegetation. Whether achieved by burning or some other means, one of the most important management goals for Sprague's pipit is to maintain grasslands that are free of woody vegetation (Dechant and others 2001f and references therein).

All published studies on the impacts of grazing have been carried out on the breeding grounds (Saab and others 1995), but the majority of studies have demonstrated that Sprague's pipits respond negatively to heavy grazing levels (Dechant and others 2001f and references therein). In New Mexico and Arizona, Sprague's pipits winter primarily in the desert grasslands along the southern border of the States. As grazing has been shown to have more dramatically negative effects on breeding Sprague's pipits in drier, less densely vegetated grasslands (Robbins and Dale 1999), it is likely that pipits wintering in the Southwest would be more vulnerable to grazing impacts than populations wintering in more mesic environments. Although pipits feed primarily on arthropods, seeds are also consumed, particularly on migration and in the winter months (Robbins and Dale 1999, Terres 1991). Grazing that prevents the formation of seed heads could thus eliminate a potentially important component of the pipit's winter diet. Overall, Sprague's pipit has proven to be tolerant of many grazing regimes subjectively described as light to moderate, depending upon local conditions (Dechant and others 2001f, Robbins and Dale 1999). Some low level of grazing is most likely acceptable for Sprague's pipit management in the Southwest, as long as monitoring of the population indicates that the species is maintaining its numbers at the site under the regime practiced (Dechant and others 2001f). On the breeding grounds, deferred rotational grazing has been suggested as appropriate (Drilling and others 1985).

Because Sprague's pipit does not nest in the Southwest, the usual issues associated with haying or mowing (that is, appropriate timing to avoid destruction of nests or young) do not apply in this case. Management recommendations for this species on the wintering grounds include maximizing the extent of appropriate grassland habitats and maintaining native grasslands or restoring haylands and pastures to native vegetation as much as possible (Dechant and others 2001f and references therein).

Associated Species—Grasshopper sparrow, chestnut-collared longspur (NMPIF 2001).

Rufous-Winged Sparrow *Aimophila carpalis*

Distribution and Population Trends—The rufous-winged sparrow, according to Allan Phillips (1968:902), is "a bird of exceptional interest . . . the most misunderstood bird in the United States." This statement was doubtless based at least in part on the highly irruptive nature of the species, leading to repeated appearances and then prolonged disappearances within its limited range. Reputed to be one of the last two distinct bird species described in the United States, the rufous-winged sparrow was first discovered in Arizona by Charles Bendire in 1872 at Fort Lowell east of Tucson (Phillips 1968). Described as abundant in the Tucson area at the time, within a matter of years the population had virtually disappeared. Following the collection of a single specimen in 1886, the species was not seen again until it was reported in 1915 on the Papago Indian Reservation (now known as the Tohono O'odham Nation) southwest of Tucson (Phillips and others 1964). By 1931 the American Ornithologists' Union had designated the rufous-winged sparrow as extirpated from Arizona (AOU 1931) and attributed the loss of the species to overgrazing (based on Swarth 1929). In 1936 the species was rediscovered, again near Tucson, and has been repeatedly documented as present in south-central Arizona ever since although its population levels and areas occupied have varied widely from year to year (Lowther and others 1999, Phillips 1968). There is some speculation that the species may never really have been extirpated from Arizona, but that its presence was missed due to the marked changes in habitat use and dramatic fluctuations in population levels of this species over time (for example, Phillips and others 1964). Furthermore, as Phillips (1968:903) points out, "no one understood the bird's requirements and everyone looked for it in the wrong places."

In the United States, the rufous-winged sparrow is found only in south-central Arizona, being primarily a Mexican species (fig. 4-21). This species is known in Arizona primarily from the eastern portions of Pinal and Pima Counties (around Oracle and Tucson) and the western half of Santa Cruz County (near Winkelman), south to Nogales and west through the Tohono O'Odham Nation and the Sauceda Mountains in Maricopa County (Latta and others 1999 and references therein; Lowther and others 1999). During irruptions, rufous-winged sparrows may be found much farther afield, occurring as far east as Sierra Vista and west to Quitobaquito (Monson and Phillips 1981). This sparrow appears to be more abundant over its range in Mexico, occurring relatively commonly in portions of central Sonora and locally in the western region of Sinaloa (Lowther and others 1999 and references therein).

Encounters with rufous-winged sparrows are so infrequent that data on this species are not presented for either Breeding Bird Surveys or Christmas Bird Counts, making population trend analysis impossible (Sauer and others 1996, 2001). Populations are nonetheless considered vulnerable because much of the former prime habitat for this species near Tucson is now unsuitable due to the expansion of urban areas, agriculture, and/or grazing (Lowther and others 1999).

USDA Forest Service Gen. Tech. Rep. RMRS-GTR-135-vol. 2. 2005

117

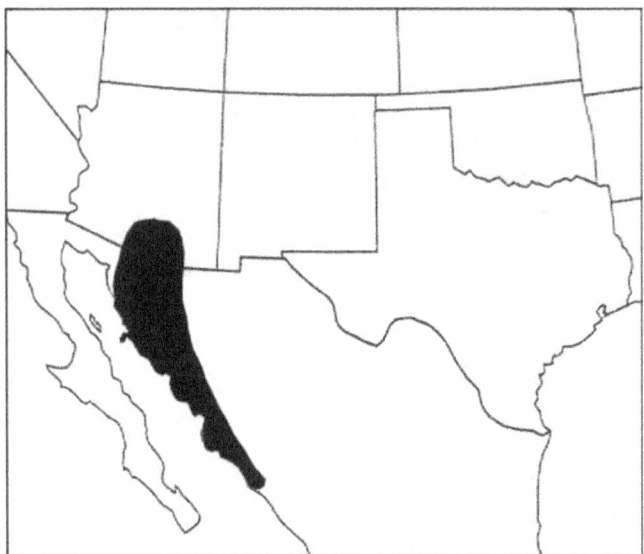

Figure 4-21. Approximate current range boundaries of the rufous-winged sparrow (from National Geographic Society 1999).

The rufous-winged sparrow is one of the priority species included in the Arizona Partners in Flight Bird Conservation Plan (Latta and others 1999).

The primary threat to this species is considered to be loss of habitat due to grazing and urban development (Lowther and others 1999). Phillips (1968) cited overgrazing as the most likely cause of local extirpations and drastic population declines witnessed in rufous-winged sparrows in the Tucson area. As evidence, he points out that this species survived in isolated pockets only in areas that had not been heavily grazed, and that the most "flourishing colonies" were formerly found in meadows of tobosa (*Hilaria mutica*), a grass that disappears under heavy grazing pressure. Even light grazing practices had led to the replacement of formerly dominant grasses such as grama (*Bouteloua* spp.) with *Aristida* (Phillips 1968), and grazing reduced the overall grass cover required to provide suitable habitat for the sparrow (Phillips and others 1964). Phillips (1968:904) further notes that the riparian habitats once utilized by rufous-winged sparrows "were soon grazed to destruction in Arizona." Overgrazing was also believed to have been the underlying cause of the presumptive extirpation of the rufous-winged sparrow from Arizona in the early 1900s (Swarth 1929).

Population losses have also been documented following the clearing of former habitat for housing development (Anderson 1965), and the Arizona Partners in Flight Bird Conservation Plan points out that many of the already limited areas in the State that currently serve as core habitat for the rufous-winged sparrow in Arizona are slated for further development (Latta and others 1999).

Brown-headed cowbirds may also be a problem for the rufous-winged sparrow, as Bendire (1882, as cited in Phillips 1968) reported that "about one-half" of the nests he found in a mesquite thicket in 1872 contained cowbird eggs. Although Phillips (1968) found little parasitism of the species in their most favored habitat, grassy swales, this is unfortunately the habitat type used by rufous-winged sparrows that has been most degraded. More recent reports cite a lower level of cowbird parasitism than that found by Bendire, however. Ohmart (1969, as cited in Lowther and others 1999) observed only seven cowbirds reared out of 90 rufous-winged sparrow nests during a 4 year study, and cowbird eggs were reported in 17 percent of nests in a study at the Santa Rita Experimental Range (Lowther and others 1999).

Preferred Habitat and Nest Placement Characteristics—The preferred habitat of the rufous-winged sparrow is generally characterized as gently sloping mixed thornscrub grasslands, composed primarily of bunchgrasses with scattered spiny shrubs and trees (Lowther and others 1999, Phillips 1968). Tobosa grass (*Hilaria mutica*) and false grama (*Cathestecum brevifolium*) are considered essential components of optimum habitat, and hackberry (*Celtis* spp.), paloverde (*Cercidium* spp.), and cholla (*Opuntia* spp.) are often present (Lowther and others 1999). In Arizona this species is typically found below 1,100 m in elevation (Lowther and others 1999) in relatively flat areas of bunchgrasses and brush, tending to avoid steep hillsides (Latta and others 1999).

Phillips (1968) described five types of habitat used by the rufous-winged sparrow: (1) grassy swales—wide, low channels flooded by desert rains and covered with tobosa grass; (2) desert washes—similar to swales but more gently sloping with bottom of drained sand and lined with paloverde, mesquite, and a brushy understory; (3) riparian habitat—flowing water, occasionally flooded bottomlands lined with bunchgrasses such as sacaton (*Sporobolus* spp.) and broad-leaved trees such as willow (*Salix* spp.) and cottonwood (*Populus* spp.), with mesquite further back; (4) farmland habitat—edges of brush along cleared fields, irrigation ditches lined with mesquite, elderberries (*Sambucus* spp.), and gray thorn (*Condalia* spp.); and (5) deep-soil habitat—scattered mesquite trees interspersed with clumps of sacaton.

Phillips (1968) specifically notes that the desert washes are marginal habitat for the species, and Lowther and others (1999) point out that the riparian, farmland, and deep-soil sites are now so altered as to no longer support populations of rufous-winged sparrows. The desert washes and surrounding uplands presently occupied by rufous-winged sparrows may represent the best remaining habitat available. However, they are poor substitutes for the lush broad riparian floodplains originally favored by this species that have now been all but eliminated within their range.

The nest of the rufous-winged sparrow is most often a solid, deep cup composed of grasses and lined with horsehair, although its exact composition depends on the materials available in the habitat. Nests are usually placed in the fork or crotch of a low shrub or tree, placed so that the rim is supported on each side and concealed by overhanging branches (Lowther and others 1999). Nest heights also vary by habitat but may range from 0.15 to 3.04 m in height (average about 0.5 to 1.5 m; Lowther and others 1999). Phillips (1968) reported nests in swale habitats at 0.6 to 2.0 m high in the edges of thick, tall desert hackberry; in desert washes, at 1.3 to 2.5 m in open paloverdes or occasionally in clumps of mistletoe (*Phoradendron* spp.) within those trees. In farmlands, nests were 1.0 to 1.3 m high in gray thorn. Nests may also be found in cholla in areas where that cactus is common (Lowther and others 1999, Wolfe 1977).

Timing of Breeding and Migration—Pair formation generally occurs in March, and eggs have been documented in nests from as early as 29 March in Arizona through 5 September, though June through August is considered the peak of egg-laying activity. In Mexico, eggs have been found as late as 16 October (Lowther and others 1999 and references therein). The nesting season "corresponds in all cases with a season of rainfall and warm to hot temperatures" (Phillips 1968:909). Ohmart (1969) reported that the birds in his study often began nest construction within 1 day of precipitation exceeding 14 mm, and in all cases within 4 days of such a rainfall event. However, Wolf (1977) found that birds in Mexico would eventually begin nesting activities even before the summer rains began if the rainy season was later than normal. Rufous-winged sparrows will most often raise second broods, even if the first brood was successful; egg dates after mid- to late July are considered to represent second nest attempts (Lowther and others 1999).

The rufous-winged sparrow is a nonmigratory resident, and territories are defended by males year-round (Lowther and others 1999). Individuals are reported to occasionally move a short distance in search of food during the winter (Moore 1946).

Area Requirements—In 1882, Bendire found no fewer than 43 nests of the rufous-winged sparrow in an area 100 m long by 400 m wide, in what Phillips (1968) calls their "original riparian habitat." In favored swale habitats, Phillips (1968) reports most territories to be less than 0.5 ha. However, as is often the case, there tends to be an inverse relationship between territory size and habitat quality. In more marginal farmland habitats, territories are closer to 1 ha (Phillips 1968). More recent estimates report average territory sizes ranging from 0.7 to 1.2 ha at a single site in Arizona

over a period of 3 years, although the type of habitat occupied there is not described (Lowther and others 1999). Active nests may be placed as close as 14 m to one another, although again the type of habitat in which this occurred is not reported (Austin, personal communication as cited in Lowther and others 1999).

Management Issues and Recommendations—It is probably no coincidence that the disappearance of the rufous-winged sparrow in Arizona in the late 1800s occurred at the same time that cattle numbers there reached record numbers (Wildeman and Brock 2000). The overstocking of the range that characterized this period resulted in extensive degradation of the broad lowland riverine floodplains that once supported the greatest numbers of rufous-winged sparrows. Such intensive overgrazing results in the elimination of the tall bunchgrasses most favored by this species, such as tobosa (Phillips 1968). Because rufous-winged sparrows are currently found in Arizona only in relatively small, remnant areas of grassland, any activity such as development or improper grazing that decreases or eliminates these habitats will negatively impact this species. Protection of remaining areas of appropriate grassland habitats for the rufous-winged sparrow should be the primary conservation goal, followed closely by restoration of such habitats.

Arizona Partners in Flight offers the following specific management recommendations for the rufous-winged sparrow (Latta and others 1999):

- Grazing should be at light to moderate levels in prime habitat and should be closely monitored to maintain appropriate use.
- Maintain blocks of habitat between developments or green belts within developments.
- Maintain current management in areas that are considered to provide core habitat for the rufous-winged sparrow, including the Santa Rita Experimental Range, Buenos Aires National Wildlife Refuge, Saguaro National Park, and Tucson Mountain Park. Additional potential core areas identified are the Tohono O'odham lands around San Xavier Mission, along the western slopes of the Baboquivari and Coyote Mountains, and on the eastern and southern slopes of the Silver Bell Mountains.

Associated Species—Cactus wren, curve-billed thrasher, pyrrhuloxia, varied bunting, canyon towhee, Scott's oriole (Latta and others 1999).

Cassin's sparrow *Aimophila cassinii*

Distribution and Population Trends—Cassin's sparrow is a true denizen of the Southwestern grasslands, being most common as a breeding bird in the arid shrubby grasslands of southeastern Colorado, eastern New Mexico, and western Texas. Its breeding

USDA Forest Service Gen. Tech. Rep. RMRS-GTR-135-vol. 2. 2005

119

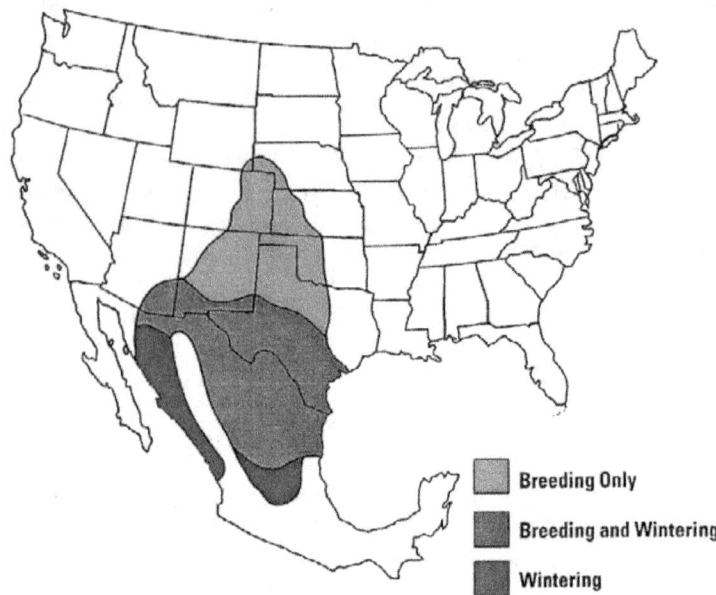

Figure 4-22. Distribution and densities of breeding Cassin's sparrows in the United States and Canada, as mean numbers of individuals detected per route per year. Data averaged from Breeding Bird Surveys over the years 1982 to 1996 (Sauer and others 2001).

Breeding Only

Breeding and Wintering

Wintering

distribution in the United States can be generally described as extending from southeastern Arizona across most of New Mexico, up into eastern Colorado and southwestern Nebraska, western Kansas, western Oklahoma, southward through the western two-thirds of Texas (fig. 4-22). This distribution extends into Mexico in the States of Chihuahua, Coahuila, in the interior south to Zacatecas and San Luis Potosí, and on the Atlantic slope from Nuevo Leon to Tamaulipas (Ruth 2000). Cassin's sparrows are migratory in the northern portions of their breeding range, retreating southward into southeastern Arizona and western and south-central Texas, being found only rarely in southern New Mexico, and extending southward into Mexico on the Pacific slope from Sonora through Sinaloa to Nayarit and south in the interior including Chihuahua, Coahuila, Zacatecas, San Luis Potosí, and Guanajuato (Ruth 2000; see fig. 4-23).

The occurrence and abundance of this species tends to fluctuate dramatically between years, making it difficult to define its actual distribution or to define population trends (Dunning and others 1999, Ruth 2000). Particularly outside of its core breeding areas (southeastern Colorado, eastern New Mexico, and western Texas), the Cassin's sparrow is highly erratic in its distribution; areas in which no Cassin's sparrows are reported for several years may suddenly have large numbers of this species breeding in other years (Dunning and others 1999). Cassin's sparrows show little breeding site fidelity between years, leading to the suggestion that they are almost nomadic (Dunning and others 1999). Defining the season of use and range of the Cassin's sparrow is challenging due to the highly cryptic nature of this species.

Inconspicuous and secretive by nature, the presence of Cassin's sparrow is most reliably detected during the breeding season by the singing and skylarking display of the males. However, in the Southwest this behavior is closely associated with the onset of summer rains, which generally commence in July in Arizona and New Mexico. Thus, the problem remains that prior to these rains, Cassin's sparrows may be present in an area but are not reliably detected (Dunning and others 1999, Ruth 2000). The actual limits of the winter range of this species are unknown because of the difficulty in identifying nonbreeding individuals (Dunning and others 1999).

The naturally variable nature of the abundance of Cassin's sparrow throughout much of its breeding range also makes it difficult to interpret the standard data gathered from Breeding Bird Surveys, as well as to detect any historical changes in distribution (Dunning and others 1999). In general, Cassin's sparrow populations appear to be stable across most of its range in the United States; although BBS data showed a significant decline surveywide in the years 1966 to 1996 (-2.5 percent, $p \leq 0.01$, $n = 203$), this downward trend appears to have been driven primarily by decreases in the Edwards Plateau and southern brushland regions of Texas (Ruth 2000). Current BBS data (1966 through 2000) demonstrate significant downward trends in this species only in Texas (-2.6 percent, $p = 0.00$, $n = 114$) and Colorado (-5.0 percent, $p = 0.02$, $n = 39$; Sauer and others 2001). In New Mexico, the Cassin's sparrow remains as the most abundant breeding bird in grasslands with a shrub component, and populations are apparently stable within the core of its range (H. Schwarz, S.O. Williams, personal communication as

Figure 4-23. Winter distribution and densities of Cassin's sparrows in the United States and Canada, based on Christmas Bird Count data. Counts are average number of birds detected per survey over the years 1982 to 1996 (from Sauer and others 2001).

Average Count

- < 1
- 1 - 3
- 3 - 10
- 10 - 30
- 30 - 100
- > 100

cited in Ruth 2000). Cassin's sparrow is a USFWS Migratory Nongame Bird of Management Concern, a Highest Priority species for New Mexico Partners in Flight, and is a priority species in the Arizona Partners in Flight Bird Conservation Plan (table 4-1).

Preferred Habitat and Nest Placement Characteristics—Cassin's sparrows are found in arid grasslands with a significant shrub component; alternatively, Cassin's sparrow habitat may be defined as shrublands with a significant understory coverage of grasses (Ruth 2000). The shrub component may be actual shrubs or vegetative forms, such as yuccas, ocotillo, cacti, or bunchgrass that approximate shrub structure. The relative proportions of grasses and shrubs used by Cassin's sparrows cover a wide range, but the structure provided by shrubs or similar plants is required by this species for both nest placement and for perches for males from which to sing or initiate their courtship flights (Ruth 2000). There is, however, an upper threshold of shrub density above which the Cassin's sparrow will not utilize the habitat; some significant area of grass cover must be available as well (Ruth 2000).

In the Southwest, most studies of Cassin's sparrow habitat have been conducted in southeastern Arizona. In this region, Cassin's sparrow is found in extensive areas of mesquite grasslands and grassy habitats in the Sonoran Zones (Monson and Phillips 1981). Bock and Webb (1984) found that plots occupied by Cassin's sparrows were characterized by a mean of 23 percent bare ground cover, 68.8 percent grass cover, 2.9 percent herb cover, and a shrub density of 23.6 shrubs per 100 m2. Shrub canopy cover was 10.3 percent on average; mean grass height was 29.1 cm. Cassin's sparrows rarely occupied plots with greater than 35 percent bare ground, and avoided areas with less than 6 percent shrub

canopy cover. In south-central Texas, the highest breeding densities of Cassin's sparrows were found in scrubby mesquite grasslands characterized by a shrub density of 717 shrubs per hectare; however, as mesquite increased in stature and density, Cassin's sparrows decreased in abundance and eventually abandoned formerly used sites (Maxwell 1979, as cited in Ruth 2000).

In southeastern Arizona, Cassin's sparrows strongly avoid heavily grazed grasslands and demonstrate a preference for ungrazed or lightly grazed upland grasslands (Bock and Bock 1988, 1999, Bock and Webb 1984). However, Ruth (2000) notes that some of the most substantial numbers of Cassin's sparrows are supported in the grasslands of eastern New Mexico, most of which are grazed to some degree. As noted by Saab and others (1995), birds respond differently to grazing in different habitats and climatic conditions. In Arizona, Cassin's sparrow was also found to show a preference for native grasslands over grasslands dominated by introduced lovegrasses (Eragrostis spp; Bock and others 1986). Cassin's sparrows are only rarely found in agricultural fields (Dunning and others 1999).

As noted above, the use of breeding habitat by Cassin's sparrows appears to be highly dependent upon patterns of precipitation. In the more arid grasslands of the Southwest, increased precipitation is positively correlated with abundance of Cassin's sparrows as well as reproductive success (Dunning and others 1999). In the more mesic, eastern portions of its range, increased precipitation may actually drive a decrease in Cassin's sparrow numbers and breeding success (Andrews and Righter 1992, Lasley and Sexton 1993, Webster 1979). Although there has been speculation that Cassin's sparrows are responding to the changes

USDA Forest Service Gen. Tech. Rep. RMRS-GTR-135-vol. 2. 2005

121

Cassin's sparrow. (Photo © Bill Schmoker, www.schmoker. org/BirdPics, used with permission)

in vegetative composition and structure that are associated with increased rainfall (for example, Dunning and others 1999), the birds generally react to the onset of summer rains within a matter of days, well before such changes take place (Ruth 2000). An alternative explanation is that these sparrows are responding to an increase in insect populations, their primary prey in the summer, which is associated with the increase in rainfall. For example, grasshoppers—an important component of the Cassin's sparrow's diet in the breeding season—respond positively to increased levels of precipitation in the Southwest (Dunning and others 1999, Ruth 2000 and references therein). Although the ultimate reason remains unknown, the erratic pattern of summer rains in the Southwest is apparently responsible for the similarly erratic or sporadic occupation of breeding habitat by Cassin's sparrows in this region (Dunning and others 1999).

Winter habitat requirements are apparently similar to those demonstrated in the breeding season, except that Cassin's sparrows retreat to the southern third of their range (Rising 1996). In southern Texas, wintering Cassin's sparrows were found in habitats ranging from grasslands with scattered patches of shrubs and mesquite to relatively dense shrublands with an overstory of taller mesquite and acacia above the primary shrub layer (Emlen 1972). Wintering birds were not found in open grasslands without shrubs (100 percent grasses and forbs) or in scrub grasslands (60 percent grasses and forbs, 40 percent low-growing woody plants, no shrubs). In Arizona, Gordon (2000a) studied wintering Cassin's sparrows in habitats described as semidesert or plains grasslands dominated by a variety of perennial bunchgrasses (*Bouteloua, Eragrostis*) with many forbs, small woody perennials, and a few scattered mesquites. As in the breeding season, wintering birds also appear to avoid using grazed grasslands (Bock and others 1984, Bock and Bock 1999, Russell and Monson 1998).

Cassin's sparrows appear to require taller, denser grasses in the winter, probably for hiding and escape cover from predators, seed availability, and thermal cover (Zwartjes and others 2005). In Arizona, Cassin's sparrows were more abundant in ungrazed grasslands that had received a high level of rainfall in the previous summer, presumably due to the resultant increases in grass cover and seed production (seeds are the dietary mainstay in the winter; Bock and Bock 1999).

The nests of Cassin's Sparrows are placed in approximately equal proportions either on the ground or low in the base of shrubs or cacti (Ruth 2000, Williams and LeSassier 1968). Ground nests are generally concealed in clumps of grass or at the base of shrubs or cacti and are not sunk below the ground surface in a scrape (Baicich and Harrison 1997, Dunning and others 1999, Rising 1996, Williams and LeSassier 1968). When placed in shrubs or cacti, nests are placed low (mean 4.0 to 15.0 cm from the ground) in plants of relatively short stature (mean 0.4 to 0.7 m in height; Ruth 2000 and references therein). Nests may be clustered, suggesting that Cassin's sparrows may at times be semicolonial (Johnsgard 1979, Williams and LeSassier 1968).

Area Requirements—Although Cassin's sparrows have been described as using extensive areas of grasslands, the impacts of habitat fragmentation on Cassin's sparrows are not known (Dunning and others 1999). In Texas, the mean territory size was 2.6 ha ± 0.5 SD (range 1.7 to 3.3, n = 21; Schnase 1984, as cited in Dunning and others 1999). In Arizona, territories were estimated to be 0.26 to 0.35 ha, although the researcher postulates that this is likely an underestimate and that the true territory size is probably closer to that reported in the Texas study (R.K. Bowers, Jr., as cited in Dunning and others 1999). The Arizona Partners in Flight Bird Conservation Plan suggests that breeding Cassin's sparrows require a minimum of 2.0 ha of dense *Grama* and bunchgrasses within a greater (minimum 16 ha) habitat matrix of mixed grasses and shrubs (Latta and others 1999).

Timing of Breeding and Migration—Breeding in this species varies widely according to local environmental conditions. In southeastern Arizona, breeding activities begin in response to the onset of the monsoon rains, which usually begin in July (Dunning and others 1999). In Texas, New Mexico, and Arizona, active nests have been found from March through September (Dunning and others 1999, Monson and Phillips 1981). In the more arid western portion of its range (Arizona and New Mexico), Dunning and others (1999) propose that Cassin's sparrow may breed only in years of unusually high precipitation.

Whether Cassin's sparrows raise more than one brood per season is unknown, although the long breeding season of this species has led some to speculate that double-brooding may be possible (Baicich and Harrison 1997, Rising 1996, Wolf 1977). The incubation period is estimated to be 11 days, and the young leave the nest approximately 9 days after hatching (Dunning and others 1999).

Exactly when Cassin's sparrows arrive and depart from their breeding and wintering grounds is hard to determine, based on the difficulty of detecting these birds when they are not actively engaged in courtship activities. Dunning and others (1999) note that the latest records in some regions do not reliably indicate when the last birds have departed, but only when the males have stopped singing. Birds probably arrive on their breeding grounds in Texas in March and return to New Mexico possibly as early as March and in large numbers by early April (Hubbard 1977). Most of the birds have left New Mexico by late September (Hubbard 1977). In Texas, Cassin's sparrows present in mid-October are considered wintering birds (Oberholser 1974). Cassin's sparrows are highly territorial and sedentary on their winter ranges (Dunning and others 1999, Gordon 2000a). Studies of color-banded birds in Arizona indicate that Cassin's sparrows here were not permanent residents but rather that wintering birds left in late April and early May, only to be replaced by a different population that then bred in the same area from July through September (Dunning and others 1999).

Management Issues and Recommendations— As shrub-grassland specialists with a relatively limited distribution concentrated in the Southwest, Cassin's sparrows are primarily threatened by the loss of habitat through conversion to agriculture, development, or desert scrublands (Ruth 2000 and references therein). Depending on local climatic conditions, poor range management and/or improper grazing practices may also contribute to loss of appropriate habitat (Bock and Bock 1988, Bock and others 1984). Because Cassin's sparrows require a combination of shrubs and grass components in their habitat, they are potentially responsive to a number of management activities that affect these proportions, including grazing, prescribed burning, shrub control, and the introduction of exotic grasses (Bock and Bock 1988, Ligon 1961, Ruth 2000).

In mesquite grasslands of southeastern Arizona, both breeding and wintering Cassin's sparrows avoided grazed plots (Bock and Bock 1988, Bock and Webb 1984, Bock and others 1984). The preferred ungrazed plots had significantly greater grass cover and herb cover than did grazed plots, and also supported greater shrub cover; grazed plots had significantly greater coverage of bare ground (Bock and Bock 1988, Bock and others 1984). Grazing may reduce habitat suitability for Cassin's sparrows by reducing vegetative height and/or density, and by altering species composition (Ruth 2000). Although such effects may actually improve habitat for Cassin's sparrows in more mesic portions of its range, where vegetation may potentially be too dense or tall, grazing should probably be avoided or carefully controlled in arid grasslands of the Southwest where the vegetation is already short and sparse (Gillihan and Hutchings 2000, Ruth 2000). Over the long term, grazing in shrubland habitats may result in an increase in shrub density to the extent that insufficient grass cover remains to provide appropriate habitat for Cassin's sparrows. Alternatively, in pure grassland habitats, grazing may result in an increase in shrub cover over the long term, which would improve the habitat for Cassin's sparrows (Ruth 2000).

Because Cassin's sparrows require at least some shrub component in conjunction with grasslands (5 percent cover has been suggested as an absolute minimum), any measures that would completely eliminate brush or shrubs (for example, chaining) are potentially detrimental (Gillihan and Hutchings 2000, Ruth 2000). However, controlled measures that would merely reduce shrub coverage in extremely dense shrub habitat (for example, selective mechanical or chemical removal) may benefit the species (Ruth 2000). The distribution of shrubs within the grasslands is apparently not important, as Cassin's sparrows have been found in habitats with both widely scattered shrubs and with shrubs occurring in dense patches interspersed with grasslands (Dunning and others 1999, Ruth 2000 and references therein).

Prescribed fire may temporarily reduce local populations of Cassin's sparrows; this species is generally absent from burned sites for the first year or two following a burn (Bock and Bock 1992, Gordon 2000b) probably due to the temporary alteration of grass cover and vegetative structure (Ruth 2000). In the long term, fire may be beneficial if it reduces overly dense shrub cover and stimulates growth of native grasses and seed production; short-term impacts may be mitigated by conducting burns in small patches to create a mosaic of burned and unburned sites (Ruth 2000).

The preservation of native grasslands with a shrub component is important for breeding Cassin's sparrows, as this species was found in significantly lower numbers in habitats dominated by exotic lovegrasses (Bock and Bock 1988, Bock and others 1986). The grasslands dominated by exotics differed from native grasslands in terms of reduced plant species diversity, shrub density, and shrub canopy cover; significantly, numbers of grasshoppers were also lower in the exotic-dominated grasslands, and grasshoppers are a diet staple for Cassin's sparrows in the breeding season (Bock and others 1986). Seeding of exotic grasses as part of a range forage improvement program should be avoided, and native grasses should be maintained or

USDA Forest Service Gen. Tech. Rep. RMRS-GTR-135-vol. 2. 2005

123

restored whenever possible to provide quality habitat for Cassin's sparrow and other grassland birds.

Associated Species—Loggerhead shrike, Botteri's sparrow, grasshopper sparrow (Latta and others 1999).

Baird's Sparrow *Ammodramus bairdii* (Winter Only)

Distribution and Population Trends—The Baird's sparrow is a true grassland specialist, one of the few species considered truly endemic to the prairies of the Great Plains (Knopf 1996a). This species occupies highly disjunct breeding and wintering grounds. Its breeding range is in the northern Great Plains, extending from eastern Montana, northern South Dakota, and western Minnesota northward into the prairies of southern Alberta and Manitoba. The majority of individuals winter in northern Mexico in the States of Chihuahua, Coahuila, Durango, and Sonora, but the winter range extends into the United States in southeastern Arizona, southwestern and south-central New Mexico, across into the Big Bend region of western Texas (American Ornithologists' Union 1998, Howell and Webb 1995, see fig. 4-24).

In Arizona, wintering Baird's sparrows are found primarily in the grasslands of the Sonoita Plains, the San Rafael Valley, and the upper Altar Valley; individuals are also found occasionally in the Sulphur Springs Valley (Jones and Green 1998, Monson and Phillips 1981). Historically this species was far more abundant in southeastern Arizona than it is today; it was described as abundant before 1878 but had become uncommon by the 1920s (Phillips and others 1964). Baird's sparrows may be found in Arizona from mid-August through early May (Jones and Green 1998). The species was formerly much more common in New Mexico as well. Described as occurring in immense numbers in the 1870s (Bailey 1928), Baird's sparrow today is considered a rare but regular migrant in the State (Jones and Green 1998). The most consistent records of Baird's sparrow in New Mexico are from the Animas Valley in Hidalgo County and Otero Mesa, Fort Bliss Military Reservation, in Otero County (Jones and Green 1998, Ligon 1961). Other recent records of Baird's sparrows are from Luna, Union, and Socorro Counties (New Mexico Department of Game and Fish 1988). Baird's sparrows may be found in the State starting in early August through late April, possibly as late as mid-May (Jones and Green 1998).

Baird's sparrow populations have experienced significant declines in the United States in recent years. Although Breeding Bird Survey data did not reveal any significant population trends over the years 1966 through 1979, Baird's sparrow numbers dropped by an average of 4.3 percent annually over the period 1980 through 2000 (p = 0.02, n = 46; Sauer and others 2001). In 1991 and again in 1999, petitions to list the Baird's sparrow as threatened under the Endangered Species Act were denied based on lack of supporting data (USFWS 1991, 1999b). The Baird's sparrow remains on the USDI Fish and Wildlife Service's list of Nongame Migratory Bird Species of Management Concern and is considered Threatened in both New Mexico and Arizona. It is a Highest Priority species for New Mexico Partners in Flight and is a priority species in the Arizona Partners in Flight Bird Conservation Plan (table 4-1).

Based on anecdotal evidence, it is likely that major declines in the abundance of Baird's sparrows have occurred over a longer time frame, and much of this change took place between the late 1800s and early 1900s before quantitative data were collected. In the late 1800s, for example, Coues (1878, as cited in Jones and Green 1998) referred to the Baird's sparrow as one of the most abundant species in the Dakota Territory. Prior to 1880, Baird's sparrows were reportedly so common in portions of North Dakota that they

Figure 4-24. Breeding and wintering ranges of the Baird's sparrow in Canada, the United States, and Mexico (from Jones and Green 1998).

Breeding

Wintering

North

outnumbered all other species of birds combined (Lane 1968). The presumably sharp drop in numbers of Baird's sparrows on their breeding grounds in the northern prairies has been attributed primarily to the conversion of its native prairie habitat to agricultural uses and degradation of grassland habitat by overgrazing (Goossen and others 1993, Jones and Green 1998, Kantrud 1981, Owens and Myres 1973, Stewart 1975, Sutter and Brigham 1998). In Canada, for example, it is estimated that more than 90 percent of the native prairie has been converted or cultivated, and numbers of Baird's sparrows have declined accordingly (DeSmet and Miller 1989). In Arizona, the primary threats to Baird's sparrows are believed to be overgrazing and loss of habitat to residential development. In New Mexico, overgrazing and conversion of native grasslands to agricultural uses are believed to be the principal threats (Jones and Green 1998).

Preferred Habitat—Unfortunately, there has been little study of this species in its winter range. The following information on wintering Baird's sparrows will be supplemented with information from studies on breeding birds where deemed appropriate and will be so noted.

Wintering Baird's sparrows are most often found in expansive areas of relatively dense, tall grasses (Jones and Green 1998, NatureServe 2001). In Arizona, habitats used may be described as open semidesert or plains grasslands, dominated by perennial bunchgrasses in the genera *Bouteloua* and *Eragrostis* (Gordon 2000a). These grasslands also supported a variety of forbs and some small woody perennials, but woody plants less than 1 m in height were restricted to a few scattered mesquite trees (*Prosopis velutina*; Gordon 2000a). In New Mexico, Baird's sparrows tend to be found primarily in mid-elevation grasslands at about 1,500 m, but on occasion have been found in mountain meadows up to about 3,600 m. In grasslands subject to grazing, Baird's sparrows are found mostly in swales with taller grass or along ungrazed roadside edges (Jones and Green 1998). On both the breeding and wintering grounds, Baird's sparrows tend to prefer either ungrazed or only lightly grazed dense grasslands with relatively few shrubs (Jones and Green 1998). In the winter, Pulliam and Mills (1977) found that Baird's sparrows were most abundant in open grasslands more than 64 m from shrub cover. Preliminary results from a study of wintering birds in southeastern Arizona show a negative relationship between the abundance of Baird's sparrows and shrub density (J. Ruth, personal communication 2002).

Some key characteristics of Baird's sparrow breeding habitat are presented here based on the assumption that winter habitat preferences may be similar to some degree (Cartwright and others 1937, as cited in Jones and Green 1998). On the breeding range,

Baird's sparrows show a preference for native mixed-grass or tallgrass prairie and are found primarily in undisturbed or lightly grazed habitats characterized by dense grasses at least 10 to 20 cm in height and with a maximum of 20 to 25 percent shrub cover (Jones and Green 1998 and references therein, Sousa and McDonal 1983). In North Dakota, the highest density of Baird's sparrows were associated with grasslands that had a relatively high but patchy coverage of forbs (20 percent) and less than 10 percent woody cover (Winter 1994, as cited in Jones and Green 1998). Traditionally Baird's sparrows are believed to exhibit an aversion to exotic grasses, although this relationship seems to hold primarily for smooth brome *Bromus inermis* and shows more mixed results for species such as crested wheatgrass *Agropyron cristatum* (Jones and Green 1998 and references therein). In Arizona, Gordon (2000a) found this species wintering in grasslands with a high proportion of the exotic Lehmann lovegrass *Eragrostris lehmanniana*. Gordon (personal communication as cited in Jones and Green 1998) speculates that the presence of exotic grasses may actually act to improve the suitability of some overgrazed habitats by providing the dense grass cover preferred by this species. Structural similarity of the vegetation may be more important in determining habitat quality for the Baird's sparrow than the actual species composition (Jones and Green 1998).

Baird's sparrows are sensitive to the structural changes in vegetation brought about by grazing. Habitats that are grazed for extended periods or subjected to excessive grazing pressure are rendered unsuitable for this species (Jones and Green 1998). Studies on the breeding grounds have shown that continuous grazing in relatively dry areas of mixed-grass prairie results in the virtual elimination of the Baird's sparrow (Dale 1984, Karasiuk and others 1977 as cited in Jones and Green 1998, Owens and Myres 1973, Smith and Smith 1966). In the Southwest, overgrazing has probably degraded wintering habitat for Baird's sparrows by promoting shrub encroachment on grasslands. Heavy grazing can also reduce habitat quality by decreasing grass density and height below the threshold preferred by this species. As wintering Baird's sparrows depend primarily upon seeds for sustenance, levels of grazing that reduce seed production may also have severe negative impacts on the population (Latta and others 1999). Grazing need not be entirely incompatible with management for this sparrow on the wintering grounds, however. In Arizona, Gordon (2000b) found no significant difference between numbers of Baird's sparrows on grazed and ungrazed grasslands; in one study year, Baird's sparrows were actually more numerous on the grazed pasture. However, the grazed pasture in this case was stocked at well below the standard stocking rate

USDA Forest Service Gen. Tech. Rep. RMRS-GTR-135-vol. 2. 2005

125

in 2 years out of the 3 years of the study, and it was rated to be in excellent condition by the Bureau of Land Management (Gordon 2000b and references therein). The 1,501 ha pasture, with a stated desired stocking rate of 1,091 animal unit months (AUM), received 1,387, 868, and 645 AUMs of grazing pressure respectively in the 3 years of the study, and grazing was concentrated primarily during the summer months. Gordon (2000b) is careful to point out that although this level of grazing did not appear to negatively impact Baird's sparrows, this species was virtually eliminated from an adjacent pasture that received more intensive grazing pressure during the same period (actual stocking rates were not reported for this pasture).

Area Requirements—Although the actual extent of the area required is unknown, Baird's sparrows are apparently quite sedentary in the winter, and individuals tend to remain within fixed home ranges once established on the wintering grounds (Gordon 2000a). Arizona Partners in Flight recommends the conservation of areas of dense *Grama* and bunchgrasses a minimum of 2.5 ha within a greater matrix of mixed grass and shrub habitat (Latta and others 1999).

Timing of Migration— In Arizona and New Mexico, wintering Baird's sparrows may arrive in early to mid-August. Most leave for their breeding grounds by late February, but some individuals may be present as late as mid-May (Jones and Green 1998, Terres 1991).

Management Issues and Recommendations— Baird's sparrows are vulnerable to habitat loss and fragmentation and show a preference for grasslands that are either of native species composition or at least composed of species that provide habitat structure and heterogeneity similar to that of native grasslands. Thus, the preservation or restoration, or both, of large expanses of native grasslands on the wintering range of the Baird's sparrow is desirable for the conservation of this species. As Baird's sparrow is relatively sedentary on the wintering grounds, it is especially vulnerable to the effects of fragmentation as it is unlikely to disperse far in search of higher quality habitat. Expansive core areas of contiguous grassland are required to sustain this species; an equal area of suitable grasslands that occur in the landscape as isolated fragments does not provide habitat of equivalent quality (Gordon 2000a). Conversion of grasslands to croplands probably represents a complete loss of usable habitat for this species and should be avoided (Goossen and others 1993).

Prescribed burning can be a potentially effective management tool for Baird's sparrow on its wintering grounds because periodic fires will help to prevent shrub encroachment and thus prevent the high densities of woody plants that Baird's sparrow avoids. Caution must be exercised, however, in tailoring the burning regime to the specific physical and vegetative characteristics of the site and in attempting to duplicate the natural fire frequency of the area (Jones and Green 1998, Madden 1996, as cited in Dechant and others 2001g, Winter 1999). If fire is used in extensive grassland areas, it may be helpful to burn small areas on a rotational basis to create a mosaic of successional stages (Johnson 1997, Madden 1996, as cited in Dechant and others 2001g, Renken and Dinsmore 1987). Alternatively, woody plants may be controlled in grasslands used by wintering Baird's sparrows through mechanical or chemical means.

Baird's sparrow appears to be tolerant of light to moderate levels of grazing. However, as this species prefers relatively dense grasses of moderate height, continuous grazing regimes or grazing at high levels of intensity are likely to result in the elimination of appropriate habitat for Baird's sparrow. One study in southern Arizona found the continued presence of wintering Baird's sparrows on pastures grazed primarily in the summer at a level of 0.4 to 0-.9 AUMs per hectare (Gordon 2000b). Long duration and/or heavy grazing levels should be avoided in areas of prime habitat for the Baird's sparrow (Latta and others 1999).

In addition to controlling shrub encroachment, perhaps the most important overall aspect of managing for Baird's sparrows in the Southwest is the implementation of range management practices that provide adequate cover for the birds and allow for greater levels of seed production to sustain wintering populations of this species (NMDGF 1988).

Associated Species—Northern aplomado falcon, horned lark, Sprague's pipit, savannah sparrow, grasshopper sparrow, chestnut-collared longspur, eastern meadowlark (Latta and others 1999, NMPIF 2001).

Acknowledgments_____

Sincere thanks to Carl Bock, Jane Bock, and Janet Ruth for their excellent and insightful reviews; their comments helped to greatly improve the quality of this chapter. Bill Howe, Christopher Rustay, and Sartor O. Williams III were all generous in sharing their knowledge with me. Additional thanks to Troy Corman, Jeff Kelly, Fritz Knopf, Janet Ruth, and Pat Zwartjes for providing information and resources to assist in my research. The species accounts for the rufous-winged sparrow and scaled quail presented here were adapted from those originally written for the Rocky Mountain Research Station's *Ecological Interactions of Ungulate Grazing and Native Species of the Southwest: Terrestrial Wildlife* (Zwartjes and others 2005). Authors of the original accounts were Walter Haussamen (scaled quail) and Michele Merola-Zwartjes (rufous-winged sparrow). Any errors or omissions remaining in this manuscript are the sole responsibility of the author.

126

USDA Forest Service Gen. Tech. Rep. RMRS-GTR-135-vol. 2. 2005

References

Agnew, W.D., W. Uresk, and R.M. Hansen. 1986. Flora and fauna associated with prairie dog colonies and adjacent ungrazed mixed-grass prairie in western South Dakota. Journal of Range Management. 39:135-139.

Aldrich, J.W. and C.S. Robbins. 1970. Changing abundance of migratory birds in North America. Smithsonian Contributions to Zoology. 26:17-26.

Allen, J.N. 1980. The ecology and behavior of the long-billed curlew in southeastern Washington. Wildlife Monographs. 73.

Ambuel, B. and S.A. Temple. 1982. Songbird populations in southern Wisconsin forests: 1954 and 1979. Journal of Field Ornithology. 53:149-158.

American Bird Conservancy. 2001. Pesticides and Birds Campaign. Available at http://www.abcbirds.org/pesticides/pesticideindex.htm. Accessed October 2001.

American Ornithologists' Union. 1931. Check-list of North American birds, 4th edition. american Ornithologists' Union, Lancaster, Pennsylvania.

American Ornithologists' Union. 1998. Check-list of North American Birds. Allen Press, Lawrence, Kansas.

Anable, M.E., M.P. McClaran, and G.B. Ruyle. 1992. Spread of introduced Lehmann lovegrass (Eragrostis lehmanniana Nees.) in southern Arizona, USA. Biological Conservation. 61:181-188.

Anderson, A.H. 1965. Notes on the behavior of the rufous-winged sparrow. Condor. 67:188-190.

Anderson, D.W. and J.J. Hickey. 1972. Eggshell changes in certain North American birds. Pages 514-540 in Proceedings of the 25th International Ornithological Congress.

Anderson, E., S.C. Forrest, T.W. Clark, and L. Richardson. 1986. Paleobiology, biogeography, and systematics of the black-footed ferret, Mustela nigripes (Audubon and Bachman), 1851. Great Basin Naturalist Memoirs. 8:11-62.

Anderson, W.L. and R.E. Duzan. 1978. DDE residues and eggshell thinning in Loggerhead Shrikes. Wilson Bulletin. 90:215-220.

Andrews, R. and R. Righter. 1992. Colorado birds. Denver Museum of Natural History, Denver, Colorado.

Anstey, D.A., S.K. Davis, D.C. Duncan, and M. Skeel. 1995. Distribution and habitat requirements of eight grassland songbird species in southern Saskatchewan. Unpublished report submitted to the Saskatchewan Wetland Conservation Corporation, Regina, Saskatchewan, Canada.

Applegate, R.D. and T.Z. Riley. 1998. Lesser Prairie-chicken Management. Rangelands. 20:13-15.

Archer, S. 1989. Have southern Texas savannas been converted to woodlands in recent history? American Naturalist. 134:545-561.

Arizona Game and Fish Department. 1988. Threatened native wildlife in Arizona. Arizona Game and Fish Department Publication, Phoenix, Arizona.

Askins, R.A. 1993. Population trends in grassland, shrubland, and forest birds in eastern North America. Current Ornithology. 11:1-34.

Askins, R.A., J.F. Lynch, and R. Greenberg. 1990. Population declines in migratory birds in eastern North America. Current Ornithology 7, 1-57. 1990.

Aspelin, A.L. and A.H. Grube. 1999. Pesticides industry sales and usage: 1996 and 1997 market estimates. U.S. Environmental Protection Agency Publication No. 733-R-99-001, Washington, D.C.

Bahre, C.J. 1987. Wild hay harvesting in southern Arizona: a casualty of the march of progress. Journal of Arizona History. 28:69-78.

Bahre, C.J. 1991. A legacy of change: historic human impact on vegetation in the Arizona borderlands. University of Arizona Press, Tucson, Arizona.

Bahre, C.J. 1995. Human impacts on the grasslands of southeastern Arizona. Pages 230-264. In: M.P. McClaran and T.R. Van Devender, eds. The Desert Grassland. The University of Arizona Press, Tucson, Arizona.

Baicich, P.J. and C.J.O. Harrison. 1997. A guide to the nests, eggs, and nestlings of North American birds. Academic Press, New York, New York.

Bailey, F.M. 1928. Birds of New Mexico. New Mexico Department of Game and Fish, Santa Fe, New Mexico.

Bailey, J.A. 1999. Status and trend of the lesser prairie-chicken in New Mexico and recommendations to list the species as threatened under the New Mexico Wildlife Conservation Act. Unpublished report submitted to the New Mexico Department of Game and Fish, Santa Fe, New Mexico.

Bailey, J.A., J. Klingel, and C.A. Davis. 2000. Status of nesting habitat for lesser prairie-chicken in New Mexico. The Prairie Naturalist. 32:149-156.

Bailey, J.A. and S.O. Williams III. 2000. Status of the lesser prairie-chicken in New Mexico, 1999. The Prairie Naturalist. 32:157-168.

Bailey, V. 1932. Mammals of New Mexico. North American Fauna. 53:119-131.

Balcomb, R. 1986. Songbird carcasses disappear rapidly from agricultural fields. Auk. 103:817-820.

Baril, A. 1993. Pesticides and wildlife in the prairies: current regulatory issues. Pages 44-48. In: G.L. Holroyd, H.L. Dickson, M. Regnier, and H.C. Smith, eds. Proceedings of the third endangered species and prairie conservation workshop. Provincial Museum of Alberta, Natural History Occasional Paper No. 19, Edmonton, Alberta.

Bartelt, G.A. 1997. Improving habitat quality of rotationally grazed pastures for grassland birds. Final report. Wisconsin Department of Natural Resources, Monona, Wisconsin.

Basili, G.D. and S.A. Temple. 1999. Winter ecology, behavior, and conservation needs of Dickcissels in Venezuela. Studies in Avian Biology. 19:289-299.

Beason, R.C. 1995. Horned Lark (Eremophila alpestris). In: A. Poole and F. Gill, eds. The Birds of North America No. 195. The Academy of Natural Sciences, Philadelphia, and The American Ornithologists' Union, Washington, D.C

Beason, R.C. and E.C. Franks. 1973. Development of young Horned Larks. Auk. 90:359-363.

Bechard, M.J. and J.K. Schmutz. 1995. Ferruginous Hawk Buteo regalis. In: A. Poole and F. Gill, eds. The Birds of North America, No. 172. The Academy of Natural Sciences, Philadelphia, and The American Ornithologists' Union, Washington, D.C.

Beintema, A.J. and G.J.D.M. Muskens. 1987. Nesting success of birds breeding in Dutch agricultural grasslands. Journal of Applied Ecology. 24:743-758.

Bell, W.R. 1921. Death to the rodents. U.S. Department of Agriculture Yearbook. 1921:421-438.

Bent, A.C. 1932. Life histories of North American gallinaceous birds. United States National Museum Bulletin No. 162.

Bent, A.C. 1937. Life histories of North American birds of prey, Part I. United States National Museum Bulletin No. 167.

Bent, A.C. 1938. Life histories of North American birds of prey, Part II. United States National Museum Bulletin No. 170.

Bent, A.C. 1950. Sprague's pipit. United States National Museum Bulletin. 197:52-62.

Bent, A.C. 1962. Life histories of North American shorebirds. Dover, New York, New York.

Berkey, G., R. Crawford, S. Galipeau, D. Johnson, D. Lambeth, and R. Kreil. 1993. A review of wildlife management practices in North Dakota: effects on nongame bird populations and habitats. Report submitted to U.S. Fish and Wildlife Service, Region 6, Denver Colorado.

Berry, M.E., C.E. Bock, and S.L. Haire. 1998. Abundance of diurnal raptors on open space grasslands in an urbanized landscape. Condor. 100:601-608.

Best, L.B. 1978. Field sparrow reproductive success and nesting ecology. Auk. 95:9-22.

Best, L.B., H. Campa III, K.E. Kemp, R.J. Robel, M.R. Ryan, J.A. Savidge, H.P. Weeks, Jr., and S.R. Winterstein. 1997. Bird abundance and nesting in CRP fields and cropland in the Midwest: a regional approach. Wildlife Society Bulletin. 25:864-877.

Best, T.L. and R.A. Smartt. 1985. Foods of scaled quail in southeastern New Mexico. Texas Academy of Sciences. 37:155-162.

Bicak, T.K. 1983. Vegetative interference: a factor affecting long-billed curlew (Numenius americanus) foraging success. Wader Study Group Bulletin. 39:57.

Biack, T.K., R.L. Redmond, and D.A. Jenni. 1982. Effects of grazing on long-billed curlew (Numenius americanus) breeding behavior and ecology in southwestern Idaho. Pages 74-85. In: J. eek and P.D. Dalke, eds. Wildlife-livestock relationships symposium:

USDA Forest Service Gen. Tech. Rep. RMRS-GTR-135-vol. 2. 2005

127

Proceedings 10. University of Idaho, Forest, Wildlife and Range Experiment Station, Moscow, Idaho.

Bock, C.E. and J.H. Bock. 1987. Avian habitat occupancy following fire in a Montana shrubsteppe. Prairie Naturalist. 19:153-158.

Bock, C.E. and J.H. Bock. 1988. Grassland birds in Southeastern Arizona: impacts of fire, grazing, and alien vegetation. Pages 43-58. In: P.D. Goriup, ed. Ecology and conservation of grassland birds. International Council for Bird Preservation, Publication No. 7, Cambridge, England.

Bock, C.E. and J.H. Bock. 1992. Response of birds to wildfire in native versus exotic Arizona grassland. Southwestern Naturalist. 37:73-81.

Bock, C.E. and J.H. Bock. 1999. Response of winter birds to drought and short-duration grazing in southeastern Arizona. Conservation Biology. 13:1117-1123.

Bock, C.E., J.H. Bock, and B.C. Bennett. 1999. Songbird abundance in grasslands at a suburban interface on the Colorado High Plains. Studies in Avian Biology. 19:131-136.

Bock, C.E., J.H. Bock, K.L. Jepson, and J.L. Ortega. 1986. Ecological effects of planting African lovegrasses in Arizona. National Geographic Research. 2:456-463.

Bock, C.E., J.H. Bock, W.R. Kenney, and V.M. Hawthorne. 1984. Responses of birds, rodents, and vegetation to livestock exclosure in a semidesert grassland site. Journal of Range Management. 37:239-242.

Bock, C.E., V.A. Saab, T.D. Rich, and D.S. Dobkin. 1993. Effects of livestock grazing on Neotropical migratory landbirds in western North America. Pages 296-309. In: D.M. Finch and P.W. Stangel, eds. Status and management of Neotropical migratory birds. USDA Forest Service, General Technical Report RM-229.

Bock, C.E. and B. Webb. 1984. Birds as grazing indicator species in southeastern Arizona. Journal of Wildlife Management. 48:1045-1049.

Bock, J.H., C.E. Bock, and J.R. McKnight. 1976. A study of the effects of grassland fires at the Research Ranch in southeastern Arizona. Journal of the Arizona Academy of Sciences. 11:49-57.

Bollinger, E.K., P.B. Bollinger, and T.A. Gavin. 1990. Effects of hay-cropping on eastern populations of the Bobolink. Wildlife Society Bulletin. 18:142-150.

Botelho, E.S. and P.C. Arrowood. 1996. Nesting success of western burrowing owls in natural and human-altered environments Pages 61-68. In: D.M. Bird, D.E. Varland, and J.J. Negro, eds. Raptors in human landscapes: adaptations to built and cultivated environments. Academic Press, San Diego, California.

Boyd, C.S. and T.S. Bidwell. 2001. Influence of prescribed fire on lesser prairie-chicken habitat in shinnery oak communities in western Oklahoma. Wildlife Society Bulletin. 29:938-947.

Briggs, S.A. and J.H. Criswell. 1979. Gradual silencing of spring in Washington. Atlantic Naturalist. 32:19-26.

Brittingham, M.C. and S.A. Temple. 1983. Have cowbirds caused forest songbirds to decline? BioScience. 33:31-35.

Brooks, B.L. and S.A. Temple. 1990. Habitat availability and suitability for Loggerhead Shrikes in the upper Midwest. American Midland Naturalist. 123:75-83.

Brown, D.E. 1982. Grasslands. Desert Plants. 4:107-141.

Brown, D.E. 1989. Arizona game birds. University of Arizona Press, Tucson, Arizona.

Bryan, G.G. and L.B. Best. 1994. Avian nest density and success in grassed waterways in Iowa rowcrop fields. Wildlife Society Bulletin. 22:583-592.

Buffington, L.D. and C.H. Herbel. 1965. Vegetation changes on semidesert grassland range from 1858 to 1963. Ecological Monographs. 35:139-164.

Burger, L.D., L.W. Burger, Jr., and J. Faaborg. 1994. Effects of prairie fragmentation on predation on artificial nests. Journal of Wildlife Management. 58:249-254.

Busby, D.G., L.M. White, and P.A. Pearce. 1990. Effects of aerial spraying of fenitrothion on breeding White-throated Sparrows. Journal of Applied Ecology. 27:743-755.

Butts, K.O. 1973. Life history and habitat requirements of Burrowing Owls in western Oklahoma. MS thesis. Stillwater, Oklahoma, Oklahoma State University.

Butts, K.O. and J.C. Lewis. 1982. The importance of prairie dog towns to Burrowing Owls in Oklahoma. Proceedings of the Oklahoma Academy of Science. 62:46-52.

Cade, T.J. and C.P. Woods. 1994. Changes in distribution and abundance of loggerhead shrikes. Journal of Ornithology. 135:288.

Campbell, H. 1952. Habitat improvement for upland game birds in New Mexico. Proceedings of the Western Association of Game and Fish Commissions. 32:115-118.

Campbell, H. 1968. Seasonal precipitation and scaled quail in eastern New Mexico. Journal of Wildlife Management. 32:641-644.

Campbell, H. 1972. A population study of Lesser Prairie-chickens in New Mexico. Journal of Wildlife Management. 36:689-699.

Campbell, H., D.K. Martin, P.E. Ferkovich, and B.K. Harris. 1973. Effects of hunting and some other environmental factors on scaled quail in New Mexico. Wildlife Monographs 34.

Campbell-Kissock, L., L.H. Blankenship, and L.D. White. 1984. Grazing management impacts on quail during drought in the northern Rio Grande Plain, Texas. Journal of Range Management. 37:442-446.

Cannings, R.J. and W. Threlfall. 1981. Horned Lark *Eremophila alpestris* breeding biology at Cape St. Marys, Newfoundland, Canada. Wilson Bulletin. 93:519-530.

Cannon, R.W. and F.L. Knopf. 1981. Lek numbers as a trend index to prairie grouse populations. Journal of Wildlife Management. 45:776-778.

Carson, R. 1962. Silent spring. Houghton Mifflin, Boston, Massachusetts.

Carter, M.F. and K. Barker. 1993. An interactive database for setting conservation priorities for western neotropical migrants. Pages 120-144. In: D.M. Finch and P.W. Stangel, eds. Status and management of neotropical migratory birds. USDA Forest Service, Rocky Mountain Forest and Range Experiment Station, GTR-RM-229, Fort Collins, Colorado.

Clayton, K.M. and J.K. Schmutz. 1999. Is the decline of Burrowing Owls *Speotyto cunicularia* in prairie Canada linked to changes in Great Plains ecosystems? Bird Conservation International. 9:163-185.

Cochran, J.F. and S.H. Anderson. 1987. Comparison of habitat attributes at sites of stable and declining long-billed curlew populations. Great Basin Naturalist. 47:459-466.

Collar, N.J., L.P. Gonzaga, N. Krabbe, A. Madrono Nieto, L.G. Naranjo, T.A. Parker III, and D.C. Wege. 1992. Threatened birds of the Americas. Smithsonian Institution Press, Washington, D.C.

Collins, C.T. and R.E. Landry. 1977. Artificial nest burrows for Burrowing Owls. North American Bird Bander. 2:151-154.

Cooke, W.W. 1915. Our shorebirds and their future. Condor. 17:237-238.

Copelin, F.F. 1963. The lesser prairie-chicken in Oklahoma. Oklahoma Wildlife Conservation Department Technical Bulletin No. 6.

Coppock, D.L., J.K. Detling, J.E. Ellis, and M.I. Dyer. 1983. Plant-herbivore interactions in a North American mixed-grass prairie II. Responses of bison to modification of vegetation by prairie dogs. Oecologia. 56:10-15.

Cox, J.R., H.L. Morton, T.N. Johnsen, Jr., G.L. Jordan, S.C. Martin, and L.C. Fierro. 1984. Vegetation restoration in the Chihuahuan and Sonoran Deserts of North America. Rangelands. 6:112-115.

Cox, J.R., G.B. Ruyle, and B.A. Roundy. 1990. Lehmann lovegrass in southeastern Arizona: biomass production and disappearance. Journal of Range Management. 43:367-372.

Craig, R.B. 1978. An analysis of the predatory behavior of the Loggerhead Shrike. Auk. 95:221-234.

Crawford, J.A. 1980. Status, problems, and research needs of the Lesser Prairie-chicken. Pages 1-7 *in* P.A. Vohs and F.L. Knopf, eds. Proceedings of the Prairie Grouse Symposium. Oklahoma State University, Stillwater, Oklahoma.

Cully, J.F. 1989. Plague in prairie dog ecosystems: importance for black-footed ferret management. Pages 47-55. In: T.W. Clar, D. Hinckley, and T. Rich, eds. The prairie dog ecosystem: managing for biological diversity. Montana Bureau of Land Management Wildlife Technical Bulletin No. 2.

Cully, J.F. 1991. Response of raptors to reduction of a Gunnison's prairie dog population by plague. American Midland Naturalist. 125:140-149.

Dale, B.C. 1984. Birds of grazed and ungrazed grasslands in Saskatchewan. Blue Jay. 42:102-105.

Dale, B.C., P.A. Martin, and P.S. Taylor. 1997. Effects of hay management on grassland songbirds in Saskatchewan. Wildlife Society Bulletin. 25:616-626.

Daubenmire, R. 1970. Steppe vegetation of Washington. Washington Agricultural Experiment Station Technical Bulletin. 62.

Davis, C.A., R.C. Barkley, and W.C. Haussamen. 1975. Scaled quail foods in southeastern New Mexico. Journal of Wildlife Management. 39:496-502.

Davis, C.A., T.Z. Riley, R.A. Smith, H.R. Suminski, and M.J. Wisdom. 1979. Habitat evaluation of Lesser Prairie-chickens in eastern Chaves County, New Mexico. New Mexico Agricultural Experiment Station, Las Cruces, New Mexico.

Davis, S.K. and D.C. Duncan. 1999. Grassland songbird abundance in native and crested wheatgrass pastures of southern Saskatchewan. Studies in Avian Biology. 19:211-218.

Day, K.S. 1994. Observations on Mountain Plovers (*Charadrius montanus*) breeding in Utah. Southwestern Naturalist. 39:298-300.

Dechant, J.A., M.L. Sondreal, D.H. Johnson, L.D. Igl, C.M. Goldade, P.A. Rabie, and B.R. Euliss. 2001a. Effects of management practices on grassland birds: Ferruginous Hawk. Northern Prairie Wildlife Research Center, http://www.npwrc.usgs.gov/resource/literatr/grasbird/ferhawk/ferhawk.htm (Version 17FEB2000), Jamestown, North Dakota.

Dechant, J.A., M.L. Sondreal, D.H. Johnson, L.D. Igl, C.M. Goldade, M.P. Nenneman, and B.R. Euliss. 2001b. Effects of management practices on grassland birds: Mountain Plover. Northern Prairie Wildlife Research Center, available at http://www.npwrc.usgs.gov/resource/literatr/grasbird/mtnplove/mtnplove.htm (Version 17FEB2000), Jamestown, North Dakota.

Dechant, J.A., M.L. Sondreal, D.H. Johnson, L.D. Igl, C.M. Goldade, P.A. Rabie, and B.R. Euliss. 2001c. Effects of management practices on grassland birds: Long-billed Curlew. Northern Prairie Wildlife Research Center, available at http://www.npwrc.usgs.gov/resource/literatr/grasbird/fplbcu/fplbcu.htm (Version 29FEB2000), Jamestown, North Dakota.

Dechant, J.A., M.L. Sondreal, D.H. Johnson, L.D. Igl, C.M. Goldade, P.A. Rabie, and B.R. Euliss. 2001d. Effects of management practices on grassland birds: Burrowing Owl. Northern Prairie Wildlife Research Center http://www.npwrc.usgs.gov/resource/literatr/grasbird/buow/buow.htm (Version 17FEB2000), Jamestown, North Dakota.

Dechant, J.A., M.L. Sondreal, D.H. Johnson, L.D. Igl, C.M. Goldade, M.P. Nenneman, A.L. Zimmerman, and B.R. Euliss. 2001e. Effects of management practices on grassland birds: Loggerhead Shrike. Northern Prairie Wildlife Research Center, http://www.npwrc.usgs.gov/resource/literatr/grasbird/logger/logger.htm (Version 17FEB2000), Jamestown, North Dakota.

Dechant, J.A., M.L. Sondreal, D.H. Johnson, L.D. Igl, C.M. Goldade, M.P. Nenneman, and B.R. Euliss. 2001f. Effects of management practices on grassland birds: Sprague's Pipit. Northern Prairie Wildlife Research Center, available at http://www.npwrc.usgs.gov/resource/literatr/grasbird/pipit/pipit.htm (Version 17FEB2000), Jamestown, North Dakota.

Dechant, J.A., M.L. Sondreal, D.H. Johnson, L.D. Igl, C.M. Goldade, M.P. Nenneman, and B.R. Euliss. 2001g. Effects of management practices on grassland birds: Baird's Sparrow. Northern Prairie Wildlife Research Center, http://www.npwrc.usgs.gov/resource/literatr/grasbird/bairds/bairds.htm (Version 17FEB2000), Jamestown, North Dakota.

DeSante, D.F. and T.L. George. 1994. Population trends in the landbirds of Western North America. Studies in Avian Biology. 15:173-190.

DeSmet, K.D. and M.P. Conrad. 1991. Management and research needs for Baird's Sparrows and other grassland species in Manitoba. Pages 83-86. In: G.L. Holroyd, G. Burns, and H.C. Smith, eds. Proceedings of the second endangerd species and prairie conservation workshop. Natural History Occasional Paper 15, Provincial Museum of Alberta, Edmonton, Alberta.

DeSmet, K.D. and W.S. Miller. 1989. Status report on the Baird's Sparrow, *Ammodramus bairdii*. Report to the Committee on the Status of Endangered Wildlife in Canada, Ottawa, Ontario.

Desmond, M. J. 1991. Ecological aspects of Burrowing Owl nesting strategies in the Nebraska panhandle. M.S. thesis. University of Nebraska, Lincoln, Nebraska. 114 p.

Desmond, M.J. and J.A. Savidge. 1996. Factors influencing Burrowing Owl (*Speotyto cunicularia*) nest densities and numbers in western Nebraska. American Midland Naturalist. 136:143-148.

Desmond, M.J. and J.A. Savidge. 1998. Burrowing Owl conservation in the Great Plains. Page 9 In: Abstracts of the Second International Burrowing Owl Symposium. Ogden, Utah.

Desmond, M.J. and J.A. Savidge. 1999. Satellite burrow use by Burrowing Owl chicks and its influence on nest site. Studies in Avian Biology. 19:128-130.

Desmond, M.J., J.A. Savidge, and K.M. Eskridge. 2000. Correlations between Burrowing Owl and Black-tailed Prairie Dog declines: a 7-year analysis. Journal of Wildlife Management. 64:1067-1075.

Desmond, J.J., J.A. Savidge, and T.F. Seibert. 1995. Spatial patterns of Burrowing Owl (*Speotyto cunicularia*) nests within black-tailed prairie dog (*Cynomys ludovicianus*) towns. Canadian Journal of Zoology. 73:1375-1379.

DeWeese, L.R., C.J. Henny, R.L. Floyd, K.A. Bobal, and A.W. Schultz. 1979. Response of breeding birds to aerial sprays of trichlorfon (Fylox) and carbaryl (Sevin-4-oil) in Montana forests. U.S. Fish and Wildlife Service, Special Science Report on Wildlife. 224:1-29.

DeWeese, L.R., L.C. McEwen, G.L. Hensler, and B.E. Petersen. 1986. Organochlorine contamination in passeriforms and other avian prey of the Peregrine falcon in the western United States. Environmental Toxicology and Chemistry. 5:675-693.

DeWeese, L.R., L.C. McEwen, L.A. Settimi, and R.D. DeBlinger. 1983. Effects on birds of Fenthion aerial application for mosquito control. Journal of Economic Entomology. 76:906-911.

Dick-Peddie, W.A. 1993. New Mexico vegetation: past, present, future. University of New Mexico Press, Albuqueruqe, New Mexico.

Dinkins, M.F., A.L. Zimmerman, J.A. Dechant, B.D. Parkin, D.H. Johnson, L.D. Igl, C.M. Goldade, and B.R. Euliss. 2000. Effects of management practices on grasslands birds: Horned Lark. Northern Prairie Wildlife Research Center, Jamestown, North Dakota. Northern Prairie Wildlife Research Center Home Page, available at http://www.npwrc.usgs.gov/resource/literatr/grasbird/hola/hola.htm (Version 16JUN2000).

DiSilvestro, R. 1996. Poison in the Pampas: what's killing the Swainson's hawk? International Wildlife. 26:38-43.

Doerr, T.B. and F.S. Guthery. 1980. Effects of shinnery oak control on Lesser Prairie-chicken habitat. Pages 59-63. In: P.A. Vohs and F.L. Knopf, eds. Proceedings of the Prairie Grouse Symposium. Stillwater, Oklahoma.

Duebbert, H.F. and J.T. Lokemoen. 1977. Upland nesting of American bitterns, marsh hawks, and short-eared owls. Prairie Naturalist. 9:33-40.

Dundas, H. and J. Jensen. 1995. Burrowing owl status and conservation. Bird Trends (Canadian Wildlife Service). 4:21-22.

Dunning, J.B. Jr., R.K. Bower Jr., S.J. Suter, and C.E. Bock. 1999. Cassin's Sparrow (*Aimophila cassinii*). In: A. Poole and F. Gill, eds. The Birds of North America, No. 471. The National Academy of Sciences, Philadelphia, Pennsylvania, and The American Ornithologists' Union, Washington, D.C.

Durrant, S.D.D. 1970. Faunal remains as indicators of Neothermal climates at Hogup Cave. Appendix II. Pages 241-245. n: C.M. Aikens, ed. University of Utah Anthropology Papers, No. 93.

Dyer, M.I. 1979. Consumers Pages 73-86. In: R.T. Coupland, ed. Grassland ecosystems of the world: analysis of grasslands and their uses. Cambridge University Pres, Cambridge, England.

Ehrlich, P.R., D.S. Dobkin, and D. Wheye. 1988. The Birder's Handbook. Simon and Schuster, Inc., New York, New York.

Ellison-Manning, A.E. and C.M. White. 2001. Breeding biology of Mountain Plovers (*Charadrius montanus*) in the Uinta Basin. Western North American Naturalist 61:223-228.

Emlen, J.T. 1972. Size and structure of a wintering avian community in southern Texas. Ecology. 53:317-329.

Environmental Protection Agency (EPA). 1989. Carbofuran: a special review technical support document. PA Office of Pesticides and Toxic Substances, Washington, D.C.

Faanes, C.A. 1983. Breeding birds of wooded draws in western North Dakota. Prairie Naturalist. 15:173-187.

Faanes, C.A. and G.R. Lingle. 1995. Breeding birds of the Platte River Valley of Nebraska. Northern Prairie Wildlife Research Center http://www.npwrc.usgs.gov/resource/distr/birds/platte/platte.htm (Version 16JUL97), Jamestown, North Dakota.

Finch, D.M., S.H. Anderson, and W.A. Hubert. 1987. Habitat suitability index models: lark bunting. U.S. Fish and Wildlife Service, Biological Report 82(10.137), Fort Collins, Colorado.

USDA Forest Service Gen. Tech. Rep. RMRS-GTR-135-vol. 2. 2005

129

Findley, J.S. 1987. The natural history of New Mexican mammals. University of New Mexico Press, Albuquerque, New Mexico.

Finzel, J.E. 1964. Avian populations of four herbaceous communities in southeastern Wyoming. Condor. 66:496-510.

Fleischner, T.L. 1994. Ecological costs of livestock grazing in western North America. Conservation Biology. 8:629-644.

Forbush, E.H. 1912. A history of game birds, wild-fowl and shore birds of Massachusetts and adjacent states. Massachusetts State Board of Agriculture, Boston, Massachusetts.

Fox, G.A., P. Mineau, B. Collins, and P.C. James. 1989. The impact of insecticide carbofuran (Furadan 480F) on the Burrowing Owl in Canada. Canadian Wildlife Service, Technical Report Series No. 72, Ottawa, Canada.

Frawley, B.J. and L.B. Best. 1991. Effects of mowing on breeding bird abundance and species composition in alfalfa fields. Wildlife Society Bulletin. 19:135-142.

Friedmann, H. 1929. The cowbirds: a study in the biology of social parasitism. C. Thomas, Springfield, Illinois.

Friedmann, H. 1963. Host relations of the parasitic cowbirds. U.S. National Museum Bulletin 233.

Friedmann, H. and L.F. Kiff. 1985. The parasitic cowbirds and their hosts. Proceedings of the Western Foundation of Zoology 2:226-304.

Gard, N.W. and M.J. Hooper. 1995. An assessment of potential hazards of pesticides and environmental contaminants. Pages 294-310. In: T.E. Martin and D.M. Finch, eds. Ecology and management of neotropical migratory birds: a synthesis and review of critical issues. Oxford University Press, New York, New York.

Gates, J.E. and L.W. Gysel. 1978. Avian nest dispersion and fledgling success in field-forest ecotones. Ecology. 59:871-883.

Giesen, K.M. 1994. Movements and nesting habitat of Lesser Prairie-chicken hens in Colorado. Southwestern Naturalist. 39:96-98.

Giesen, K.M. 1998. Lesser Prairie-Chicken (Tympanuchus pallidicinctus). In: A. Poole and F. Gill, eds. The Birds of North America, No. 364. The Academy of Natural Sciences, Philadelphia, Pennsylvania, and The American Ornithologists' Union, Washington, D.C.

Giesen, K.M. 2000. Population status and management of lesser prairie-chicken in Colorado. The Prairie Naturalist. 32:137-148.

Gillihan, S.W., D.J. Hanni, S.W. Hutchings, T. Toombs, and T. VerCauteren. 2001. Sharing your land with shortgrass prairie birds. Rocky Mountain Bird Observatory, Brighton, Colorado.

Gillihan, S.W. and S.W. Hutchings. 2000. Best management practices for shortgrass prairie birds: a landowner's guide. Colorado Bird Observatory, Brighton, Colorado.

Gleason, R.S. and D.R. Johnson. 1985. Factors influencing nesting success of Burrowing Owls in southeastern Idaho. Great Basin Naturalist. 45:81-84.

Glendening, G.E. 1952. Some quantitative data on the increase of mesquite and cactus on a desert grassland range in southern Arizona. Ecology. 33:57-74.

Glinski, R.L. 1998. Ferruginous Hawk. Pages 105-108. In: R.L. Glinski, ed. The raptors of Arizona. University of Arizona Press, Tucson, Arizona.

Goodwin, J.G. Jr. and C.R. Hungerford. 1977. Habitat used by native Gambel's and Scaled quail and released masked bobwhite quail in southern Arizona. USDA Forest Service Research Paper RM-197, Rocky Mountain Forest and Range Experiment Station, Fort Collins, Colorado.

Goossen, J.P., S. Brechtel, K.D. DeSmet, D. Hjertass, and C. Werschler. 1993. Canadian Baird's Sparrow recovery plan. Recovery of Nationally Endangered Wildlife, Report No. 3. Canadian Wildlife Federation, Ottawa, Ontario.

Gordon, C.E. 2000a. Movement patterns of wintering grassland sparrows in Arizona. Auk. 117:748-759.

Gordon, C.E. 2000b. Fire and cattle grazing on wintering sparrows in Arizona grasslands. Journal of Range Management. 53:384-389.

Graber, R.R., J.W. Graber, and E.L. Kirk. 1973. Illinois birds: Laniidae. Illinois Natural History Survey Biological Notes. 83:1-18.

Grant, R.A. 1965. The Burrowing Owl in Minnesota. Loon. 37:2-17.

Graul, W.D. 1975. Breeding biology of the Mountain Plover. Wilson Bulletin. 87:6-31.

Graul, W.D. and L.E. Webster. 1976. Breeding status of the Mountain Plover. Condor. 78:265-267.

Green, G.A. and R.G. Anthony. 1989. Nesting success and habitat relationships of Burrowing Owls in the Columbia Basin, Oregon. Condor. 91:347-354.

Green, G.A., and R.G. Anthony. 1997. Ecological considerations for management of breeding burrowing owls in the Columbia Basin. Pages 117-121 in J.L. Lincer and K. Steenhof, eds. The Burrowing Owl, its biology and management: including the Proceedings of the First International Symposium. Raptor Research Report Number 9.

Grue, C.E., W.J. Fleming, D.G. Busby, and E.F. Hill. 1983. Assessing hazards of organophosphate pesticides to wildlife. Transactions of the North American Wildlife Natural Resources Conference. 48:200-220.

Grue, C.E., P.L. Gilbert, and M.E. Seeley. 1997. Neurophysiological and behavioral changes in non-target wildlife exposed to organophosphate and carbamate pesticides: Thermoregulation, food consumption, and reproduction. American Zoologist. 37:369-388.

Grue, C.E. and B.K. Shipley. 1984. Sensitivity of nestling and adult starlings to dicrotophos, an organophosphate insecticide. Environmental Research. 35:454-465.

Gryzbowski, J.A. 1991. Ecology and management of isolated populations of the black-capped vireo (Vireo atricapillus) in Oklahoma. Oklahoma Department of Conservation Performance Report E-1-6.

Hands, H.M., R.D. Drobney, and M.R. Ryan. 1989. Status of the Loggerhead Shrike in the northcentral United States. U.S. Fish and Wildlife Service, Missouri Cooperative Fish and Wildlife Research Unit, University of Missouri, Columbia, Missouri.

Hart, A.D.M. 1993. Relationship between behavior and the inhibition of acetyl-cholinesterase in birds exposed to organophosphorus pesticides. Environmental Toxicology and Chemistry. 12:321-336.

Haug, E.A. 1985. Observations on the breeding ecology of Burrowing Owls in Saskatchewan. M.S. thesis. Saskatoon, Saskatchewan, Canada, University of Saskatchewan.

Haug, E.A. and A.B. Didiuk. 1991. Updated status report on the burrowing owl Athene cunicularia hypugaea in Canada. Committee on the Status of Endangered Wildlife in Canada.

Haug, E.A., B.A. Millsap, and M.S. Martell. 1993. Burrowing Owl (Speotyto cunicularia). In: A. Poole and F. Gill, eds. The Birds of North America, No. 61. The Academy of Natural Sciences, Philadelphia, Pennsylvania, and The American Ornithologists' Union, Washington, D.C.

Haug, E.A. and L.W. Oliphant. 1987. Breeding biology of Burrowing Owls in Saskatchewan. Pages 269-271. In: G.L. Holroyd, W.B. McGillivray, P.H.R. Stepney, D.M. Ealey, G.C. Trottier, and K.E. Eberhart, eds. Endangered species in the Prairie Provinces. Provincial Museum of Alberta Occasional Paper No. 9, Edmonton, Alberta.

Haug, E.A. and L.W. Oliphant. 1990. Movements, activity patterns, and habitat use of Burrowing Owls in Saskatchewan. Journal of Wildlife Management. 54:27-35.

Haukos, D.A. and L.M. Smith. 1989. Lesser Prairie-Chicken nest site selection and vegetation characteristics in tebuthiuron-treated and untreated sand shinnery oak in Texas. Great Basin Naturalist. 49:624-626.

Hawks Aloft. 1998. Nest site selection, reproductive success, and territory reoccupation of Ferruginous Hawks in three regions of New Mexico. Report submitted to the Bureau of Land Management, New Mexico Department of Game and Fish, the National Fish and Wildlife Foundation, the U.S. Fish and Wildlife Service, and the Turner Foundation. Albuquerque, New Mexico.

Henny, C.J., F.P. Ward, K.E. Riddle, and R.M. Prouty. 1982. Migratory Peregrine Falcons, Falco peregrinus, accumulate pesticides in Latin America during winter. Canadian Field Naturalist. 96:333-338.

Herkert, J.R. 1991. Study suggests increases in restored prairie fragments to conserve breeding bird communities. Restoration and Management Notes. 9:107.

Herkert, J.R. 1994. The effects of habitat fragmentation on midwestern grassland bird communities. Ecological Applications. 4:461-471.

Herkert, J.R., D.W. Sample, and R.E. Arner. 1996. Management of midwestern grassland landscapes for the conservation of migratory birds. Pages 89-116. In: F.R. Thompson III, ed. Managing midwestern landscapes for the conservation of neo-tropical migratory birds. USDA Forest Service North Central Forest Experimental Station, General Technical Report GTR-NC-187, St. Paul, Minnesota.

Hill, E.F. and W.J. Fleming. 1982. Anticholinesterase poisoning of birds: field monitoring and diagnosis of acute poisoning. Environmental Toxicology and Chemistry. 1:27-38.

Hobbs, R.J. and L.F. Huenneke. 1992. Disturbance, diversity, and invasion: implications for conservation. Conservation Biology. 6:324-337.

Hoffman, D.M. 1963. The lesser prairie-chicken in Colorado. Journal of Wildlife Management. 27:726-732.

Holland, E.A. and J.K. Detling. 1990. Plant response to herbivory and below ground nitrogen cycling. Ecology . 71:1040-1049.

Holochek, J.L., R.D. Piper, and C.H. Herbel. 1989. Range management principles and practices. Prentice Hall, Englewood Cliffs, New Jersey.

Hooper, M.J., L.W. Brewer, G.P. Cobb, and R.J. Kendall. 1990. An integrated laboratory and field approach for assessing hazards of pesticides exposure to wildlife. Pages 271-283 In: L. Somerville and C.H. Walker, eds. Pesticide effects on terrestrial wildlife. Taylor and Francis, London, England.

Horton, R.E. 2000. Distribution and abundance of lesser prairie-chicken in Oklahoma. The Prairie Naturalist. 32:189-195.

Howard, R.P. and M.L. Wolfe. 1976. Range improvement practices and Ferruginous Hawks.Journal of Range Management. 29:33-37.

Howell, S.N.G. and S. Webb. 1995. A guide to the birds of Mexico and northern Central America. Oxford University Press, Oxford, England.

Hubbard, J.P. 1977. The status of Cassin's sparrow in New Mexico and adjacent states. American Birds. 31:933-941.

Hubbard, J.P. 1978. Revised check-list of the birds of New Mexico. New Mexico Ornithological Society Publication No. 6.

Hubbard, J.P. and C.G. Schmitt. 1984. The black-footed ferret in New Mexico. New Mexico Game and Fish Department, unpublished report to the New Mexico Bureau of Land Management, Santa Fe, New Mexico.

Humphrey, R.R. 1958. The desert grassland. Botanical Review. 24:193-253.

Humphrey, R.R. 1987. 90 years and 535 miles: vegetation changes along the Mexican border. University of New Mexico Press, Albuquerque, New Mexico.

Hungerford, C.R. 1964. Vitamin A and productivity in Gambel's quail. Journal of Wildlife Management. 28:141-147.

Hunter Jr., M.L. and J.W. Witham. 1985. Effects of a carbaryl induced depression of arthropod abundance on the behavior of Parulinae warblers. Canadian Journal of Zoology. 63:2612-2616.

Hurley, R.J. and E.C. Franks. 1976. Changes in the breeding ranges of two grassland birds. Auk. 93:108-115.

Jackson, A.S. and R. DeArment. 1963. The lesser prairie-chicken in the Texas panhandle. Journal of Wildlife Management. 27:733-737.

James, P.C. and R.H.M. Espie. 1997. Current status of the burrowing owl in North America: an agency survey. Pages 3-5. In: J.L. Lincer and K. Steenhof, eds. The burrowing owl: its biology and management. Raptor Research Report No. 9. Raptor Research Foundation.

James, P.C. and T.J. Ethier. 1989. Trends in the winter distribution and abundance of burrowing owls in North America. American Birds. 43:1224-1225.

James, P.C. and G.A. Fox. 1987. Effects of some insecticides on productivity of Burrowing Owls. Blue jay. 45:65-71.

James, P.C., G.A. Fox, and T.J. Ethier. 1990. Is the operational use of strychnine to control ground squirrels detrimental to Burrowing Owls? Journal of Raptor Research. 24:120-123.

James, T.R. and R.W. Seabloom. 1968. Notes on the burrow ecology and food habits of the Burrowing Owl in southwestern North Dakota. Blue Jay. 26:83-84.

Janes, S.W. 1985. Habitat selection in raptorial birds. Pages 159-188. In: M.L. Cody, ed. Habitat selection in birds. Academic Press, New York, New York.

Jensen, J.K. 1925. Late nesting of scaled quail. Auk. 42:129-130.

Jewett, S.G. 1936. Bird notes from Harney County, Oregon, during May 1934. Murrelet. 17:41-47.

Johnsgard, P.A. 1979. Birds of the Great Plains. University of Nebraska Press, Lincoln, Nebraska.

Johnsgard, P.A. 1980. A preliminary list of the birds of Nebraska and adjacent Plains states. University of Nebraska, Lincoln, Nebraska.

Johnson, D.H. 1997. Effects of fire on bird populations in mixed-grass prairie. Pages 181-206. In: F.L. Knopf and F.B. Samson, eds. Ecology and conservation of Great Plains vertebrates. Springer-Verlag, New York, New York.

Johnson, D.H. and L.D. Igl. 1995. Contributions of the Conservation Reserve Program to populations of breeding birds in North Dakota. Wilson Bulletin . 107:709-718.

Johnson, D.H. and L.D. Igl. 2001. Effects of management practices on grassland birds. Northern Prairie Wildlife Research Center Home Page, available at http://www.npwrc.usgs.gov/resource/literatr/grasbird/grasbird.htm (Version 11APR2001). Northern Prairie Wildlife Research Center, Jamestown, North Dakota.

Johnson, D.H. and M.D. Schwartz. 1993. The Conservation Reserve Program: habitat for grassland birds.Great Plains Research. 3:273-295.

Johnson, R.G. and S.A. Temple. 1986. Assessing habitat quality for birds nesting in fragmented tallgrass prairies. Pages 245-249. In: J.A. Verner, M.L. Morrison, and C.J. Ralph, eds. Wildlife 2000: Modeling habitat relationships of terrestrial vertebrates. University of Wisconsin Press, Madison, Wisconsin.

Johnson, R.G. and S.A. Temple. 1990. Nest predation and brood parasitism of tallgrass prairie birds.Journal of Wildlife Management. 54:106-111.

Johnston, D.W. 1975. Organochlorine pesticide residues in small migratory birds, 1974-1973. Pesticide Monitoring Journal. 9:79-88.

Jones, A. 2000. Effects of cattle grazing on North American arid ecosystems: a quantitative review. Western North American Naturalist. 60:155-164.

Jones, R.E. 1963. Identification and analysis of Lesser and Greater Prairie-chicken habitat. Journal of Wildlife Management. 27:757-778.

Jones, S.L. and M.T. Green. 1998. Baird's Sparrow status assessment and conservation plan. May, 1998. Administrative Report. U.S. Department of Interior, Fish and Wildlife Service, Denver, Colorado.

Kantrud, H.A. 1981. Grazing intensity effects on the breeding avifauna of North Dakota native grasslands. Canadian Field Naturalist. 95:404-417.

Kantrud, H.A. and K.F. Higgins. 1992. Nest and nest site characteristics of some ground-nesting, non-passerine birds of northern grasslands. Prairie Naturalist. 24:67-84.

Kantrud, H.A. and R.L. Kologiski. 1982. Effects of soils and grazing on breeding birds of uncultivated upland grasslands of the northern Great Plains. USDI Fish and Wildlife Service Research Publication no. 15, Washington, D.C.

King, J.W. and J.A. Savidge. 1995. Effects of the Conservation Reserve Program on wildlife in southeast Nebraska. Wildlife Society Bulletin. 23:377-385.

Knight, R.L. and Gutzwiller, K.G. 1995. Wildlife and recreationists: coexistence through research and management. Covelo, California, Island Press.

Knopf, F.L. 1994. Avian assemblages on altered grasslands. Studies in Avian Biology. 15:247-257.

Knopf, F.L. 1996a. Prairie Legacies—Birds. Pages 135-148. In: F.B. Samson and F.L. Knopf, eds. Prairie conservation: preserving North America's most endangered ecosystem. Island Press, Washington, D.C.

Knopf, F.L. 1996b. Grazing nongame bird habitats. Pages 51-58 in P.R. Krausman, ed. Rangeland wildlife. The Wildlife Society, Denver, Colorado.

Knopf, F.L. 1996c. Mountain Plover (Charadrius montanus). in A. Poole and F. Gill, eds. The birds of North America, No. 211. The Academy of Natural Sciences and The American Ornithologists' Union, Philadelphia, Pennsylvania and Washington, D.C.

Knopf, F.L. and B.J. Miller. 1994. Charadrius montanus—montane, grassland, or bare-ground plover? Auk. 11:504-506.

USDA Forest Service Gen. Tech. Rep. RMRS-GTR-135-vol. 2. 2005

131

Knopf, F.L. and J.R. Rupert. 1995. Habits and habitats of Mountain Plovers in California. Condor. 97:743-751.

Knopf, F.L. and J.R. Rupert. 1996. Reproduction and movements of mountain plovers breeding in Colorado. Wilson Bulletin. 108:28-35.

Knopf, F.L. and J.R. Rupert. 1999. Use of cultivated fields by breeding mountain plovers in Colorado. Studies in Avian Biology. 19:81-86.

Knowles, C. 1986. Some relationships of black-tailed prairie dogs to livestock grazing. Great Basin Naturalist. 46:198-203.

Knowles, C.J. and P.R. Knowles. 1984. Additional records of Mountain Plovers using prairie dog towns in Montana. Prairie Naturalist. 16:183-186.

Knowles, C.J., C.J. Stoner, and S.P. Gieb. 1982. Selective use of black-tailed prairie dog towns by Mountain Plovers. Condor. 84:71-74.

Koerth, B.H., W.M. Webb, F.C. Bryant, and F.S. Guthery. 1983. Cattle trampling of simulated ground nests under short duration and continuous grazing. Journal of Range Management. 36:385-386.

Koford, C.B. 1958. Prairie dogs, whitefaces, and blue grama. Wildlife Monographs. 3:1-78.

Konrad, P.M. and D.S. Gilmer. 1984. Observations on the nesting ecology of Burrowing Owls in central North Dakota. Prairie Naturalist. 16:129-130.

Korschgen, L.J. 1970. Soil food-chain pesticide relationships in aldrin-treated fields. Journal of Wildlife Management. 34:186-199.

Kotliar, N.B., B.W. Baker, A.D. Whicker, and G. Plumb. 1999. A critical review of assumptions about the prairie dog as a keystone species. Environmental Management. 24:177-192.

Krueger, K. 1986. Feeding relationships among bison, pronghorn, and prairie dogs: an experimental analysis. Ecology. 67:760-770.

Lane, J. 1968. Baird's Sparrow. United States National Museum Bulletin. 237:745-765.

Lanyon, W.E. 1995. Eastern Meadowlark (Sturnella magna). in A. Poole and F. Gill, eds. The birds of North America, No. 160. Academy of Natural Sciences, Philadelphia, PA, and American Ornithologists' Union, Washington, D.C.

Lasley, G.W. and C. Sexton. 1993. The nesting season. American Birds. 47:1128.

Latta, M.J., C.J. Beardmore, and T.E. Corman. 1999. Arizona Partners in Flight Bird Conservation Plan version 1.0. Nongame and endangered wildlife program technical report. Arizona Game and Fish Department, Phoenix, Arizona.

Laursen, K. 1981. Birds on roadside verges and the effect of mowing on frequency and distribution. Biological Conservation. 20:59-68.

Leary, A.W., R. Mazaika, and M.J. Bechard. 1998. Factors affecting the size of Ferruginous Hawk home ranges. Wilson Bulletin. 110:198-205.

Lehmann, V.W. 1953. Bobwhite population fluctuations and vitamin A. Transactions of the North American Wildlife Conference. 18:199-246.

Ligon, J.S. 1927. Wildlife of New Mexico, its conservation and management. New Mexico State Game Commission, Santa Fe, New Mexico.

Ligon, J.S. 1937. Tragedy of upland game birds throughout the west and southwest. Transactions of the North American Wildlife Conference. 2:476-480.

Ligon, J.S. 1961. New Mexico birds and where to find them. University of New Mexico Press, Albuquerque, New Mexico.

Loftin, S.R., C.E. Bock, J.H. Bock, and S.L. Brantley. 2000. Desert grasslands. Pages 53-96 In: R. Jemison and C. Raish, eds. Livestock management in the American Southwest: ecology, society, and economics. Elsevier, Amsterdam, The Netherlands.

Lokemoen, J.T. and H.F. Duebbert. 1976. Ferruginous Hawk nesting ecology and raptor populations in northern South Dakota. Condor. 78:464-470.

Lovejoy, T.C., R.O. Bieregaard Jr., A.B. Rylands, J.R. Malcolm, C.E. Quintela, L.H. Harper, K.S. Brown Jr., A.H. Powell, G.V.N. Powell, H.O.R. Schubart, and M.B. Hays. 1986. Edge and other effects of isolation on Amazon forest fragments. Pages 257-285. In: M.E. Soulé, ed. Conservation biology: The science of scarcity and diversity. Sinauer Associates, Sunderland, Massachusetts.

Lowther, P.E., K.D. Groschupf, and S.M. Russell. 1999. Rufous-winged Sparrow (Aimophila carpalis). In: A. Poole and F. Gill, eds.

The birds of North America, No. 422. The Academy of Natural Sciences, Philadelphia, and The American Ornithologists' Union, Washington, D.C.

MacCracken, J.G., D.W. Uresk, and R.M. Hansen. 1984. Burrowing Owl nesting habitat use in Conata Basin, South Dakota. Abstracts of the Society for Range Mangaement 37th annual Meeting, Rapid City, South Dakota.

MacCracken, J.G., D.W. Uresk, and R.M. Hansen. 1985. Vegetation and soils of Burrowing Owl nest sites in Conata Basin, South Dakota. Condor. 87:152-154.

Mack, R.N. 1981. Invasion of Bromus tectorum L. into western North America: an ecological chronicle. Agro-Ecosystems. 7:145-165.

Mack, R.N. and J.N. Thompson. 1982. Evolution in steppe with few large, hooved mammals. American Naturalist. 119:757-773.

Madden, E.M., A.J. Hansen, and R.K. Murphy. 1999. Influence of prescribed fire history on habitat and abundance of passerine birds in northern mixed-grass prairie. Canadian Field Naturalist. 113:627-640.

Maher, W.J. 1973. Matador Project: Birds I. Population dynamics. Canadian Committee for the International Biological Programme, Matador Project, Technical Report 34. University of Saskatchewan, Saskatoon, Saskatchewan.

Maher, W.J. 1979. Nesting diets of prairie passerine birds at Matador, Saskatchewan, Canada. Ibis. 121:437-452.

Manzano-Fischer, P., R. List, and G. Ceballos. 1999. Grassland birds in prairie-dog towns in northwestern Chihuahua, Mexico. Studies in Avian Biology. 19:263-271.

Marlette, G.M. and J.E. Anderson. 1986. Seed banks and propagule dispersal in crested wheatgrass stands. Journal of Applied Ecology. 23:161-175.

Martin, D.J. 1973. Selected aspects of Burrowing Owl ecology and behaviour in central New Mexico. Condor. 75:446-456.

Martin, S.J. 1983. Burrowing Owl occurrence on white-tailed prairie dog colonies. Journal of Field Ornithology. 54:422-423.

Mastrota, F.N. 1999. Wildlife mortality incidents caused by pesticides: an analysis of the EIIS database. U.S. Environmental Protection Agency, Washington, D.C.

Mayfield, H.F. 1965. The brown-headed cowbird with old and new hosts. Living Bird. 4:13-28.

McCallum, D.A., W.D. Graul, and R. Zaccagnini. 1977. The breeding status of the long-billed curlew in Colorado. The Auk. 94: 599-601.

McCarthey, T.D. and T.E. Corman. 1996. Arizona breeding bird atlas project 1996 project report. Nongame Endangered Wildlife Program Technical Report 108, Arizona Game and Fish Department, Phoenix, Arizona.

McEwen, L.C., C.E. Knittle, and M.L. Richmond. 1972. Wildlife effects from grasshopper insecticides sprayed on short-grass range. Journal of Range Management. 25:188-194.

McLeod, J.M. 1967. The effect of phosphamidon on bird populations in jack pine stands in Quebec. Canadian Field Naturalist. 81:102-106.

McPherson, G.R. 1995. The role of fire in the desert grasslands. Pages 130-151 in M.P. McClaran and T.R. Van Devender, eds. The desert grassland. University of Arizona Press, Tucson, Arizona.

Mearns, E.A. 1907. Mammals of the Mexican boundary of the United States, Part I. United States National Museum Bulletin No. 56.

Medina, A.L. 1988. Diets of scaled quail in southern Arizona. Journal of Wildlife Management. 32:753-757.

Mellink, E. and H. Madrigal. 1993. Ecology of Mexican prairie dogs. Journal of Mammalogy. 74:631-635.

Merriam, C.H. 1902. The prairie dog of the Great Plains. Pages 257-270 in Yearbook of the U.S. Department of Agriculture 1901. U.S. Government Printing Office, Washington, D.C.

Milchunas, D.G., O.E. Sala, and W.K. Lauenroth. 1988. A generalized model of the effects of grazing by large herbivores on grassland community structure. American Naturalist. 132:87-106.

Miller, A.H. 1951. A comparison of the avifaunas of Santa Cruz and Santa Rosa islands, California. Condor. 53:117-123.

Miller, B., G. Ceballos, and R. Reading. 1994. The prairie dog and biotic diversity. Conservation Biology. 8:677-681.

Millikin, R.L. and J.N.M. Smith. 1990. Sublethal effects of fenitrothion on forest passerines. Journal of Applied Ecology. 27:983-1000.

Møller, A.P. 1989. Nest site selection across field-woodland ecotones: The effect of nest predation. Oikos. 56:240-246.

Monson, G. and A.R. Phillips. 1981. Annotated checklist of the birds of Arizona. University of Arizona Press, Tucson, Arizona.

Moore, R.T. 1946. The Rufous-winged Sparrow, its legends and taxonomic status. Condor. 48:117-123.

Mora, M.A., M.C. Lee, J.P. Jenny, T.W. Schultz, J.L. Sericano, and N.J. Clum. 1997. Potential effects of environmental contaminants on recovery of the aplomado falcon in south Texas. Journal of Wildlife Management. 61:1288-1296.

Mote, K.D., R.D. Applegate, J.A. Bailey, K.M. Giesen, R. Horton, and J.L. Sheppard. 1999. Assessment and conservation strategy for the lesser prairie-chicken (*Tympanuchus pallidicinctus*). Kansas Department of Wildlife and Parks, Emporia, Kansas.

Moulding, J.D. 1976. Effects of a low-persistence insecticide on forest bird populations. Auk. 93:692-708.

Mulhern, D.W. and C.J. Knowles. 1996. Black-tailed prairie dog status and future conservation planning. Pages 19-29. In: D.W. Uresk, G.L. Schenbeck, and J.T. O'Rourke, eds. Conserving biodiversity on native rangelands: symposium proceedings; August 17, 1995; Fort Robinson State Park, Nebraska. USDA Forest Service, Rocky Mountain Forest and Range Experiment Station, RM-GTR-298, Fort Collins, Colorado.

National Geographic Society. 1999. Field Guide to the Birds of North America (Third Edition). National Geographic Society, Washington, D.C.

NatureServe: An online encyclopedia of life [web application]. 2001. Version 1.5. Available: http://www.natureserve.org/. (Accessed November 23, 2001). Association for Biodiversity Information, Arlington, Virginia.

Neilson, R.P. 1986. High-resolution climatic analysis and Southwest biogeography. Science. 232:27-34.

New Mexico Department of Game and Fish. 1988. Handbook of species endangered in New Mexico, F-150. New Mexico Department of Game and Fish, Santa Fe, New Mexico.

New Mexico Department of Game and Fish. 2002. Threatened and endangered species of New Mexico: biennial review and recommendations. New Mexico Department of Game and Fish, Santa Fe, New Mexico.

New Mexico Partners in Flight. 2001. Draft Land Bird Conservation Plan for the State of New Mexico, Version 1.0. Available at http://www.hawksaloft.org/pif.html. Compiled by Christopher Rustay, Albuquerque, New Mexico.

Norman, R.F. and R.J. Robertson. 1975. Nest-searching behavior in the brown-headed cowbird. Auk. 92:610-611.

Noss, R.F. and A.Y. Cooperrider. 1994. Saving nature's legacy: Protecting and restoring biodiversity. Island Press, Covelo, California.

Oberholser, H.C. 1974. The bird life of Texas. University of Texas Press, Austin, Texas.

Olawsky, C.D. and L.M. Smith. 1991. Lesser Prairie-chicken densities on tebuthiuron-treated and untreated san shinnery oak rangelands. Journal of Range Management. 44:364-368.

O'Leary, C.H. and D.W. Nyberg. 2000. Treelines between fields reduce the density of grassland birds. Natural Areas Journal. 20:243-249.

Olendorff, R.R. 1993. Status, biology and management of Ferruginous Hawks: a review. Raptor Research and Technical Assistance Center, Special Report. USDI Bureau of Land Management, Boise, Idaho.

Olson, S.L. and D. Edge. 1985. Nest site selection by Mountain Plovers in northcentral Montana. Journal of Range Management. 38:280-282.

Olson-Edge, S.L. and D. Edge. 1987. Density and distribution of the Mountain Plover on the Charles M. Russell National Wildlife Refuge. Prairie Naturalist. 19:233-238.

O'Meilia, M.E., F.L. Knopf, and J.C. Lewis. 1982. Some consequences of competition between prairie dogs and beef cattle. Journal of Range Management. 35:580-585.

Owens, R.A. and M.T. Myres. 1973. Effects of agriculture upon populations of native passerine birds of an Alberta fescue grassland. Canadian Journal of Zoology. 51:697-713.

Paine, L.K., D.J. Undersander, D.W. Sample, G.A. Bartelt, and T.A. Schatteman. 1996. Cattle trampling of simulated ground nests in rotationally grazed pastures. Journal of Range Management. 49:294-300.

Palmer, R.S. 1988. Ferruginous Hawk. Pages 135-151. In: Handbook of North American birds. Volume 5, Part 2. Yale University Press, New Haven, Connecticut.

Pampush, G.J. and R.G. Anthony. 1993. Nest success, habitat utilization and nest-site selection of long-billed curlews in the Columbia Basin, Oregon. The Condor. 95:957-967.

Parmenter, R.R. and T.R. Van Devender. 1995. Diversity, spatial variability, and functional roles of vertebrates in the desert grassland. Pages 196-229 in M.P. McClaran and T.R. Van Devender, eds. The desert grassland. University of Arizona Press, Tucson, Arizona.

Parrish, T.L., S.H. Anderson, and W.F. Oelklaus. 1993. Mountain Plover habitat selection in the Powder River Basin, Wyoming. Prairie Naturalist. 25:219-226.

Patnode, K.A. and D.H. White. 1991. Effects of pesticides on songbird productivity in conjunction with pecan cultivation in southern Georgia: a multiple-exposure experimental design. Environmental Toxicology and Chemistry. 10:1479-1486.

Paton, P.W.C. and J. Dalton. 1994. Breeding ecology of long-billed curlews at Great Salt Lake, Utah. Great Basin Naturalist. 54:79-85.

Patterson, M.P. and L.B. Best. 1996. Bird abundance and nesting success in Iowa CRP fields: the importance of vegetation structure and composition. American Midland Naturalist. 135:153-167.

Payne, N.F. and F.C. Bryant. 1994. Techniques for wildlife habitat management of uplands. McGraw-Hill, New York, New York.

Peterjohn, B.G. and J.R. Sauer. 1999. Population status of North American grassland birds from the North American Breeding Bird Survey 1966-1996. Studies in Avian Biology. 19:27-44.

Phillips, A.R. 1968. *Aimophila carpalis carpalis* (Coues) Rufous-winged Sparrow. U.S. National Museum Bulletin. 237:902-919.

Phillips, A.R., J. Marshall, and G. Monson. 1964. The birds of Arizona. University of Arizona Press, Tucson, Arizona.

Pimentel, D. 2001. Environmental effects of pesticides on public health, birds, and other organisms. Talk given at conference proceedings: Rachel Carson and the Conservation Movement: Past, Present, Future. Shepherdstown, West Virginia, August 2001.

Pimentel, D., H. Acquay, M. Biltonen, P. Rice, M. Silva, J. Nelson, V. Lipner, S. Giordano, A. Horowitz, and M. D'Amore. 1992. Environmental and economic costs of pesticide use. BioScience. 42:750-760.

Pimentel, D., L. McLaughlin, A. Zepp, B. Lakitan, T. Kraus, P. Kleinman, F. Vancini, W.J. Roach, E. Graap, W.S. Keeton, and G. Selig. 1991. Environmental and economic effects of reducing pesticide use. BioScience. 41:402-409.

Plumpton, D.L. and D.E. Andersen. 1998. Anthropogenic effects on winter behavior of ferruginous hawks. Journal of Wildlife Management. 62:340-346.

Plumpton, D.L. and R.S. Lutz. 1993. Nesting habitat use by Burrowing Owls in Colorado. Journal of Raptor Research. 27:175-179.

Porter, D.K. and R.A. Ryder. 1974. Avian density and productivity studies and analyses on the Pawnee Site in 1972. U.S. International Biological Program, Grassland Biome Technical Report 252. Colorado State University, Fort Collins, Colorado.

Porter, D.K., M.A. Strong, J.B. Giezentanner, and R.A. Ryder. 1975. Nest ecology, productivity, and growth of the Loggerhead Shrike on the shortgrass prairie. Southwestern Naturalist. 19:429-436.

Power, M.E., D. Tilman, J.A. Estes, B.A. Menge, W.J. Bond, L.S. Mills, G. Daily, J.C. Castilla, J. Lubchenco, and R.T. Paine. 1996. Challenges in the quest for keystones. BioScience. 466:9-20.

Prescott, D.R.C. and A.J. Murphy. 1996. Habitat associations of grassland birds on native and tame pastures of the aspen parkland in Alberta. NAWMP-021. Alberta NAWMP Centre, Edmonton, Alberta.

Prescott, D.R.C. and A.J. Murphy. 1999. Bird populations in seeded nesting cover on North American Waterfowl Management Plan properties in the aspen parkland of Alberta. Studies in Avian Biology. 19:203-210.

Pulliam, H.R. and G.S. Mills. 1977. The use of space by wintering sparrows. Ecology. 58:1393-1399.

Pylypec, B. 1991. Impacts of fire on bird populations in a fescue prairie. Canadian Field Naturalist. 105:346-349.

USDA Forest Service Gen. Tech. Rep. RMRS-GTR-135-vol. 2. 2005

133

Ratti, J.T. and K.P. Reese. 1988. Preliminary test of the ecological trap hypothesis. Journal of Wildlife Management. 52:484-491.

Ratti, J.T. and J.M. Scott. 1991. Agricultural impacts on wildlife: problem review and research needs. Environmental Professional. 13:263-274.

Redmond, R.L. 1986. Egg size and laying date of long-billed curlews (*Numenius americanus*): implications for female reproductive tactics. Oikos. 46:330-338.

Redmond, R.L., T.K. Bicak, and D.A. Jenni. 1981. An evaluation of breeding season census techniques for long-billed curlews (*Numenius americanus*).Studies in Avian Biology. 6:197-201.

Redmond, R.L. and D.A. Jenni. 1982. Natal philopatry and breeding area fidelity of long-billed curlews (*Numenius americanus*): patterns and evolutionary consequences. Behavioral Ecology and Sociobiology. 10:277-279.

Redmond, R.L. and D.A. Jenni. 1986. Population ecology of the long-billed curlew (*Numenius americanus*) in western Idaho. The Auk. 103:755-767.

Renaud, W.E. 1980. The long-billed curlew in Saskatchewan: status and distribution. Blue Jay. 38:221-237.

Renken, R.B. and J.J. Dinsmore. 1987. Nongame bird communities on managed grasslands in North Dakota. Canadian Field-Naturalist. 101:551-557.

Rich, T. 1986. Habitat and nest-site selection by Burrowing Owls in the sagebrush steppe of Idaho. Journal of Wildlife Management. 50:548-555.

Riley, T.Z. and C.A. Davis. 1993. Vegetative characteristics of lesser prairie-chicken brood foraging sites. Prairie Naturalist. 25:243-248.

Riley, T.Z., C.A. Davis, M. Ortiz, and M.J. Wisdom. 1992. Vegetative characteristics of sucessful and unsuccessful nests of Lesser Prairie-chickens. Journal of Wildlife Management. 56:383-387.

Riley, T.Z., C.A. Davis, and R.A. Smith. 1993a. Autumn and winter foods of the lesser prairie-chicken (*Tympanuchus pallidicinctus*) (Galliformes: Tetraonidae). Great Basin Naturalist. 53:186-189.

Riley, T.Z., C.A. Davis, and R.A. Smith. 1993b. Autumn-winter habitat use of Lesser Prairie-Chickens (*Tympanuchus pallidicinctus*, Tetraonidae). Great Basin Naturalist. 53:409-411.

Rising, J.D. 1996. A guide to the identification and natural history of the sparrows of the United States and Canada. Academic Press, New York, New York.

Robbins, C.S., J.R. Sauer, R.S. Greenberg, and S. Droege. 1989. Population declines in North American birds that migrate to the neotropics. Proceedings of the National Academy of Sciences (USA). 86:7658-7662.

Robbins, M.B. and B.C. Dale. 1999. Sprague's Pipit *Anthus spragueii*. In: A. Poole and F. Gill, eds. The Birds of North America, No. 439. The Academy of Natural Sciences, Philadelphia, and American Ornithologists' Union, Washington, D.C.

Robinson, S.K., S.I. Rothstein, M.C. Brittingham, L.J. Petit, and J.A. Grzybowski. 1995a. Ecology and behavior of cowbirds and their impact on host populations. Pages 428-460. In: T.E. Martin and D.M. Finch, eds. Ecology and management of neotropical migratory birds. Oxford University Press, New York, New York.

Robinson, S.K., F.R. Thompson III, T.M. Donovan, D.R. Whitehead, and J. Faaborg. 1995b. Regional forest fragmentation and the nesting success of migratory birds. Science. 267:1987-1990.

Rodenhouse, N.L., L.B. Best, R.J. O'Connor, and E.K. Bollinger. 1993. Effects of temperate agriculture on neotropic migrant landbirds. Pages 280-295. In: D.M. Finch and P.W. Stangel, eds. Status and management of neotropical migratory birds. USDA Forest Service Rocky Mountain Research Station GTR-RM-229, Fort Collins, Colorado.

Rodriguez Estrella, R., F. Chavez Ramirez, and G.L. Holroyd. 1998. Current knowledge of the burrowing owl in Mexico: what is needed for a conservation plan? Abstract and notes. Second International Burrowing Owl Symposium, September 29-30, 1998, Ogden, Utah. Canadian Wildlife Service, Environment Canada.

Rotenberry, J.T. and J.A. Wiens. 1980. Temporal variation in habitat structure and shrubsteppe bird dynamics. Oecologia. 47:1-9.

Rothstein, S.I. 1975. An experimental and teleonomic investigation of avian brood parasitism. Condor. 77:250-271.

Rothstein, S.I. 1977. Cowbird parasitism and egg recognition of the Northern Oriole. Wilson Bulletin. 89:21-32.

Rothstein, S.I. 1982. Successes and failures in avian egg and nestling recognition with comments on the utility of optimality reasoning. American Zoologist. 22:547-560.

Russell, S.M. and G. Monson. 1998. The birds of Sonora. University of Arizona Press, Tucson, Arizona.

Ruth, J.M. 2000. Cassin's Sparrow (*Aimophila cassinii*) status assessment and conservation plan. Biological Technical Publication BTP-R6002-1999. U.S. Fish and Wildlife Service, Denver, Colorado.

Ryan, M.R. 1986. Nongame management in grassland and agricultural ecosystems. Pages 117-136. In: J.B. Hale, L.B. Best, and R.L. Clawson, eds. Management of nongame wildlife in the Midwest. Northcentral Section of the Wildlife Society, Grand Rapids, Michigan.

Ryder, R.A. 1980. Effects of grazing on bird habitats. In: R.M. DeGraaf and N.G. Tilghman, eds. Management of western forests and grasslands for nongame birds. USDA Forest Service, Intermountain Forest and Range Experiment Station General Technical Report INT-86, Ogden, Utah.

Saab, V.A., C.E. Bock, T.D. Rich, and D.S. Dobkin. 1995. Livestock grazing effects in western North America. Pages 311-353. In: T.E. Martin and D.M. Finch, eds. Ecology and management of neotropical migratory birds: a synthesis and review of critical issues. Oxford University Press, New York, New York.

Saiwana, L., J.L. Holechek, A. Tembo, R. Valdez, and M. Cardenas. 1998. Scaled quail use of different seral stages in the Chihuahuan desert. Journal of Wildlife Management. 62:550-556.

Salt, W.R. and A.L. Wilk. 1958. The birds of Alberta. Department of Economic Affairs, Edmonton, Alberta.

Samson, F.B. 1980. Island biogeography and the conservation of prairie birds. Pages 293-305. In: C.L. Kucera, ed. Proceedings of the Seventh North American Prairie Conference. Southwest Missouri State University, Springfield, Missouri.

Samson, F. and F. Knopf. 1994. Prairie conservation in North America. BioScience. 44:418-421.

Sandoz, M. 1954. The buffalo hunters. Hasting House, New York, New York.

Sands, J.L. 1968. Status of the lesser prairie-chicken. Audubon Field Notes. 22:454-456.

Sauer, J.R. and S. Droege. 1992. Geographic patterns in population trends of neotropical migrants in North America. Pages 26-42. In: Hagan III, J.M. and D.W. Johnston, eds. Ecology and conservation of neotropical migrant landbirds. Smithsonian Institution Press, Washington, D.C.

Sauer, J.R., J.E. Hines, and J. Fallon. 2001. The North American Breeding Bird Survey, Results and Analysis 1966 - 2000. Version 2001.2. Available at http://www.mbr.nbs.gov/bbs/bbs.html, USGS Patuxent Wildlife Research Center, Laurel, Maryland.

Sauer, J.R., J.E. Hines, G. Grough, I. Thomas, and B.G. Peterjohn. 1997. The North American Breeding Bird Survey Results and Analysis. Version 96.4. Patuxent Wildlife Research Center, Laurel, Maryland.

Sauer, J.R.; B.G. Peterjohn, S. Schwartz, and J.E. Hines. 1995. The grassland bird home page. Version 95.0 http://www.mbr. nbs.gov/bbs/grass/grass.htm. Patuxent Wildlife Research Center, Laurel, Maryland.

Sauer, J.R., S. Schwartz, and B. Hoover. 1996. The Christmas Bird Count Home Page. Version 95.1. Available at http://www.mbr-pwrc.usgs.gov/bbs/cbc.html. Patuxent Wildlife Research Center, Laurel, Maryland.

Saunders, A.A. 1914. The birds of Teton and northern Lewis and Clark counties, Montana. Condor. 16:124-144.

Sawyer, P.E. 1973. Habitat-use by scaled quail and other birds in southeastern New Mexico. M.S. thesis. New Mexico State University, Las Cruces, New Mexico.

Schemnitz, S.D. 1961. Ecology of the scaled quail in the Oklahoma panhandle. Wildlife Monographs. 8.

Schemnitz, S.D. 1994. Scaled quail *Callipepla squamata*. In: A. Poole and F. Gill, eds. The birds of North America, No. 106. The Academy of Natural Sciences, Philadelphia, Pennsylvania, and the American Ornithologists' Union, Washington, D.C.

Schlesinger, W.H., J.F. Reynolds, G.L. Cunningham, L.F. Huenneke, W.M. Jarrell, R.A. Virginia, and W.G. Whitford. 1990. Biological feedbacks in global desertification. Science. 247:1043-1048.

134

USDA Forest Service Gen. Tech. Rep. RMRS-GTR-135-vol. 2. 2005

Schmutz, J.K. and R.W. Fyfe. 1987. Migration and mortality of Alberta Ferruginous Hawks. Condor. 89:169-174.

Schmutz, J.K., R.W. Fyfe, D.A. Moore, and A.R. Smith. 1984. Artificial nests for Ferruginous and Swainson's hawks. Journal of Wildlife Management. 48:1009-1013.

Schmutz, J.K. and D.J. Hungle. 1989. Populations of Ferruginous and Swainson's hawks increase in synchrony with ground squirrels. Canadian Journal of Zoology. 67:2596-2601.

Scott, D.M. 1977. Cowbird parasitism on the gray catbird at London, Ontario. Auk. 94:18.

Sealy, S.G. 1992. Removal of yellow warbler eggs in association with cowbird parasitism. Condor. 94:40-54.

Shackford, J.S. 1991. Breeding ecology of the Mountain Plover in Oklahoma. Bulletin of the Oklahoma Ornithological Society. 24:9-13.

Shackford, J.S. 1994. Nesting of long-billed curlews on cultivated fields. Bulletin of the Oklahoma Ornithological Society. 27:17-20.

Shackford, J.S., D.M. Leslie Jr., and W.D. Harden. 1999. Range-wide use of cultivated fields by Mountain Plovers during the breeding season. Journal of Field Ornithology. 70:114-120.

Sharps, J.C. and D.W. Uresk. 1990. Ecological review of black-tailed prairie dogs and associated species in western South Dakota. Great Basin Naturalist. 50:339-345.

Sheffield, S.R. 1997. Current status, distribution, and conservation of the burrowing owl (*Speotyto cunicularia*) in Midwestern North America. Pages 399-407. In: J.R. Dundan, D.H. Johnson, and T.H. Nicholls, eds. Biology and conservation of owls of the Northern Hemisphere. USDA Forest Service, North Central Forest Experiment Station, General Technical Report NC-190, St. Paul, Minnesota.

Silloway, P.M. 1900. Notes on the long-billed curlew. Condor. 2:79-82.

Sissons, R., K. Scalise, and T.I. Wellicome. 1998. Nocturnal foraging habitat use of the Burrowing Owl in a heavily cultivated region of southern Saskatchewan. Pages 22-23. Abstracts of the Second International Burrowing Owl Symposium. Ogden, Utah.

Skinner, R.M. 1975. Grassland use patterns and prairie bird populations in Missouri. Pages 171-180. In: M.K. Wali, ed. Prairie: a multiple view. University of North Dakota Press, Grand Forks, North Dakota.

Skinner, R.M., T.S. Baskett, and M.D. Blendon. 1984. Bird habitat on Missouri prairies. Terrestrial Series 14. Missouri Department of Conservation, Jefferson City, Missouri.

Smith, G., J.L. Holechek, and M. Cardenas. 1996. Wildlife numbers on excellent and good condition Chihuahuan Desert rangelands: an observation. Journal of Range Management. 49:489-493.

Smith, H. and J. Smith. 1966. A breeding bird survey on uncultivated grasslands at Regina. Blue Jay. 24:129-131.

Sousa, P.J. and W.N. McDonal. 1983. Habitat suitability index models: Baird's Sparrow. U.S. Fish and Wildlife Service, FWS/OBS-82/10.44, Washington, D.C.

Stewart, R.E. 1975. Breeding birds of North Dakota. Tri-college Center for Environmental Studies, Fargo, North Dakota.

Stone, W.B. 1979. Poisoning of wild birds by organophosphate and carbamate pesticides. New York Fish and Game. 26:37-47.

Stormer, F.A. 1984. Night-roosting habitat of scaled quail. Journal of Wildlife Management. 48:191-197.

Stotz, D.F., J.W. Fitzpatrick, T.A. Parker III, and D.K. Moskovits. 1996. Neotropical birds: ecology and conservation. University of Chicago Press, Chicago, Illinois.

Sugden, J.W. 1933. Range restriction of the long-billed curlew. Condor. 35:3-9.

Sutter, G.C. 1997. Nest-site selection and nest-entrance orientation in Sprague's pipit. Wilson Bulletin. 109:462-269.

Sutter, G.C. and R.M. Brigham. 1998. Avifaunal and habitat changes resulting from conversion of native prairie to crested wheatgrass: patterns at songbird community and species levels. Canadian Journal of Zoology. 76:869-875.

Sutton, G.M. 1927. Flocking, mating and nest-building habits of the Prairie Horned Lark. Wilson Bulletin. 34:131-141.

Swarth, H.S. 1929. The faunal areas of southern Arizona: a study in animal distribution. Proceedings of the California Academy of Sciences. 18:267-383.

Szmedra, P.I. 1991. Pesticides use in agriculture. Pages 649-677. In: D. Pimentel, ed. CRC handbook of pest management in agriculture. CRC Press, Boca Raton, Florida.

Taylor, M.A. 1980. Lesser prairie-chicken use of man-made leks. Southwestern Naturalist. 24:706-707.

Taylor, M.A. and F.S. Guthery. 1980. Status, ecology and management of the lesser prairie-chicken. USDA Forest Service, Rocky Mountain Forest and Range Experiment Station, General Technical Report RM-77, Fort Collins, Colorado.

Tellman, B., D.M. Finch, C. Edminster, and R. Hamre. 1998. The future of arid grasslands: identifying issues, seeking solutions. 1996 Oct. 9-13; Tucson, AZ. Fort Collins, Colorado, USDA Forest Service, Rocky Mountain Research Station, Proceedings RMRS-P-3.

Temple, S.A., B.M. Fevold, L.K. Paine, D.J. Undersander, and D.W. Sample. 1999. Nesting birds and grazing cattle: accommodating both on midwestern pastures. Studies in Avian Biology. 19:196-202.

Terborgh, J. 1989. Where have all the birds gone? Princeton University Press, Princeton, New Jersey.

Terres, J.K. 1991. The Audubon Society Encyclopedia of North American Birds. Alfred A. Knopf, Inc., New York, New York.

Thompson, E.E. 1893. Additions to the list of Manitoban birds. Auk. 10:49-50.

Thomsen, L. 1971. Behavior and ecology of Burrowing Owls on the Oakland municipal airport. Condor. 73:177-192.

Timken, R.L. 1969. Notes on the long-billed curlew. Auk. 86:750-751.

Tisdale, E.W. 1961. Ecological changes in the Palouse. Northwest Sciences. 35:134-138.

Trulio, L.A. 1997. Strategies for protecting western burrowing owls (*Speotyto cunicularia hypugaea*). Pages 461-465. In: J.R. Dundan, D.H. Johnson, and T.H. Nicholls, eds. Biology and conservation of owls in the Northern Hemisphere. USDA Forest Service, North Central Forest Experiment Station, General Technical Report NC-190, St. Paul, Minnesota.

Ure, J., P. Briggs, and S.W. Hoffman. 1991. Petition to list as endangered the Ferruginous Hawk (*Buteo regalis*), as provided by the Endangered Species Act of 1973, as amended in 1982. Ferruginous Hawk Project, Salt Lake City, Utah.

U.S. Fish and Wildlife Service. 1991. Endangered and threatened wildlife and plants: animal candidate review for listing as endangered or threatened species. Proposed Rule. Federal Register. 56:58804-58836.

U.S. Fish and Wildlife Service. 1992. Endangered and threatened wildlife and plants: notice of finding on petition to list the Ferruginous Hawk. Federal Register. 57:37507-37513.

U.S. Fish and Wildlife Service. 1995. Migratory nongame birds of management concern in the United States: the 1995 list. U.S. Fish and Wildlife Service, Washington, D.C.

U.S. Fish and Wildlife Service. 1998. Endangered and threatened wildlife and plants; 12-month finding for a petition to list the Lesser Prairie-Chicken as threatened and designate critical habitat. Federal Register. 63:31400-31406.

U.S. Fish and Wildlife Service. 1999a. Endangered and threatened wildlife and plants; proposed threatened status for the Mountain Plover. Federal Register. 64:7587-7601.

U.S. Fish and Wildlife Service. 1999b. Endangered and threatened wildlife and plants; 90-Day finding for a petition to list the Baird's Sparrow as threatened with critical habitat. Federal Register. 64:27747-27749.

U.S. Fish and Wildlife Service. 2000. Endangered and threatened wildlife and plants; 12-month finding for a petition to list the black-tailed prairie dog as threatened. Federal Register. 65:5476-5488.

U.S. Fish and Wildlife Service. 2001. Endangered and threatened wildlife and plants; review of plant and animal species that are candidates or proposed for listing as endangered or threatened, annual notice of findings on recycled petitions, and annual description of progress on listing actions; proposed rule. Federal Register. 66:54807-54832.

U.S. Fish and Wildlife Service. 2002. Species information: threatened and endangered animals and plants. Available at http://ecos.fws.gov/wildlife.html. Accessed August 2002.

USDA Forest Service Gen. Tech. Rep. RMRS-GTR-135-vol. 2. 2005

135

Van Pelt, W.E. 1999. The black-tailed prairie dog conservation assessment and strategy - fifth draft. Nongame and Endangered Wildlife Program, Arizona Game and Fish Department, Phoenix, Arizona.

Verbeek, N.A.M. 1967. Breeding biology and ecology of the Horned Lark in alpine tundra. Wilson Bulletin. 79:208-218.

Vickery, P.D., J.R. Herkert, F.L. Knopf, J. Ruth, and C.E. Keller. 1999a. Grasslands birds: an overview of threats and recommended management strategies. In: R.E. Bonney Jr., D.N. Pashley, R. Cooper, and L. Niles, eds. Strategies for bird conservation: the Partners in Flight planning process. Cornell Laboratory of Ornithology, Ithaca, New York. Available at http://birds.cornell.edu/pifcapemay.

Vickery, P.D., M.L. Hunter Jr., and S.M. Melvin. 1994. Effects of habitat area on the distribution of grassland birds in Maine. Conservation Biology. 8:1087-1097.

Vickery, P.D., P.L. Tubaro, J.M.C. Da Silva, B.G. Peterjohn, J.G. Herkert, and R.B. Cavalcanti. 1999b. Conservation of grassland birds of the Western Hemisphere. Studies in Avian Biology. 19:2-26.

Vyas, N.B. 1999. Factors influencing estimation of pesticide-related mortality. Toxicology and Industrial Health. 15:186-191.

Wakely, J.S. 1978. Activity budgets, energy expenditures, and energy intakes of nesting Ferruginous Hawks. Auk. 95:667-676.

Wallis, C.A. and C.R. Wershler. 1981. Status and breeding of Mountain Plovers (*Charadrius montanus*) in Canada. Canadian Field Naturalist. 95:133-136.

Wallmo, O.C. 1957. A study of blues. Texas Game and Fish. 15:4-7.

Wallmo, O.C. and P.B. Uzell. 1958. Ecological and social problems in quail management in west Texas. Transactions of the North American Wildlife Conference. 23:320-327.

Warner, R.E. 1992. Nest ecology of grassland passerines on road rights-of-way in central Illinois. Biological Conservation. 59:1-7.

Warner, R.E. 1994. Agriculture, land use, and grassland habitat in Illinois: future shock for midwestern birds? Conservation Biology. 8:147-156.

Warner, R.E. and S.L. Etter. 1989. Hay cutting and the survival of pheasants. Journal of Wildlife Management. 53:455-461.

Warnock, R. 1997. Is habitat fragmentation a factor in the decline of the Burrowing Owl in Saskatchewan? Blue Jay. 55:222-228.

Warnock, R.G. and P.C. James. 1997. Habitat fragmentation and Burrowing Owls (*Speotyto cunicularia*) in Saskatchewan. Pages 477-486. In: J.R. Duncan, D.H. Johnson, and T.H. Nicholls, eds. Biology and conservation of owls of the Northern Hemisphere. USDA Forest Service, North Central Forest Experiment Station, General Technical Report NC-190, St. Paul, Minnesota.

Weatherhead, P.J. 1989. Sex ratios, host-specific reproductive success, and impact of brown-headed cowbirds. Auk. 106:358-366.

Weaver, T., E.M. Payson, and D.L. Gustafson. 1996. Prairie ecology: the shortgrass prairie. Pages 67-76. In: F.B. Samson and F.L. Knopf, eds. Prairie conservation: preserving North America's most endangered ecosystem. Island Press, Washington, D.C.

Webb, E.A. and C.E. Bock. 1990. Relationship of the Botteri's sparrow to sacaton grassland in Southeastern Arizona. Pages 199-209. In: P.R. Krausman and N.S. Smith, eds. Managing wildlife in the Southwest. Arizona Chapter of the Wildlife Society, Phoenix, Arizona.

Webster, F.S. 1979. The nesting season. American Bird. 33:879.

Wedgwood, J.A. 1976. Burrowing Owl in south-central Saskatchewan. Blue Jay. 34:26-44.

Wedgwood, J.A. 1978. The status of the Burrowing Owl in Canada. A report prepared for the Committee on the Status of Endangered Wildlife in Canada, Ottawa, Canada.

Wellicome, T.I. 1994. Is reproduction in Burrowing Owls limited by food supply? Picoides. 7:9-10.

Wellicome, T.I. 1997. Status of the burrowing owl (*Speotyto cunicularia hypugaea*) in Alberta. Wildlife Status Report No. 11. Alberta Environmental Protection, Wildlife Management Division, Edmonton, Alberta.

Wellicome, T.I. and E.A. Haug. 1995. Second update of status report on the Burrowing Owl. Committee on the Status of Endangered Wildlife in Canada, Ottawa, Ontario.

Wellicome, T.I., G.L. Holroyd, K. Scalise, and E.R. Wiltse. 1997. The effects of predator exclusion and food supplementation on Burrowing Owl (*Speotyto cunicularia*) population change in Saskatchewan. Pages 487-497. In: J.R. Duncan, D.H. Johnson, and T.H. Nicholls, eds. Biology and conservation of owls of the Northern Hemisphere. USDA Forest Service, North Central Forest Experiment Station, General Technical Report NC-190, St. Paul, Minnesota.

Weltzin, J.F., S. Archer, and R.K. Heitschmidt. 1997. Small-mammal regulation of vegetation structure in a temperate savanna. Ecology. 78:751-763.

Wershler, C., W.W. Smith, and C. Wallis. 1991. Status of the Baird's Sparrow in Alberta: 1987/1988 update with notes on other grasslands sparrows and Sprague's Pipit. Pages 87-89. In: G.L. Holroyd, G. Burns, and H.C. Smith, eds. Proceedings of the second endangered species and prairie conservation workshop. Natural History Occasional Paper 15, Provincial Museum of Alberta, Edmonton, Alberta.

Westemeier, R.L. 1985. Management plan for native prairie-chicken in Illinois. Illinois Natural History Survey, Springfield, Illinois.

Whicker, A.D. and J.K. Detling. 1988. Ecological consequences of prairie dog disturbances. BioScience. 38:778-785.

White, D.H., K.A. King, C.A. Mitchell, and A.J. Krynitsky. 1981. Body lipids and pesticide burdens of migrant Blue-winged Teal. Journal of Field Ornithology. 52:23-28.

White, D.H. and A.J. Krynitsky. 1986. Wildlife in some areas of New Mexico and Texas accumulate elevated DDE residues, 1983. Archives of Environmental Contaminants and Toxicology. 15:149-157.

Wickersham, C.W. 1902. Sickle-billed curlew. Auk. 19:353-356.

Wiens, J.A. 1970. Avian populations and patterns of habitat occupancy at the Pawnee site, 1968-1969. U.S. International Biological Program, Grassland Biome Technical Report 63. Colorado State University, Fort Collins, Colorado.

Wiens, J.A. 1971. Avian ecology and distribution in the comprehensive network, 1970. U.S. International Biological Program, Grassland Biome Technical Report 77. Colorado State University, Fort Collins, Colorado.

Wiens, J.A. 1973. Pattern and process in grassland bird communities. Ecological Monographs. 43:237-270.

Wilcove, D.S. 1985. Nest predation in forest tracts and the decline of migratory songbirds. Ecology. 66:1211-1214.

Wildeman, G. and J.H. Brock. 2000. Grazing in the southwest: history of land use and grazing since 1540. Pages 1-26. In: R. Jemison and C. Raish, eds. Livestock management in the American Southwest: ecology, society, and economics. Elsevier, Amsterdam, The Netherlands.

Williams, F.C. and A.L. LeSassier. 1968. Cassins Sparrow. Pages 981-990. In: O.L. Austin, Jr., ed. Life histories of North American cardinals, grosbeaks, buntings, towhees, finches, sparrows, and allies. Dover, New York, New York.

Winter, M. 1999. Relationship of fire history to territory size, breeding density and habitat of Baird's Sparrow in North Dakota. Studies in Avian Biology. 19:171-177.

Winter, M., D.H. Johnson, and J. Faaborg. 2000. Evidence for edge effects on multiple levels in tallgrass prairie. Condor. 102:256-266.

With, K.A. and D.R. Webb. 1993. Microclimate of groundnests: the relative importance of radiative cover and wind breaks for three grassland species. Condor. 95:401-413.

Wobeser, G. and A.G. Wobeser. 1992. Carcass disappearance and estimation of mortality in a simulated die-off of small birds. Journal of Wildlife Diseases. 28:548-554.

Woffinden, N.D. and J.R. Murphy. 1989. Decline of a Ferruginous Hawk population: a 20-year summary. Journal of Wildlife Management. 53:1127-1132.

Wolf, L.L. 1977. Species relationships in the avian genus *Aimophila*. Ornithological Monographs. 23.

Wray II, T., Strait, K.A., and R.C. Whitmore. 1982. Reproductive success of grassland sparrows on a reclaimed surface mine in West Virginia. Auk. 99:157-164.

Wydeven, A.P. and R.B. Dahlgren. 1985. Ungulate habitat relationships in Wind Cave National Park. Journal of Wildlife Management. 49:805-813.

136

USDA Forest Service Gen. Tech. Rep. RMRS-GTR-135-vol. 2. 2005

Yahner, R.H. 1983. Seasonal dynamics, habitat relationships, and management of avifauna in farmstead shelterbelts. Journal of Wildlife Management. 47:85-104.

York, J.C. and W.A. Dick-Peddie. 1969. Vegetation changes in southern New Mexico during the past hundred years. In: W.G. McGinnies and B.J. Goldman, eds. Arid lands in perspective. The American Association for the Advancement of Science, Washington, D.C., and The University of Arizona Press, Tucson, Arizona.

Yosef, R. 1996. Loggerhead Shrike (*Lanius ludovicianus*). In: A. Poole and F. Gill, eds. The Birds of North America, No. 231. The Academy of Natural Sciences, Philadelphia, Pennsylvania, and The American Ornithologists' Union, Washington, D.C.

Yosef, R. and T.C. Grubb. 1994. Resource dependence and territory size in Loggerhead Shrikes. Auk. 111:465-469.

Zimmerman, J.L. 1983. Cowbird parasitism of Dickcissels in different habitats and at different nest densities. Wilson Bulletin. 95:7-22.

Zwartjes, P.W., J-L.E. Cartron, P.L.L. Stoleson, W.C. Haussamen, and T.E. Crane. 2005. Ecological interactions of ungulate grazing and native species of the Southwest: terrestrial wildife. Gen. Tech. Rep. RMRS-GTR-142. Fort Collins, CO: U.S. Department of Agriculture Forest Service Rocky Mountain Research Station. 71 p. plus CD.

USDA Forest Service Gen. Tech. Rep. RMRS-GTR-135-vol. 2. 2005

137

Appendix 4-A. Common and scientific names of birds in text, listed in alphabetical order of the scientific names

Common name	Scientific name
Northern harrier	*Circus cyaneus*
Swainson's hawk	*Buteo swainsoni*
Ferruginous hawk	*Buteo regalis*
Golden eagle	*Aquila chrysaetos*
American kestrel	*Falco sparverius*
Northern Aplomado falcon	*Falco femoralis septentrionalis*
Prairie falcon	*Falco mexicanus*
Ring-necked pheasant	*Phasianus colchicus*
Sage grouse	*Centrocercus urophasianus*
White-tailed ptarmigan	*Lagopus leucurus*
Sharp-tailed grouse	*Tympanuchus phasianellus*
Greater prairie-chicken	*Tympanuchus cupido*
Lesser prairie-chicken	*Tympanuchus pallidicinctus*
Scaled quail	*Callipepla squamata*
Northern bobwhite	*Colinus virginianus*
Masked bobwhite	*Colinus virginianus ridgwayi*
Montezuma quail	*Cyrtonyx montezumae*
Killdeer	*Charadrius vociferus*
Mountain plover	*Charadrius montanus*
Upland sandpiper	*Bartramia longicauda*
Long-billed curlew	*Numenius americanus*
Common snipe	*Gallinago gallinago*
Wilson's phalarope	*Phalaropus tricolor*
Mourning dove	*Zenaida macroura*
Burrowing owl	*Athene cunicularia*
Short-eared owl	*Asio flammeus*
Lesser nighthawk	*Chordeiles acutipennis*
Common nighthawk	*Chordeiles minor*
Common poorwill	*Phalaenoptilus nuttallii*
Broad-tailed hummingbird	*Selasphorus platycercus*
Ladder-backed woodpecker	*Picoides scalaris*
Southwestern willow flycatcher	*Empidonax traillii extimus*
Say's phoebe	*Sayornis saya*
Ash-throated flycatcher	*Myiarchus cinerascens*
Cassin's kingbird	*Tyrannus vociferans*
Western kingbird	*Tyrannus verticalis*
Scissor-tailed flycatcher	*Tyrannus forficatus*
Loggerhead shrike	*Lanius ludovicianus*
Bell's vireo	*Vireo bellii*
Gray vireo	*Vireo vicinior*
Black-capped vireo	*Vireo atricapillus*
Chihuahuan raven	*Corvus cryptoleucus*
Common raven	*Corvus corax*

Horned lark	*Eremophila alpestris*
Cactus wren	*Campylorhynchus brunneicapillus*
Sedge wren	*Cistothorus platensis*
Mountain bluebird	*Sialia currucoides*
Northern mockingbird	*Mimus polyglottos*
Bendire's thrasher	*Toxostoma bendirei*
Curve-billed thrasher	*Toxostoma curvirostre*
American pipit	*Anthus rubescens*
Sprague's pipit	*Anthus spragueii*
Yellow warbler	*Dendroica petechia*
Common yellowthroat	*Geothlypis trichas*
Yellow-breasted chat	*Icteria virens*
Canyon towhee	*Pipilo fuscus*
Rufous-winged sparrow	*Aimophila carpalis*
Cassin's sparrow	*Aimophila cassinii*
Botteri's sparrow	*Aimophila botterii*
Brewer's sparrow	*Spizella breweri*
Black-chinned sparrow	*Spizella atrogularis*
Vesper sparrow	*Pooecetes gramineus*
Lark sparrow	*Chondestes grammacus*
Black-throated sparrow	*Amphispiza bilineata*
Sage sparrow	*Amphispiza belli*
Lark bunting	*Calamospiza melanocorys*
Savannah sparrow	*Passerculus sandwichensis*
Grasshopper sparrow	*Ammodramus savannarum*
Arizona Grasshopper sparrow	*Ammodramus savannarum ammolegus*
Baird's sparrow	*Ammodramus bairdii*
Henslow's sparrow	*Ammodramus henslowii*
Le Conte's sparrow	*Ammodramu leconteii*
Fox sparrow	*Passerella iliaca*
Song sparrow	*Melospiza melodia*
White-crowned sparrow	*Zonotrichia leucophrys*
McCown's longspur	*Calcarius mccownii*
Chestnut-collared longspur	*Calcarius ornatus*
Pyrrhuloxia	*Cardinalis sinuatus*
Varied bunting	*Passerina versicolor*
Dickcissel	*Spiza americana*
Bobolink	*Dolichonyx oryzivorus*
Red-winged blackbird	*Agelaius phoeniceus*
Eastern meadowlark	*Sturnella magna*
Eastern meadowlark (Southwestern subspecies)	*Sturnella magna lilianae*
Western meadowlark	*Sturnella neglecta*
Brewer's blackbird	*Euphagus cyanocephalus*
Brown-headed cowbird	*Molothrus ater*
Scott's oriole	*Icterus parisorum*
Brown-capped rosy-finch	*Leucosticte australis*

Bob Calamusso

Chapter 5:
Fishes of Southwestern Grasslands: Ecology, Conservation, and Management

Introduction

The world possesses an amazing number and variety of freshwater fishes. Fish, the most diverse taxon on Earth, exhibit more species than all vertebrate taxa combined (Hocutt and Wiley 1986, May 1988, Nelson 1994, Matthews 1998) (table 5-1). Worldwide, an estimated 28,500 fish species are in 57 orders and 482 families (Nelson 1994). The North American freshwater fish fauna is also relatively rich and highly diverse ranging from primitive forms such as the *Petromyzontidae* (lampreys) to more modern and advanced forms such as the *Percidae* (perches) (Miller 1959, Gilbert 1976, Briggs 1986, Cavender 1986, Nelson 1994). Currently, there are about 1,000 known freshwater fish species representing 50 families in 201 genera in an area from Canada and Alaska south to the Isthmus of Tehuantepec (Gilbert 1976, Lee and others 1980, Briggs 1986, Mayden 1992a,b). Some of these fish families are endemic to North America whereas others are also found on bordering continents (Briggs 1986). Despite persistent research for more than 100 years, numbers of described fishes in North America continue to increase over time. For example, Lee and others (1980) described 770 North American fishes, whereas just over a decade later Mayden (1992a,b) listed 971.

Regionally significant differences in North American freshwater fish species numbers and diversity are evident. The fish fauna east of the Continental Divide, consisting of eight speciose genera that comprise the majority of freshwater fish species on the continent, is species rich compared to the fish fauna of the Southwestern grasslands of New Mexico, Texas, and Oklahoma and the fish fauna west of the Continental Divide (Smith 1981b, Briggs 1986, Minckley and others 1986, Moyle and Herbold 1987, Etnier and Starnes 1993). Concentrations or "hot spots" of fish species diversity east of the Divide occur in the Appalachian and Ozark highlands and in Eastern streams. Here, some river systems contain as many as 100 to 200 fish species (Robison and Beedles 1974, Hocutt and others 1986, Schmidt 1986, Starnes and Etnier 1986, Mayden 1987, Robison and Buchanan 1988, Etneier and Starnes 1993, Matthews 1998). Diversity of fishes is also high throughout the Mississippi-Missouri River drainage, the region's major basin, where at least 260

Table 5-1. Fish versus tetrapod diversity. Numbers given are for described species worldwide in each taxon. (Adapted from Nelson 1994 and May 1988)

Species	Numbers
Fishes	28,618
Amphibians	2,800
Reptiles	6,000
Birds	4,500
Mammals	4,500

USDA Forest Service Gen. Tech. Rep. RMRS-GTR-135-vol. 2. 2005

141

Figure 5-1. Western Mississippi Basin.

1986, Minckley and others 1986, Moyle and Herbold 1987). The fauna west of the Divide has only about one-fourth as many species as the waters of Eastern North America (Miller 1959, Briggs 1986, Minckley and others 1986). For example, Burr and Mayden (1992) suggest that the Colorado River basin has approximately 32 native fish species, whereas 375 native fishes could be found in the Mississippi River. Matthews and Gelwick (1990) indicated that a typical reach (200 m) in a medium or large stream in Eastern North America contained 20 species of fish, whereas a reach in semiarid or arid lands of the Midwestern to Western North America may only contain eight to 12 species. Moyle and Herbold (1987) suggested that a sample of fishes in Western North America could contain fewer than 10 species, whereas in the Mississippi River basin two to three times as many fishes could be found.

The variation in fish species diversity and numbers between the Mississippi Basin and Southwestern grasslands east of the Continental Divide and the fish fauna west of the Continental Divide can be linked to a myriad of obvious and less apparent factors such as historic and recent evolutionary geology, effects of inland seas, climate, past and present erosive processes, and extant local fish faunas (Endler 1977, Briggs 1986, Minckley and others 1986, Smith and Miller 1986). In general, the fish fauna east of the Divide experienced a relatively calm geologic history. During the Pleistocene, the fish fauna of the East was able to avoid a high number of extinctions due to the region's large watershed size, stability, and lack of barriers to fish migration to refugia during glaciation and subsequent recolonization of habitats as ice sheets retreated northward (Smith 1981). In contrast, the fish fauna of the eastern Rocky Mountain slopes and west of the Continental Divide experienced more intense geological events during their evolution. West

species of fresh water fishes are found (Cross 1967, Smith 1981b, Cross and others 1986, Robison 1986, Moyle and Herbold 1987). Moving west into the western Mississippi Basin (fig. 5-1) the number of native fish species decline to about 235 and continues to decline as one moves westward into Western short-grass prairie and Southwestern grasslands east of the Continental Divide (fig. 5-2).

In contrast, the fish fauna west of the Continental Divide is characterized by relatively depauperate fish assemblages rich in endemic species, many of which are confined to a single spring, stream, or drainage (Minckley 1973, Pister 1974, Smith 1981a,b, Briggs

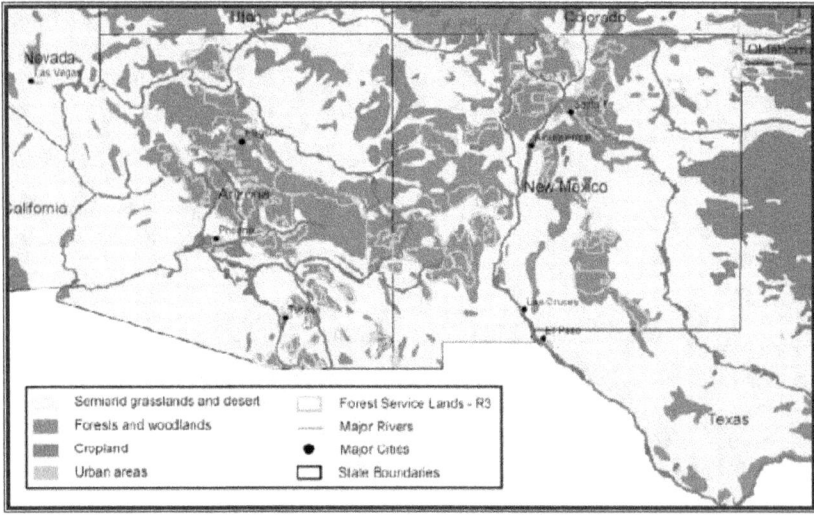

Figure 5-2. Semiarid grasslands, deserts, and major rivers of the Southwestern United States.

of the Divide, the fish fauna evolved in small isolated basins that were influenced by periods of extreme tectonic uplift, regional erosion, mountain building, volcanism, and increasing aridity (Dickinson 1981, Minckley and others 1986). In contrast to events east of the Continental Divide, these processes created barriers to fishes moving in search of refugia and prevented dispersal and recolonziation of waters subsequent to these geologic events (Smith 1981b, Dott and Batten 1981). Isolation, fragmentation, and allopatric speciation prevailed in this region. Many fish populations were extirpated, others were isolated or restricted to small habitats where genetic variation of the population was limited and speciation was allowed to proceed (Miller 1946a,b, 1959, Simberloff 1966, Moyle 1976, Smith 1978, 1981a,b, Minckley and others 1986). These factors, coupled with loss of genetic variation, contributed to rapid evolutionary change (Hubbs and Miller 1948, Hubbs and others 1974). These events account for a fish fauna that is characterized by special adaptations, endemism, and relatively depauperate populations.

Population Trends

As illustrated, the Southwestern fish fauna evolved in a region with highly variable climate and a dynamic geologic history. These environmental influences are reflected in the specializations and unique adaptations of the native Southwestern fish fauna. Unfortunately, the adaptations that have allowed these fishes to survive the harsh hydrologic conditions of the Southwest uplands and grasslands also made them vulnerable to large-scale human-induced ecological changes (Johnson and Rinne 1982, Minckley and Deacon 1991).

Native fishes of the Southwestern United States have experienced a severe reduction in both range and numbers since the region was first surveyed in the 19th century (Williams and others 1985). Significant fish faunal changes were first observed in the early 1900s (Miller 1946a, 1961, Minckley and Deacon 1968, Minckley and Deacon 1991, Koster 1957, Tyus and others 1982, Sublette and others 1990). By this time, extirpation and decline of native forms due to habitat alteration and competition with nonnative fish species had already begun (Miller 1961, Scurlock 1998). As early as 1904, nonnative common carp (*Cyprinus carpio*), brown bullhead (*Ameiurus nebulosus*), mosquito fish (*Gambusia affinis*), and green sunfish (*Lepomis cyanellus*) were collected in the Gila River of Arizona and New Mexico (Miller and others 1991). By 1926, 50 percent of the native fish fauna had been extirpated in the Salt River near Tempe, AZ, and by the late 1950s only two (14 percent) of the 14 original native fishes remained (Minckley and Deacon 1968). By the turn of the century, four fish species inhabiting grassland stream reaches

including shovelnose sturgeon (*Scaphirhynchus platorynchus*), spotted gar (*Lepisosteus osculates*), bonytail chub (*Gila elegans*), and freshwater drum (*Aplodinotus grunniens*), had been extirpated in New Mexico (Koster 1957, Sublette and others 1990). Noticing this downward trend prompted Miller (1946b) to call for studies of Western fishes to ensure their persistence.

It was not until the middle of the 20th century, however, when large-scale continental and regional changes in the native fish faunas occurred and were finally recognized by the scientific community (Miller 1961, 1972, Minckley and Deacon 1991). Miller (1961) examined and provided data on changes in the Southwestern fish fauna. In a more extensive effort, Miller (1972) provided a preliminary effort to identify threatened fishes of the 50 States and again highlighted the decline of Southwestern native fishes, provided reasons for the decline, and listed species of threatened fishes for each of the 50 States in the United States (Miller 1972). He listed 305 fishes as threatened. Nine fish species were listed as threatened in Arizona and five in New Mexico. Miller and others (1989) documented the extinction of three genera, 27 species, and 13 subspecies of fishes from North America during the past 100 years.

Today, most native Western fishes have become listed as threatened or endangered by the USDI Fish and Wildlife Service, and others are given protection afford by individual States (Johnson and Rinne 1982, Williams and others 1989, Minckley and Douglas 1991, USFWS 2003). Of the 150 fishes recognized by Lee and others (1980) west of the Continental Divide, 122 are considered to be in danger of extirpation (Minckley and Deacon 1991). A large percentage (34 percent) of the fishes currently listed by the USDI Fish and Wildlife Service are from the Western United States (USFWS TESS 2003). Viability of many of these populations is questionable. Many species not afforded protection under the Endangered Species Act or by State regulations are also believed to be in decline.

In New Mexico, a minimum of 66 and possibly as many as 70 native fishes were extant when Euro-American settlers arrived (approximately 1525) (Sublette and others 1990, Propst 1999). Using the latter value, since that time, two (3 percent) native fish species have gone extinct, 12 (17 percent) have been extirpated from the State, 25 (36 percent) are considered to be in decline, and 31 (44 percent) are listed as stable (table 5-2). Of the remaining native fish fauna, 23 (41 percent) are listed as threatened or endangered by the State of New Mexico (Propst 1999). Of these, 10 (18 percent) are listed as threatened and endangered by the USDI Fish and Wildlife Service, and one additional species is proposed for listing (table 5-2). Many of these are species found in reaches that flowed through grasslands of the Southwest (Koster 1957, Sublette and others 1990, Propst 1999).

USDA Forest Service Gen. Tech. Rep. RMRS-GTR-135-vol. 2. 2005

143

Table 5-2. Status of native fishes in New Mexico.

Species Scientific name	Common name	Status USFWS	Status NM
Scaphirhynchus platorynchus	Shovelnose sturgeon		Ex
Lepsiosteus oculatus	Spotted gar		Ex
Lepisosteus osseus	Longnose gar		
Anguila rostrata	American eel		
Dorosoma cepedianum	Gizzard shad		
Oncorhynchus clarki virginalis	Rio Grande cutthroat trout		
Oncorhynchus gilae	Gila trout	En	Th
Oncorhynchus clarki	Colorado River cutthroat		Ex
Astyanax mexicanus	Mexican tetra		Th
Agosia chrysogaster	Longfin dace		
Campostoma anomalum	Central stoneroller		
Cyprinella Formosa	Beautiful shiner		Ext
Cyprinella lutrensis	Red shiner		
Dionda episcopa	Roundnose minnow		
Extrarius aestivalis	Speckled chub		
Macrhybopsis aestivalis tetranemus	Arkansas River speckled chub		Th
Gila elegans	Bonytail chub		Ex
Gila nigrescens	Chihuahua chub		En
Gila Pandora	Rio Grande chub		
Gila nigrescens	Chihuahua chub	Th	En
Gila intermedia	Gila chub		Ex
Gila robusta	Roundtail chub		En
Hybognathus amarus	Rio Grande silvery minnow	En	En
Hybognathus placitus	Plains minnow		
Meda fulgida	Spikedace	Th	Th
Notropis amabilis	Texas shiner		Ex
Notropis girardi	Arkansas shiner	Th	En
Notropis jemezanus	Rio Grande shiner		
Notropis orca	Phantom shiner	Ext	Ext
Notropis simus simus	Bluntnose shiner	Ext	Ext
Notropis simus pecosensis	Pecos Bluntnose shiner		Th
Notropis stramineus	Sand shiner	Th	
Phenacobius mirabilis	suckermouth minnow		Th
Phoxinus erythrogaster	Southern redbelly dace		En
Pimephales promelas	Fathead minnow		
Platygobio gracilis	Flathead chub		
Ptychocheilus lucius	Colorado cikeminnow	En	En
Rhinichthys cataractae	Longnose dace		
Rhinichthys osculus	Speckled dace		
Semotilus atromaculatus	Creek chub		
Tiaroga cobitis	Loach minnow	Th	Th
Carpoides carpio	River carpsucker		
Catostomus commersoni	White sucker		
Catostomus plebeius	Rio Grande sucker		
Catostomus clarki	Desert sucker		
Catostomus discobolus	Zuni bluehead sucker		En
Catostomus insignis	Sonoran sucker		
Catostomus latipinnis	Flannelmouth sucker		
Cycleptus elongatus	Blue sucker		En
Xyrauchen texanus	Razorback sucker		
Ictiobus bubalus	Smallmouth buffalo		Th
Moxostoma congestum	Gray redhorse		
Ictalurus furcatus	Blue catfish		
Ictalurus lupus	Headwater catfish		
Ictalurus melas	Black bullhead		
Ictalurus punctatus	Channel catfish		
Pylodictus olivaris	Flathead catfish		

144

USDA Forest Service Gen. Tech. Rep. RMRS-GTR-135-vol. 2. 2005

Table 5-2. *Continued.*

Species Scientific name	Common name	Status USFWS	NM
Cyprinodon pecosensis	Pecos pupfish	Th	Th
Cyprinodon tularosa	White sands pupfish		Th
Cyprinodon sp.	Palomas pupfish	Ext	Ext
Fundulus zebrinus	Plains killifish		
Lucania parva	Rainwater killifish		
Poeciliopsis occidentalis	Gila topminnow	En	Th
Gambusia affinis	Mosquito fish		
Gambusia noblis	Pecos gambusia	En	En
Lepomis cyanellus	Green sunfish		
Lepomis macrochirus	Blugill		
Lepomis meglotis	Longear sunfish		
Micropterus salmoides	Largemouth bass		
Etheostoma lepidum	Greenthroat darter		Th
Percina macrolepida	Bigscale logperch		Th
Aplodinotus grunniens	Freshwater drum		Ex
Cottus bairdi	Mottled sculpin		

En=Endangered, Th =Threatened, Ext = Extinct, Ex = Extirpated (For more detailed description of Federal and State threatened and endangered status of native fishes see Propst 1999.)

Similar to New Mexico, the native fish fauna of Arizona has been greatly modified over the past 120 years. Of the 36 fishes native to the waters of Arizona, one (3 percent) is now extinct, three (8 percent) have been extirpated from the State, 21 (58 percent) are in decline, and 11 (25 percent) are considered stable (table 5-3). Of the remaining native fishes, 25 (69 percent) are listed as Wildlife of Special Concern in Arizona, 19 (53 percent) are listed as threatened or endangered by the USDI Fish and Wildlife Service, and one is classified as a candidate for listing (table 5-3).

The decline of native fishes and native fish communities can be linked to resource extraction, alteration of stream channels, and water diversion by indigenous peoples and Euro-Americans settling in the region (approximately 1521) (Minckley and Douglas 1991, Rinne and Platania 1995, Calamusso and Rinne 1999). Introduction of nonnative aquatic species and associated competition and hybridization have resulted in the decline, alteration, and extirpation of many native fish species and entire assemblages. Remaining populations of native fish are often isolated, then decline to low levels leading to categorization as threatened, endangered, or at risk (Miller 1961, Deacon and others 1979, Williams and Sada 1985, Williams and others 1985, 1989, Miller and others 1989, Rinne and Minckley 1991). Often resource management agencies do not have complete knowledge of populations that in fact warrant listing or some type of protection.

Biological Threats: Introduction of Nonnative Fish Species

Other than dewatering of a stream reach or desiccation of some type of standing body of water the primary threat to the persistence of native fishes in Southwestern grasslands has been the introduction and range expansion of nonnative fishes. In fact, Minckley and Douglas (1991) suggested that the spread of nonnative fishes may be more detrimental than all other environmental perturbations combined. The effects of dewatering, habitat loss, and pollution are sometimes temporary, but once a nonnative species is established it is difficult or impossible to remove it from many systems (Rinne and Turner 1991).

Nonnative fishes have been introduced into the waters of North America since the late 1600s. Fuller and others (1999) listed 536 fish taxa (representing 75 families) that have been transplanted into the United States outside their native range. Unfortunately, rates of introduction have continued to increase over the past 45 years due to more efficient transportation and demand for nonnative forms for sport, fish farming, bait, and aquarium use (Fuller and others 1999, Heidinger 1999, Li and Moyle 1999, Nico and Fuller 1999). Of the myriad of intentional fish stockings, only a few have been positive, and no unplanned introductions have been considered beneficial (Steirer 1992, Courtnay and Williams 1992). Introductions have, on the whole, caused many problems for native fishes (Deacon 1979, Deacon and others 1979, Williams and

USDA Forest Service Gen. Tech. Rep. RMRS-GTR-135-vol. 2. 2005

145

Table 5-3. Status of native fishes in Arizona.

Species		Status	
		USFWS	AZ
Elops affinis	Machete		
Mugil cephalus	Striped mullet		
Oncorhynchus gilae apache	Apache trout	Th	X
Oncorhynchus gilae gilae	Gila trout	En	X
Campostoma ornatum	Mexican stoneroller		
Cyprinella formosa	Beautiful shiner	Th	X
Gila cypha	Humpback chub	En	X
Gila ditaenia	Sonora chub	Th	X
Gila elegans	Bonytail chub	En	X
Gila intermedia	Gila chub	C	X
Gila nigra	Headwater chub		
Gila purpurea	Yaqui chub	En	X
Gila robusta	Roundtail chub		X
Gila seminuda	Virgin chub	En	X
Meda fulgida	Spikedace	Th	X
Lepidomeda mollispinis mollispinis	Virgin spinedace		X
Lepidomeda vittata	Little Colorado spinedace	Th	X
Plagopterus argentissimus	Woundfin	En	X
Ptychocheilus lucius	Colorado sikeminnow	En	X
Rhinichthys osculus	Speckled dace		
Tiaroga cobitis	Loach minnow	Th	X
Catostomus bernardini	Yaqui sucker		X
Catostomus clarki	Desert sucker		
Catostomus discobolus	Bluehead sucker		
Catostomus d. yarrowi	Zuni Mountain sucker		
Catostomus insignis	Sonora sucker		
Catostomus latipinnis	Flannelmouth sucker		X
Catostomus sp.	Little Colorado sucker		
Xyrauchen texanus	Razorback sucker	En	X
Ictalurus pricei	Yaqui catfish	Th	X
Cyprinodon eremus	Quitobaquito pupfish	En	X
Cyprinodon macularius	Desert pupfish	En	X
Cyprinodon sp.	Monkey spring pupfish	Ext	Ext
Poeciliopsis occidentalis occidentalis	Gila topminnow	En	X
Poeciliopsis occidentalis sonoriensis	Yaqui topminnow	En	X

En = Endangered, Th = Threatened, Ext = Extinct, X = Species of Special Concern by State of Arizona, Ex = Extirpated

others 1989). The nonnative fishes currently found in almost all major watersheds of the Continental United States have led to the decline and listing of native fish populations across North America (Taylor and others 1984, Courtenay and others 1984, Courtenay and Stauffer 1990, Hendrickson and Brooks 1991, U.S. Congress, OTA 1993). Today, 70 percent of the fishes listed under the Endangered Species Act have been negatively impacted by nonnative fishes (Lassuy 1995, USFWS 2003, Tyus and Saunders 2000). Further, it is estimated that the extinction of 20 native fishes in the 1900s is primarily due to interactions with nonnative forms (Miller and others 1989).

Impacts of nonnative fish on native fishes/communities depend on the physiological, behavioral, and ecological capabilities of the nonnative species and the biological and physical components of the ecosystem and its inhabitants (Taylor and others 1984, Haines and Tyus 1990, Rinne and others 1998). Nonnative fish often have adaptations that provide advantages in the aquatic environment in which they are introduced. These capabilities (reproductive, environmental tolerances, behavior) enable them to exploit environmental resources more effectively than native inhabitants. This efficient exploitation can lead to higher reproductive success and greater growth rates, which then allow nonnative species to biologically "swamp" resident fishes. The end result is replacement of native forms by nonindigenous species.

Many examples of these phenomena exist in the Southwest. Native Gila topminnow (*Poeciliopsis occidentalis occidentalis*) have been eliminated through aggression and predation by mosquito fish (*Gambusia affinis*) (Minckley and others 1977, Meffe and others 1983, Weedman and others 1996, 1997a,b). Brown trout (*Salmo trutta*), a native trout of Europe, have wider environmental tolerances, especially water temperature, and are more aggressive and piscivorous. They have replaced native trout across North America, and in the Southwest have been implicated in the demise of Rio Grande cutthroat trout (*Oncorhynchus clarki virginalis*), Gila trout (*O. gilae*), and Apace trout (*O. apache*) (Behnke and Zarn 1976). Red shiner has been implicated in the replacement of native fishes through competitive exclusion throughout low elevation grassland streams in the Southwest. Predation by species nonnative channel (*Ictalurus punctatus*) and flathead catfish (*Pylodictus olivaris*) directly prey on larval young and adult native fishes. Both of these species have been implicated in the demise of the razorback sucker (*Xyrauchen texanus*) (Marsh and Langhorst 1988). Some species of introduced chiclid have year-round breeding seasons. These fish reproductively swamp native fishes by sheer number, which appears also to be the case in the replacement of Rio Grande sucker (*Catostomus plebeius*) by nonnative white sucker (*Catostomus commersoni*) in the Rio Grande drainage of Colorado and New Mexico.

Habitat alteration, it is hypothesized, often allows nonnative fishes to dominate indigenous fish faunas (Maddux and others 1993). Minckley and Carufel (1967) concluded that red shiner contributed to the demise of native fish populations throughout the Southwest. In many areas Red shiners have replaced woundfin (*Plagopterus argentissimus*), spikedace (*Meda fulgida*), and loach minnow (*Rhinichthys (tiaroga) cobitis*), all of which are Federally listed species in Arizona and New Mexico (Deacon 1988, Marsh and others 1989, Douglas and others 1994). While the mechanisms of replacement are not known, Rinne (1991) and Douglas and others (1994) indicated that red shiner adults occupied habitats used by juvenile spikedace and loach minnow in the Verde River. Nonnative trout have been shown to have detrimental affects on the Little Colorado River spinedace (*Lepidomeda vittata vittata*) in terms of predation and displacement (Blinn and others 1993). Centrarchids, especially, have been problematic for native fishes. This taxon has been introduced throughout Southwestern streams for sport, and by nature they are predacious, which has had severe impacts on all native forms. In the Verde River of Arizona, smallmouth bass (*Micropterus dolmieui*) and Green sunfish (*Lepomis cyanellus*) have eliminated a complete native fish fauna (Rinne and others 1999).

Similar to continental trends, establishment of nonnative fishes and replacement of native fishes has occurred on a regional scale throughout the Southwestern grasslands since the late 1800s (Rinne

1990, Fuller and others 1999). Nonnative fishes were imported for sport, biological control, and bait along with accidental introductions of unwanted species (Deacon and others 1964). Currently, 84 nonindigenous fishes are now found in the waters of Arizona and 78 in New Mexico (tables 5-4 and 5-5) (Minckley 1973, Hanson 1980, Sublette and others 1990, Fuller and others 1999). In New Mexico, introduced fishes account for more than half of the total fish fauna in the Rio Grande, Mimbres, Tularosa, San Juan, Zuni, San Francisco, and Gila Rivers (Propst and others 1987, Platania 1991, Sublette and others 1990, Rinne and Platania 1995, Propst 1999). In the Pecos and Canadian Rivers, nonnative fishes comprise 42 percent and 48 percent of the current fish fauna, respectively (Sublette and others 1990). Similar effects are seen in Arizona. Nonnative fishes comprise 82 percent of the fauna in the Colorado River basin, 68 percent in the Little Colorado, 50 percent in the San Juan, 40 percent in the Gila, 38 percent in the Bill Williams, 25 percent in the Rio Yaqui basin, and 10 percent in the Virgin River. The Sonotya and Rio Magdalena basins are free of nonnative fishes.

Native fish of the montane and grassland reaches of the Eastern Rocky Mountains and Western North America may be at greater risk from the introduction of nonnative species than native fishes in other parts of the country because of their isolated evolutionary history (Moyle and others 1986, Minckley and Douglas 1991). Additionally, depauperate native Western species live in dynamic watershed and aquatic environments, both of which make them vulnerable to replacement by nonnative fishes (Minckley and Deacon 1968, Moyle and Nichols 1973, 1974, Moyle 1976). Many native fishes in the West have not developed protective mechanisms against predation, general competition, and genetic hybridization, and they have low tolerance to biological interactions with nonnative fishes (Miller 1961, Deacon and Minckley 1974, Deacon 1979, Minckley and others 1986, Smith and Miller 1986, Sublette and others 1990). To a large degree, many Southwestern fishes exist as relict populations in single habitats, which exacerbates their precarious state (Deacon and Minckley 1974).

Effects of nonnative fishes on native fish communities are not well understood and are typically observed from major alterations in the native fish fauna. Direct effects from the interactions with nonnative fishes come in the form of predation (Schoenherr 1981, Minckley 1983, Blinn and others 1993), competition (Deacon and others 1964), hybridization (Rinne and Minckley 1985, Dowling and Childs 1992), elimination, reduced growth and survival, changes in community structure, and no effect (Moyle and others 1986). Impacts on various life stages also occur in time and space. Indirect effects, such as stress or other behavioral interactions are more difficult to document. The outcome of many of these

Table 5-4. Current distribution introduced nonnative grassland fishes by drainage basin in New Mexico. (Table adapted from Sublette and others 1990)

Species	Rio Grande	Canadian	Pecos	San Juan	Mimbres	Tularosa	Gila
Threadfin shad	X	X	X	X			
Cutthroat trout	X	X	X	X			
Coho Salmon	X	X	X	X			
Rainbow trout	X	X	X	X	X		X
Kokanee salmon	X	X	X	X			X
Brown trout	X	X	X	X	X		X
Brook trout	X	X	X		X		X
Lake trout	X						
Northern pike	X	X	X	X			
Zebra danio	X						
Goldfish			X				
Grass carp							
Carp	X	X	X		X		X
Fathead minnow	X	X	X	X	X		X
Bullhead minnow	X						
Yellow bullhead	X	X					X
Guppy	X						
Sailfin molly	X						
Inland silverside			X				
White bass	X	X	X				
Striped bass	X		X				
Rock bass			X				
Warmouth	X						
Smallmouth bass	X	X	X	X			X
Spotted bass			X				
White crappie	X	X	X		X		X
Black crappie	X	X	X				
Walleye	X	X	X				

Key: X = presence.

Table 5-5. Current distribution of nonnative grassland fishes by drainage basin in Arizona.

Species	Colorado	Little Colorado	Bill Williams	San Juan	Sonoyta	Yaqui	Gila	Virgin
White sturgeon								
American eel	X		X					
Threadfin shad	X						X	
Coho salmon								
Sockeye salmon								
Rainbow trout	X	X		X			X	
Cutthroat trout								
Brown trout								
Brook trout								
Arctic grayling								
Northern pike								
Banded tetra	X ?							
Carp	X	X	X				X	X
Goldfish								
Grass carp								
Golden shiner	X	X		X			X	

Table 5-5. *Continued.*

Species	Colorado	Little Colorado	Bill Williams	San Juan	Sonoyta	Yaqui	Gila	Virgin
Utah chub	X ?							
Red shiner	X	X	X				X	X
Redside shiner	X ?						X	X ?
Sand shiner		X ?						
Fathead minnow	X	X	X			X	X	
Bigmouth buffalo							X	
Black buffalo							X	
Smallmouth buffalo							X	
Flathead catfish	X						X	
Channel catfish	X	X	X				X	
Blue catfish	X ?							
Black bullhead	X	X				X	X	
Yellow bullhead	X	X					X	
Brown bullhead	X							
Plains Killifish	X	X						
Mosquitofish	X	X	X			X	X	X
Pacu								
Variable platyfish								
Green swordtail								
Sailfin molly	X						X	
Mexican molly	X						X	
Guppy	X						X	
Striped bass	X							
White bass	X							
Yellow bass							X	
Smallmouth bass	X						X	
Spotted bass	X						X	
Largemouth bass	X							
Warmouth								
Green sunfish	X	X	X				X	X
Bluegill	X	X	X			X	X	
Redear sunfish	X						X	
Pumpkinseed							X	
Rockbass								
White crappie							X	
Black crappie	X	X					X	
Sacramento perch								
Walleye							X	
Yellow perch	X	X					X	
Sargo								
Bairdiella								
Corvina								
Convict cichlid							X	
Mozambique mouthbrooder	X						X	
Blue talapia								
Red-breasted tilapia							X	
Striped mullet	X							
Spotted sleeper	X							
Longjaw mudsleeper	X							
Mottled sculpin	X							

Key: X = presence. X? = questionable.

USDA Forest Service Gen. Tech. Rep. RMRS-GTR-135-vol. 2. 2005

149

negative interactions is that remaining populations of native fish are often isolated, decline to low levels leading to categorization as threatened, endangered, or at risk (Miller 1961, Deacon and others 1979, Williams and others 1985, Miller and others 1989, Rinne and Minckley 1991).

Habitat Threats

General Landscape Change and Habitat Loss

Beginning in the 1880s, marked ecological changes over the Southwestern landscape occurred. By the 1890s, regional degradation was evident (Hasting and Tuner 1965). Dense stands of Southwestern grasslands, lush riparian areas, free flowing rivers and unaltered watersheds that were in place at the time of the Spanish explorers and later by Anglo settlers, had long since been irrevocably altered by livestock grazing and the damming and diverting of river water for human consumption (Griffiths 1904, Mehrhoff 1955, Scurlock 1998, Ambos and others 2002). Cottonwood gallery forests that once lined Southwestern rivers died due to channel incision and dropping water tables and were being replaced by nonnative phreatophytic species such as salt cedar (*Tamarisk* sp.).

Examples were noted throughout the Southwest. The San Pedro River, once a slow moving river with cienegas, had been changed to a steep-walled entrenched channel through which water moved rapidly, thus transporting large amounts of sediment into the Gila River. By the end of the 19th century, the once perennial San Pedro River had changed to an intermittent system exhibiting dry reaches throughout the year. Events such as these were relatively unknown prior to 1890 (Hastings and Turner 1965). In the grasslands of New Mexico, similar events occurred in the Rio Puerco (Rio Grande drainage) and Rio Chaco (San Juan drainage) watersheds (Bryan 1928, Scurlock 1998).

Water Use

The original aquatic habitats of the Southwestern grasslands once consisted of large rivers (5th order), streams, cienegas, and springs. Since settlement by Native Americans and Euro-Americans, these resources have undergone extreme modification (Leopold and others 1964, Hastings and Turner 1965, Sublette and others 1990, Minckley and Deacon 1991). Water development and its use for agriculture began as early as 900 A.D. when pueblo dwelling Native Americans collected surface runoff or diverted water from Southwestern rivers for agriculture and domestic uses. As the Spanish-Americans began settling the region (approximately 1521), increased demand was placed on limited Southwestern waters resources (Dozier 1983, Carlson 1990, Scurlock 1998). The use of metal tools, domesticated animals, and engineering skills used by Spanish-American settlers made even a greater impact on water resources in the region. In New Mexico, the *acequia* or irrigation ditch was so important that they were dug prior to the construction of human dwellings. By the end of the 1600s, all or portions of present-day New Mexico's perennial streams were being diverted into irrigation networks (Scurlock 1998). As Anglo-Americans (nonnative, non-Hispanic peoples) entered the Southwest in the early 1820s, more demand was laced on water resources for expanding commercial agricultural and economic interest (Hastings 1959, Scurlock 1998). New irrigation systems were constructed, and older systems expanded by private companies whose economic well being was tied directly to the growing economy (Briggs and Van Ness 1987, Clark 1987, Scurlock 1998). Technological advances allowed wells to be dug that tapped underlying aquifers. Windmills also gave access to underground water resources. By 1880 water shortages had begun in the Southwest (Westphall 1965).

Large-scale change in natural stream flow and surface water dispersion occurred during the latter part of the 19th and beginning of the 20th centuries when dams were built on the major rivers of New Mexico and Arizona (Mueller and Marsh 2002). Then, with the passage of the Reclamation Act of 1903, the free-flowing waters and cienegas of the American Southwest were changed forever (Hastings and Tuner 1965). The perennial shortage of water for human use inherent in the region along with the post-World War II population boom precipitated the need for larger dams and diversion systems. Large-scale dams and diversion projects were built to store water, control sedimentation and flooding, generate power, and disperse water for irrigation. Today, dams and diversions are found on all major rivers and many of their tributaries throughout the Southwest (fig. 5-3 and 5-4). Large, artificial impoundments now make up the major surface waters in the Southwestern grasslands (Minckley 1973, Sublette and others 1990). Expanding agriculture, especially in the lower elevation grassland valleys, has necessitated the pumping of groundwater because of the shortages in surface water allocations; often times the result is the extraction of water that exceeds rates at which water recharges. Some aquifers are essentially being "mined" for their fossil water. Pumping of aquifers has placed many rivers and springs in the grasslands of the Western United States at risk by lowering regional and local water tables.

Interbasin transfer projects, such as the Central Arizona Project (fig. 5-5) now transport water across hundreds of kilometers into foreign basins. Natural drought cycles (one of which at publication time is in

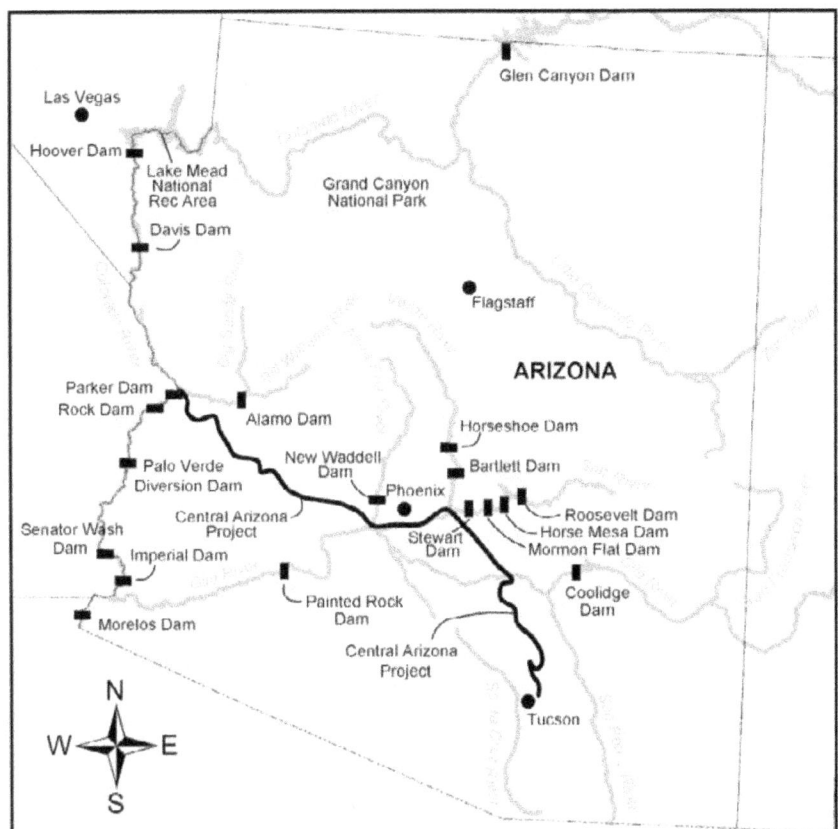

Figure 5-3. Major dams and diversions on rivers in Arizona.

Figure 5-4. Major dams and diversions on rivers in New Mexico.

Figure 5-5. Central Arizona Project.

Table 5-6. Dams and diversions on major rivers in the New Mexico.

Structure	River	Date built
Heron	Rio Grande	1971
El Vado	Rio Grande	1935
Abiquiu Resrvoir	Rio Grande	1963
Cochiti Dam	Rio Grande	1975
Galisteo Dam	Rio Grande	1970
Nambe Falls Dam	Rio Nambe	1974
Jemez Canyon Dam	Jemez	1953
Angostura Diversion	Rio Grande	1938
Isleta Diversion	Rio Grande	1934
San Acacia Diversion	Rio Grande	1934
Elephant Butte Dam	Rio Grande	1916
Caballo Dam	Rio Grande	1938
Leasburg Diversion	Rio Grande	1919
McMillan Dam	Pecos	1908
Brantley Dam	Pecos	1991
Avalon Dam	Pecos	1888
Sumner Dam	Pecos	1937

progress in the Southwest) add additional stress to a system that is largely overallocated and overused. Though completed with the best of intentions, all of these activities have disrupted the natural flows of grassland rivers and altered their physical properties. Today much of Arizona's and New Mexico's grassland river flows are found in canals, ditches, and drains.

In New Mexico, major dams or diversions exist on every large mainstem river in the State (table 5-6; fig. 5-4). There are also 32 small watershed projects with 71 flood control dams and 41 miles of diversions that were constructed since 1957. On the Rio Grande there are 13 major dams and diversions in New Mexico. Along the upper and middle reaches of the Rio Grande, six dams and three major diversions have been built. There are 321 km of canals (9.6 km concrete lined), 928 km of laterals (6 km lined), and 648 km of open and concrete pipe drains. The objective of these projects is to provide irrigation water, control sediment, and prevent flooding in the Middle Rio Grande Valley. Over 36,000 ha of agricultural lands are irrigated by water diverted from this reach of the Rio Grande. On the lower Rio Grande in New Mexico and West Texas, there are two major dams, six diversion dams, 222 km of canals,

731 km miles of laterals, 744 km of drains, and one hydroelectric power generating facility. Most drains in this reach of river are unlined earthen structures. These structures provide irrigation water for 79,320 ha of farm land in addition to power generation for cities and industry in the region. Water is also provided to irrigate 10,117 ha in the Juarez Valley, Mexico. Today, the lower Rio Grande is essentially a conveyance ditch from the headwaters of Elephant Butte to the Texas border. In the grassland reaches of the Pecos River, four dams have been constructed in New Mexico. There are 242 km of laterals, 59 km of canals, and about 38 km of drains in this system. Water stored in Pecos River reservoirs irrigates almost 10,000 ha in the region.

As with New Mexico, all major rivers and many tributaries in Arizona now are impounded, controlled, diverted, and in some cases overallocated (table 5-7; fig. 5-3). On the Colorado River there six dams, on the Bill Williams River one, four on the Salt River, two on the Verde River, and two on the Gila River. Impoundments on the Colorado River and its tributaries now account for the major surface waters in Arizona. The Colorado River—the once turbid and swift-flowing water that meandered through braided channel system bordered by riparian vegetation and marshes—has now been dammed, diverted, channelized, and confined by levees (Mueler and Marsh 2002). The largest artificial bodies of water in Arizona—Lakes Havasu, Powell, Mead, and Mohave—are all located on the Colorado River. Remote reaches of the Colorado River retain characteristics of a free-flowing stream as does the Salt River Canyon and the upper reaches of the Verde River.

Effect on Fishes—Water, above all, is of course the key habitat element needed to sustain fishes (Heede

Table 5-7. Major dams and diversions of the Lower Colorado River Basin, Arizona.

Structure	River	Date built
Granite Reef Diversion	Salt River	1908
Theodore Roosevelt Dam	Salt River	1911
Horse Mesa Dam	Salt River	1927
Mormon Flat Dam	Salt River	1925
Stewart Mountain Dam	Salt River	1930
Horseshoe Dam	Verde River	1946
Bartlett Dam	Verde River	1939
Laguna Dam	Colorado River	1909
Boulder Dam	Colorado River	1936
Imperial Dam	Colorado River	1938
Parker Dam	Colorado River	1938
Headgate Rock Diversion	Colorado River	1944
Palo Verde Diversion	Colorado River	1957
Coolidge Dam	Gila River	1928
Painted Rock Dam	Gila River	1960
New Waddell Dam	Agua Fria River	1928
Alamo Dam	Bill Williams River	1968

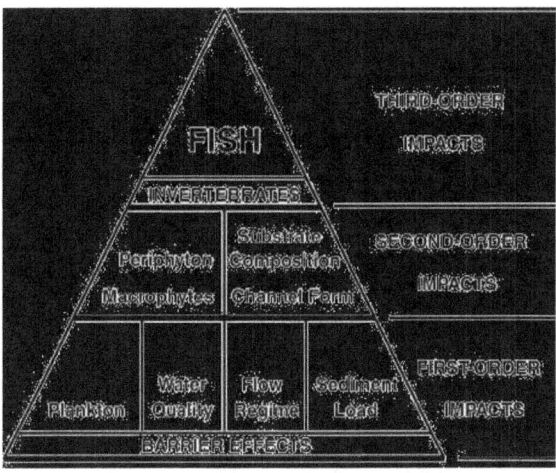

Figure 5-6. Impacts of impoundments on riverine systems.

and Rinne 1990, Rinne 1990, 2000). The impact of impounding, diverting, dewatering, and draining of Southwestern waters along with mining of ancient aquifers has eliminated or drastically altered the aquatic habitats needed for survival of native Southwestern grassland fishes. The affect of these activities has accelerated the early decimation of native fishes found in grassland reaches throughout Southwestern rivers (Minckley and Deacon 1968).

Damming—Dams present a suite of problems for native fishes. First order impacts begin soon after the dam is in place (Neel 1963, Orth and White 1993). The physical structure acts as a barrier to upstream migration, and the impoundment can prevent downstream migration. Natural cycles of flooding and drought flows are now determined by power and water demands of cities and agriculture (Johnson and Rinne 1982). Other first order effects are altered sediment load, changes in water quality, and plankton (fig. 5-6). Second order impacts alter channel morphology and change substrate composition. Third order impacts relate to the cumulative effects of first and second order effects. It is the third order effects that impact fish and invertebrates. The physical structure interferes or prevents upstream migration, and often times the impoundment above precludes downstream migration due to vastly different water quality than preimpoundment conditions. For example, the Rio Grande once had large runs of female American eel (*Anguilla rostrata*). Other species affected by dams on the Rio Grande and Pecos Rivers were freshwater drum (*Aplodintus grunniens*), river carpsucker (*Carpoides carpio*), blue sucker (*Cycleptus elongates*), grey redhorse (*Moxostoma congestum*). Dams on the Lower Colorado system have

been particularly destructive to the long-lived big river fishes such as flannelmouth sucker (*Catostomous latipinnis*), razorback sucker (*Xyrauchen texanus*), Colorado pikeminnow (*Ptychoceilus lucius*), humpback chub (*Gila cypha*), and bonytailed chub (*G. elegans*). Dams alter the riverine environment upstream and downstream of the structure. Stratification and point of release from the dam also determine water quality and temperature (fig. 5-7). For example, hypolimnetic releases have low relative water temperatures, are often anoxic, and can also have elevated nutrient, iron, manganese, and hydrogen sulfide concentrations (Reid and Wood 1976, Orth and White 1993). These conditions may be unsuitable for native fishes and native macroinvertebrates, but may be excellent for introduced cool-water game fishes. In addition to unfavorable habitat conditions, native fish now face the threat of predation and competition from these alien forms. Releases such as these occur at Stewart Mountain Dam on the Salt River and Caballo Dam on

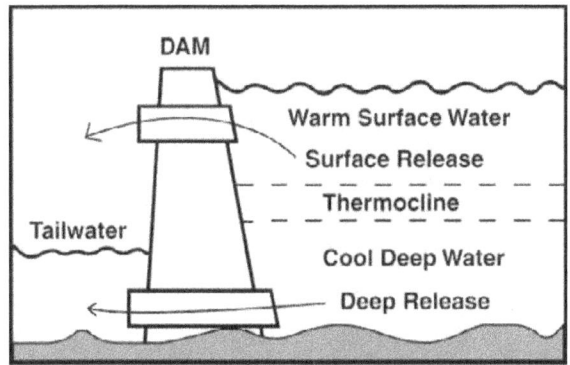

Figure 5-7. Impacts of dams on upstream and downstream water temperature.

USDA Forest Service Gen. Tech. Rep. RMRS-GTR-135-vol. 2. 2005

153

the Rio Grande. Water chemistry and conditions that once favored native grassland fishes below Elephant Butte and Caballo Reservoirs now support species cool-water species such as trout and walleye (*Stizostedion vitreum*), along with various sunfishes and catfishes. In many reaches of Southwestern rivers (such as the Rio Grande, Salt, Colorado), dams have dewatered hundreds of kilometers of river channel while permanently inundating others. Flood plain areas that may have acted as nursery or rearing areas are now inaccessible along most major rivers.

Diversion—Diversion of stream waters during irrigation season desiccates many riverine habitats causing local extirpations and extinctions in reaches that have become permanently dewatered. Impacts are more severe during drought years. For example, Rio Grande silvery minnow living below the San Acia diversion on the Rio Grande often run the risk of coping with decreasing flows and drying of the channel during drought years. Fish are unable to ascend the diversion as larvae. As the stream dries many individuals are lost and recruitment is reduced. Similar situations occur on the Salt River below Stewart Mountain Dam and in the lower reaches of the Colorado River near the Mexican border. During irrigation season many fishes become stranded in irrigation canals as water flows are decreased and headgates are closed. The effects of dewatering appear too be more pronounced in the middle to lower elevations of Southwestern streams (fig. 5-3 and 5-4). These reaches flow through grassland and desert ecotypes that are farther from headwater sources and are more prone to natural dewatering. The placement of diversion systems above these reaches increases the probability of dewatering. Canals and laterals often times are earthen structures, but many miles of these are concrete lined. Lining canals with concrete, while increasing irrigation efficiency, prevents water from filtering into the water table. Seepage from unlined irrigation systems recharges aquifers, flows into drains, and recharges rivers from which it was diverted, thus supporting fish and riparian communities.

Earthen canals are regularly dredged to clean and maintain efficient flow of water. During this operation, riparian vegetation is either partially or completely removed so that equipment can complete the dredging operation. Fish communities in these systems (common along the Ro Grande) often harbor native fishes. Applications of herbicides to control aquatic weeds and pesticides to control mosquitoes are common. Such chemicals alter water quality and often make conditions uninhabitable for certain fishes (Minckley and Deacon 1968).

Irrigation systems present a suite of problems for native fishes that once were abundant in the unaltered river systems from which present systems are watered. The irrigation systems that are often lined with concrete and are highly regulated cause organic components that would typically be found in natural riverine systems to be almost nonexistent in the artificial environment. Mechanical and chemical vegetation removal and dredging of such systems are regularly conducted to clean, facilitate flow, and effect efficient transfer of the precious commodity—water. The threat of dewatering and drying is ever present. Even in primitive, earthen irrigation canals, aquatic habitats have been highly simplified, flow regimes altered, and the fish community impacted through the introduction of nonnative fishes and other alien aquatic species such as crayfish and other invertebrates. Though these problems for native fish are salient, irrigation systems do allow fishes to persist, even if that occurs at reduced levels. The drains that parallel the Rio Grande in New Mexico for all practical purposes harbor the fish community of its middle and lower reaches.

Pumping—Pumping of groundwater lowers water tables; this causes interruption in arid land streams. Springs and marshes can also become desiccated from lowering of water tables. The upshot is the demise of many aquatic habitats and the loss of native fishes populations One of the classic examples of this, while not in the grasslands reaches of Arizona or New Mexico, was the near extirpation of the Devil's Hole pupfish (*Cyprinodon diabolis*). In 1969, corporate farm interests intended to pump the Ash Meadows aquifer, located in southeastern Nevada near Las Vegas, to increase farm production. The result would have been the lowering of the water table, which in turn would dewater the spring, ultimately leading to the extinction of this indigenous endemic pupfish species. Fortunately, for the Devil's Hole pupfish, concerned scientists and citizens were able to bring a halt to this action.

Grazing, Riparian Corridors, and Fish Relationships

The ecological conditions of Southwestern watersheds and riparian corridors have undergone dramatic changes since the settlement of the region by Native Americans and Euro-Americans (Carton and others 2000). Many of these changes have been attributed to grazing of domestic livestock over the past 460 years. The first livestock grazed in the region were part of the Spanish expeditions that entered the region in 1539. Spanish settlers grazed 4,000 sheep, 1,000 cattle, 1,000 goats, and 150 mares with colts in the Middle Rio Grande reach of present-day New Mexico around 1598 (Baxster 1987, Bayer and Montoya 1994, Scurlock 1998, Floyd and others 2003). Overgrazing was observed in the area as early as 1630 (Stewart 1936, Scurlock 1998). From 1785 to 1900 some 6,000 goats grazed the foothills of the Sandia Mountains. These lands later came under the jurisdiction of the

Cibola National Forest (Scurlock 1998). In addition to Spanish settlers, many contemporary Native American peoples grazed livestock. As many as 30,000 head of sheep grazed the lands of the Hopi Pueblos during the 1700s (Schickendanz 1980). By 1820 there was an estimated one million sheep grazing in New Mexico, and by the mid 1800s about three million sheep grazed the grasslands and riparian areas of that region (Baxter 1987, Scurlock 1986, 1998). The ending of hostilities between the United States government and Native Americans along with the completion of transcontinental railways and their spur routes led to sharp increases in livestock from 1870 to 1890 (Scurlock 1998). By 1880 five million sheep and 250,000 head of cattle grazed the grasslands and river valleys of New Mexico (Bailey and Bailey 1986).

Arizona experienced a long history of grazing by domestic livestock similar to New Mexico (Young 1998, Wildeman and Brock 2000). Spanish horses were first grazed in present-day Arizona in 1515, cattle in 1521. Goats and sheep, imported by Spanish settlers and expeditions, were grazed on the Arizona grasslands by 1700 (Barnes 1926, Peplow 1958). Peplow (1958) reported that the most important (and probably the most well stocked) ranches were at present-day San Bernardino, Babocomari, San Pedro, Arivaca, Calabasas, Sapori, Radenton, San Rafael de la Zanje, Sonoita, Tubac, and ranches in the San Simon Valley, Aqua Prieta, and Pueblo Viejo. After wars with the Apache and Navajo Tribes, most if not all of the haciendas were abandoned (Wildeman and Brock 2000). Subsequently, large herds of domestic livestock roamed freely across the grasslands of Arizona.

Anglo settlement and livestock grazing began in the early 1870s (Young 1998). Cattle driven from Texas were grazed the Salt River watershed and 100,000 head of cattle grazed the headwaters of the San Pedro River in southern Arizona (Wildeman and Brock 2000). By 1891 about 1.5 million cattle grazed the grasslands and watersheds of southern Arizona (Cox and others 1983, Ferguson and Ferguson 1983, Hendrickson and Minckley 1985).

By the early 1870s, even untrained observers noted that range conditions across the Southwest were rapidly deteriorating. Overstocking of upland and riparian grassland habitats and drought (late 1880s) was implicated to be the primary cause of decline (Leopold 1946, Hastings 1959, Gresswell and others 1989, Scurlock 1998, Kruse and Jemison 2000). Arroyo cutting and erosion of topsoil began to occur as vegetation was stripped from watershed slopes. Overutilized riparian areas, which had formerly acted as filter strips in their pristine state, were unable to trap the large quantities of soil moving down slope into stream channels (Hastings 1959, Miller 1961, York and Dick-Peddie 1969, Dick-Peddie 1993, Minckley 1969, Sublette and

others 1990, Bahre 1991, 1995, Friedman and others 1997, Wildeman and Brock 2000). Southwestern grasslands east of the Rocky Mountains (Great Plains type grasslands) faired better than desert grasslands of western New Mexico and Arizona. Great Plains type grasslands evolved under the grazing pressure of large herds of native ungulates (Milchunas and others 1988, Loftin and others 2000).

In contrast, desert grasslands west of the Continental Divide evolved under light grazing pressure from native ungulates. Thus, making the latter susceptible to degradation by livestock grazing (Elmore 1992, Bock and Bock 1993, Loftin and others 2000). Grassland reaches of streams at intermediate and higher elevations in the American Southwest suffered far less impact than middle and lower elevation grassland stream reaches. Many of these stream reaches are found within National Forest System lands and Native American lands. Greater amounts of precipitation, relative to lower elevation grasslands, made these riparian zones more resistant to the effects of grazing and other land use practices. Steeper gradient reaches also are less accessible to grazing livestock and use by agriculture.

As one can see, the long history of grazing in the Southwest has had definite impacts on Southwestern watersheds. Today, many riparian areas in the Southwest are considered to be functionally impaired due to environmental stressors such as overgrazing (Leopold 1974, Galliziolli 1977, Davis 1977, Hibbert 1979, Platts 1983, Clarkson and Wilson 1995, Patten 1998, Baker and others 2000). Grazing of livestock affects watershed condition and function through the direct removal of vegetation and the mechanical action of trampling (Johnston 1962, Johnson and others 1978, Tromble and others 1974, Hibbert 1979, Ryder 1980, Reid 1993, Peiper 1994, Belsky and others 1999). Removal of riparian vegetation and trampling through grazing can reduce bank stability and the channel-narrowing capacity of a stream (Platts 1979, 1982, Platts and others 1983, Abdel-Magid and others 1987a,b, Medina 1995, Neary and Medina 1995, Clary and Kinney 2000). Hoof action disturbs stream substrate, loosens and/or compacts soils, which in turn reduces infiltration, increases surface runoff, and accelerates movement of soils into watersheds (Wilcox and Wood 1988, Neary and Medina 1996, Payne and Lapointe 1997, Loftin and others 2000). Typical changes in stream morphology and aquatic habitat are streambank sloughing, widening and shallowing of the streambed, channel entrenchment, velocity reduction (Behnke and Raleigh 1978, Platts 1981a,b, Allen-Diaz and others 1998). The result is a less complex aquatic habitat. Fine sediments (less than 2 mm) that would typically be suspended in the water column and transported downstream are deposited on

USDA Forest Service Gen. Tech. Rep. RMRS-GTR-135-vol. 2. 2005

155

the streambed as water velocity decreases. Erosion of bank materials, due to loss of ground cover and increased surface runoff, adds to the fine sediment portion of the stream bedload (Dune and Leopold 1978, Pogacnik and Marlow 1983, Williams and Sada 1985, Abdel-Magid and others 1987b, Schultz and Leininger 1990, Platts 1991, Medina 1995, Neary and Medina 1996). Fines in bedload fill interstitial spaces and sedimentation of channel substrate begins (Lisle 1989, Bevenger and King 1995). Increases in temperature can occur due to alteration of species composition and reduction in plant density through direct removal of vegetation by grazing livestock (Amaranthus and others 1989, Schultz and Leininger 1990). Overgrazing of livestock of watersheds in arid and semiarid regions such as the Southwestern grasslands may have more severe consequences to watersheds, riparian habitats, and their inhabitants than in more mesic habitats where plant vigor is assumed to be greater (Behnke and Raleigh 1978).

Physical and chemical changes caused by grazing in grassland watersheds, riparian areas, and instream habitats clearly may have a direct affect on the quality and quantity of fish habitat (Meehan and Platts 1978, Platts and Nelson 1985, Platts 1981a,b, 1991, Bestchta and Platts 1986). Although the linkage between fish and grazing is not well defined and many cases cannot be correlated (Rinne 1988a b, 1999a,b, 2000), evidence does suggest that as grazing negatively impacts fish habitat, it also affects fish populations (Stuber 1985). For example, Platts (1981a) reported that a stream reach receiving high intensity grazing from sheep had a channel width five times greater, stream depth one-fifth as deep, and stream shore depth one-third as deep in heavily grazed reaches compared to moderately or lightly grazed adjoining reaches. Livestock grazing in riparian areas can reduce overhanging banks that can serve as cover for fish, and cause stream banks to become reposed with a decrease in stream shore depth (Overton and others 1994). Platts (1991) concluded, as did Behnke (1977), that degradation of riparian habitats through grazing was one of the major vectors causing the decline of native fishes in the Western United States. Grazing causes temporal and spatial changes in the riparian canopy and composition, which in turn may elevate stream temperature, and thus may have negative effects on the persistence or productivity of some fish populations, particularly cold water species (Meehan and others 1977, Meehan 1996). For example, Platts and Nelson (1989a,b) found that salmonid biomass was correlated with riparian canopy density in Great Basin streams. The authors suggested that solar insolation was a limiting factor in these waters. Sponholtz and Rinne (1997) reported that on reaches that were grazed by livestock in the Verde River, Arizona streambank vegetation was 60

percent lower, channel width 50 percent greater, and stream velocity was 85 percent lower than in grazed reaches. Fish density in the grazed reaches was 50 percent lower than at the ungrazed sites.

Although fine sediment (less than 2 mm) is a natural component of bedload (Hynes 1972), an overabundance of fines can affect the quality and complexity of aquatic environments and its inhabitants (Downes and others 1998). Abiotic changes (that is, sedimentation) can decrease the diversity and abundance of macroinvertebrates that serve as food for fishes (Brown and Moyle 1991). Allen-Diaz and Jackson (1998) reported that insect family richness was significantly reduced on moderately grazed plot versus lightly or ungrazed plots. Rinne (1988a) reported similar findings in the Rio De Las Vacas, Santa Fe National Forest, New Mexico. Fine sediment can also impair reproductive success of gravel spawning fish. Meehan (1991) indicated that excessive percentage of fines negatively impacted the reproduction and recruitment in salmonid populations. In contrast, Rinne (1999b) could not identify if fines had negative impacts on spikedace and loach minnow and could not say it was a major limiting factor. Abundant populations of these two species are found in the Gila-Cliff Valley, New Mexico, where grazing is present (Propst and others 1986). Further, Rinne (2000) cautions that often times we are dealing with difficult-to-determine thresholds and discrete percentages of fines that negatively affect various stages of a fish life cycle. Too, streams with a greater percentage of suitable spawning gravels may be able to tolerate higher levels of sedimentation and still recruit fish into the population.

There is a scarcity of research on grazing effects on Southwestern fishes, especially nonsalmonids (Rinne 2000), and it some cases, when dealing with cypriniform species, grazing may not have an impact on this group of fishes. Although empirical information is scarce on the effects of grazing in arid land watersheds (Rinne 1999a, 2000), much research has been conducted in the Intermountain, Northern Rocky Mountain, and Pacific Northwest (Platts 1991, Rinne 1999a, 2000). This information can be used to lend insight into grazing effects in the Southwest. Platts (1991) and Rinne (1998, 1999a, 2000) both state that more scientific rigor and better study design were needed in past studies and will be needed in future research. Nonetheless, negative effects of grazing on watershed condition, riparian vegetation, and aquatic habitats alluded to above have been documented by many practitioners throughout the Western United States (Ames 1977, Platts 1979, 1982, 1991, Szarro 1989, Chaney and others 1990, Naimen and Descamps 1990, Elmore 1992, Belsky and others 1999). In a review article published in the *Journal of Soil and Water Conservation*, Belsky and others (1999) concluded that most scientific studies document

156

USDA Forest Service Gen. Tech. Rep. RMRS-GTR-135-vol. 2. 2005

that livestock grazing continues to be detrimental to stream and riparian ecosystems in the West. It may well be that the linkages between grazing and its direct effect on native fishes are still obscure (Medina and Rinne 1999, Rinne 1999a,b, 2000). Nevertheless, both watershed health and the protection of native fishes should be our primary objectives. Managers and land owners should assess whether these two ecosystem components will be negatively affected before deciding to graze livestock in Southwestern watersheds.

Management and Conservation_____

The first step in management of fish is the recognition that a species is imperiled locally or nationally. Managers must have up-to-date lists of species so that appropriate action can be taken to implement conservation measures (Miller 1972, Pister 1976, 1981). Since the late 1960s States across the country along with the Federal government has been enacting legislation and enforcing protection of endangered species, subspecies, and critical habitat. Laws such as the Endangered Species Preservation Act of 1966, Endangered Species Conservation Act of 1969, and the Endangered Species Act of 1973 (amended in 1978 and 1979) were put in place with the purpose of conserving endangered and threatened species and their ecosystems (Johnson and Rinne 1982) as well as maintaining natural habitats and creating refugia for some critically threatened fishes (Miller 1972, Miller and Pister 1991). An example of this is the refugia created for the Owens Valley pupfish. In 1971, Congress established the Desert Pupfish National Monument to save threatened pup-fishes living east of Death Valley (Deacon and Bunnell 1970). Similar actions could be put into play for fishes inhabiting Southwestern grasslands. Optimal habitat is infinitely more effective than imposition of restrictive regulations in the enhancement of fish populations especially with officially designated Threatened and Endangered species (Deacon and others 1979). Critical habitat has been designated for spikedace and loach minnow in the Southwest, and restocking programs for native fish are ongoing. Gila topminnow is being repatriated throughout its range in New Mexico and Arizona. Rio Grande sucker and chub are being planted into native waters in the upper Rio Grande basin, as are Rio Grande silvery minnow, razorback sucker, and Colorado pike minnow. These restockings have had mixed results due to the availability of optimum habitats or the continued competition with nonnative fishes. Nevertheless, these must be continued if we are to have any chance at successfully restoring native fishes.

Problems are inherent when trying to save native fish. First, because many native Southwestern fishes are nongame species considered by many, even in resource agencies, as "rough fish," garnering support from private land owners or individuals and companies leasing public lands can be a challenge. Second, funding conservation efforts for native fish is a challenge because of budgetary constraints, political climate of the time, and, again, the view of these fishes as somewhat less desirable than game fish. Third, the frequent lack of information and communication among scientists might even be encouraged by what is perceived as small "cliques" of researchers whose intention is development of their own view on how the species should be managed. Fourth, water is an ever-decreasing resource in the Southwest, and many water laws permit beneficial water use without regard to fish and wildlife.

Finally, what is especially grim are the logistics and realities of trying to preserve native fishes in Southwestern grasslands, especially fishes that inhabit the grassland reaches. The grassland reaches of most Southwestern streams occur at low elevations in broad river valleys that have been occupied by humans for a long time and that typically have the highest human concentrations. Major cities such as Albuquerque, Las Cruces, El Paso, Tucson, and Phoenix have significant impacts on the water supply and quality of these low elevation grassland reaches. Major water withdrawals occur in these reaches; development and alteration of stream morphology is extensive along with the removal of riparian habitats. Pollution—both chemical and biological (encroachment of nonnative aquatic species)—is an ever-increasing concern. There are probably hundreds of thousands of nonnative fishes in these large-order, low-elevation grassland reaches. The chance of removing nonnative fishes to ensure the survival of native forms is small at best and, being realistic, probably impossible. The best land managers, fishery professionals, and society at large could expect is to identify isolated reaches on smaller tributary streams where logistics and isolation might result in some chance of success. Recovery is viable in small, remote locations, but at a large scale loss will continue and native fish community diversity will decline (Johnson and Rinne 1982).

This is a sad note, but one must face realities when prioritizing conservation projects when funding and worker availability are often limited. With that in mind, the rest of this chapter looks at a number of native fish in detail.

Loach Minnow (*Rhinichthys (tiaroga) cobitis*)

Distribution and Population Trends—*Rhinichthys (tiaroga) cobitis* is endemic to the upper Gila River drainage of southwestern New Mexico, southeastern and east-central Arizona, and northeastern Sonora (Miller and Winn 1951, Koster 1957, Minckley 1973, Propst 1999). Its historic distribution in New Mexico

USDA Forest Service Gen. Tech. Rep. RMRS-GTR-135-vol. 2. 2005

157

has been reported as the mainstem of the San Francisco River and Gila River along with many of the lower elevation tributaries (Koster 1957, Propst and others 1988). Minckley (1973) indicated that loach minnow were historically found in the Gila River above Aqua Fria Creek, Salt River, Verde River, San Pedro River, San Francisco River, and Blue River. In Mexico, the species was known from the upper reaches of the San Pedro River in northern Sonora (Miller and Winn 1951, Propst 1999). Today the range of *T. cobitis* has been much reduced and the population trend is declining. In Arizona, loach minnow remain in Aravaipa Creek, Eagle Creek, White River, Blue River, and the North Fork of East Black River; however, populations continue to decline over its range. Loach minnow was listed by New Mexico as a threatened species (19 NMAC 33.1) in 1975 and is Federally listed as a threatened species (USFWS 1986). In Arizona it is listed as a species of special concern (AZGFD 1996).

Preferred Habitat—*Rhinnichthys (tiaroga) cobitis* is found in moderate to large streams where gradients range from 1 to 3 or 4 percent (Rinne 1989, Rinne and Deason 2000). Loach minnow are a cryptic species associated with riffle habitats (Minckley 1973, Propst and others 1988, Propst and Bestgen 1991, Propst 1999) where they live in the interstitial spaces of large gravel and cobble substrate (LaBounty and Minckley 1972, Minckley 1973, Rinne 1989, Turner and Tafanelli 1983, Rinne and Deason 2000). Loach minnow have a reduced air bladder, streamlined body form, and large fins, which allow them to exploit high velocity, riffle habitats where it breeds and feeds on aquatic insects, principally fly and mayfly larvae and nymphs; however, stone, caddis and blackfly larvae are also part of loach minnow diet. The species moves in bursts of swimming from one substrate material to another much as do darters of the Eastern United States. Loach minnow are most closely associated with other native riffle dwelling species. It coinhabits similar aquatic space with desert suckers and speckled dace (Rinne 1992, Propst 1999).

Breeding Biology—In New Mexico, loach minnows reproduced during a 4 to 6 week period during late March and early June when waters temperatures reach 16 to 20 ^{0}C (Britt 1982, Propst and Bestgen 1991, Propst 1999). In contrast to New Mexico, Vives and Minckley (1990) found loach minnow spawning in the autumn in Aravipa Creek, Arizona. Bestgen and Propst (1991) indicate that runoff volume, timing, and duration of flow influences the onset of spawning for loach minnow. Loach minnow lay adhesive eggs on the undersides of rocks in flowing water habitats (42.7 cm/sec or less) and at depths of 6.1 to 21.3 cm (Britt 1982, Propst and Bestgen 1991, Propst and others 1988, Propst 1999). Propst and Bestgen (1991) observed that when water velocities slow (less than 5 cm/s), egg

mortality increased. Clutch size ranges from nine to 260 eggs per nest (Britt 1982, Propst and others 1988). Britt (1982) reported fecundity of females ranging from 144 to 1,200 eggs. Eggs of loach minnow hatch in 4 to 5 days at 21 ^{0}C (Propst and others 1988). Males may provide care during the incubation period (Propst and others 1985). Larvae average 5.4 mm TL at hatching (Propst 1999). Larvae use low velocity habitats after hatching (Propst and others 1988). Maximum life span of loach minnow ranges from 2 to 4 years (Minckley 1973, Britt 1982, Propst and others 1988).

Management Issues and Recommendations—Two major factors appear to determine the persistence of loach minnow: presence of nonnative species and the degradation of historic loach minnow habitat. Propst (1999) reports that at least 15 nonnative fishes are in the New Mexico portion of the loach minnow range with a similar number occurring in its historic Arizona range. An eminent threat is from introduced catfishes (Family: Ictaluridae), principally flathead catfish (*Pylodictis olivaris*), channel catfish (*Ictalurus punctatus*), black bullhead (*I. melas*), yellow bullhead (*I. natalis*), and brown bullhead (*I. nebulosus*) (Propst and others 1988). Flathead catfish are highly piscivorous and become so at an early age. Channel catfish often feed in riffles, habitat used by loach minnow. Propst (1999) indicates that where channel and flathead catfish co-occur, loach minnow are rare or extirpated. In addition to these predacious species, nonnative centrarchids are established throughout the range of loach minnow (Minckley 1973, Sublette and others 1990).

Land use activities such as cattle grazing, timber harvest, and road building, all of which contribute fine sediments to river systems, have also been implicated in the decline of loach minnow. Fine sediments fill the interstitial spaces where loach minnow live, feed, and breed, thereby decreasing available habitat and impacting spawning success. Also, dewatering of streams for consumptive uses eliminates spawning areas and core habitat.

Management activities directed toward removal of nonnative fishes, decreasing fine sediment in watersheds, and maintaining free-flowing unaltered stream systems appear to be critical for the conservation of loach minnow, along with translocating populations into suitable habitats free of nonnative fishes (Prospt 1999).

Rio Grande Silvery Minnow (*Hybognathus amarus*)

Distribution and Population Trends—Native to New Mexico, the species has been historically found in the Rio Grande drainage downstream from Velarde, NM, to the Gulf of Mexico, in the Rio Chama downstream from Abiquiu, and the Pecos River downstream

Rio Grande silvery minnow.

from Santa Rosa (absent in the reach from Red Bluff Reservoir to Sheffield) to its confluence with the Rio Grande in Texas. The Rio Grande silvery minnow also occurs in coastal drainages of Texas from the Brazos River west to the Rio Grande drainage of New Mexico (Sublette and others 1990, Bestgen and Platania 1991, Platania 1995, Propst 1999). Bestgen and Platania (1991) report *Hybognathus amarus* as formerly common in the Rio Grande from Cochiti to Socorro and in the Pecos River from Fort Summer to Carlsbad. Likewise it was common near the confluence of the Pecos and Rio Grande in Texas (Trevino-Robinson 1959, Edwards and Contreras-Balderas 1991). Rio Grande silvery minnow appear to have been extirpated in the Pecos River and the lower Rio Grande below Elephant Butte Reservoir, the former occurring in the 1970s and the latter by the 1950s (Propst and others 1987, Edwards and Contreras-Balderas 1991, Bestgen and Platania 1991, Propst 1999). Currently, *H. amarus* occupies less than 10 percent of its historic range (Propst 1999). The species is found only in perennial sections of the Rio Grande and incidentally in irrigation systems in the Middle Rio Grande reach from Cochiti to the head of Elephant Butte Reservoir (Sublette and others 1990, Platania 1991, 1993). Rio Grande Silvery minnow is listed by the USFWS as endangered (USFWS 2003), and by the New Mexico Department of Game and Fish as State Endangered, Group II (19 NMAC 33.1) (Propst 1999).

Preferred Habitat—Rio Grande silvery minnow are schooling fish and use a variety of habitats (Sublette and others 1990). Dudley and Platania (1997, 2000) report Rio Grande silvery minnow using mainstream habitats with water depths ranging from 0.2 to 0.8 m, water velocities of 0 to 30 cm/sec, and over silt/sand substrate. Propst (1999) indicates that a seasonal shift to slower velocity habitats with debris cover occurs in winter. While individuals are sometimes found in irrigation canals, often young and some adults have apparently been entrained during irrigation activities (Lang and Altenbach 1994, Propst 1999). Rio Grande silvery minnow are herbivores feeding on diatoms, larval insects skins, and live and decaying plant material (Sublette and others 1990).

Breeding Biology—Spawning activity of Rio Grande silvery minnow occurs at the end of spring and the beginning of summer with water temperatures ranging from 20 to 24 ^{0}C (Propst 1999). Platania and Altenbach (1998) report that the species is a pelagic spawner, and the eggs are semibuoyant and nonadhesive. Females are attended by multiple males with several encounters (Propst 1999). Females are reported as producing three to 18 clutches in a 12-hour period. Propst (1999) reports that the majority (more than 90 percent) of spawning individuals were age-1 adults. Further, it appears that mortality can be as high as 98 percent of breeding individuals (Propst 1999). Similar to other larval fishes, larvae of Rio Grande silvery minnow drift for several days and then migrate to low velocity habitats at the stream margins.

Management Issues and Recommendations—Propst (1999) lists factors related to the decline of Rio Grande silvery minnow. He suggests that nonnative fishes, impoundments, declining water quality, reduction of flow, and range fragmentation due to mainstem and diversion dams have together contributed to the decline and potential extirpation of Rio Grande silvery minnow in the Rio Grande drainage. Bestgen and Platania (1991) and Cook and others (1992) provide evidence that a combination of poor water quality, altered flow regimes, and hybridization with plains minnow, *Hybognathus placitus*, accounted for its elimination in the Pecos River.

Conservation strategies that maintain minimum flow, natural hydrographs, and improved water quality are needed to sustain Rio Grande silvery minnow. Maintenance of river flows will also alleviate loss through predation when minnows are concentrated in shrinking habitats.

Rio Grande Sucker (*Catostomus (Pantosteous) plebeius*)

Distribution and Population Trends—The Rio Grande sucker is native to Colorado, New Mexico, and Mexico. Historically, the species was widely distributed in the Rio Grande Basin of Colorado and New Mexico (Koster 1957, Sublette and others 1990, Langlois and others 1994). In New Mexico, its current distribution is the Rio Grande above the 36th parallel and its tributaries north of the 33rd parallel (Propst 1987, Sublette and others 1990, Platania 1991, Calamusso unpublished data). Rio Grande suckers are found in the Mimbres River, and introduced populations are established in the Rio Hondo (Pecos drainage), Gila River basin, and San Francisco drainage (Sublette and others 1990). Rio Grande sucker also inhabit six river basins draining four States of Mexico (Hendrickson and others 1980, Abarca and others 1995). The Rio Grande sucker appears to be declining across its range. At one

USDA Forest Service Gen. Tech. Rep. RMRS-GTR-135-vol. 2. 2005

159

time the species was found in only one drainage in Colorado (Hot Creek) (Swift-Miller and others 1999a,b). In New Mexico, the species appears to be declining across its range (Michael Hatch, personal communication). Calamusso and others (2002) documented the decline and replacement of Rio Grande sucker by white sucker, *Catostomus commersoni*, in Rio Grande tributary streams in northern New Mexico. Rio Grande sucker was designated as State endangered by the Colorado legislature in 1993 when it was found that only one population remained (Swift and others 1999) in the State. While more common in New Mexico, Rio Grande sucker are considered rare in the Rio Grande mainstem (Rinne and Platania 1995) and is declining in the tributaries of the Middle and Upper Rio Grande basin (Calamusso 1992, 1996, Calamusso and Rinne 1996, 1999).

Breeding Biology—Temperature is the controlling factor as indicated by latitudinal and elevation differences in spawning time. Spawning begins in February in the southern portion of the species range and occurs progressively later northward (Smith 1966). Rio Grande sucker were found spawning in Animas Creek, Sierra County, NM, in February when water temperature reached 9 ^{0}C (Calamusso unpublished data) and in June in streams on the Santa Fe National Forest when water temperature also reached 9 ^{0}C (Calamusso 1996). Rinne (1995b) reported spawning in the Rio de las Vacas peaking in June during the declining spring flows, and Rausch (1963) found the species spawning in the Jemez River in May. In two streams on the Santa Fe National Forest, suckers spawned where dominant substrate ranged in size from 2.0 to 18.9 mm, water velocity ranged from 21.0 to 62.0 cm/s (mean 37.0 cm/s, and depth ranged from 9.0 to 28.2 cm (mean 16.2 cm) (Calamusso 1992). Koster (1957) indicated that Rio Grande sucker also spawned in the fall. Males and females become sexually mature at age 3 (Rausch 1963). Maximum life span of females is 7 years, with a corresponding mean standard length of 159 mm (Rausch 1963).

Preferred Habitat—Rio Grande sucker live in small to large middle elevation (2,000 to 2,600 m) streams over substrates that range from sand/small gravel to cobble (Sublette and others 1990). Calamusso (1996) and Calamusso and Rinne (in review) evaluated habitat use of Rio Grande sucker in six study streams on the Carson and Santa Fe National Forests of northern New Mexico. Rio Grande suckers were found in low gradient (3.2 percent or less) stream reaches and were associated with pool and glide habitat, low water column velocity (less than 20 cm/s), moderate depth (mean: 24.5 cm; range 7 to 62 cm), and cobble substrate. These habitats were used disproportionately to available habitats. Abundance of Rio Grande sucker was inversely related with stream gradient and mean water column velocity. Density and biomass of Rio

Grande sucker was positively related with increasing amounts of pool and glide habitat at the reach level, as was greater biomass.

Management Issues and Recommendations—The Rio Grande sucker was the only catostomid endemic to the Rio Grande (Koster 1957, Sublette and others 1990, Langlois and others 1994). Rio Grande suckers probably once occupied all low gradient (less than 3.2 percent), middle-elevation tributaries to the Rio Grande in Colorado and New Mexico north of the 33rd parallel (Calamusso and others 2002). The decline in range and numbers of the Rio Grande sucker is related to introduction of nonnative fishes, especially white sucker, into the Rio Grande drainage (Calamusso 1996, Calamusso and Rinne 1999, Calamusso and others 2002). In all streams where Rio Grande sucker have been extirpated or are declining, white sucker are now present (Calamusso and others 2002). Although nonnative brown trout, *Salmo trutta*, are believed to pry upon Rio Grande suckers, Calamusso and Rinne (1999) could not detect a negative correlation between presence of the nonnative trout and the native sucker. Management directed at protecting remaining populations of Rio Grande sucker using fish migration barriers is warranted. In addition, Rio Grande sucker should be reintroduced along with Rio Grande cutthroat during restorations for the latter. Recovery efforts for both these species should consider the effect of nonnative species and stream gradient on their persistence and abundance when considering reintroduction sites.

Rio Grande Chub (*Gila pandora*)

Distribution and Population Trends—Rio Grande chub are native to the Rio Grande basin of Colorado, New Mexico, and Texas. In New Mexico the species is also found in the Pecos River and Canadian drainages, although it may have been introduced in the latter. While no recent systematic review of its status in New Mexico has been conducted, the species appears to be stable and widespread throughout the montane tributaries of the Middle and Upper Rio Grande basin. In contrast, Rio Grande chub is considered rare or may even be extirpated in the Rio Grande mainstem (Rinne and Platania 1995, Propst 1999) and in tributaries in the southern portion of the State below Albuquerque. Recent ichthyofaunal surveys of streams draining the east slopes of the Black range, Sierra County, NM, indicate that Rio Grande chub are being replaced by nonnative longfin dace, *Agosia chrysogaster*, (Calamusso unpublished data). Propst (1999) suggests that legal protection for the species in New Mexico may be warranted. In Colorado Rio Grande chub is considered to be in general decline and listed as threatened (Zuckerman 1983, Zuckerman and Langlois 1990, Sublette and others 1990).

Breeding Biology—Rio Grande chub spawn in spring and early summer (Sublette and others 1990). Rinne (1995a) found that spawning of Rio Grande chub reached its peak on the descending limb of the spring hydrograph in the Rio de las Vacas, New Mexico. Rio Grande chub are known to hybridize with longnose dace, *Rhinichthyes cataractae*, when the two occur in reduced habitats due to dewatering or drought conditions (Cross and Minckley; 1960, Suttkus and Cashner 1981).

Preferred Habitat—Similar to many members of the Genus *Gila,* Rio Grande chub are found in low velocity habitats (pools, glides, runs) of small to moderate sized streams where gradients rarely exceed 2 percent and are often associated with instream woody debris or aquatic vegetation (Woodling 1985, Calamusso 1996). Rio Grande chub are midwater carnivores that, similar to many salmonids, feed on insect drift, zooplankton, and small fishes (Sublette and others 1990). *Gila pandora* also feed on detritus (Sublette and others 1990).

Management Issues and Recommendations—Declines in Rio Grande chub populations appear to be due in large part to the introduction and range expansion of nonnative fishes more than overall degradation of habitat quality (Zuckerman 1983, Zuckerman and Langlois 1990, Propst 1999, Calamusso unpublished data). The latter may decrease population persistence through decreased habitat quality and decreased spawning success. Future conservation strategies should consider protection of tributary Rio Grande chub populations from intrusion by nonnative cyprinids, centrarchids, and salmonids, particularly brown trout. Many barriers currently protecting Rio Grande chub (and Rio Grande sucker) populations are unstable beaver dams, debris jams, and water diversions. As with Rio Grande sucker, Rio Grande chub should be introduced to suitable habitat during restoration activities for Rio Grande cutthroat trout. Restoration efforts should be conducted on a watershed scale to ensure stream connectivity and enhance opportunities for metapopulation development.

Spikedace (*Meda fulgida*)

Distribution and Population Trends—The spikedace is endemic to the Gila River Basin of New Mexico and Arizona (Koster 1957, Minckley 1973) and possibly northern Sonora (Propst 1999). Historically, it was common in the Gila River drainage of Arizona downstream to Tempe. It was also found in the Agua Fria, upper Verde, and Salt Rivers (Barber and Minckley 1966, Minckley and Deacon 1968, Minckley 1973). In New Mexico, spikedace were common in the San Francisco River, Gila River, and the lower reaches of the three forks of the Gila River (Anderson 1978, Propst and others 1986). Today, the range of the

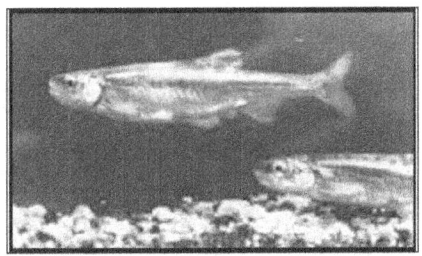

Spikedace. (Copyright John Rinne. Used with permission.)

spikedace has been severely reduced (Propst 1999). In Arizona it now is found only in the upper Verde River, Aravaipa Creek, and Eagle Creek (Barber and Minckley 1966, Minckley 1973, Marsh and others 1991). In New Mexico, spikedace have been extirpated in the San Francisco River (Anderson 1978, Propst and others 1986). Propst (1999) reported the distribution of spikedace in the Gila River mainstem as sporadic. The species is found in low numbers in the East Fork of the Gila River and regularly collected in the West Fork of the Gila River, although it appears to be in decline. Spikedace may be extirpated from the Middle Fork of the Gila River (Propst and others 1986, Propst 1999). The species is common to abundant in the upper Gila River in the Gila–Cliff Valley (Propst 1986, Rinne 1999). Spikedace is listed by New Mexico and Arizona as threatened. It is Federally listed as Federal Threatened 31 July 1986.

Preferred Habitat—Spikedace is a small (50 to 60 mm adult size) pelagic cyprinid species that uses moderately deep, low gradient riffles and runs with gradient ranging from 0.3 to 0.5 percent in permanently flowing streams (Sublette and others 1990, Rinne 1991, 1999b). They are associated with sand and gravel substrates (Rinne 1991). Turner and Tafanelli (1983) indicated that velocities most often used by spikedace ranged from 40 to 82 cm/sec with preferred depths ranging from 15 to 18.0 cm. Larvae use low velocity habitats near stream margins with stream depth typically less than 32.0 cm. Rinne and Kroeger (1988) reported spikedace using velocities more than 25 cm/sec with mean water depths of 27 cm.

Habitat use varies geographically and temporally for spikedace along with variation due to age of individuals (Propst and others 1986, Propst 1999). The species is insectivorous with its principal diet composed of mayflies, midges, and caddis flies along with taking other aquatic and terrestrial insects opportunistically (Barber and Minckley 1983).

Breeding Biology—The breeding season for spikedace occurs from February to March at elevations less than 1,000 m, and from April to June at elevations greater than 1,500 m (Anderson 1978, Propst and Bestgen 1991). At the onset of spawning, females move into riffle areas attended by several males. Spawning

USDA Forest Service Gen. Tech. Rep. RMRS-GTR-135-vol. 2. 2005

161

takes place in riffles with moderate velocity (25 to 50 cm/sec) over small cobble/gravel substrate (Barber and others 1970, Propst and Bestgen 1991). Eggs of the species are demurral and are broadcast over the substrate, dropping into the interstitial spaces (Anderson 1978) where they incubate for about 4 to 7 days (Snyder 1981). Fecundity is related to age and size. Eggs produced by female spikedace can range from 100 to 300 mature ova (Minckley 1973, Propst and others 1986). Propst and others (1986) reports one age 2 individual 55 mm SL female containing 319 mature ova, and age 1 females averaging 101 mature ova. Spikedace are 5 to 7 mm TL upon emergence and grow at a rate of 1 mm per day (Propst and others 1986).

Management Issues and Recommendations— The decline in spikedace distribution and abundance is related to the alteration of aquatic and riparian habitats and the introduction of nonnative fishes (Propst 1999). Alteration of habitat for this species includes: ranching and farming practices that have removed instream flow; increased channelization; and increased siltation caused by grazing, road building, and recreational activities; construction of dams; and the introduction of nonnative fishes. The latter both preys upon and competes with spikedace for resources (Sublette and others 1990, Propst 1999). Management practices that address these vectors of decline are needed to ensure the persistence of spikedace. Currently, the USDI Fish and Wildlife Service has designated reaches in the Southwest as designated critical habitat.

References

Abarca, F.J., K.L. Young, I. Parra, R.H. Bettaso, and K. Cobble. 1995. Yaqui River fishes relevant to the Madrean Province: U.S.—Mexico collaborations. In: Debano, L.F. and others (tech. coord.), Biodiversity and management of the Madrean Archipelago: The sky islands of Southwestern United States and Northwestern Mexico. 1994 Sept. 19-23, 1994; Tucson, AZ. Gen. Tech. Rep. RM-GTR-264. Fort Collins, CO: U.S. Department of Agriculture, Forest Service, Rocky Mountain Forest and Range Experiment Station. 669 p.

Abdel-Magid, A.H. Schuman, G.E., and R.H. Hart. 1987a. Soil bulk density and water infiltration as affected by grazing systems. Journal of Range Management 40(4):307-309.

Abdel-Magid, A.H. Schuman, G.E., and R.H. Hart. 1987b. Soil and vegetation responses to simulated trampling. Journal of Range Management 40(4): 307-309.

Allen-Diaz, B. H. and R. D. Jackson. 1998. Cattle grazing effects on oak woodland spring ecosystems. In: Proceedings of the American Water Resources Association Specialty Conference on Rangeland Management and Water Resources. May 27-29, 1998, Reno, NV. American Water Resources Association. 146 p.

Allen-Diaz, B.H., R.D. Jackson and J.S. Fehmi. 1998. Detecting channel morphology change in California's hardwood rangeland spring ecosystems. Journal of Range Management 51:514-518.

Amaranthus, M.H., H. Jubas, and D. Arthur. 1989. Stream shading, summer streamflow and maximum water temperature following intense wildfire in headwater streams. In: N.H. Berg (tech. coord.) Proceedings of the Symposium on fire and Watershed Management, Gen. Tech. Rep. PSW-109, Berkeley, California.

Ambos, N., G. Robertson, and J. Douglas. 2002. Dutchwoman Butte: A relict grassland in Central Arizona. Rangelands. 22 (2): 3-8.

Ames, C.R. 1977. Wildlife conflicts in riparian management: grazing. Pp. 49-51, In: B.R. Johnson, and D.A. Jones (tech. coords.). USDA Forest Service Gen. Tech. Rep. RM-43. Importance, preservation, and management of riparian habitat: a symposium. Denver, Colorado.

Anderson, 1978. The distribution and aspects of the life history of *Media fulgida* in New Mexico, M.S. Thesis, New Mexico State University, Las Cruces.

Arizona Game and Fish Department (AZGF). 1996. Wildlife of Special Concern in Arizona. Nongame and Endangered Wildlife Program, Arizona Game and Fish Department, Phoenix.

Bahre, C.J. 1991. A legacy of change: historic human impact on vegetation of the Arizona borderlands. University of Arizona Press, Tucson.

Bahre, C.J. 1995. Human impacts on the grasslands of southeastern Arizona. In: M.P. McClaran and T.R. Van Devender (eds). The desert grassland. University Arizona Press, Tucson.

Bailey, G. and R.G. Bailey. 1986. A history of the Navajos: the reservation years. School of American Research Press, Santa Fe, NM.

Baker, Malchus, B.B. Jr. and P.F. Ffolliott. 2000. Contributions of watershed management research to ecosystem-based management in the Colorado River Basin. Pp. 117-128. In: Ffolliott, P.F., M.B. Baker Jr., C.B. Carlton, M.C. Dillon, K.L. Mora (tech. coords.). 2000. Land stewardship in the 21st century: The contributions of watershed management; 2000 March 13-16; Tucson, AZ. Proceedings. RMRS-P-13. Fort Collins, CO: U.S. Department of Agriculture, Forest Service, Rocky Mountain Research Station, 438 p.

Barber, W.E. and W.L. Minckley. 1966. Fishes of Arivaipa Creek, Graham and Pinal Counties, Arizona. The Southwestern Naturalist. 11:313-314.

Barber, W.E. and W.L. Minckley. 1983. The feeding ecology of a southwestern cyprinid fish, the spikedace, *Meda fulgida*, in Arizona. Copeia. 1970:9-18.

Barber, W.E., D.C. Williams, and W.L. Minckley. 1970. Biology of the spikedace, *Media fulgida*, in Arizona. Copeia. 1970: 9 – 18.

Barnes, W.C. 1926. The Story of the Range. Washington, D.C.: GPO, 1926. iv, 60 pp.

Baxster, J.O. 1987. Las Carneradas: Sheep trade in New Mexico, 1700-1860. University of New Mexico Press, Albuquerque.

Bayer, L. and F. Montoya. 1994. Santa Ana: The people, pueblo, and the history of Tamaya. University of New Mexico Press, Albuquerque.

Behnke, R.J. 1977. Fish faunal changes associated with land use and water development. Great Plains – Rocky Mountain Geological Journal. 6(2):133-136. In: W.S. Platts 1981. Influence of Forest and rangeland management on anadromous fish habitat in western North America: Effects of livestock grazing. USDA Gen. Tech. Rep. PNW-124. 25 pp.

Behnke, R.J. and R.F. Raleigh. 1978. Grazing and the riparian zone: Impact and management perspectives. Pp. 262-267. In: Proceedings of the symposium, Strategies for protection and management of floodplain wetlands and other riparian ecosystems. 11-13 December 1978. Callaway Gardens, GA. USDA Forest Service. Gen. Tech. Rep. WO-12.

Behnke, R.J. and M. Zarn. 1976. Biology and management of threatened and endangered western trout. Gen. Tech. Rep. RM-28. Fort Collins, CO: U.S. Department of Agriculture, Forest Service, Rocky Mountain Forest and Range Experiment Station.

Belsky, A.J., A. Matzke, and S. Uselman. 1999. Survey of Livestock Influences on Stream and Riparian Ecosystems in the Western US. Journal of Soil and Water Conservation. 54: 419-31.

Bestchta, R.L. and W.S. Platts. 1986. Morphological features of small streams: significance and function. Water Resources Research. 22:369-379.

Bestgen, K.R. and S.P. Platania. 1991. Status and conservation of the Rio Grande silvery minnow, *Hybognathus amarus*. The Southwestern Naturalist. 36: 225-232.

Bevenger, G.S. and R.M. King. 1995. A pebble count procedure for assessing watershed cumulative affects. USDA Forest Service Research Paper RM-319:1-17.

Blinn, D.W., C. Runck, D.A. Clark, and J.N. Rinne. 1993. Effects of rainbow trout predation on the Little Colorado Rive spinedace. Transactions of the American Fisheries Society. 122(1): 139-143.

162

USDA Forest Service Gen. Tech. Rep. RMRS-GTR-135-vol. 2. 2005

Bock, C.E. and J.H. Bock. 1993. Cover of perennial grasses in southeastern Arizona in relation to livestock grazing. Conservation Biology. 7:371-381.

Briggs, C.L. and J.R. Van Ness. 1987. Land, water, and culture: New perspectives on Hispanic land grants. University of New Mexico Press, Albuquerque.

Briggs, J.C. 1986. Introduction to the zoogeography of North American Fishes. Pages 1-6 In: C.H. Hocutt and E.O. Wiley (eds). The Zoogeography of North American Fishes. John Wiley and Sons, New York.

Britt, K.A. 1982. The reproductive biology and aspects of life history of *Tiaroga cobitis* in southwestern New Mexico. M.S. Thesis, New Mexico State University, Las Cruces.

Brown, L.R. and P.B. Moyle. 1991. Changes in habitat and micro-habitat partitioning within an assemblage of stream fishes in response to predation by Sacramento squawfish (*Ptychocheilus grandis*). Canadian Journal of Fisheries and Aquatic Sciences. 48: 849-856.

Bryan, K. 1928. Date of channel trenching (arroyo cutting) in the arid southwest. Science. 62: 338-344.

Burr, B.M. and R.L. Mayden. 1992. Phylogenetics and North American freshwater fishes. Pages 287-324 In: R.L. Mayden, (ed) Systematics Historical Ecology, and North American Freshwater Fishes. Stanford University Press, Stanford, California.

Calamusso, B. 1992. Current distribution of the *Catostomus plebeius* and *Gila pandora* on the Carson National Forest, New Mexico with preliminary comments on habitat preferences. Proceedings of the Desert Fishes Council. 24:63-64.

Calamusso, B. 1996. Distribution, abundance, and habitat of Rio Grande sucker (*Catostomus plebeius*) in the Carson and Santa Fe National Forests, New Mexico. M.S. Thesis, New Mexico State University, Las Cruces, NM.

Calamusso, B. and J.N. Rinne. 1996. Distribution of the Rio Grande cutthroat trout and its co-occurrence with the Rio Grande sucker and Rio Grande chub on the Carson and Santa Fe national forests. Pp. 157-167. In: D.W. Shaw and D.M. Finch (tech. coords.) Desired future conditions for Southwestern riparian ecosystems: Bringing interests and concerns together. Gen. Tech. Rep. RM-GTR-272. Fort Collins, CO: US Department of Agriculture, Forest Service Rocky Mountain Research Station.

Calamusso, B. and Rinne J.N. 1999. Native montane fishes of the Middle Rio Grande Ecosystem: Status, Threats, and Conservation. pp. 231-237 In: Finch, D.M. and others (Technical Coordinators), Rio Grande Ecosystems: Linking land, water, and people. Toward a sustainable future for the Middle Rio Grande Basin. 1998 June 2-5; Albuquerque, NM. Proceedings RMRS-P-7. Ogden, Utah: U.S. Department of Agriculture, Forest Service, Rocky Mountain Research Station. 254 p.

Calamusso, B. and J.N. Rinne. In Review. Macro and Micro-Habitat use by Rio Grande sucker in the Carson and Santa Fe National Forests, New Mexico.

Calamusso, B., J.N. Rinne, and P.R. Turner. 2002. Distribution and abundance of Rio Grande sucker (*Catostomus plebeius*) in the Carson and Santa Fe National Forests, New Mexico. Southwestern Naturalist 47 (2): 182-186.

Carlson, A.W. 1990. The Spanish-American homeland: Four centuries in New Mexico's Rio Arriba. John Hopkins University Press, Baltimore.

Carton, J.E., S.H. Stoleson, P. L Stoleson, and D.W. Shaw. 2000. Riparian Areas. In: Jemison, R. and C. Raish (eds) Livestock management in the American Southwest: Ecology, Society, and Economics. Elsevier, Amsterdam.

Cavender, T.M. 1986. Review of the fossil history of North American Fishes, in the Zoogeography of North American Freshwater Fishes In: C.H. Hocutt and E.O. Wiley (eds), John Wiley and Sons, New York, pp. 701-24.

Chaney, E., W. Elmore, and W.S. Platts. 1990. Livestock grazing on Western Riparian Ranges. 1990. U.S. Environmental Protection Agency, Northwest Resource Information Center, Eagle, Idaho.

Clarkson, R.W. and J.R. Wilson. 1995. Trout biomass and stream habitat relationships in the White Mountains area, east-central Arizona. Transactions of the American Fisheries Society 124:599-612.

Clary, W.P. and J.W. Kinney. 2000. Streambank response to simulated grazing. Pp. 292 -295. In: P.F. Ffolliott, M.B. Baker Jr., C.B.

Carlton, M.C. Dillon, K.L. Mora. (tech. coords.) Land stewardship in the 21st century: The contributions of watershed management; 2000 March 13-16; Tucson, AZ. Proceedings. RMRS-P-13. Fort Collins, CO: U.S. Department of Agriculture, Forest Service, Rocky Mountain Research Station. 438 p.

Cook, J.A., K.R. Bestgen, D.L. Propst, and T.L. Yates. 1992. Allozymic divergence and systematics of the Rio Grande silvery minnow, *Hybognathus amarus* (Teleostei: *Cyprinidae*). Copeia 1992:36-44.

Courtenay, W. Jr., D. Hensley, J. Taylor, and J. McCann. 1984. Distribution of exotic fishes in the Continental United States. Pp. 41 – 77 In: W.R. Courtney Jr. and J. Stauffer (eds) Distribution, Biology, and Management of exotic fishes. John Hopkins University Press, Baltimore, Maryland.

Courtenay, W.R., Jr., and J.R. Stauffer, Jr. 1990. The introduced fish problem and the aquarium fish industry. Journal of the World Aquaculture Society 21(3):145-159.

Courtenay, W.R. and J.D. Williams. 1992. Dispersal of exotic species from aquaculture sources, with emphasis on freshwater fishes. Pp 49 – 81 In: A. Rosenfield and R. Mann (eds) Dispersal of living organisms into aquatic ecosystems. University of Maryland Sea Grant Publication, College Park.

Cox, J.R., H.L. Morton, J.T. LaBurme and K.G. Renard. 1983. Reviving Arizona's rangelands. Journal of Soil and Water Conservation 38: 342-345.

Cross, J.N. 1967. Handbook of the fishes of Kansas. Misc. Pub. Museum Natural History, University of Kansas 45. 357 p.

Cross, F.B., R.L. Mayeden, and J.D. Stewart. 1986. Fishes inn the Western Mississippi Drainage. Pages 363-412 In: C.H. Hocutt and E.O. Wiley, eds. The Zoogeography of North American Fishes. John Wiley and Sons, New York.

Cross, F.B. and W.L. Minckley. 1960. Five natural hybrid combinations in minnows (*Cyprinidae*). University of Kansas Publication Museum of Natural History, 13: 1-18.

Davis, G.A. 1977. Management alternatives for the riparian habitat in the southwest. Pp. 59-67. In: Johnson, R.R., and D.A. Jones (tech. cords.) Importance of preservation and management of riparian habitat: a symposium. Gen. Tech. Rep. RM-43. USDA Forest Service, Fort Collins, CO.

Deacon, J.E. 1979. Endangered and threatened fishes of the West. Great Basin Naturalist Memoirs 3, 41-64.

Deacon, J.E. 1988. The endangered woundfin and water management in the Virgin River, Utah, Arizona, and Nevada. Fisheries 13(1): 18-24.

Deacon, J.E. and S. Bunnell. 1970. Man and pupfish, a process of destruction. Cry California 5, 14-21.

Deacon, J.E., C. Hubbs, and B.J. Zahuranec. 1964. Some effects of introduced fishes on the native fish fauna of southern Nevada. Copiea 1964: 384-388.

Deacon, J.E., G.C. Kobetich, J.D. Williams, S. Contreras, and other members of the Endangered Species Committee of the American Fisheries Society. 1979. Fishes of North America Endangered, Threatened, or of Special Concern: 1979. Fisheries, Volume 4, No 2.

Deacon, J.E. and W.L. Minckley. 1974. Desert Fishes, Pp. 385-487 In: Desert Biology, Volume 2, Academic Press, N.Y.

Dickinson, W.R. 1981. Plate tectonics and the continental margin of California, Pages 1–28 In: W.R. Ernst (ed) The Geotectonic development of California. Prentice-Hall, Inc., Englewood Cliffs, NJ.

Dick-Peddie, W.A. 1993. New Mexico Vegetation: past, present, and future. University of New Mexico Press, Albuquerque.

Dott, R.H. Jr. and R.L. Batten. 1981. Evolution of the earth, 3rd ed. McGraw-Hill, New York.

Douglas, M.E., P.C. Marsh, and W.L. Minckley. 1994. Indigenous fishes of western North America and the hypothesis of competitive displacement: *Meda fulgida* (*Cyprinidae*) as a case study. Copeia 1994: 9-19.

Dowling, T.E. and M.R. Childs. 1992. Impact of hybridization of a threatened trout of the southwestern United States. Conservation Biology 6(3): 355-364.

Downes, B.J., P.S. Lakes, E.S.G. Schreiber, and A. Glaister. 1998. Habitat structure and regulation of local species diversity in a stony, upland stream. Ecological Monographs 68(2), 237-257.

Dozier, E.P. 1983. The Pueblo Indians of North America. Waveland Press, New Haven.

Dudley, R.K. and S.P. Platania. 1997. Habitat use of the Rio Grande Silvery Minnow. Report to the New Mexico Department of Game and fish, Santa Fe and the U.S. Bureau of Reclamation (Albuquerque Filed Projects Office) Albuquerque, NM. 188 pp.

Dudley, R.K. and S.P. Platania. 2000. Downstream transport of drifting semibouyant cyprinid eggs and larvae in the Pecos River, NM. Report to the U.S. Bureau of Reclamation. 61 pp.

Edwards, R.J., and S. Contreras-Balderas. 1991. Historical changes in the icthyofauna of the lower Rio Grande (Rio Bravo del Norte), Texas and Mexico. Southwestern Naturalist 36: 201-212.

Elmore, W. 1992. Pp. 442-457. In: Naiman, R.J. (ed). Watershed Management: Balancing Sustainability and Environmental Change. Springer- Verlag, New York.

Endler, J.A. 1977. Geographic Variation, Speciation, and clines. Princeton University Press, Princeton, NJ.

Etnier, D.A. and W.C. Starnes. 1993. The Fishes of Tennessee. University of Tennessee Press, Knoxville.

Ferguson, D. and N. Ferguson. 1983. Sacred Cows At The Public Trough. Maverick Publishers Bend, Oregon.

Floyd, M.L., T.L. Fleischner, D. Hanna, and P. Whitefield. 2003. Effects of historic livestock grazing on vegetation at Chaco Culture National Park, New Mexico.

Friedman, J.M., M.L. Scott, and G.T. Auble. 1997. Water management and cottonwood forest dynamics along prairie streams. Pp. 49-71, In: F.L. Knopf and F.B. Samson (eds). Ecology and conservation of Great Plains vertebrates. Ecological Studies, Volume 125. Springer, New York.

Fuller, P.L., L.G. Nico, and J.D. Williams. 1999. Nonindigenous fishes introduced into inland waters of the United States. American Fisheries Society, Special Publication 27.

Gallizioli, S. 1977. Statement on improving fish and wildlife benefits in range management. Pp. 90-96. In: Townsend, J.F. and R.J. Smith (eds). Proceedings, improving fish and wildlife benefits in range management seminar. FWS/OBS/77-1. U.S. Fish and Wildlife Service.

Gilbert, C.R. 1976. Composition and derivation of the North American freshwater fish fauna. Florida Science, 39(2): 104-111.

Gresswell, R.E.B.A. Barton, and J.L. Kershner. (eds) 1989. Practical Approaches to Riparian Resource Management. U.S. Bureau of Land Management: Billings, MT.

Griffiths, D. 1904. Range investigations in Arizona. USDA. Bureau of plant industry. Bulletin 67.

Haines, G.B. and H.M. Tyus. 1990. Fish associations and environmental variables in age-0 Colorado squawfish habitats, Green River, Utah. Journal of Freshwater Ecology 5: 427-435.

Hanson, B. 1980. Fish survey of the streams in the Zuni River drainage, New Mexico. Report prepared for the Water and Power Resources Service, Boulder City, NV. U. S Fish and Wildlife Service, Albuquerque, NM.

Hastings, J.R. 1959. Vegetation change and arroyo cutting in Southeastern Arizona. Journal of the Arizona Academy of Science, (1) 60 – 67.

Hastings, J.R. and R.M. Turner. 1965. The Changing Mile. University of Arizona Press, Tucson, Arizona.

Heede, B. and J.N. Rinne. 1990. Hydrodynamic and fluvial morphologic processes: implications for fisheries management and research. North American Journal of Fisheries Management. 10:249-268.

Heidinger, R.C. 1999. Stocking for sport fisheries enhancement. Pages 375-401 In: C.C. Kohler and W.A. Hubert (eds) Inland fisheries management in North America, American Fisheries Society, Bethesda, MD.

Hendrickson, D.A. and J.E. Brooks. 1991. Transplants of short-lived fishes of southwest North American deserts - a review, assessment and recommendations. Pp. 283-298 In: Battle Against Extinction - Desert Fish Management in the American Southwest. W.L. Minckley and J.E. Deacon (eds). University of Arizona Press, Tucson.

Hendrickson, D.A. and W.L. Minckley. 1985. Cienegas – Vanishing climax communities of the American Southwest. Desert Plants 5:131-175.

Hendrickson, D.A., W.C. Minckley, R.R. Miller, D.J. Siebert, and P.H. Minckley. 1980. Fishes of the Rio Yaqui Basin, Mexico and the United States. Journal of Arizona-Nevada Academy of Science 15(3): 65-106.

Hibbert, A.R. 1979. Managing vegetation to increase flow in the Colorado River Basin. USDA Forest Service, Gen. Tech. Rep. RM-66.

Hocutt, C.H., R.E. Jenkins, and J.R. Stauffer, Jr. 1986. Zoogeography of the fishes of the Central Appalachians and Central Atlantic Coastal Plain. Pages 161-211 In: C.H. Hocutt and E.O. Wiley (eds). The Zoogeography of North American Fishes. John Wiley and Sons, New York.

Hocutt, C.H. and E.O. Wiley. 1986. The Zoogeography of North American Freshwater Fishes. John Wiley and Sons, New York.

Hubbs, C.L. and R.R. Miller. 1948. The zoological evidence: correlation between fish distribution and hydrographic history in the desert basins of western United States. Bulletin of the University of Utah, 30: 17 – 66.

Hubbs, C.L., R.R. Miller, and L.C. Hubbs. 1974 Hydrographic history and relict fishes of the north-central Great Basin. California Academy of Science Memoirs 7: 1-259.

Johnson, J.E. and J.N. Rinne. 1982. The endangered species act and southwestern fishes. Fisheries. 7, 1-10.

Johnson, S.R., H.L. Gary, and Stanley L. Ponce. 1978. Range cattle impacts on stream water quality in the Colorado front range (U.S.A.). USDA, Forest Service, Rocky Mountain Forest and Range Experiment Station Research Note RM-359.

Johnston, A. 1962. Effects of grazing intensity and cover on the water-intake rate of fescue grassland. Journal of Range Management 15 (2).

Koster, W.J. 1957. Guide to the fishes of New Mexico. University of New Mexico Press, Albuquerque.

Kruse, W.H. and R. Jemison. 2000. Grazing systems of the southwest. In: Jemison, R. and C. Raish, (eds). Livestock management in the American Southwest: Ecology, Society, and Economics. Elsevier, Amsterdam.

LaBounty, J.F. and W.L. Minckley. 1972. Native fishes of the upper Gila River system, New Mexico. Symposium on rare and endangered wildlife of the Southwestern United States, September 22-23 1972, Albuquerque. Santa Fe, NM: New Mexico Department of Game and Fish, pp. 134-146.

Lang, B.K. and C.S. Altenbach. 1994. Ichthyofauna of the Middle Rio Grande Conservancy District irrigation system: Cochiti Dam to Elephant Butte State Park, July-August 1993. Albuquerque Projects Office, U.S. Bureau of Reclamation, Albuquerque, NM.

Langlois, D., J. Alves, and J. Apker. 1994. Rio Grande sucker recovery plan. Colorado Division of Wildlife, Denver.

Lassuy, D.R. 1995. Introduced species as a factor in extinction and endangerment of native fish species. American Fisheries Society Symposium. 15:391-396.

Lee, D.S., C.R. Gilbert, C.H. Hocutt, R.E. Jenkins, D.E. McAllister, J.R. Stauffer. 1980. Atlas of North American freshwater fishes. North Carolina Museum of Natural History, Raleigh, NC.

Leoplod, A. 1946. Erosion as a menace to the social and economic future of the Southwest. Journal of Forestry. 44:627-633

Leopold, A.S. 1974. Ecosystem deterioration under multiple use. Proceedings of the Wild Trout Symposium, Pp. 96-98. U.S. Department of the Interior Fish and Wildlife Service and Trout Unlimited, Denver, Colorado.

Leopold, L.B., M.G. Wolman, and J.P. Miller. 1964. Fluvial processes in geomorphology. W.H. Freeman and Co., San Francisco.

Li, H.W. and P.B. Moyle. 1999. Management of Introduced Fishes. Pp. 345-374. In: C. Kohler and W. Hubert (eds). Inland Fisheries Management in North America. American Fisheries Society. Bethesda, MD.

Lisle, T.E. 1989. Sediment transport and resulting deposition in spawning gravels, north central California. Water Resources Research 25(6), 1303-1319.

Loftin, S.R., C.E. Bock, J.H. Bock, and S.L. Brentley. 2000. Desert Grasslands. pp. 53-96 In: R. Jemison and C. Raish (eds). Livestock management in the American Southwest: Ecology, Society, and Economics. Elsevier Science B.V., Amsterdam.

Maddux, H.R., L.A. Fitzpatrick, and W.R. Noonan. 1993. Colorado River endangered fishes critical habitat draft biological support document. U.S. Fish and Wildlife Service, Salt Lake City, UT 225 pp.

Marsh, P.C., F.J. Arbaca, M.E. Douglas, and W.L. Minckley. 1989. Spikedace (*Meda fulgida*) and loach minnow (*Tiaroga cobitis*) relative to shiner (*Cyprinella lutrensis*). Arizona Game and Fish Department, Phoenix.

Marsh, P.C., J.E. Brooks, D.A. Hendrickson, and W.L. Minckley. 1991. Fishes of Eagle Creek, Arizona, with records for threatened spikedace and loach minnow (*Cyprinidae*). Journal of the Arizona Academy of Science. 23: 107 – 116.

Marsh, P.C. and D.R. Langhorst, 1988. Feeding and fate of wild larval razorback sucker. Environmental Biology of Fishes. 21(1):59-67.

Matthews, W.J. 1998. Patterns in freshwater fish ecology. Chapman and Hall, New York.

Matthews, W.J. and F.P. Gelwick. 1990. Fishes of Crutcho Creek and the North Canadian River near Oklahoma City: urbanization, and temporal variability. Southwestern Naturalist. 35, 403-10.

May, R.M. 1988. How many species are there on Earth? Science. 241: 1441-1449.

Mayden, R.L. 1987. Historical ecology and North American highland fishes: a research program in community ecology. In: W.J. Matthews and D.C. Heins (eds) Community and Evolutionary Ecology of North American Stream Fishes, University of Oklahoma Press, Norman, pp. 210-222.

Mayden, R.L. 1992a. An emerging revolution in comparative biology and the evolution of North American freshwater fishes, in *Systematics, Historical Ecology and North American Fishes* R.L. Mayden (ed) Stanford University Press.

Mayden, R.L. 1992b. Systematics, Historical Ecology and North American Fishes. R.L. Mayden (ed) Stanford University Press.

Medina, A.L. 1995. Native aquatic plants and ecological condition. USDA Forest Service, Rocky Mountain Forest and Research Station Gen. Tech. Rep. 272:329-335.

Medina, A.L. and J.N. Rinne. 1999. Ungulate/fishery interactions in southwestern riparian ecosystems: Pretensions and realities. Proceedings of the North America Wildlife and Natural Resources Conference 62:307-322.

Meehan, W.R. 1991. Influences of forest and rangeland management on salmonid fishes and their habitats. American Fisheries Society Special Publication 19., Bethesda, Maryland.

Meehan, W.R. 1996. Influence of riparian canopy on macroinvertebrate composition and food habits of juvenile salmonids in several Oregon streams. USDA Forest Service. Research Paper PNW-RP-496. 14 p.

Meehan, W.R. and W.S. Platts. 1978. Livestock grazing and the aquatic environment. Journal of Sol and Water Conservation 33(6):274-278.

Meehan, W.R., F.J. Swanson, and J.R. Sedell. 1977. Influence of riparian vegetation on aquatic ecosystems with particular reference to salmonid fishes and their food supply. Pp. 137-145 In: Johnson, R.R. and D.A. Jones (tech. coord.). Importance, preservation, and management of riparian habitats: A symposium. 9 July 1977. Tucson, AZ. USDA Forest Service. Gen. Tech. Rep.

Meffe, G.K., D.A. Hendrickson, and D.L. Minckley. 1983. Factors resulting in the decline of the endangered Sonoran topminnow *Poeciliopsis occidentalis* (Atheriniformes: Poeciliidae) in the United States. Biological Conservation. 25: 135-159.

Mehrhoff, L.A. Jr. 1955. Vegetation change on a southern Arizona grassland – an analysis of causes. University of Arizona, Tucson. Masters Thesis.

Milchunas, D.G., O.E. Sala, and W.K. Lauenroth. 1988. A generalized model of the effects of grazing by large herbivores on grassland community structure. American Naturalist. 132:87-106.

Miller, R.R. 1946a. Correlation between fish distribution and Pleistocene hydrography in eastern California and southwestern Nevada, with a map of the Pleistocene waters. Journal of Geology. 54: 43 – 53.

Miller, R.R. 1946b. The need for ichthyological studies of the major rivers of western North America. Science. 104, 517-519.

Miller, R.R. 1959. Origin and affinities of the freshwater fish fauna of western North America. Pages 187 – 222 In: C.L. Hubbs, ed. Zoogeography. Pub. 51 (1958). Washington, DC: American Association for the Advancement of Science.

Miller, R.R. 1961. Man and the changing fish fauna of the American Southwest. Papers of the Michigan Academy of Science, Arts, and Letters. 46, 365-404.

Miller, R.R. 1972. Threatened Freshwater Fishes of the United States. Transactions of the American Fisheries Society, No. 2. 14p.

Miller, R.R. and B. Chernoff. 1979. Status of populations of the endangered Chihuahua chub, Gila nigrescens. Proceedings of the Desert Fishes Council 11: 74-84.

Miller, R.R., C. Hubbs, and F.H. Miller. 1991. Ichthyological Exploration of the American West: The Hubbs-Miller Era, 1915-1950.

Miller, R.R. and E.P. Pister. 1971. Management of the Owens pupfish, *Cyprinodon radiosus*, in Mono County, California. Transaction of the American Fisheries Society. 100(3): 502-507.

Miller, R.R., J.D. Williams, and J.E. Williams. 1989. Extinction in North American Fishes during the past century. Fisheries. 14: 22-38.

Miller, R.R. and W.E. Winn. 1951. Additions to the known fish fauna of Mexico: three species and one subspecies from Sonora. Journal of the Washington Academy of Science. 41:83 – 84.

Minckley, W.L. 1969. Attempted re-establishment of the Gila topminnow within its former range. Copeia. 1969(1):193-194.

Minckley, W.L. 1973. Fishes of Arizona. Sims Printing Co., Phoenix, AZ.

Minckley, W. L. 1983. Status of the razorback sucker, Xyrauchen texanus, (Abott) in the lower Colorado, Southwestern Naturalist 28: 165-187.

Minckley, W.L. and Carufel. 1967. The Little Colorado River spinedace, *Lepidomeda vittata*, in Arizona. The Southwestern Naturalist. 12(3):291-302.

Minckley, W.L. and J.E. Deacon. 1968. Southwestern fishes and the enigma of "Endangered Species." Science. 159: 1424 – 1432.

Minckley, W.L. and J.E. Deacon. 1991. Battle against extinction: Native fish management in the American West. University of Arizona Press, Tucson.

Minckley, W.L. and M. Douglas. 1991. Discovery and extinction of western fishes: a blink of the eye in geologic time. Pages 717 In: W.L. Minckley and J.E. Deacon (eds) Battle against extinction: Native fish management in the American West. University of Arizona Press, Tucson.

Minckley, W.L., D.A. Hendrickson, and C.E. Bond. 1986. Geography of Western North American Freshwater Fishes: Description and relationships to intercontinental tectonism. Pages 519-613 In: C.H. Hocutt and E.O. Wiley, eds. The Zoogeography of North American Fishes. John Wiley and Sons, New York.

Minckley, W.L., J.N. Rinne, and J.E. Johnson. 1977. Status of the Gila topminnow and its co-occurrence with mosquitofish. USDA Forest Service Research paper RM-198, Fort Collins, CO.

Moyle, P.B. 1976. Inland fishes of California. University of California Press.

Moyle, P.B. and B. Herbold. 1987. Life-history patterns and community structure in stream fishes of Western North America. Comparison with Eastern North America and Europe, in: W.J. Matthews and D.C. Heins (eds) Community and Evolutionary Ecology of North American Stream Fishes, University of Oklahoma Press, Norman, pp 25-32.

Moyle, P.B., H.W. Li, and B.A. Barton. 1986. The Frankenstein effect: impact of introduced fishes on native fishes in North America. Pp. 415426 In: R.H. Stroud (ed). Fish culture in fisheries management. American Fisheries Society, Bethesda, Md.

Moyle, P.B., and R. Nichols. 1973. Ecology of some native and introduced fishes of the Sierra Nevada foothills in central California. Copeia. 1973(3):478-490.

Moyle, P.B., and R. Nichols. 1974. Decline of the native fish fauna of the Sierra-Nevada foothills, central California. American Midland Naturalist. 92(1):72-83.

Mueller, G.A., and P.C. Marsh. 2002. Lost, a desert river and its native fishes: A historical perspective of the lower Colorado River. Fort Collins, CO: U.S. Geological Survey. Information and Technology Report USGS/BRD/ITR 2002-0010. 69 p.

Neary, D.G. and A.L. Medina. 1995. Geomorphic response of a montane riparian habitat to interactions of ungulate vegetation, and hydrology. USDA Forest Service, Rocky Mountain Forest and Research Station Gen. Tech. Rep. 272:143-147.

Neary, D.G. and A.L. Medina. 1996. Geomorphic response of a montane riparian habitat to interactions of ungulates, vegetation, and hydrology. Pp. 143-147. In: Shaw, D.W. and D.M. Finch (tech. coord.) Desired future conditions for Southwestern ecosystems: Bringing interests and concerns together. USDA Forest Service. Gen. Tech. Rep. RM-GTR-272.

USDA Forest Service Gen. Tech. Rep. RMRS-GTR-135-vol. 2. 2005

165

Neel, J.K. 1963. Impact of reservoirs. Pages 575–593. In: Frey, D.G. (ed) Limnology in North America. Wisconsin Press, Madison.

Nelson, J.S. 1994. Fishes of the World, 3rd ed. John Wiley and Sons, New York. Meeting of the American Society of Ichthyologists and Herpetologists, Austin, TX.

Nico, L.G. and P. Fuller. 1999. Spatial and temporal patterns of nonindigenous fishes introductions in the United States. Fisheries. 24:16-27.

Orth, D.J. and R.J. White, 1993. Stream Habitat Management. In: C.C. Kohler and W.A. Hubert (eds) Inland Fisheries Management in North America Bethesda, Maryland, USA: American Fisheries Society.

Overton, K.C., G.L. Chandler, and J.A. Pisano. 1994. Northern/Intermountain Region's fish habitat inventory: Grazed, rested, and ungrazed reference stream reaches, Silver King Creek, CA. USDA Forest Service. Gen. Tech. Rep. INT-GTR-311. 27 p.

Patten, D.T. 1998. Riparian ecosystems of semi-arid North America: diversity and human impacts. Wetlands. 18:498-512.

Payne, B.A. and M.F. Lapointe. 1997. Channel morphology and lateral stability: effects on distribution of spawning and rearing habitat for Atlantic salmon in wandering cobble-bed river. Canadian Journal of Fisheries and Aquatic Science. 54:2627-2636.

Peiper, R. 1994. Ecological Implications of livestock grazing. Pp. 177-211. In: Vavra, W.A. Laycok, and R.D. Peiper (eds). Ecological Implications of Livestock Herbivory in the West. Society for Range Management.

Peplow, Edward H. Jr. 1958. Livestock Industry in Arizona. In: History of Arizona, Volume III. Lewis Historical Publishing Company, New York.

Pister, E.P. 1974. Desert fishes and their habitats. Transactions of the American Fisheries Society. 102(3): 531-540.

Pister, E.P. 1976. The rationale for the management of non-game fish and wildlife. Fisheries. 1(1):11-14.

Pister, E.P. 1981. The conservation of desert fishes. Pp. 411- 444 In: R.J. Naiman and D.L. Soltz (eds). Fishes in North American Deserts. John Wiley and Sons, New York.

Platania, S.P. 1991. Fishes of the Rio Chama and upper Rio Grande, New Mexico, with preliminary comments on their longitudinal distribution. Southwestern Naturalist 36: 186-193.

Platania, S.P. 1993. The fishes of the Rio Grande between Velarde and Elephant Butte Reservoir and their habitat associations. Report to the New Mexico Department of Game and Fish, Santa Fe and Bureau of Reclamation (Albuquerque Projects Office) Albuquerque Ichthyofaunal Studies Program, Museum of Southwestern Biology, University of New Mexico, Albuquerque.

Platania, S.P. 1995. Reproductive biology and early life-history of the Rio Grande silvery minnow, *Hybognathus amarus*. Albuquerque District, U.S. Army Corps of Engineers, Albuquerque, NM.

Platania, S.P. and C.S. Altenbach. 1998. Reproductive strategies and egg types of seven Rio Grande basin cyprinids. Copeia. 1998: 559-569.

Platts, W.S. 1979. Livestock grazing and riparian stream ecosystems. P.39-45. In: Proc. Forum-Grazing and Riparian Stream Ecosystems. Trout Unlimited. Inc. In: Kauffman, J.B. & W.C. Krueger. 1984. Livestock impacts on riparian ecosystems and streamside management implications...a review. Journal of Range Management. 37:430-483.

Platts, W.S. 1981a. Effects of livestock grazing. Pp. 389-423 In: W.R. Meehan (ed). Influence of forest and rangeland management on anadromous fish habitat in western North America. Gen. Tech. Rep. PNW-124. USDA Forest Service, Pacific Northwest Forest and Range Experiment Station.

Platts, W.S. 1981b. Effects of sheep grazing on riparian-stream environment. USDA Forest Service. Research Note INT-307. 6 p.

Platts, W.S. 1982. Sheep and cattle grazing strategies on riparian stream environments. P. 251-270. In: Wildlife-Livestock Relationships Symposium. Proc. 10. University of Idaho Forest, Wildlife & Range Exp. Sta. Moscow. In: Kauffman, J.B. & W.C. Krueger. 1984. Livestock impacts on riparian ecosystems and streamside management implications...a review. Journal of Range. Management. 37:430-483.

Platts, W.S. 1983. Vegetation requirements for fisheries habitats. Pp. 184-188. In: Proceedings of the Symposia on managing intermountain rangelands – improvement of range and wildlife habitats. 15-17 September 1981; Twin Falls, ID. 22-24 June 1982; Elko, NV. USDA Forest Service Gen. Tech. Rep. INT-57.

Platts, W.S. 1991. Livestock grazing. Pp. 389-423. In: Influences of forest and rangeland management on salmonid fishes and their habitats. American Fisheries Society Special Publication. 19.

Platts, W.R. and R.L. Nelson. 1985. Stream habitat and fisheries response to livestock grazing and instream improvement structures. Big Creek, Utah. Journal of Soil and Water Conservation, 40(4), 374-379.

Platts, W.S., and R.L. Nelson. 1989a. Characteristics of riparian plant communities and streambanks with respect to grazing in northeastern Utah. Pp. 73-81. In: Gresswell, R.E., B.A. Barton, J.L. Kershner (eds). Riparian resource management: an educational workshop. USDI Bureau of Land Management. Billings, MT.

Platts, W.S., and R.L. Nelson. 1989b. Stream canopy and its relationship to salmonid biomass in the Intermountain West. North American Journal of Fisheries Management, 9: 446-457.

Platts, W.S., Nelson, R.L., Casy, O. Crispin, V. 1983. Riparian-stream habitat conditions on Tabor Creek, Nevada, under grazed and ungrazed conditions. In: Western association of fish and wildlife agencies annual conference proceedings, 63rd; Teton Village, WY: The Association; 162-174.

Pogacnik, T.M. and C.B. Marlow. 1983. The effects of time grazing on stream channel stability and suspended sediment loading. Proceedings of the annual meeting of the Society for Range Management. 14-16 February 1983. Albuquerque, NM.

Propst, D.L. 1999. Threatened and Endangered fishes of New Mexico. Technical Report No.1. New Mexico Department of Game and Fish, Santa Fe. 84 p.

Propst, D.L. and K.R. Bestgen. 1991. Habitat and biology of the loach minnow, *Tiaroga cobitis*, in New Mexico. Copeia. 1991: 29-39.

Propst, D.L., K.R. Bestgen, and C.W. Painter. 1986. Distribution, status, biology, and conservation of the spikedace (*Meda fulgida*) in New Mexico. Endangered Species Report No. 15, U.S. Fish and Wildlife Service, Albuquerque, New Mexico.

Propst, D.L., K.R. Bestgen, and C.W. Painter. 1988. Distribution, status, biology, and conservation of the loach minnow, *Tiaroga cobitis* Girard, in New Mexico. USFWS, Albuquerque, Endangered Species Report No. 17, pp.1-75.

Propst, D.L., G.L. Burton, and B.H. Pridgeon. 1987. Fishes of the Rio Grande between Elephant Butte and Caballo Reservoirs, New Mexico. The Southwestern Naturalist .32: 408-11.

Propst, D.L, P.C. Marsh, and W.L. Minckley. 1986. Arizona survey survey for spikedace and loach minnow (Tiaroga cobitis): Fort Apache and San Carlos Indian Reservations and Eagle Creek, 1985. Report, U.S. Fish and Wildlife Service, Albuquerque, New Mexico 8 p.

Rausch, R.R. 1963. Age and growth of the Rio Grande mountain-sucker, *Pantosteus plebeius* (Baird and Girard). M.S. Thesis, University of New Mexico, Albuquerque.

Reid, L.M. 1993. Research and cumulative watershed effects. Gen. Tech. Rep. PSW-GTR-141. Albany, CA: Pacific Southwest Research Station, Forest Service, U.S. Department of Agriculture. 118 p.

Reid, G.K. and R.D. Wood. 1976. Ecology of inland waters and estuaries. D. Van Nostrand, New York.

Rinne, J.N. 1988a. Effects of livestock grazing exclosure on aquatic macroinvertebrates in a montane stream, New Mexico. Great Basin Naturalist. 48(2), 146-153.

Rinne, J.N. 1988b. Grazing effects on stream habitat and fishes: research design considerations. North American Journal of Fisheries Management. 8: 240-247.

Rinne, J.N. 1989. Physical habitat use by loach minnow, *Tiaroga cobitis* (Pisces: Cyprinidae), in southwestern (USA) desert streams. Southwestern Naturalist. 34(1): 109-117.

Rinne, J.N. 1990. An approach to management and conservation of a declining regional fish fauna: Southwestern United States, pp55-60. In: Maruyama and others (eds). Wildlife Conservation: Present trends and perspectives for the 21st century. International Symposium on Wildlife, 5th International Congress Zoology, August 21-25, 1990 Tskuba and Yokohama, Japan.

Rinne, J.N. 1991. Physical habitat use by spikedace, *Meda fulgida* in southwestern desert streams with reference to probable habitat competition by red shiner, *Notropis lutrensis* (Pisces: Cyprinidae). Southwestern Naturalist 36(1): 7-13.

166

USDA Forest Service Gen. Tech. Rep. RMRS-GTR-135-vol. 2. 2005

Rinne, J.N. 1992. Physical habitat utilization of fish in a Sonoran Desert Stream, Arizona, southwestern United States. Ecology of Freshwater Fishes 1: 35 – 41.

Rinne, J.N. 1995a. Reproductive biology of the Rio Grande chub, *Gila pandora*, (*Cypriniformes*) in a montane stream, New Mexico. The Southwestern Natualist 40(1):107-110.

Rinne, J.N. 1995b. Reproductive biology of the Rio Grande sucker, *Catostomus plebeius*, (*Cypriniformes*) in a montane stream, New Mexico. The Southwestern Naturalist 40(2):102-105.

Rinne, J.N. 1998. Grazing and fishes in the southwest: Confounding factors for research, 75-84. In: Potts, D.F. (ed). Proceedings American Water Resources Agency Specialty Conference: Rangeland Management and Water Resources American Water Resources Agency/Society for Range Management Specialty Conference on Rangeland and Water Resources. May 26-30, Reno, NV. Herndon, VA.

Rinne, J.N. 1999a. Fish and grazing relationships: The facts and some pleas. Fisheries 24(8): 12-21.

Rinne, J.N. 1999b. The status of spikedace, *Meda fulgida*, in the Verde River, 1999. Implications for research and management. Hydrology and Water Resources in the Southwest 29.

Rinne, J.N. 2000. Fish and grazing relationships in southwestern national forests. Pp. 329- 371 In: Jemison, R. and C. Raish (eds). Livestock management in the American Southwest: Ecology, Society, and Economics. Elsevier Science B.V., Amsterdam..

Rinne, J.N., P. Boucher, D. Miller, A. Telles, J. Montzingo, R. Pope, B. Deason, C. Gatton, and B. Merhage. 1999. Comparative fish community structure in two southwestern desert rivers *In*: S. Leon, P. Stine, and C. Springer (eds) Restoring native fish to the lower Colorado River: Interactions of native and non-native fishes: A symposium and Workshop.

Rinne J.N. and B.P. Deason. 2000. Habitat availability and utilization by two native, threatened fish species in two southwestern rivers. Hydrology and Water Resources in Arizona and the Southwest. 30: 43-52.

Rinne, J.N. and K. Kroger. 1988. Physical habitat used by spikedace, *Meda fulgida*, In: Aravaipa Creek, Arizona. Proceedings of the 68th Annual Conference of the Western Association of Fish and Wildlife Agencies, Albuquerque.

Rinne, J.N. and W.L. Minckley. 1985. Patterns of variation and distribution in Apache trout (*Salmo apache*) relative to co-occurrence with introduced salmonids. Copeia 1985(2): 285-292.

Rinne J.N. and W.L. Minckley. 1991. Native Fishes of Arid Lands: A Dwindling Natural Resource of the Desert Southwest. USDA Forest Service, Gen. Tech. Rep. RM-206: 1-45. Rocky Mountain Forest and Range Experiment Station, Fort Collins, CO.

Rinne, J.N. and S.P. Platania. 1995. Fish Fauna. pp. 165 – 175 In: Ecology, diversity, and sustainability of the Middle Rio Grande Basin. Gen. Tech. Rep. RM-GTR-268. Fort Collins, CO: U.S. Department of Agriculture, Forest Service, Rocky Mountain Forest and Range Experiment Station. 186 pp.

Rinne, J.N. and P.R. Turner. 1991. Reclamation and alteration as management techniques,and a review of methodology in stream renovation, Pp. 219-244 In: W.L. Minckley and J.E. Deacon (eds). Battle Against Extinction--Native Fish Management in the American West. University of Arizona Press.

Roberts, B.C. and R.G. White. 1992. Effects of angler wading on survival of tout eggs and pre-emergent fry. North American Journal of Fisheries Management 12. 450-459.

Robison, H.W. 1986. Zoogeographic implications of the Mississippi River Basin. Pp 267-285 In: C.H. Hocutt and E.O. Wiley, eds. The Zoogeography of North American Fishes. John Wiley and Sons, New York.

Robison, H.W. and J.K. Beedles. 1974. Fishes of the Strawberry River System in northcentral Arkansas. Proceedings of the Arkansas Academy of Science. 28: 65-70.

Robison, H.W. and T.M. Buchanan. 1988. Fishes of Arkansas. University of Arkansas Press, Fayetteville.

Ryder, R.A. 1980. Effects of grazing on bird habitats. Pp 51-65. In: Workshop proceedings, Management of western forests and grasslands for nongame birds. 11-14 February 1980. Salt Lake City, UT. USDA Forest Service. Gen. Tech. Rep. INT-86.

Schickendanz, J.G. 1980. History of grazing in the southwest. Pp 1- 9, In: Kirk C. McDaniel and Chris Allison (eds). Grazing management systems for southwest rangelands: A symposium. The Range Improvement Task Force, Albuquerque, NM.

Schmidt, R.E. 1986. Zoogeography of the Northern Appalachians. Pages 137-159 In: C.H. Hocutt and E.O. Wiley (eds). The Zoogeography of North American Fishes. John Wiley and Sons, New York.

Schoenherr, A.A. 1981. The role of competition in the replacement of native fishes by introduced species. Pp 173-203 In: R.J. Naiman and D.L. Soltz (eds). Fishes of North American Deserts. John Wiley and Sons, New York.

Schultz, T.T. and W.C. Leininger. 1990. Differences in riparian vegetation between grazed areas and exclosures. Journal of Range Management. 43(4), 295-299.

Scurlock, D. 1986. Settlements and Missions, 1606 – 1680. In: J.L. Williams (ed) New Mexico in maps, 2nd edition. University of New Mexico Press.

Scurlock, D. 1998. From Rio to the Sierra: an environmental history of the middle Rio Grande Basin. USDA Forest Service Gen. Tech. Rep. RMRS-GTR-5, Rocky Mountain Research Station, Fort Collins, Colorado

Simberloff, D.S. 1974. Equilibrium theory of island biogeography and ecology. Annual Review of Ecological Systematics. 5: 161 – 182.

Smith, G.R. 1966. Distribution and evolution of the North American catostomid fishes of the subgenus *Pantosteus*, genus *Catostomus*. Systematical Zoology. 20:282-297.

Smith, G.R. 1978. Biogeography of intermountain fishes. Great Basin Naturalist Memoirs. 2: 17 – 46.

Smith, G.R. 1981a. Effects of habitat size on species richness and adult body size of desert fishes. Pages 125 – 172 In: R.J. Naiman and D.L. Soltz (eds). Fishes in North American Deserts.

Smith, G.R. 1981b. Late Cenozoic freshwater fishes of North America. Annual Review of Ecological Systematics. 12:163-193. John Wiley and Sons, New York.

Smith, M.L. 1981. Late cenozoic fishes in the warm deserts of North America: A reinterpretation of desert adaptations. Pages 11 – 38 In: R.J. Naiman and D.L. Soltz (eds). Fishes in North American Deserts.

Smith, M.L. and R.R. Miller. 1986. The evolution of the Rio Grande basin as inferred from its fish fauna. Pages 457- 486 In: C.H. Hocutt and E.O. Wiley (eds). The Zoogeography of North American Fishes. John Wiley and Sons, New York.

Snyder, D.E. 1981. Contributions to a guide to the cypriniform fish larvae of the upper Colorado River system in Colorado. Biological Science Series No. 3, U.S. Bureau of Land Management, Denver, Colorado.

Sponholtz, P.J. and J.N. Rinne. 1997. Refinement of aquatic macrohabitat definition in the Upper Verde River, Arizona. Pp. 17-24 In: Hydrology and water resources in Arizona and the Southwest. Volume 28. Proceedings of the 1998 Meetings of the Arizona Section, American Water Resource Association and the Hydrology Section, Arizona-Nevada Academy of Sciences, April 17, 1999, Flagstaff, Arizona.

Starnes, W.C. and D.A. Etnier. 1986. Drainage evolution and fish biogeography of the Tennessee and Cumberland Rivers Drainage Realm. Pp 325-361 In: C.H. Hocutt and E.O. Wiley, eds. The Zoogeography of North American Fishes. John Wiley and Sons, New York.

Steirer, F.S., Jr. 1992. Historical perspective on exotic species. Pp 1-4 In: M.R. DeVoe, ed. Introductions and transfers of marine species. South Carolina Sea Grant Consortium. Charleston.

Stewart, G. 1936. History of range use. Pp. 119-133 In: U.S. Forest Service: The Western Range. 74th Congress, 2nd session, Senate Document 199.

Stuber, R.J. 1985. Trout habitat, abundance, and fishing opportunities in fenced vs. unfenced riparian habitat along Sheep Creek, Colorado. Pp. 310-314. In: Johnson, RR, C.D. Ziebell, D.R. Patton, P.F. Ffolliott, and R.H. Hamre (tech. Coords.). Riparian ecosystems and their management: Reconciling conflicting uses. 16-18 April 1985. Tucson, AZ. USDA Forest Service. General Technical Report RM-120.

Sublette, J.E., M.D. Hatch, and M. Sublette. 1990. The Fishes of New Mexico. University of Arizona Press, Tucson.

Suttkus, R.D. and R.C. Cashner. 1981. The intergeneric hybrid combination, *Gila pandora* x *Rhinichthys cataractae* (*Cyprinidae*), and comparisons with parental species. Southwestern Naturalist. 26(1): 78-82.

Swift-Miller, S.M., B.M. Johnson, and R.T. Muth. 1999a. Factors affecting the diet and abundance of northern populations of the Rio Grande sucker (*Catostomus plebeius*). Southwestern Naturalist. 44:148-156.

Swift-Miller, S.M., B.M. Johnson, R.T. Muth, and D. Langlois. 1999b. Distribution, abundance, and habitat use of Rio Grande sucker (*Catostomus plebeius*) in Hot Creek, Colorado. Southwestern Naturalist. 44:42-48.

Szarro, R.C. 1989. Riparian forest and scrubland community types of Arizona and New Mexico. Desert Plants. 9(3-4):72-138.

Taylor, J.N., W.R. Courtenay, Jr., and J.A. McCann. 1984. Known impact of exotic fishes in the continental United States. Pp. 322-373 In: W.R. Courtenay, Jr. and J.R. Stauffer, eds. Distribution, biology, and management of exotic fish. Johns Hopkins University Press, Baltimore, Maryland.

Trevino-Robinson, D.T. 1959. The icthyofauna of the lower Rio Grande, Texas and Mexico. Copeia. 1959: 253-256

Tromble, J.M., K.G. Renard, and A.P. Thatcher. 1974. Infiltration for three rangeland soil-vegetation complexes. Journal of Range Management. 27(4):318-321.

Turner, P.R. and R.J. Tafanelli. 1983. Evaluation of the instream flow requirements of the native fishes of Aravipa Creek, Arizona by the incremental methodology. U.S. Fish and Wildlife Service, Albuquerque, 114 pp.

Tyus, H. M. and J.F. Saunders. 2000. Nonnative fish control and endangered fish recovery. Fisheries 25: 17-24.

Tyus, H.M., B.D. Burdick, R.A. Valdez, C.M. Haynes, T.A. Lytle, and C.R. Berry. 1982. Fishes of the Upper Colorado River Basin: Distribution, abundance, and status. Pp 12- 70 In: W.H. Miller, H.M. Tyus, and C.A. Carlson (eds) Fishes of the Upper Colorado River system: Present and Future. Western Division of the American Fisheries Society, Bethesda, MD.

United States Congress, Office of Technology Assessment. 1993. Harmful non-indigenous species in the United States. U.S. Government Printing Office, OTA-F-565, Washington, DC.

United States Fish and Wildlife Service (USFWS). 1986. Endangered and threatened wildlife and plants; Determination of threatened status for the loach minnow. Federal Register 51: 39468-39478.

United States Fish and Wildlife Service (USFWS). 2003. Threatened and Endangered Species System.

Vives, S.P. and W.L. Minckley. 1990. Autumn spawning and others reproductive notes on loach minnow, a threatened cyprinid fish of the American Southwest. The Southwestern Naturalist. 35: 451-454.

Weedman, D.A., A.L. Girmendonk, and K.L. Young. 1997a. Gila topminnow sites in Arizona: Provisional extirpation report 1996-97 field season. Nongame and Endangered Wildlife Program Technical Report 116. Arizona Game and Fish Department, Phoenix.

Weedmand, D.A. and K.L. Young. 1997b. Status of the Gila topminnow and desert pupfish in Arizona. Nongame and Endanageed Wildlife Program Technical Report 118. Arizona Game and Fish Department, Phoenix.

Westphall, V. 1965. The Public Domain in New Mexico: 1854-1891. Albuquerque: University of New Mexico Press, 1965.

Wilcox, B.P. and M.K. Wood. 1988. Hydrologic impacts of sheep grazing on steep slopes in semiarid rangelands. Journal of Range Management. 41:303-306.

Wildeman, G. and J. H Brock. 2000. Grazing in the southwest: history of land use and grazing since 1540. In: Jemison, R. and C. Raish (eds). Livestock management in the American Southwest: Ecology, Society, and Economics. Elsevier Science B.V., Amsterdam.

Williams, J.E., D.B Brooks, J.E. Echelle, A.A. Echelle, R.J. Edwards, D.A. Hendrickson, and J.J. Landye. 1985. Endangered aquatic ecosystems in North American deserts, with a list of vanishing fishes of the region. Journal of the Arizona-Nevada Academy of Sciences. 20: 1-62.

Williams, J.E., J.E. Johnson, D.A. Hendrickson, Salvador Contreras-Balderas, J.D. Williams, M. Navarro-Mendoza, D.E. McAllister, and J.E. Deacon. 1989. Fishes of North America, endangered, threatened, or of special concern: 1989. Fisheries. 14, 2-20.

Williams, J.E. and D.W. Sada. 1985. Endangered species technical bulletin, Volume X, No. 11, United States Fish and Wildlife Service.

Williams, J.E., D.W. Sada, C.D. Williams, and Other Members of the Western Division Endangered Species Committee. 1988. American Fisheries Society guidelines for the introductions of threatened and endangered fishes. Fisheries. 13: 5-11.

Woodling, J. 1985. Colorado's little fishes. A guide to the minnows and other lesser known fishes in the state of Colorado. Colorado Division of Wildlife, Department of Natural Resources, Denver.

York, J.C. and W.A. Dick-Peddie. 1969. Vegetation change in New Mexico during the past 100 years. In: Arid lands in perspective. University of Arizona Press, Tucson.

Young, W.D. 1998. The history of cattle grazing in Arizona. Pp. 3 – 17 In: Hydrology and water resources in Arizona and the Southwest. Volume 28. Proceedings of the 1998 Meetings of the Arizona Section, American Water Resource Association and the Hydrology Section, Arizona-Nevada Academy of Sciences, April 18, 1998, Glendale, Arizona.

Zuckerman, L.D. 1983. Rio Grande fishes management: progress report, November 1982 to June 1983. Colorado State University, Fort Collins. 53 pp.

Zuckerman, L.D. and D. Langlois. 1990. Status of Rio Grande sucker and Rio Grande chub in Colorado. Research Report, Colorado Division on Wildlife, Montrose.

www.ingramcontent.com/pod-product-compliance
Lightning Source LLC
Chambersburg PA
CBHW080249290526

45790CB00005B/1754